RESISTANCE, FLIGHT, CREATION

Resistance, Flight, Creation

Feminist Enactments of French Philosophy

Edited by

DOROTHEA OLKOWSKI

CORNELL UNIVERSITY PRESS

Ithaca and London

First published 2000 by Cornell University Press
First printing, Cornell Paperbacks, 2000

Printed in the United States of America

Library of Congress Cataloging-in-Publication Data

Resistance, flight, creation : feminist enactments of French philosophy / edited by Dorothea Olkowski

    p. cm.
    Includes bibliographical references and index.
    ISBN 0-8014-3742-3 — ISBN 0-8014-8645-9 (pbk.)
    1. Feminist theory.   2. Philosophy, French–20th century.
  I. Olkowski, Dorothea.

HQ1190 .R472 2000
305.42′01—dc21   99-059369

Cornell University Press strives to use environmentally responsible suppliers and materials to the fullest extent possible in the publishing of its books. Such materials include vegetable-based, low-VOC inks and acid-free papers that are recycled, totally chlorine-free, or partly composed of nonwood fibers. Books that bear the logo of the FSC (Forest Stewardship Council) use paper taken from forests that have been inspected and certified as meeting the highest standards for environmental and social responsibility. For further information, visit our website at www.cornellpress.cornell.edu.

Cloth printing   10 9 8 7 6 5 4 3 2 1
Paperback printing   10 9 8 7 6 5 4 3 2 1

For
Eleanore Holveck,
who started it

Contents

Part III   Emancipating Phenomenology

Part IV   Creative Collaborations

Part V   Resistance, Flight, Creation

Acknowledgments

The idea supporting this volume, that feminist philosophy is philosophy per se and not just a branch or a field of philosophy, is an idea that has been with me from the time I first began reading and writing feminist philosophy. This idea was further reinforced at a conference organized by Eleanore Holveck at Duquesne University on the topic of feminism and phenomenology. Each of the speakers—Hazel Barnes, Michèle Le Doeuff, Sonia Kruks, and Monika Langer—presented their arguments for and against phenomenological and existential practices within the context of feminist concerns and needs, but they also argued as philosophers who recognize the necessity of making a philosophy that is inclusive enough to incorporate those concerns and needs. Thus, when Eleanore suggested that I edit a volume of feminist philosophy, I immediately focused on the possibility of collecting essays in which philosophical content would reflect this relation between feminist concerns and needs and philosophy. I thank Eleanore Holveck for her support of my own philosophical career, both as an example and as someone who let me know that she thought I had the ability to do philosophy and to do it well. The importance of such encouragement can never be overestimated. I would also like to thank Hazel Barnes, another wonderful example of a philosopher whose experience of herself as a feminist is imbued in everything she writes. I also want to thank Helen Fielding, a young philosopher whose philosophical work is as thorough and thoughtful as the enormous and in-depth bibliography she painstakingly compiled for this volume. Finally, I give special thanks to my editors at Cornell, first Alison Shonkwiler, who initially took on this project with me, and then especially Catherine Rice, who came to the volume as it was under way and aided in its production with infinite patience and care.

D. O.

RESISTANCE, FLIGHT, CREATION

Introduction:
What Are Feminist Enactments?

DOROTHEA OLKOWSKI

This volume actualizes a dual idea: that of "feminist enactments" and that of "enactments of French philosophy." Each of these ideas has arisen out of and in relation to actual practices of philosophy that have engaged or subjected feminist philosophers since Simone de Beauvoir wrote *The Second Sex*. To say that philosophical practices "subjected" feminist philosophers is not a claim about oppression; rather, it is a statement acknowledging that a subject is formed or qualified by the parameters of her affective or qualitative life. Therefore, if French philosophy has been able to manifest its importance in the lives and work of feminist thinkers, this is because it so often concerns itself with the affective dimension and its relation to freedom in thought and freedom in practices. Much twentieth-century French philosophy is characterized by an affective subjectivity committed to strategies of freedom. This volume acknowledges that it is precisely this commitment that makes French philosophy so compelling for feminist thinkers who wish to enact, to put into motion, their own strategies of freedom. These feminist enactments, then, attest to the manner in which feminist philosophy emphasizes the value of affective life as a primary condition in the creation of freedom as well as for the role it can play in the disruption of methodology and prescribed systems of truth.

The affective dimension, defined as the unorganized flow of purely qualitative sensory-motor stimuli, makes such freedom possible, for it cannot be subject to a force or form of expression that orders it a priori, whether that force is philosophical or social. Henri Bergson takes affectivity to be "all the events of our daily life as they occur in time," and as such they are memory-images.[1] Affective images neglect no qualitative detail, fact, or gesture. As unique, they are unrepeatable; as unrepeatable, they manifest freedom by disregarding what is immediately familiar and mundane, offering instead "the will to dream."[2] The unrepeatable and imaginative memory out of which we dream and create must be fugitive to remain free of the other

1

kind of memory, the learned memory that becomes a habitual and repetitive response to demands for thought and action serving already known interests in philosophy or social life. The contemporary feminist philosophy celebrated in this collection, as a field of inquiry and as a practice, operates outside of the constraints of the canon of philosophy and outside of the practices that reinforce that canon. Taking its power from affective, qualitative life, it charges our thinking and practices with the force of freedom, the new, the creative.

Both the imaginative affective lives and the creative practices producing the essays in this collection arose in situations—institutional and other—that can be described less as exclusionary than as circumstances of control that gave way to freedom. The circumstances of control are, of course, everywhere, and also, as habitual and socially inscribed, they are broadly practiced. They are not terribly conspicuous in any way that one can point to and say, "Well obviously women are not welcome here." Nor is it a matter of the often-heard refrain, "There is no feminism in France, French women are not interested in it, they repudiate feminism." Nor is it the even more subtle concern that "French philosophy has come to the limits of unraveling the framework provided by Descartes and must return to that framework." Of course, in the name of order or truth, institutions of higher education granting degrees in philosophy, even those with commitments to philosophies of freedom, have deemed it reasonable to make exclusions with respect to women. The work of three French feminist philosophers, Simone de Beauvoir, Michèle Le Doeuff, and Hélène Cixous, attests to this. Le Doeuff, for one, has written extensively about women and the philosophical educational system. Her ideas on this subject are particularly conducive to setting thought in motion because her writing practice takes the form of a conversation or exchange that readers are invited to participate in and contribute to, so that together reader and writer enact or create philosophy.

Examining the relations between women and philosophy, Le Doeuff remarks on the theoretico-amorous character of the attachment of students to their professors. "In fact, you—Tom, Dick and Harry—who were at the Sorbonne or prepared for the *agrégation* with me. . . . Was it not only too easy sometimes to sense—in the knotting of a tie, in a hairstyle or some such fad—the symbol of allegiance to some cult-figure?"[3] In this way, Le Doeuff explains, not only women are determined in their studies by useful allegiances to a mentor. But this is only part of the story. In a time when nearly all the professors teaching graduate courses and, certainly, all of those eligible for cult status were male, then it was also much more difficult for a woman student to engage in habitual, repetitive practices, in the tie-knotting or pipe-smoking kinds of mimicry. In fact, for many women students, such mimicry appeared ludicrous, even pathetic, although this may have been only because women never found mentors, or as Le Doeuff calls it, *amours*. But my point is elsewhere.

In France, the real point of control, Le Doeuff explains, arises at the level of the institutional framework. Corresponding to this, in America, is the process of graduate admissions, of grants and stipends, of procuring and offering jobs, of being assigned rather than selecting one's courses, all with an eye to one's future philosophical production. The second- or third-tier institution, the lack of grants, and jobs with heavy teaching loads or constantly shifting courses ensure that one will have little time or energy for the enactment of philosophy. Yet, there is a price to be paid for the habituation demanded by the "right" institutional framework. Le Doeuff implies that women who stayed within the permitted range freely open to them in philosophy—that limited field of the personal relationship to a philosopher and to "his" philosophy—never became more than "amateurs." Yet often, I think, women are offered institutional rewards for their devotion to mentors whose analyses of freedom did not apply to women because, as Le Doeuff maintains, those same philosophers needed admirers and were gratified to be seen as a plentitude by them.

From the point of view of affective and creative life, the benefit of such offers is debatable.[4] This is why it is not enough for a woman simply to earn her living by philosophizing. A woman who is a philosopher might need to choose her exclusion from the field, dare to be excluded in order to avoid amateur status. In this, a certain deliberate blindness or opacity to mentors and their philosophical positions may be the necessary condition for women to create their own philosophy, their own ideas. In such a circumstance, even if it arises by accident, the situation amounts to freedom. The close connection between mentors with established methodologies and philosophical positions—even when those methods and positions are constituted in the name of freedom—is fundamentally alien to what I am calling "feminist enactments." The essays in this book reflect this situation, for they cannot easily be codified within the delimitations of a single methodology. Phenomenological description is often relied upon by these authors to delimit a particular field of life; yet, when feminists enact philosophy, they generally do so without habituation to a single philosophical perspective. Instead, having eluded amateur status, they carefully observe and analyze methodologies with particular concern for the outcomes or effects of those methods. The result of this is a "feminist" methodology that not only embraces phenomenology for the sake of its descriptive powers but also modifies and mixes it with other supposedly alien methods by means of a fluid framework that makes possible the passage from one kind of analysis to another based on qualitative correspondences rather than a priori concepts.

Exemplary, in this respect, is Simone de Beauvoir. Considered by many contemporary feminist philosophers to have led the way in creating contemporary French feminism, Beauvoir deserted her freedom at least temporarily when she first attempted to do philosophy. As she relates it in *Memoirs of a Dutiful Daughter*,[5] after days and days of "discussions" with Sartre, Beauvoir decides that she is beaten, that her opinions were based on prejudice, bad faith, or thoughtlessness; that her reasoning was shaky; and that her ideas for a theory of pluralist morality were confused in comparison with the ideas of Sartre and his friends. Beauvoir claims to give in to Sartre because she prefers "learning" to "shining" in argumentation and because she mistakenly concludes that to philosophize is to shine along a singular path and that any argument that can be ripped to shreds as Sartre has done with hers cannot be philosophy. Le Doeuff thinks that Beauvoir's strange idea that she had to "liquidate her past" and turn herself into a sort of tabula rasa did not constitute freedom for Beauvoir. This would mean, I think, that Beauvoir at least temporarily turned away from affective, creative memory, from her unique qualitative memory-images. The unfortunate effect is that Beauvoir let Sartre fulfill his promise to take her in hand, a promise that Le Doeuff takes to be both "banal and terrifying." "For being 'taken in hand' by someone else takes one out of philosophy, to the extent that the latter is a confrontation of a will to think with a lack of both knowing and a master."[6]

Yet, Beauvoir remains the one to whom many contemporary feminists turn in search of not so much a mentor but an image of a woman who is or became a feminist "doing" French philosophy and doing it in the mainstream among men. We look to Beauvoir's "enactments," and in many respects, she has provided numerous examples of how to create a feminist philosophy of one's own while working through the "discipline" of French philosophy. Rather than accepting Sartre's taking her in hand, Beauvoir wrote her freedom in philosophical literature. As Debra Bergoffen has argued, Beauvoir wrote novels and works like *The Second Sex*, whose philosophical focus is ethical, whose method is phenomenological, and whose commitments are existential.[7] This places Beauvoir firmly within the realm of philosophy, one constituted by radically reinventing and combining the ideas of those who would take her in hand. Perhaps Beauvoir's philosophical integrity comes from her engagement in women's situatedness, a condition that surely no other French philosopher took seriously. The question she posed in *The Second Sex*: "What is a woman?" and the answer she provided: "One is not born a woman, one becomes one," initiated as much criticism as admiration, but it opened up feminist philosophical questions for the first time, whether Beauvoir was describing women's situation of inequality with men biologically, historically, or as a social structure.

Proving the fact of Beauvoir's philosophical status for feminist French philosophy, Le Doeuff uses her own examination of Sartre's denial of Beauvoir to describe her own philosophical imagination. Her unique approach was born when a male secondary-school teacher determined that Kant was too difficult for Le Doeuff and refused her request for the *Critique of Pure Reason*. Le Doeuff courageously relates that she has never read it since; that she cannot bring herself to read more than fragments of it and in a fragmentary manner. This revelation is more interesting when one thinks of the positive and creative use Le Doeuff has made of this technique of reading, a technique that was meant to deny her access to philosophy. Rather than systematizing the world in clear conceptual categories, Le Doeuff breaks it up into numerous reflections drawn from myriad sources and methodologies including, but in no way limited to, philosophical texts. Such stories haunt the writing of each of the women who have contributed to this volume insofar as each of us began our philosophical investigations within the confines of educational institutions that sometimes excluded us and sometimes tried to take us in hand. Yet, the surprising result of this is that these encounters made us find our own ways of practicing philosophy outside of the theoretico-amorous relation.

As I have argued, the overlapping or intersection of disciplines and methods is the norm for feminist enactments of French philosophy, but this does not mean that such work is formless. For example, the incursion of French philosophy into literary studies and from there its leakage back into philosophy brings to mind precisely the schematics of Kant. It was Kant who among modern philosophers led the way to the view that philosophy is quite possibly dependent on something outside of itself like works of art, which, for the sake of their beauty, make possible an assessment of truth. What Kant did not have in mind in proposing this was that "beauty" itself would be up for grabs, that different interpretations of beauty would muddy the clear waters of the universal, though largely male, aesthetic feeling. In a radical way, recent French philosophy and feminist philosophy have contributed to muddying the water, but in so doing, they have embraced the result. I certainly do not mean by this that contributors to this volume merely advocate the principle of undecidability. Rather, these feminist philosophers are imaginatively "creating" new philosophical concepts with what I previously described as "feminist" methodologies. Feminist concepts are supplanting traditional philosophical concepts, and simultaneously, feminists are asking about the use-value of these new concepts: What does the concept or theory do? Who is doing the interpreting? Who is using the concept? With such an approach, philosophy is transformed, and these feminist philosophers are not just doing "feminist theory," they have invaded the entire field of philosophy and have set philosophy in motion, transforming it out of their affective memory-images into creative enactments. Without this, they would simply continue to "interpret" the philosophy of the past for some ideal but unactualized audience or community, or worse, they would think in a mode that vainly attempts to reproduce the past in the present, to bring back the past without creating anything new of it. Either way, all they would have produced is a repetition of the same text in other words.

Thus, in "The Laugh of the Medusa,"[8] Hélène Cixous addresses women's writing in precisely these terms; it is a way for women to actualize their freedom. She asks about women's writing as a creative act and in terms of "what it will do."[9] She writes:

> I have been amazed more than once by a description a woman gave me of a world all her own which she had secretly been haunting since early childhood. A world of searching, the elaboration of a knowledge, on the basis of a systematic experimentation with the bodily functions, a passionate and precise interrogation of heterogeneity. This practice, extraordinarily rich and inventive, in particular as concerns masturbation, is prolonged or accompanied by a production of forms, a veritable aesthetic activity, each stage of rapture inscribing a resonant vision, a composition, something beautiful. Beauty will no longer be forbidden.[10]

Cixous exhorts this woman and all women—women who have invented new forms—not to be ashamed of their torrents, not to be horrified by the "fantastic tumult" of their drives, not to think that they are sick or mad, but to write! Admitting that she did not write before the age of twenty-seven, Cixous acknowledges having thought what Le Doeuff's philosophy teacher told her, what Sartre told Beauvoir: that writing is for great men. Writing from the position of devotee assures that the system of great men is not disrupted; even a woman can write safely. But once the writing begins, there is no longer any assurance of what will take place; commentary can spiral out of control and transform itself into imaginative creativity; devotion may end in critique or paradox.

Cixous urges women to use their bodies and to write through their bodies. Far from being a claim for a new feminine materialism or a rejection of rationality, I take this to be an appeal to women to bodily remove themselves from the role of devotee, to take their affectivity and volcanic heterogeneity out of the institutional domain of what is habitually given to them, to cease even looking for something to be "given," because most such gifts are a trap. By bodily removing herself from the given world and haunting a world all her own, woman can write. "Her" writing can redefine the rational as "cosmic," "worldwide," not simply masculine or feminine. If, as I have suggested, feminist philosophy announces as the "matter" of its inquiry, that it will at least for a short time dare to take up the question of the use-value of newly created concepts, as an ongoing process, as an investigation into who speaks, then certainly feminist philosophy is dangerous to those who prefer that women function within the discourse of man as the signifier that refers to its opposite, that is only given existence as the opposite of all things male.[11]

The question remains, what about feminist enactments of French philosophy by women who are not French? In 1966, when the Johns Hopkins University sponsored the first American conference on structuralism, only a few graduate institutions offered classes in structuralist and linguistic theory, though "continental critics, particularly the structuralists in France . . . argued for a more philosophical unification of the human sciences, under a comprehensive theory of structure and signification, joining the work of Lévi-Strauss with the linguistic theory of Ferdinand de Saussure."[12] Nonetheless, structuralism and linguistics arrived via literature and not philosophy departments, and this explains why most so-called continental philosophy programs followed the lead of their analytic brothers and did not offer courses in either structuralism or linguistics, thereby leaving philosophy students more or less untrained and in the dark when the "post" phases arrived. Those feminists who did manage to learn these disciplines did so outside of philosophy. The U.K., Australia, and to a lesser extent Canada generally seem to have done a better job of educating philosophers in linguistics and structuralism, though even there these ideas arrived by way of literary theory or anthropology and only slowly made their way into general philosophy. Add to this the idea that these critical methods did not merely require the usual competence in logic and the history of philosophy, but made exceptional demands upon the philosopher for familiarity with linguistics, semiotics, psychoanalysis, intellectual history, anthropology, literature and art, scientific and mathematical innovations, and concrete knowledge of social and political realities, and you can begin to make sense of why the new French philosophy was so slow to be taken up and remains, to this moment, steeped in controversy and suspicion.[13]

Furthermore, as I have indicated previously, when feminists "do" French philosophy, they are even less likely to retain whatever methodological frameworks exist. They are most likely, as these essays show, to mix theories that previously remained pure and to combine epistemology with politics, ontology with art, or linguistics with cultural phenomena. All this gives rise to the serious issue of how to organize a book that celebrates, even insists upon, both creative imagination and concepts enacting freedom. It seems necessary, then, to organize the various parts of *Resistance, Flight, Creation* to reflect the fact that women are creating new structures of thought out of their own affective engagements and concrete practices in the world. Although these engagements and practices involve existing, perhaps even canonic, French philosophy, the complexity of the individual methods and the fact that they often combine several points of view and unexpected points of departure and arrival make each of these essays a resource for creative thinking that is exemplary through its radical redefinition of what counts as a rational concept and a useful method in philosophy. In a world where reason has been forced to reflect, sometimes painfully, upon its own self-interested procedures, the essays in this volume will serve as an intervention in canonical rationality and as a resource for new and ever-creative methods and points of view, not just for feminism or French philosophy but for philosophy in general.

It is with great pleasure that I introduce this collection with an essay by the American philosopher Hazel Barnes. Known first as the translator of *Being and Nothingness,* Barnes is one of those rare philosopher-academics who has achieved respect and admiration far beyond the ostensible limits of her own discipline. In "Philosophy and Gender: A First-Person View," Barnes explicitly locates herself as having the point of view of a "professor with a longtime investment in existentialism, as well as, inevitably, the situation of a white woman." From these points of view, she poses the question of the relation of feminist philosophy to the philosophical tradition as a whole and whether or not feminist enactments of philosophy will, in the end, shatter that philosophical tradition.

Describing a surely idiosyncratic upbringing that was equal parts "Jesus [and] . . . William James," Barnes finds that it was the latter's arguments that religious conversions, visions, and ecstatic trances are a form of partial insight into the possibilities of consciousness that finally held sway. Sartrean existentialism appealed to Barnes precisely because it provided a philosophical foundation for the pragmatists' assumption that we make ourselves, that we are radically free but also radically responsible. The Sartrean notions of authenticity and bad faith and the insistence that the choice of a system of ethics is a creative act, perhaps the greatest one, culminated, for Barnes, in the conclusion that women, too, make themselves. Finding this position affirmed in Beauvoir's, *The Second Sex,* Barnes writes that in 1950 she considered herself to be in that most fortunate of situations: a liberated woman. Yet, as she realized, Barnes was a liberated woman with a "male-trained mind."

From this background, Barnes finds it interesting that whereas once women were thrilled to be given access to a field men had kept to themselves, today the question has arisen of why women should bother to study works that constitute a purely male discourse, or why racial and ethnic minorities should apply themselves to the study of what has so scrupulously excluded them. Certainly, Barnes argues, there are too few women and minority philosophers read in even the most liberal curriculum, yet this may not be the case in the near future. With this in mind, Barnes delineates, what are for her, the major areas of philosophy that women are now contributing to and the philosophical issues they are raising, including that new-old question of the gender status of reason. Barnes also notes some areas of philosophy where women still seem to be missing and asks why. She concludes with an exegesis of several issues in philosophy that she considers crucial to current feminist debates, namely: equality or sexual difference, essentialism or social constructivism, and finally, whether the term *human* can be inclusive of male and female. In stating her positions in each of these three areas of debate, Barnes manifests her existentialist commitments but also her interest in looking at these problems through the perspectives of other feminist and nonfeminist thinkers. In so doing, Barnes engages in a feminist enactment of French philosophy from the position of a situated woman who continuously creates herself from the emerging data of life and who affirms her responsibility for her positions and actions.

The essays in part 1 take up, in a very general way, the text-based concerns of a deconstructive philosophy. However, given the affective and qualitative commitments of these feminist philosophers, an original and particular freedom with respect to knowing and dwelling emerges in each case. Hélène Cixous's "From My Menagerie to Philosophy," artfully translated by Keith Cohen, is, like Barnes's essay, an account of philosophy that incorporates biographical elements. Beginning with a citation from Jacques Derrida's "What Is Poetry?" which announces that to know poetry one is expected to know how to renounce knowledge without forgetting that knowledge, Cixous regrets that contemporary culture makes the impossible demand upon anyone who would know poetry to be both ignorant and knowing.[14] This is a demand to be someone and to still be anonymous, like the hedgehog who rolls itself up in a ball by the side of the road in order to escape detection and ends up being run over. We must, she implies, pay more attention to hedgehogs and to poetry in writing and thinking. Animals remind us of this. Always there, animals place a limit on neglect; like Abraham's ass on Mount Moriah or like her own cat, they constitute a menagerie, and the problematic she poses is how to go from one's menagerie to philosophy.

There are the many requests coming from her cat that she cannot fulfill and the visible signs of feline language that she cannot speak. A reasonable beginning for a poet who is finite, whose soul and body are separate. The poet coos, hums, meows; at least her words charm. And unlike the would-be knower of poetry who must both know and not know, with the menagerie detachment is entirely pure: "She lets me leave without violence without rift. . . . I return: she at once reties the bands." How to make philosophy of such gentleness and accord, the order of love in which in caressing one is caressed? How to make a philosophy out of the experience of mourning enacted not because the poet has refused or forgotten something of her animal needs, but from a confident mourning that arises out of an event-encounter with boundaries, with the poet's own powerlessness? It will not be a matter of exchanging one kind of knowledge for another, so not a matter of translation. Certain things, writes Cixous, are in the body where deep intelligence lies, and the craving that cannot be translated for giving and being received wells up.

The cat and the characters in the poet's book do what they want; they scoot out the door to discover the future of which they have no knowledge. They do not know poetry, do not put it into boxes and handle it, do not force it to roll itself into a ball then run it down. What counts for the poet (to the point of philosophy), Cixous affirms, is love between those who share a life reciprocally. Unable to speak a common language, they use their bodies, they contact one another in mute and chaste emotion. This is "the poetry of poetry." It is, perhaps, one way of enacting philosophy that does not produce the kind of knowledge that gets packed up in boxes and held and that does not kill the hedgehog but charms and affirms.

Iris Young begins her essay "House and Home: Feminist Variations on a Theme" with the poetic image of Penelope sitting by the hearth weaving while her man roams the earth, adventuring. Historically and mythologically associated with confinement, house and home have become deeply ambivalent values for women, to the point where they often feel they must lock themselves out of their own hearths in order to exercise any freedom. Feminist philosopher Luce Irigaray made a first attempt to reimagine Martin Heidegger's deconstructive privileging of the nondwelling, world-founding subject by explicitly stating that dwelling is the condition of the possibility of what it supplements. Man makes a house and fills it with things, including woman, in order to establish his own identity. Although Irigaray associates this impulse with substituting for the lost mother, Young articulates another more immediate source: The attachment of personal identity to commodified houses and their contents might best be thought to belong to the hegemony of bourgeois society.

To create her own concepts of home, Young calls up and fashions an affective memory-image, the story of her mother, an educated woman but a "bad housekeeper," accused of neglect, arrested, and separated from her children until she escaped suburban "bliss" and retreated back to the anonymity of the city. Appealing to Beauvoir's existentialist account of the oppression of housework, which supplies the material base for male transcendence, Young rethinks the entire problematic by placing limits on domestic immanence. Home is not, after all, merely a hotel room; it is a personal arrangement of material belongings that often either have stories of their own or serve as the background of stories. So, a significant aspect of dwelling is preserving: cleaning, repairing, arranging, keeping personal mementos. When contemporary feminists reject the value of affirming home because of its association with oppression or privilege, Young cautions them to rethink the entire conception of home as a "critical value." That is, to criticize the global culture and the limited philosophical framework in which the positive values of home—safety, individuation, privacy—are not extended to all but limited to those who have the means to consume and so to control these aspects of affective and practical life.

Existential-phenomenology and psychoanalysis have gained acceptance in feminist circles, in part because they do not ignore affective life. In fact, they each claim to constitute an affective, heterogeneous subject. But from the point of view of the essays in part 2, "Enactments between Existentialism and Psychoanalysis," they fail to give that subject adequate freedom when they insist upon oppositional distinctions such as immanence-transcendence and subject-object. In "Splitting the Subject: The Interval between Immanence and Transcendence," Gail Weiss both carries out an original critique of the existential-phenomenological use of the immanence-transcendence distinction and conceives of the subject as a bodily ego whose constitution exceeds the limits of the Lacanian project. Weiss begins with an analysis of Iris Young's account of "throwing like a girl" in which Young characterizes living as a woman in contemporary Western, industrial, patriarchal society as a tension between immanence and transcendence that arises from the self-referred quality of "feminine" bodily comportment. Weiss concentrates on the bias attached to the acts (transcendencies) that require paying close attention to one's body. Given that all actions have a socially referred character, does not the social situation profoundly affect how one pays attention to one's own body?

For women, the socially referred character of their bodily existence often dominates or overwhelms their own experience of their body's capabilities. This bodily alienation reflects that of the Lacanian mirror stage in which "I am watching this imaginary other watching me," resulting in a subject split between the bodily modalities of "I can" and "I cannot." Rather than focusing on how this fragments the subject and reduces her to her body, Weiss creates a practice in which fragmentation and objectification are not necessarily oppressive and possibly are self-affirming. Weiss argues that bodily integrity is created through developing a greater sensitivity to one's bodily changes, capacities, movements, and gestures, and she thinks anew Merleau-Ponty's chiasmic encounter between being touched and touching and being seen and seeing. Relived, as an experience of fission, the narcissism of the mirror produces a stronger sense of self rather than one that is merely negatively mediated by the presence and perspective of others. By appropriating and remaking the tools of existential and phenomenological analysis that have been used against women and minorities, Weiss enacts new and positive accounts and concepts that arise with and out of the positive practices that women engage in their own lives and bodies.

In "Simone de Beauvoir: Disrupting the Metonymy of Gender," Debra Bergoffen is interested in engaging the fullest possibilities of Beauvoir's thought beyond existentialism, humanism, and Marxism by bringing to thought aspects of Beauvoir's critique of patriarchy that are usually not recognized or thematized as relevant to feminist thought. Bergoffen discovers two specific elements in Beauvoir: (1) that patriarchy distorts the meaning of subjectivity for both men and women, and (2) that patriarchy conceals and distorts the ethical dimensions of the erotic. Out of these two critiques, Bergoffen produces an ethics of the erotic. Bergoffen argues that Beauvoir's complicated view of the patriarchal gender system acknowledges its perversity and immorality, yet recognizes that it is not merely the effect of myth and habit. Rather, gender can be understood as referring to the materially given that passes itself off as immutably given. Materially given flesh is not the so-called natural body of gender but a "boundary" body produced within a metonymic system, an economy of part-whole substitutions that satisfies the desire for identity, clarity, and distinction. Using the psychoanalytic analysis of infantile libidinal attachment to part-objects (attachments that must be outgrown in the direction of a preference for the whole object) to reorganize the Lacanian mirror stage as a part-whole distinction, Bergoffen argues that the latter is a deliberate refusal on the part of the infant of its being as a whole object, such that identifying with the imago is the beginning of self-alienation. The ego-imago is the part passing itself off as the whole psychic reality that functions to repress the voice of the whole. Gender, like the ego, is a part-object, and the so-called whole objects (patriarchically gendered men and women) are, like the ego, part-objects passing for wholes, or as Bergoffen now writes this: "(w)holes."

Like Weiss, Bergoffen configures anew the elements of the immanence-transcendence distinction because, in Beauvoir's account, girls do not have a clearly visible bodily sign of transcendence. Unable to alienate herself in a part of herself, the girl's entire body is the site of self-alienation and retrieval. Although patriarchy codes the woman's sexual and reproductive organs as immanent, it forgets the ambiguities of the male organ: that it is not always erect, that there are "wet" dreams. And, it forgets that women's ability to give birth is a mark of transcendence. For patriarchy, the ambiguously sexed transcendent and immanent bodies of men and women are gendered as transcendent or immanent. This, she argues, is patriarchy's bad faith, a contingent historical response to the lost securities of childhood that rule in patriarchy's version of the erotic. Bergoffen's attention to the affectivities of women's erotic experience produces the conclusion that we have paid a high price—passion itself—for patriarchy's version of the erotic, and she insists that the securities of gender are no fair recompense for what is lost of erotic ethics.

Although phenomenology (whether Hegelian dialectics or Merleau-Pontean habituation) has often been embraced by feminists for its articulation of otherness or its willingness to theorize the body, as a method, it is not without limits. The essays in part 3, "Emancipating Phenomenology," refute the negation, the essentialism, and the bodily confinement phenomenology weaves around its articulation of women. Morny Joy's chapter, "Love and the Labor of the Negative: Irigaray and Hegel," creates a version of Luce Irigaray's philosophical invention with respect to the role of the negative in Hegel. It produces a philosophy that liberates women from essentialist claims. Joy maintains that Hegel, embraced by so many feminists, artificially introduces alienation in service to a higher, though equally suspicious, unity. In Irigaray's interpolation, negativity is radically revised and reconceived. Joy argues that Irigaray's growing preoccupation with establishing a right order of relationship, an ethics, between men and women and between particular men and women moves her away from Hegel's conception of desire and love as something that denies women full participation. Because Hegel conceives of love as a labor of the universal, it is unavailable to woman who must love this or that particular man or child. Irigaray, however, affirms the singular and rethinks the negative, not as negation but as the element that each gender must encounter on its own terms, as singular, heterogeneous, and unique, as what I have been calling qualitative affective life.

Joy claims that Irigaray is carrying out a radical revision of Hegel that is an enactment of her own thought. Thus, Irigaray's reflections on Hegel's reading of *Antigone* are not a refutation of Hegel's distortion of Sophocles' text, nor are they a pretext for vindicating the bonding of sister to sister, nor are they a direct confrontation with Hegel's pronouncements, as previous feminist readers have claimed. For Joy, Irigaray is going beyond the limits of the project that these thinkers attribute to her to reveal the double logic at work in Hegel's thought. She shows how women are assimilated by male social values that forbid them access to universal (and cosmic) consciousness, then destroyed by the values that have assimilated them without their consent. Because this method permeates Irigaray's creative work, in particular, what Joy takes to be her drive for social reform and for the personal (singular) refinement of the sometimes destructive forces of desire into love, Joy concludes that Irigaray's method can be appreciated for its determination to right the wrongs of instrumental dualism in service to male hierarchy. Irigaray's refusal of any final Hegelian-type synthesis in favor of a "sensible transcendental" is the sign of Irigaray's creation of a philosophy of plurality and transformation through concrete and singular relations.

In the chapter titled, "'The Sum of What She Is Saying': Bringing Essentials Back to the Body," Helen A. Fielding maintains that the contemporary era is one oriented toward rationalizing and systematizing all existence, and the more this takes place, the more the body has come under scrutiny. That is, in spite of numerous attempts by feminist and other philosophers to rethink such crucial categories as mind/body dualism, the body has been reproduced, in French theory, as an object of social discourse. The challenge that Fielding sets into motion is to enact a philosophy of the body in terms of embodiment. Fielding believes that, as a method, a reconfigured phenomenology can go a long way towards filling the gaps that exist between two extreme conceptions of the body: that of a static reality preexisting the discursive and that of a purely culturally or socially inscribed body. On the one hand, there are feminists who argue that most feminists are engaging in a "nominal" not a "real" essentialism of the body. Because language can be purely formal due to the way it categorizes, this may be a distinction without a difference. Other feminists have found no better ground for the body in experience than in essence. This is because, they warn, the whole province of "authentic" experience cannot be trusted, for experience is always an interpretation formed in terms of the background of the interpreter and by her society.

In order to distinguish between the "body as object" and a radically different concept of the body, that of the body-subject, Fielding draws our attention to the ways in which the body-subject "opens out onto and into the world, the ways in which the corporeal subject interacts with others and with her environment." There is a crucial change of thinking here, for no longer is the body the focus of interest, instead the corporeal subject is at stake. Merleau-Ponty claims that for a corporeal subject, cognition, far from being the superior function, overlaps and so interacts with perception, motility, social, and affective relations. Fielding thinks that this overlapping and interacting are the corporeal being's own structures, and they provide the means for a corporeal rethinking of essences, if not of language. These would-be essences adhere to particular geographies and particular historical contexts. As such, an embodied essence is neither linguistic nor formal but is a manner of inhabiting the world, the capacity or skill to be with things and others. This essence is a type of generality that is never closed as long as the embodied subject is living, moving, and perceiving. In a far-reaching step, Fielding argues that such essences are not in the body at all but are the connections, the joints between bodies and cultural and historical zones, connecting the embodied subject to the rest of life. By means of the paradoxical conception of an embodied essence, philosophy can keep from reducing the body to either discourse or to an object, and Fielding can create a concept of human beings as intertwined with the world and as embodied subjects.

The final chapter in this section is that by Monika Langer. Langer begins "Making the Phenomenological Reduction Experientially Real" with an account of three feminists who each make use of the work of Maurice Merleau-Ponty. One of the chief difficulties in using Merleau-Ponty's work for feminist purposes is that he ignores women's experiences of embodiment by failing to describe women's historical and social situation. This is a more serious allegation than it first appears to be insofar as these omissions amount to a suppression of difference that can never provide an "ideal ontological grounding" for enacting a feminist philosophy. The suppression of women's experiences also radically brings into question the notion of "the body" as a concept that conceals more than it reveals about women's concrete, lived experience. Langer argues that the conflict at the heart of Merleau-Ponty's phenomenology is that he claims to describe concrete, lived experience, while actually describing seemingly universal structures of bodily existence. Thus it is no big surprise to feminists that this universal subject turns out to be masculine.

If Merleau-Ponty's philosophy is to be of use to feminist philosophers, it has to be on some other basis. Langer makes the completely singular connection between the practice of feminist "consciousness raising" as "a sustained reflection on, and revalorization of, one's own prereflective experience of living as a woman in patriarchal society" and takes this prereflective grounding as the reworking of Merleau-Ponty's method of phenomenological reduction. It is her task to theorize this method and to describe the practices and freedoms it opens up. Langer turns to Merleau-Ponty's "Cézanne's Doubt." Cézanne is valorized for practicing phenomenological reduction in art, a practice that is the opposite of Descartes's, whose doubt leads to the establishment of rigid dichotomies between mind and body, reason and sensibility. Cézanne bracketed common sense and scientific attitudes while drawing attention to the sensible and primordial world underlying science. The reason engendered by such a phenomenological reduction is of a different order than Descartes, but nonetheless, it is reason.

At the prereflective level, Langer argues, dualism is overcome insofar as immanence and transcendence mutually imply one another, leading

Cézanne to claim that "the landscape thinks itself in me." Yet, following Derrida, Langer is not happy with Merleau-Ponty's linking of the "me" of the painter and philosopher to the "we men" of the horizon of humanity. Her point is that such a link is not a slight matter, for the direct and regularized link undermines phenomenological reduction. She proceeds by incorporating the notion "sinuosity," from Jeffner Allen, to describe paintings such as *Zunoqua of the Cat Village,* by artist Emily Carr, using this notion to overturn the false binary of nature-culture. In the painting, cultural elements such as human habitations and the carved figure of Zunoqua are inseparable from the animal, vegetable, and even monstrous world, and all the sinuous elements of the painting radiate the perception of a vital rhythm characterizing the realm of phenomenological reduction. Such images are neither chaos nor Cartesianism, but as Langer proposes, they serve as the basis for a revised phenomenological reduction and call upon us (female and male) to learn new modes of engaging with the world.

Part 4 of the volume, "Creative Collaborations," consists of two chapters that thematize as they develop the process of writing as collaboration—an idea that has operated throughout this volume insofar as these enactments of philosophy are collaborations with those French philosophers whose work inhabits yet is exceeded by each of these reflections. Penelope Deutscher's chapter, "Disappropriations: Luce Irigaray and Sarah Kofman," rethinks the philosophy of Sarah Kofman as a feminist enactment of collaborative writing and not merely as mimicry of or commentary on contemporary French philosophy. Deutscher accomplishes this by way of a remarkable elucidation of Luce Irigaray's embodiment of the feminine as occupying and exceeding the categories philosophy has established for women. Like Paul de Man and Jacques Derrida, who are in agreement regarding the contradictory tensions in Rousseau's work, but differ with regard to the question of "appropriation," Luce Irigaray and Sarah Kofman both agree and disagree with respect to the work of Freud. Deutscher notes that Kofman repeatedly distances herself from Luce Irigaray's interpretation of Freud's "Femininity" essay, even while acknowledging many parallels. Thus, as de Man directs repeated jabs at Derrida in order to promote Rousseau, so Kofman does the same for Irigaray's reading of Freud in order to revalorize Freud. And yet, she does so using the same tools as Derrida—notably the distinction between what the text declares and what it describes—as well as those of de Man, who insists that Rousseau is in control of the complexities of his text.

Ultimately, Deutscher argues, it appears that the interest in identifying Freud and Rousseau as deconstructive writers leads Kofman and de Man to resist reading them deconstructively, and thus to a new and creative use of their work. Yet the debate, as Deutscher opens it up, is as much about deconstruction as it is about Rousseau's or Freud's texts. In particular, any deconstructive reading takes up that text's complexities in a manner that introduces quasi-ethical issues of appropriation. Why, Deutscher asks, does Kofman take such pains to disappropriate her own (and Irigaray's) complex reading of Freud and to insist on Freud's complexity? Why does Kofman identify her own style of reading with deconstruction and insist that her work is a repetition of a text, whether that of Freud, Kant, Rousseau, Plato, Nietzsche, or Compte, while Deutscher clearly thinks that it is wrong to relegate Kofman to the ranks of faithful commentator rather than creative thinker? Because, Deutscher insists, for Kofman, texts that do not "cross-fertilize" one another—as when in her reading of Nietzsche and Freud, Nietzsche becomes partly Freud and Freud becomes partly Nietzsche—do not interest her. Yet, for Kofman, the work of *disappropriation* continues insofar as it is her own "self" as well as that of the texts she reads that are illusions; destabilized as unified, proper selves they become complex, poly-vocal, and textually self-conflicting.

Ultimately, Kofman's critique of deconstructive appropriation may be misplaced insofar as the boundaries between reader and read are—as Kofman certainly knew—unstable. Kofman thinks that Irigaray is not in-serting enough of herself into the texts she reads, so is not risking the iden-tificatory/compromising/transformative mimicry of writing. Kofman may be said to have failed to refigure the feminine in her analyses in order to refigure philosophy, yet, Deutscher argues, she does this in order to demon-strate that philosophical reason is in close proximity to the sexual posi-tioning of the philosopher, or, as I have argued above, philosophy, if it is to be creative, must risk embracing the individual's affective freedom. This is a gesture of freedom that the institution of philosophy tries too often to deny to women philosophers, and so it fails to recognize this gesture when a philosopher eludes capture and stages the feminine.

Tamsin Lorraine collaborates with the French philosopher Gilles Deleuze who, as she states, "writes only in collaboration and never as what we might call an autonomous author." In writing "Becoming-Imperceptible as a Mode of Self-Presentation: A Feminist Model Drawn from a Deleuzian Line of Flight," Lorraine begins by focusing on Deleuze's manner of self-presentation as collaborative. More than the fact of Deleuze's collabora-tion with Félix Guattari or Claire Parnet, each book is a form of expression of the differenciating of differences such that no unified text can be con-structed. Deleuze contests a unified identity and suggests that affective life is much more a matter of a collaborative encounter with the world than of autonomous and individual agency. Lorraine is drawn to Deleuze's work because, "Deleuze thinks that traditional philosophy impedes and even prevents thinking." She finds in Deleuze a mode of thought that works with processes of becoming—the imperceptible—what cannot be reduced to a relation of similarity with something else it resembles and so fits into a known order and is given a general name. This singularity is the difference, and paradoxically, preserving such difference is precisely what makes collaborative writing occur. To make her point, Lorraine emphasizes the fundamental affective encounter with the world that compels thought. Such an encounter, Lorraine insists, is grasped as wonder, love, hate, or suffering and not as a category of reason or a principle of intellectual understanding. Furthermore, Deleuze's transcendental empiricism, that "the form of identity in objects relies upon a ground in the unity of a thinking subject," opens the way for Lorraine's claim that imperceptibility, the affective encounter, undoes the assumption that the various faculties of a self will converge in order to recognize an already knowable object. Rather, multiplicity at the level of the object implies a complementary multiplicity at the level of the subject, so both can be construed as multiple dimensions eliding categorical definition and identity.

Lorraine argues that, as creative thinkers, we must make use of the affective encounter by refusing traditional boundaries. The writer has to allow for the use-value of difference to be produced rather than fall back upon habits that would strip singularities of their difference and reduce them to familiar but banal concepts. This is why, according to Lorraine, Deleuze emphasizes not the beginning nor the end of any writing, but rather what she calls the points of contact, the moment in which people, ideas, and events interact thereby putting one another into question. Thus, although the category of "woman" has been mapped onto a terrain marked by gender warfare, it remains available for any particular woman to present herself in terms of the connections she has created or will create. The focus here is on the moment and place where something new happens, where something is enacted or created from an alternative point of view in the moment of connection. Insofar as the project of this volume is to demonstrate that women are creating new structures of thought out of their multiple affective engagements and practices in the world, Lorraine's work articulates and affirms this endeavor in every respect.

Each of the chapters in part 5, titled "Resistance, Flight, Creation," take up "feminist methodology" as a challenge to resist traditional methodologies, to flee habituating frameworks, and to create new forms of life and thought. They are profoundly engaged in creating new concepts for new practices and, in many respects, they are the most daring experiments in the book. Ewa Plonowska Ziarek begins with an account of Foucault that she interpolates with Deleuze's reading of Foucault for the sake of her own revaluation of values. In "Between the Visible and the Articulable: Matter, Interpellation, and Resistance in Foucault's *Discipline and Punish*," Ziarek takes up the concern of many contemporary feminist thinkers that Foucault's analysis of the technologies of individuals seems to evacuate psychic space and eliminate the possibility of agency. Foucault's purported ethos appears to be realized largely in a negative manner that demonstrates the insufficiency of various liberal attempts at freedom. Yet Ziarek is convinced that Foucault inspires something feminists will find useful, beginning with a diagnosis of patriarchal culture and ending with an account of how to transform that culture.

Much of the power of Foucault's work that lead Ziarek to a theory of social and cultural transformation lies in his articulation of causality and its relation to subjectivity. She argues that it is a misreading of Foucault to see him providing utilitarian principles for his own use, and she turns to Deleuze to explain why. Deleuze extrapolates from Foucault not a homology of language and visibility endorsed by utilitarianism but rather a disjunction between them, especially with respect to law and the prison. As an immanent cause, disciplinary power is neither visible nor discursive. It only becomes so when actualized in a specific historical formation such as the panopticon and its discourse of delinquency. These two do not have the same genealogy or object of punishment nor the same form; they are two different semiotic systems.

Deleuze calls Foucault's concept of power an immanent dispersed cause, a cause that produces neither continuity nor calculable results as it acts within institutional frameworks and specific formations of knowledge. As immanent cause, power produces a stabilization of forces and force relations that otherwise would remain unstable. Such stabilized forces diverge into forms of content and forms of expression, that is, forms of power and forms of knowledge that are irreducible. However, as immanent cause, power is not reducible to its effects, and the power substrate of forces remains in its sphere as the possibility of resistance and therefore social transformation. This points to what is often overlooked in the discussion of power's relation to bodies: there is a difference between visible and discursive bodies that corresponds to the deployment of the disciplinary regime acting on the body and the deployment of sex into discourse, enabling the organization of power over life. The regulation of isolated bodies fixed in cells and subject to continuous observation trains bodies to be docile and inscribes them as the materialized relation of forces incapable of resistance. Crucially, Ziarek also recognizes that insofar as Foucault reconceptualizes matter as the actualization of specific relations between forces, the materialization of "bodies" precedes the matter-form distinction. If power is actualized in bodies in multiple modes, there is no final bodily form, and the reversal of forces, a new materialization, is always available. Likewise, discourse operates to manage life forces by hystericizing women's bodies, sexualizing childhood, or psychiatrizing perversions effecting a new set of relations between power and pleasure, history and life. This is why, Ziarek concludes, in Foucault's discussion of the soul or unified moral conscience the soul appears as the ghostly double of the subjected body, the fictitious unity of a fictitious unity. And the function of the soul has been, in modern thought, replaced by sex, both being instruments in the management of the collectivity. But, insofar as the divergence remains between forms of expression and forms of content, between discourse and visibility, we can ask what makes possible the emergence of a new configuration of forces, what yields to the creation of new concepts and frameworks? Ziarek maintains that there are not-yet realized forces, forces that are not fully expended in the production of any specific historical body or any historical type of subject. They emerge in the gaps or fissures between the visible and the discursive, and they constitute the possibility of resistance and of freedom for materialized bodies and historically constituted subjects.

The final chapter in this volume returns us to the concerns expressed by Hazel Barnes at the beginning. It formulates practices of feminist enactments that meet the realities of cultural diversity. Whereas French philosophy creates theories of freedom, feminist and minority theorists pragmatically commit themselves to making it possible for diverse peoples to live freely. Thus, Jane Drexler's "Carnival: The Novel, Wor(l)ds, and Practicing Resistance" is a work aimed at the affective, theoretical, and practical lives that are creating the future. Drexler takes on one of the chief issues in contemporary French philosophy. That is, if contemporary social orders are arranged to ignore or marginalize real differences relative to set of pre-established categories of identity, then is there any hope for social change? Can the suppressed and maginalized others gain a place in society without losing their own particular difference? Drexler's approach to this issue is unique and original. Her radical reconsideration of Mikhail Bakhtin's concept of the carnival puts this idea into motion using ontological arguments drawn from Gilles Deleuze and Félix Guattari.

Drexler starts with the familiar argument that, for Bakhtin, a multitude of different language systems and voices that resist submission to any dominant ideology or language system exist within different classes and social orders. Such "heteroglossia" disrupts and cracks open the categories and organization of any ideology or language system to dismantle the social body in a manner than can be positive. Bakhtin locates heteroglossia in the narrative novel where multiple common languages, parody, hyperbole, and hybrid constructions, as well as the words and actions of various characters, exemplify differing and conflicting social roles and attitudes. In feminist literature these strategies have created a strategy for rearticulating women's voices in literature and because literature is part of society, in society as well. Drexler argues that the dialogical resistance of heteroglossia lays the foundation for Bakhtin's conception of the "carnival," and that carnival, the site at which characters become subjects of discourse and not merely objects of the dominant discourse, opposes authoritative institutions and so is a real and powerful force for undermining hierarchical social orders. Drexler's strongest arguments against the predominant postmodernist view of the creative power of carnival come from her use of Deleuze's and Guattari's ontology. Carnival is not defined as a totalized system with a finalized telos, but is a process that flows and cuts across the web of heteroglossic voices and persons, a web of multiplicities that does not allow any single one to dominate exclusively. Deleuze and Guattari would call it a plane of consistency, a body without organs that is actualized only in the real practices of life, whether those of the novel or those of the political activist. And heteroglossia is what exposes this plane, this refusal of hierarchy that experiments with life. In reworking Bakhtin in this manner, Drexler not only retrieves his work from the postmodernist dilemma of utopian idealism, but also herself participates in the venerable actions and practices of feminist activism. She rescues Bakhtin's theory from a moribund and nonproductive reading in order to put it to use, to put it into action, for thought and for life.

The book concludes with an extensive bibliography of feminist enactments of French philosophy compiled by Helen A. Fielding. When I first proposed assembling such a bibliography to Helen, I envisioned it as consisting of largely Anglo-American feminist writing. However, Fielding quickly expanded the range to accommodate the many feminist perspectives she encountered in the French and German languages as well. The results, I think, speak for themselves and speak loudly to the variety and range of feminist interests in French philosophy among English-, French-, and German-speaking scholars. To the best of my knowledge, this is the most complete bibliography of its kind ever collected, and I both thank and honor Fielding for her considerable efforts toward publishing it in this collection.

PART I

Creating Concepts
from Home

Philosophy and Gender:
A First-Person View

HAZEL E. BARNES

In this day of identity politics, point of view is everything. So at the outset, I acknowledge that whatever I may say will reflect the views of a professor with a longtime investment in existentialism as well as, inevitably, the situation of a white American woman. Moreover, what perhaps most differentiates me from the majority of contemporary women philosophers is that I am closer to the end of my life than they are to the beginning of theirs. I do not speak apologetically of my point of view. I *like* it. The intention behind my title is precisely to show how my view of philosophy and gender both clashed with and conformed to the prevailing one at the time I was starting my career, how I would place myself now in today's infinitely more complex situation, and how those two things are related. When I was in college, it was a matter for serious debate as to whether there could be a *feminine philosopher*. Today, although a few like to think that a *feminist philosophy* is an oxymoron, the serious question for most thoughtful persons is whether it can be introduced into the philosophical tradition without effectively shattering that tradition and whether this might not be a good thing.

I am not addressing myself solely to women and will not dwell at length on the practical aspects of the difference between the situation of a hopeful female Ph.D. fifty years ago and those of young women today who are considering the possibility of becoming professors of philosophy. But perhaps a few words on the difference between my situation then and the current one may be relevant and of some interest as a reminder of how far we have come.

Though I had never suffered from any discrimination in my graduate work at Yale, I realized how many built-in limitations surrounded me when, as a new Ph.D., I began to hunt for a job. I knew that all-male schools were closed to me, which eliminated most of the established private universities. (Yale, for example, allowed women to pursue graduate work but never hired

25

them as instructors. There were *no* female undergraduates.) State and municipal universities might have a few women on their faculties, but only a tiny minority. Women's colleges, including the most distinguished, had many women on their faculties. Such an appointment I would welcome. Yet I did not feel altogether easy about a career in the confines of a girls' school. Women professors at Wilson College, which I had attended, had seemed to me, at least from September to June, to lead a somewhat nunlike existence. I confirmed that fear when I found myself teaching at a women's college in Charlotte, North Carolina. I remember the day when a well-intentioned student whispered to me that I had been seen having a beer with my hamburger for a Sunday night snack; she advised me to be careful not to get into trouble by doing things like that.

That first summer after my graduation I wished in vain for *anything* to turn up—until it finally did in early September. My anxious waiting was not helped when I had occasion, after commencement, to introduce my parents to my dissertation director. My father expressed the hope that the professor would be able to help me find a position. The reply was succinct. "I never promise to find jobs for Jews or women," he said. My first appointment was in classics, but I rather quickly moved on to positions that allowed me to combine classics and philosophy and eventually were solely in philosophy. (I have never been sure whether my interdisciplinary career shows me to be a Renaissance woman or a successful fraud, but that is another story.) When I sought to enter philosophy departments, I discovered that they were particularly unwelcoming. An example is a report that came to me from a close friend who had a relative on the all-male committee that was considering me for an assistant professorship at a large state university. All was going well when suddenly one key figure blocked the way. He would be glad to vote for Miss Barnes, he said, if the appointment were in anything but philosophy. "But," he declared, "women simply cannot think philosophically." He was far from atypical.

Although I have no reason for complaint at how things actually turned out for me, I know that I was lucky; not all women of my generation were. The difference in the opportunities open then for us and for women today is immense. In theory, there is no built-in obstacle today save what women themselves put there. Women may indeed encounter covert prejudice but not overt opposition. In practice, they undoubtedly have to prove themselves as considerably above average in order to be judged the equal of a run-of-the-mill man, but this they can do if they think it is worth the effort. That the effort required may be considerable I would be the last to deny. But I would hope that not many women would choose a merely competent male professor as a measuring stick for themselves. There is one other major difference. We older women generally assumed that the choice before us was marriage or a career, and we fought for the right to choose the latter without being labeled freaks. Many women now confront the problem of whether and how they may combine the two, a choice that poses new problems, but ones for which they are free to try to find their own solutions.

To me the more interesting question concerns the change in what philosophy as a discipline offered to me then as compared with what it holds today. How does the presence of women philosophers make a difference in how women *and* men might regard the tasks the field proposes to them?

I will indulge here in a bit more autobiography. Looking back, it seems to me that my attraction to philosophy and ultimate embrace of Sartrean existentialism hardly differed from what would have been if I had been born a boy. The primary oppression I experienced as a child was not sexist. In this respect I was singularly favored. My father, for example, tried to inspire us children by telling how, in ancient times, Hamilcar said to his sons that he wanted them to become eagles. The remarkable thing is that in urging each of us to strive to fly high, my father made no distinction between his son and his two daughters. Moreover, I had three still-unmarried aunts who were teachers. They seemed to me to have much more interesting lives than the other women who fussed around with babies. So I had the motivation to find my own pattern. The counterforce to hold me back was the extreme fundamentalist religious sect to which my family was committed—the Free Methodist Church. This imposed practical limits on my behavior, and its doctrine was appalling. What disturbed me most was not the threat of Hell and the Day of Judgment; these, like death, were too far off to be immediately threatening. What did weigh upon me was two other things: first, the insistence that one must be perfect and that secret unworthy impulses were as bad as overt sinful acts. I remember particularly those verses from the New Testament: "Be ye therefore perfect as your Father in Heaven is perfect." And, "As a man thinketh in his heart, so is he." I would have been grateful this time if the sexist language had excluded me, but regrettably it did not. No wonder I developed a constant feeling of guilt—though whether I felt I had wronged God or my parents or myself I could not have said. The second source of conflict, though this came when I was just a bit older, was the claim that it was only through a personal revelation, which came in a dramatic conversion, usually accomplished while praying at the altar, that you could *know* the truth. (I'm thinking of the kind of public "praying through" and emotional testimonials described, for example, in James Baldwin's *Go Tell It on the Mountain*.) I found myself in a "catch-22" situation; something in me resisted this call to total self-surrender, yet how could I know what I was rejecting without trying it?

Happily, I was brought up not only on Jesus but also on William James. I recall the time my father, an admirer of James, paid (or underpaid) my sister and me a dime apiece for memorizing and reciting once a day for a week a short passage from James's essay "On Habit." Not dogmatically but subtly my father instilled in me notions of self-reliance and responsible self-determination, an optimistic confidence in our human capacity to realize the ideal of infinite progress. Such ideas were not quite compatible with the religious teachings of otherworldliness and self-abasement, but perhaps in part because of this contradiction I somehow found my way.

By the time I finished college, I had abandoned my belief in a personal God. I find it amusing that, although I was influenced partly by my discovery of Darwin, my apostasy was effected primarily by my study of Greek philosophy and finally by the work of the Roman poet Lucretius, the Epicurean "Evangelist of Atheism," as my teacher called him. But somewhat as Sartre said that although he had got rid of God before he was twelve, it took him years before he was free of the Holy Ghost, so I found myself later drawn to a philosophy tinged with mysticism. I did my doctoral dissertation on Plotinus, a third-century Greek philosopher who, to my mind, is the most rational mystic in history—or at least in the Western tradition. Coincidentally, Albert Camus centered his thesis on Plotinus. I don't know whether his fascination with this Neoplatonist was as compelling to him as mine was to me. I do know that I was so caught up in it that I could not regard my work with it as a purely scholarly investigation, but felt that I must either embrace a modernized version of it or reject it for its opposite extreme. I did the latter, probably because, despite its intellectual depth, Plotinus' philosophy displayed the two negative factors that had repelled me in the fundamentalist religion of my childhood: it neglected this world for a mythical eternity, was life denying rather than life expansive, and its truth claim rested ultimately on faith in a nonrational revelation to be attained in the ecstasy of union with the undefinable One. This latter, that old bogey of mine, was finally dispelled, strangely enough, by my reading of James's *Varieties of Religious Experience*. For although he was sympathetic to such things, James acknowledged that the recorded conversions, visions, ecstatic trances, and the like are all at best partial insights into the possibilities of our consciousness, that many of them are negative instead of reassuring, and that inevitably people's interpretations of what the experience means are determined by their individual histories and orientations. I began to read more of James and Dewey. Insofar as my naturalistic outlook could be given any label before I encountered Sartrean existentialism, I suppose it was pragmatist.

This is not the occasion to explore all the reasons why I found existentialism, Sartre's work in particular, so appealing back then in the late forties. I will mention only a few of the most obvious: it seemed to me to provide a philosophical foundation for what was only assumed in pragmatism—

that we do indeed make ourselves. Sartre's claim that we are radically free and responsible is inextricable from his view of consciousness as a non-substantial activity, not to be confused with the ego, which is its product, not its producer. Our basic consciousness, he says, is able to distance itself from the personality structure it has created, to reappraise and to modify it. This idea especially attracted me, for in introspection I had always found that the self I discovered within me was a burden without being a recourse. I mean that in self-reflection I discovered many things that I had to take into account as I tried to judge what I had been and what I wanted to be. But I found no authoritative voice to give me guidance, no sure intuition of an identity that might serve as a pattern. Rather, to use my later Sartrean language, there was only a lack to be filled. I liked Sartre's plea for authenticity. I was delighted by his analysis of bad faith as an alternative to the Freudian notion of repression and the unconscious. I particularly admired his insistence that values are not given but chosen and his suggestion that possibly the greatest creative act for any individual is the invention of an ethical system to live by. I found profound and convincing his description of how human relations are poisoned by the subject-object conflict, also the possibilities he sketched out for living in good faith with each other. And so on . . . I will speak of only one more important reason for my enthusiastic response. This is one that will serve as a transition from these autobiographical reflections to the more general question of philosophy and gender.

Sartre's view of what the human being is seemed to me to present the first solid philosophical argument I had seen to justify the claim that women, too, "make themselves." Not that Sartre himself specifically worked out the implications for women. But everything in his description of consciousness in the world demanded feminism as a corollary. I soon learned that Simone de Beauvoir had provided it in *The Second Sex,* in which she examined how "one is not born but becomes a woman." In 1950 I felt that I was thoroughly liberated, philosophically and as a woman. I was convinced that only time was required until society at large would accept the demonstrable truth that women could and should engage in men's fields as equals. Sartre and Beauvoir offered philosophical support for what I had always believed without being able to defend my conviction. What more did I need now? I was smugly complacent. Neither then nor in the preceding years did I feel discontented with philosophy because it had paid so little attention to women and their concerns, nor did it occur to me then that much of it might seem inadequate or false if looked at from a woman's point of view. Obviously I had what today is called a male-trained mind. Not only at Yale, but even earlier at my undergraduate women's college, all academic knowledge, like reason itself, was considered to be gender-neutral, especially philosophy, which claimed to deal solely with the objective and universal. As a woman, I wanted access to the field that men had formerly kept almost wholly to themselves. I never expected women to transform the landscape.

Simone de Beauvoir was a precursor of the feminist revolution. The feminists who came after her radicalized the situation of women with respect to philosophy, with consequences for their male colleagues as well. Whether undertaking to study or to teach it, women and men alike currently see before them possibilities and choices unimagined in my time. Obviously I cannot say how this looks from within, but my purpose is to describe how the philosophical scene seems to me who have not, after all, shut my eyes and ears since the publication of *The Second Sex* at the midpoint of this century.

What strikes me first of all is the reappearance of an old question in a new form: *Should* a woman study the works of the philosophical tradition? Not *can* she do it? But should she *bother* to devote time to this purely male discourse that, with very few exceptions, has ignored women when it has not downgraded them? (I recognize that a comparable question has been raised by racial and ethnic minorities with respect to the entire Western tradition in the humanities. Much of what I say might be relevant in this connection, but here I will concentrate only on the gender issue.)

In the Western tradition overt negative statements about women are of two sorts:[1] Some are clearly expressions of a writer's personal prejudice or neurosis and unrelated to his philosophical thought; for example, the absurd vituperations of Schopenhauer and Nietzsche. The best response to such ridiculous remarks is to laugh at them. Other philosophers, most notably Aristotle, have offered philosophical argument to account for what they took to be the evident intellectual and moral inferiority of females, never questioning the oppression that prevented women from developing their intellectual and ethical capacities as they might have under different circumstances. The proper response here is obvious—to challenge and to correct the misconceptions; philosophers (both male and female) have been effectively doing so for some time now, but the task is hardly finished. The majority of all philosophers who have not overtly or covertly been influenced by religious precommitments have tacitly assumed philosophy to be gender-neutral but have ignored the possibility that women might have anything significant to contribute, either by way of support or question. Why should women not ignore them in return? A handful of disgusted feminists might be willing to go so far. Most of them will not, for a variety of obvious reasons. Just as it is important to set the record straight when we find that historical accounts of events have been distorted, so it is imperative to examine whether and how the one-sidedness of philosophers may have been injurious over the centuries. It would be most interesting, too, to show how the inclusion of a new gender-conscious point of view might reveal the poverty of a particular philosophy taken as a whole or might, as could easily be possible, indicate how it could be expanded or enriched if looked at in other contexts. We need to read past philosophers critically, maybe even aggressively, but, in my opinion, our approach should not be so hostile that we fail to salvage what may still be of value to us. Let me clarify with an example:

Julia, a colleague of mine, asked me to read an outline she had drawn up for presenting Plato's *Symposium* to her humanities class. (She was not seeking my approval as an older colleague but checking with me as a classicist.) Starting with the absurdity of Plato's depiction of men discussing love with no women present (presumably women by themselves would never do the same), she intended for the rest of the class period to make the dialogue a target for an attack on Greek sexism. Philosophical and literary questions she ignored. Possibly she would get to them on the second day allotted to the work; it is hard to see how by then any of the students would feel inclined to find anything of value in the *Symposium*. Julia's approach might be regarded sympathetically as an understandable overreaction to the centuries of male-biased interpretation of philosophical and literary works but that is beside the point. Admittedly, Athens supported "the reign of the phallus"[2] to a degree that was almost pathological, and its rampant sexism must be weighed in the balance of any appraisal of ancient Greek civilization. But to do this to the *Symposium?* From every point of view such a travesty is indefensible. In the first place, Plato was one of the rare early philosophers to assign *any* importance to women. True, he believed that fewer women than men were capable of attaining the highest degrees of intellect. Still, he did make room for philosopher queens as well as kings in his *Republic.* But quite aside from all that, I recall the excitement and absolute awe with which I first read the *Symposium.* (So *this* is philosophy, I marveled.) It seems to me that my colleague was depriving all of her students of their birthright. I still regard this dialogue as one of the very greatest works of art. To try to block access to it is as though we would screen off the warriors in the tomb at Xian in China because we know that the Emperor who ordered them rewarded the artisans with death.

In any case, nobody, not even Descartes, who claimed to do so, can "do philosophy" intelligently without taking into account what has already been done.

Women who come to philosophy today do indeed still confront one obvious problem: the paucity of women philosophers to be read. The earlier part of this century gave us Hannah Arendt, Simone Weil, and Simone de

Beauvoir, for example, but they are all but lost in the total picture. Women philosophers hold but a tiny space even in the most liberal curriculum, just as women do in art museums and in lists of composers. While I predict that this will not be the case in the farther future, I have to admit that this remains at present a negative factor for female philosophy students. On the other hand, if we are to speak of the opportunity to write or to teach philosophy, there has never at any date or place been a richer prospect for women; and I am not speaking merely of the practical side. I think that some of the new advantages extend to men, too, not only to those belonging to minority groups but to white Anglo-Saxons as well. But let me for a moment consider the choice before a woman student wanting to work in philosophy.

First, she has before her two kinds of models: There are women who have distinguished themselves in the fields long established by men and in much the same way as men; for example, Martha Nussbaum working in ancient philosophy or Ruth Marcus in what I will loosely call the analytic field. Or she may work as a feminist who uses philosophy; for example, Alison Jaggar or Judith Butler. Some women have entered the house of philosophy as well-behaved guests, anxious to fit in with the plans and lifestyles of their hosts; others insist that the furniture be rearranged and propose to repaint the walls. And they suggest that if men will help, everyone will be better off and live more pleasantly. There is room for both types, the discipline needs both, but it is the latter who raise difficult questions and set the tasks to be done. Most obvious are these:

The first is relatively easy: In cleansing philosophy of its bias, we need to ferret out those instances in which philosophers have identified "human" with "male." Beauvoir, of course did this magnificently in *The Second Sex,* pointing out that in all spheres men have defined "human" in such a way as to make woman a deviant. Even the supposedly gender-neutral analysis of propositions in analytic or language philosophy needs to be scrutinized. But to hunt down negative examples is not enough. Philosophical discussion should be positively expanded to include those concerns of women that have been ignored.[3]

Second, in the field of ethics, we confront the knotty problem of "women's values." Is there such a thing? Certainly the work of recent psychologists and sociologists (e.g., Carol Gilligan's *In a Different Voice*) so indicates. But there is no agreement as to their origin—genetic (biological) or cultural. If it is genetic, does this mean that we are faced forever with two separate and competing schools of ethics for which mutual tolerance is the most we can expect? Or is a new androgyny a realistic ideal? If the supposed feminine values are culturally induced, then are we to regard them as temporary protective devices of the weak, fated to disappear when sexual equality becomes a reality? I am thinking of such things as the claim that in making ethical decisions, women tend to be more relational, concerned with people and consequences more than with principles, with the particular rather than the universal. Is this to acknowledge that after all women are not cut out to be philosophers, or that philosophy should be more inclusive, should learn from what women's experience has taught them? Nel Noddings, for example, proposes that women, because of their midway position—serving as authority for their children but subordinate to their husbands—have developed skills and insights as mediators. Are these transferable to traditional ethical debates? And what of Nodding's much discussed philosophy of caring? Some feminists reject it as offering a disguised form of the old ideal of female self-sacrifice. Others believe that Nodding's work may throw new light on the question of personal responsibility and the search for the more inclusive claim that have always been a central concern for ethics.[4]

Third, I suppose the most radical challenge from feminist philosophers has been the question of the nature and proper role for reason or rationality. Some French feminists have identified reason, as traditionally defined, with male thinking and condemned it as phallogocentric. They have been particularly concerned with ways in which language has reinforced a narrow, restrictive view of what constitutes logical thought and its appropriate application. They and feminists generally (and some male fellow travelers as well) have been working effectively on two fronts: first, of course, to pinpoint past and present instances of how what has passed for rationality is in fact nothing but thought patterns that men have preferred. More important (and here even men who are not self-proclaimed supporters of feminism have been active) philosophers are questioning the supposed divorce between reason and emotion, arguing that frequently both are necessary in arriving at a valid judgment, some regarding the two as virtually inextricable. The psychologist Robert Coles has gone so far as to speak not only of emotional but of moral thought. Moral cognition—*there* is a bold idea! Yet wasn't it something of this sort that Plato was trying to do in the *Symposium?*

Finally, a few more radical feminists have accused traditional philosophers of pursuing abstractions so remote from everyday living that they have made of the discipline a sort of word game. This charge, if it was ever justified, is no longer so. Applied philosophy has come into its own. We have medical, legal, and business ethics. And the oldest questions, after a period of being thrust outside as unfashionable, unanswerable, and unprofitable for discussion, or simply worn out, have come back in new forms and demanded urgent answers. How do we define life and death? When does animal existence become also human? Where does the human species stand in relation to nature? These and related ancient problems are relevant to decisions we have to make daily, ranging in context from abortion, assisted suicide, and euthanasia to problems of the origin and rights of sexual preference, of animal rights, and of ecology. I cannot resist raising also a new one: the ethics of human cloning—if the recent experiment on sheep should lead us to that point. (It's appropriate, I think, that the manufacture of identical copies should begin with sheep.) If human cloning becomes a reality, would the impulse to clone oneself be proof of colossal egotism or a manifestation of Aristotle's great-souled man? In matters so vital to all of us, I think everyone must agree that *all* voices should be heard, sometimes to insure that what passes for gender encompassing is indeed that and sometimes because what seems like an anomaly can prove to be a key to a larger vista. An example here is the story of what happened when Gertrude Stein was in William James's psychology class at Harvard. After conducting an experiment, the students concluded that because all were in agreement except for Gertrude Stein, her reactions could safely be disregarded. James insisted that, on the contrary, Miss Stein's replies *must* be included as an important part of the evidential data. I do not know just what was involved in this instance; certainly Stein later enabled us all to see things in a new way.

Of course, nothing will change unless women continue to engage themselves. I thought of this recently in a particular context. To me one of the most exciting areas in philosophy just now is the exploration of the nature of consciousness and intelligence, whether thought of as cognitive psychology or as philosophy. I have been following in recent issues of *The New York Review of Books* the discussion of consciousness and artificial intelligence by John Searle and other philosophers. And I have noticed that not a single woman was represented. Was this due to editorial bias? Or are women philosophers so engaged in immediate feminist problems that they have no interest in this fundamental question? I am not sure. But do I know that I do not want to see consciousness itself become a subject for men only.

In what I have said, I have not pretended to be objective in the sense of being disengaged. If I have not used the words *we feminists,* this is not because I do not consider myself a feminist; quite the contrary. But although *feminist* is still sometimes used as a pejorative even now, it is, in some circles, a term one has to prove one's right to apply to oneself. In claiming it for myself, I recognize that *my* feminism is peculiarly my own, colored by my generation, by my existentialist philosophy, and by my individual experiences and personal prejudices. In some ways I simply do not fit even in the mainstream. I am, for example, too puritanical (or should I say, too fastidious, or too romantic) to feel comfortable with the idea of sex as entertainment; I am too pedantic to use *their* as a singular possessive or *herstory* because I know that *history* is not a gender-laden word like *wo-man* but a derivative of the neutral Greek *historia* (inquiry). Furthermore, as we all know, feminists are divided among themselves. Perhaps I can best show where I stand today, as a woman and as a would-be philosopher, by indicating how I would position myself with respect to three major controversies.[5]

First, the question of whether I think feminism should be based primarily on the assumption of equality or on the recognition of sexual differences. Both my education and my involvement with existentialism inevitably lead me to incline strongly to the side of equality. I am initially suspicious of any argument stressing innate differences between male and female; this, after all, was the assumption supporting women's oppression. In its strongest form it smacks of the fallacious "separate but equal" claim utilized by former segregationists. And I would argue that difference itself can be accommodated under the goal of insuring to everyone equal opportunity for self-making. Clearly, we must distinguish between biological and situational differences; my objections are solely to attributing a deterministic force to the former. Some neo-Freudian and Lacanian feminists seem to come dangerously close to reinstituting the old Freudian "anatomy is destiny," a view I resist whether it is in the form presented by some of the French feminists or by Camille Paglia. I stubbornly insist that becoming a woman means designing one's place creatively, not building a nest by instinct. That centuries of male dominance have rendered language phallogocentric is undeniable. To claim, following Lacan, that a girl's psychological development differs from that of a boy because of the association of the "word" of the father with the penis is not, in my opinion, an improvement over the infamous "penis envy" ascribed to all females by Freud, even if enfolded in new theories of language.

I do believe there is a legitimate feminist standpoint in discussions of ethics, values, and rationality. A feminism that emphasizes difference seems to me progressive so long as it deals with differences stemming from women's situation. And I would certainly include in that situation the special knowledge derived from having been a mother. (It would be interesting, by the way, to compare the personal values held by men who have lived for years as single parents of young children with those of men who have not.) One might even argue (as Sartre in fact did) that women, like minorities, are in a privileged position to open up new areas of thought because as partial outsiders in the established system of rewards, they are inwardly less imprisoned by it.

If I feel so strongly concerning the so-called feminine values, I am even more emphatic when it comes to such things as innate abilities to reason and to think abstractly. In this connection I have surely been influenced not only by my so-called male education but also by family attitudes in my childhood. My father would never admit that his religious faith was incommensurate with rationality. When faced with the theory of evolution, for instance, he did not reject it outright but argued that, when understood, the evolutionary process might well be seen as the outward manifestation of God's hidden plan. I recall vividly the evening when, as an adult, I first discussed with him fully and openly the philosophical differences between us. Afterwards, when I had gone to bed, he came and stood at the door of my room. "I do want you to know, Hazel," he said, "that I realize you cannot go contrary to your reason. If we didn't follow our reason, why—I don't know what we would do. . . ." And his words trailed off in bewilderment in the face of the unimaginable. I recognize now that there are "many ways of knowing"[6] and that we need to expand our understanding of what does and what does not constitute rationality as such. But I am unwilling to identify it with masculinity and hand it over to men for their exclusive use. This would be once again to define women by what they lack. Are women to be saddled with irrationality? Or to be limited solely to intuition and feeling? It was, after all, a woman poet, Edna St. Vincent Millay, who wrote as the opening line of her sonnet, "Euclid alone has looked on Beauty bare."

To avoid misunderstanding, I should add that it is, of course, obligatory to explore and to legislate in areas where biological differences create special problems. That medical research, for instance, should include women subjects and not assume that their susceptibility to heart attacks will be covered by knowledge gleaned from the study of men is as obvious as it is that there should be special provisions for pregnancy. To treat women with the assumption that they *are* men is not to treat them equally.

A second area of controversy concerns the question of whether we should view sexual practices and preferences as "essential" or as "socially constructed." In the debate over essentialism versus social constructionism the question of biological sexual determination reappears in another form. In this context those committed to the essentialist view are not concerned with innate differences between the sexes but with forms of individual sexuality; that is, with sexual preference. Essentialists argue that we are born, physically made, to be heterosexual or homosexual or—I suppose logically one would have to add—bisexual (chemically hermaphroditic?). Social constructionists insist that human sexuality is not reducible to animal sexuality; that is, it holds that any individual's form of sexuality is the result of a choice (or series of choices) made within a social context. Here again I am influenced by the existentialist insistence that we make ourselves. Firmly, though somewhat uneasily (because of practical political implications), I take my stand here with the social constructionists. To be sure, scientific reports appear from time to time suggesting that homosexuality is genetic; they have yet to meet with universal acceptance by other scientists.

I am far more persuaded by the arguments and evidence presented in *Dual Attraction: Understanding Bisexuality,* by Weinberg, Williams, and Pryor, who claim that sexual preference is neither fixed nor stable and that it is known to fluctuate radically within an individual's lifetime. What they claim fits my personal observations.[7] I realize that we cannot know absolutely. I believe that in this instance Freud was right: that all of us are born with bisexual potentialities, that we develop as heterosexual, homosexual, or bisexual (ambisextrous, to use my friend Lynn Martin's term) according to a complexity of chance factors and continued personal choices. Many homosexuals (among them some whom I know personally) say that I am totally wrong; they point to themselves as living proof of their being what they are and always have been; they declare that they *know* their preference to be as much something given as the color of their eyes. They may be right. Or they could be mistaking a long-established reaction for one that was always inescapably there. In many instances they may have convinced themselves of the essentialist view because it has become politically expedient. The social constructionist theory, which I myself assume to be a radical one, has been somehow transformed into a trap set by conservatives. If homosexuality is a choice, a lifestyle, the argument goes (or so gays often believe and fear it will go), then a largely homophobic society has the right to declare it culpable and punishable. But on what basis other than sheer caprice? Not with the support of any natural or divine law. Not if all values and ethics are human creations, as social constructionists are not alone in maintaining. I sometimes wonder whether, in a few cases, homosexuals' eagerness to look on themselves as ready-made is not an unacknowledged carryover of the old habit of internalizing society's verdict on them as undesirable deviants—as if to say, like the handicapped, "We can't be blamed." In the absence of proof, it seems to me that it would be better to state confidently: "This is our choice—as justified and as unjustified as yours."

Probably what I have given as my own view overstates the case. Certainly I would not be so foolish as to hold that, by a simple wish or act of will, persons could suddenly find their desires and sexual responses rearranged. Perhaps, if we accept Freud's claim that each of us biologically, or psychosomatically, is born with sexual inclinations of both sorts, one kind may initially be more strongly present in one individual than in another. Even so, the question of how or why one or the other preference did or did not develop into a stable sex orientation would remain. I like what my editor, David Brent, said to me in this connection, "Nothing human is purely genetic."

Finally, this question: Is there any significant way in which the term *human* or *humanity* (or *person*) is inclusive of *male* and *female* other than as referring to a biological species? Identity politics seems to deny it, and sometimes it seems to risk reducing the notion of commonality to the point at which the possibility of communication between diverse groups becomes problematic. Yet we *do* communicate; we *are* capable of empathic concern for persons or groups quite different from ourselves; and we do in fact, every day of our lives, mentally abstract the common essence of material objects, of animals, and of a wide variety of human feelings and experiences. I am unwilling to acknowledge that the notion of an all-embracing humanity is useless today, though I admit that it can be and often is misused.

Obviously, if *human* is equated with the self-description of a particular group, this is a vicious perversion. Similarly, if *human* is employed as a determining designation, it can be noxious. Sartre, for example, objected to the idea that we have a fixed human nature, either in the sense that there exists some discernible blueprint prescribing what we all ought to be, or that we are so governed by instincts and innate psychological traits that it is futile to hope that human patterns of behavior can significantly change. I suspect that it is always unwise to assume the existence of any clear and universally accepted definition of the meaning of human as a starting point, never more so than when one group feels itself so advanced in its understanding of what is good for humans that it imposes its prescriptions on others. Still, if the notion of humanity is allowed to function as a sort of regulative idea, it may be helpful, even indispensable. It does so in legal matters, though today we are more aware of cases in which the law must be a "respecter of persons" if it is to distribute equal justice instead of assuming the situational equality of all those who stand before it. I myself felt the need of some governing notion of *human* at the very moment that I recognized the validity of the argument that a woman's point of view on the Western tradition must be included in teaching it. However difficult it may be to abstract from our multisituated experiences those things that we share simply as humans, I think we do and must live by some such regulating idea. We rely on it implicitly when we expect that in introducing into the curriculum works from cultures formerly alien to us, we can read them with comprehension and empathy. It is assumed in the very efforts we make to transcend ourselves.

In papers that came to light after his death, Sartre chose the expression *integral humanity* to designate a legitimate goal for any ethics in the future. Here *integral humanity* is neither a restrictive term nor a label for a loosely defined existing condition. Sartre intends it to contrast with the subhumanity that is our present reality. Integral humanity would characterize a society in which communal responsibility would exist in harmony with freedom for individuals to develop to the maximum their unique possibilities for growth. Or, as Sartre would prefer to put it, this would be a society in which humanity would make itself, becoming its own product, rather than the product of its products.[8] This is, of course, a utopian ideal to be approximated, not a realizable state of perfection. But in the sense that it represents an ideal synthesis in which the right to difference is one of the ingredients of commonality, I think that *integral humanity* as a goal to be achieved may have meaning in any discourse. Of course, it must be held in constant tension with the knowledge that "humanity" is never a finished thing. What is humanity? asked James. He answered that we won't know "until the last man has had his last say." How tiresome! We have come far enough to know that the sentence has to be rewritten: "We won't know what humanity will have been until the last humans have had their last say." The time of integral humanity is not yet. But as John Dewey pointed out, to believe that an ideal is achievable is the first and necessary step toward realizing it.

From My Menagerie to Philosophy

HÉLÈNE CIXOUS

[Che cos'è la poesia?] *To answer that sort of question*—in two words, right?—*you are expected to know how to renounce knowledge. And to know how to do it well, without ever forgetting it: demobilize culture, but, as you cross the road, don't ever forget in your learned ignorance what you sacrifice* en route. [...]

I am a dictation [une dictée], *pronounces poetry* [...].

This answer sees itself as dictated to be poetic. And for that reason it's required to address itself to someone, singularly to you but as though to the being lost in anonymity, between city and nature, an imparted secret, at once public and private, absolutely *one and the other, absolved from within and from without, neither one nor the other, the animal cast off on the road, absolute, solitary, rolled up in a ball,* close beside (it)self. *And precisely* for that reason, *it may get itself run over—the hedgehog* [hérisson], istrice.[1]

Animals are becoming more and more important in my books, it's natural: they are always there when you leave on a very risky journey, whether you clear out all at once or set out very carefully. Life on the other side is difficult, you feel a bit lonely, or very lonely, as you climb the slopes of Mount Moriah. And if the ass weren't there to keep Abraham company, it would be infernal. But the ass is there, placing a limit on neglect. The Bible does not report the conversation that Abraham had with the ass on Mount Moriah. But you just have to follow them, and you can hear them speaking: I want to render the ass's words to Abraham. You don't say anything asinine to an ass, right? Or to a cat either.

Conversation au téléphone:
—*C'est moi ton âne, dit-il.*
Elle est surprise parce qu'elle pensait que l'âne c'était elle:
—*Tu es mon âne, toi?*
—*Je l'aime infiniment.*
—*Mais je n'ai pas dit: tu aimes mon âne. J'ai dit: Tu es mon âne??*

—*Ah oui. Mais un tout petit. Mais j'ai de grandes oreilles.*
—*Finalement tu es toute ma ménagerie.*
Ma plus grande difficulté est de passer de ma ménagerie à la philosophie.[2]

*   *   *

Imitations of Thea [3]

It's urgent. These are orders that she's giving, but we're free to follow them or not. The imperative of hope. Right afterward she forgives. God is begging me. How beautiful is her confidence. She speaks to me only with the utmost seriousness, intensity, and reasonableness. Requesting help only for what is truly beyond her control. It's an honest way of not reducing the other to slavery. Her sublime way of tolerating no satisfaction: without resentment. A spiritual equilibrium. Divine versatility.

She asks me for the fulfillment of her dreams: to be a butterfly, stop this rain, could I have squirrel paws, fly without wings. Alas, I'm unable to fulfill such fair and concrete desires. My magic is abstract. Too bad, she says, without bitterness. I take full stock of my powerlessness. I am so finite that I don't have in me even the idea of having wings. She has her body for a soul. I am separate.

What a struggle, though, toward speech, when faced with speech. She speaks to me in her foreign tongue, and knowingly she talks to me, patiently, as a mute person, as if to a person who doesn't understand her language, she sends me innumerable messages, trying to gain access to that ear in my head that hasn't yet been born, to tear that membrane, that bandage that straitjackets her language, and with all my eyes I listen to the Pythian riot as it shouts me directions. She stretches out her body to become the arrow toward that which isn't there, and I'm struck on the side of the head. I in turn coo hum meow a stream of dewy words to charm the ear she lends me.

Turned toward the world that stretches out after the world, her nose lifted toward god, she cries mutely:—See see see see see see see see see see see—Ah! me too! me too! We are born to see, to want to see, and to be unable to see, in order to be forced to cross over the final barrier—but where is it, is it down there, a veil stretched between these continents and the Other? or is it in my eyes? Staring straight at you, mutely I cry: I want to see you! see see see see!

She wants to get going. Outside: black tomcats with the supple paws of a cheetah, paws full of naked blades. There is the older brother, looking nasty, the father, an old fox. The younger one, a big stubborn muscular creature, hides in the thicket, he'll strike from behind. I'll use my little knife to take down the big hefty one, she tells me, and I know she will, but I'm not brave enough. I look at the slim little knife, sure it could go through that male, but will I have the heft I need to push it all the way in? As I torture myself trying to resist, she cries in front of the deadly door: come come; I tighten my grip, I'm going to give in, I don't have the courage to resist, when suddenly she gives in to me and comes over and lies down tenderly on my chest. The joy that overwhelms me: from one second to the next, the suffering is forgotten I am forgiven.

She coos:

I was gone: homecoming celebration.

Games and joys: the way she starts racing around and hiding and jumping, the way she shows off to celebrate my coming home, a dance of rejoicing, she appears, she gives it her all, I'm racing around for you and I'm jumping for you and I'm beautiful and powerful for you, she dresses herself up in order to dress me up.

Expert lover: the way in which she holds out her fourth paw for me to take, is an order of love, hold my paw, put your hand on my belly, I obey, with the caress I am caressed. There is a perfection between us that I feel: the sensation of a sensuous perfection that we share, the delicious sensation of exactness.

Attachment—detachment: incredible suppleness: she lets me leave without violence without rift: she undoes the ties without reproach, without apprehensiveness: accord. Gentleness of detachment, purity of soul. I return: she at once reties the bands.

She's somebody who makes no accusations. She understands—smells in her flesh the perfume of my goodwill, senses the goodness that I want for her. Senses: uncontrolled uncontrollable forces that remain up there above us inflict upon us pains and pleasures.

Weaning

The weaning that reached us unexpectedly this week deprives us. A strange, profound experience of *mourning*. Because of the "Mad Cows," I suddenly stopped getting cans of "cat food." At the crack of dawn, no can. The food I prepare *in its place* will not do: I try raw chicken, cooked chicken, cut into big pieces small pieces pureed, it's not the right thing: it's not that she rejects it out of hand as when she doesn't like something: not liking ("it's not good") is an affirmation, it's a negative liking, a commitment. What wells up in her is an absence, absence of desire, absence toward herself, absence incorporated through her whole body. Sweetly during the day she absorbs a few drops that I hold out to her with my fingertip. But it's not the right thing. She lowers her head and yields to her ill fortune. We've been in mourning for two days. She has lost something. It's a hardship. It's a cutting-off. I too am "cut off" from the can.

And I become acquainted with weaning: one might have imagined she would clamor, beg, become cross, show her hunger, her need. But no. It's inside herself, within her own being, that something is cut: she knows it, she knows that the proof is being disputed in her heart her thought her soul, the object is not exterior. It is not, she knows, something I've forgotten, it's an event in her life, the law, an encounter with boundaries and renunciation. The proof of her confidence in me: I would never be able to let her down, forget her, cause her any harm out of carelessness. If then there was no can yesterday, it's the result of Invisible Forces, difficulties waiting around the corner for the live little being. She and I are struck by the same blow. My powerlessness she internalizes, it's hers too. It's the breast that has been confiscated. Sadly she remains next to me, uniting us in the ritual.

No resentment, no error. She knows that I am hurt by her hurt.

Even the shrimp are grief stricken. One might have expected she would clamor and beg for them. But no. Her entire world has been stricken with ill fortune. The shrimp that, even last night, were her joy and her passion, neither interest nor console her. Her life has been touched.

No substitution: the thing is irreplaceable.

Thea's Smile

She likes me to smile at her: what is a smile: the open door.

She wants the doors to stay open. Anguish when faced with closed doors. Anguish when faced with *the sign* door closed. Her cry: let me come and go at will.

What I am for her at Night: her nighttime object, her thing, she loves me because she can make me her thing. Her thing? her support, her little mound, the ground she lies against, the earthly body that she curls up to [*épouse*]. The way she lies on my hip, in the greatest comfort. And the greatest comfort is that I am so thoroughly hers that she turns her back to me, her backside, with the tail carefully coiled, turned toward my face, her face turned toward the universe, sphinx of dawn, she stands watch, icon of what is to come.

The kisses are her word of thanks, her head bent down, the kisses from her little mouth, tiny shudder of her minuscule lips, innumerable kisses that show (re)cognition:[4] I know I know the continuity we are of the same species gratefulness for life, partnership.

She knows that I speak a language to her, sensual and sublime nourishment she busies herself gathering words, the voice, like me, I delight in her voice in her language. At times I speak to her in her language and she in mine, mutely, with her eyes.

Like what happens when making love: the rapture of the heart/ear as it gathers the nectar of your moan.

The Other knowledge; the other language

The way Thea and I "understand" each other: what gets understood, between our foreign tongues, and *without translation* (whereas when I was "speaking" with Joanna's parents, sitting with them on the couch in their little apartment in Thessalonica, I didn't understand anything, there was a message, messages, and they expected me to respond, but the Greek they spoke they spoke only with words, while in India, in Kerala, the little black women spoke with their fingertips and their arms and their eyes).

How Thea addresses me: with her whole body, without requiring a response, with her back or else I'm sitting at a table and her face might come up to speak to my face, she jumps up on the table, we're nose-to-nose lips-to-lips, I follow her, we kiss, *we imitate each other,* but if she imitates me while I'm imitating her, there is a slight animalhumanization that takes place upon contact with one another. This is possible: it's because in her there's something human—emotive elements, instantaneous "thoughts," human echoes and presentiments—whereas in me, always palpitating in my tissues, in my organs, is my ancestral animality.

Not with (in) my head, in the body: that's where deep intelligence lies.

What actors communicate to the audience, with their bodies—as the result of imprinting, the engraving of words in their bodies. Bodies talk to one another wondrous joy before the writing of bodies—gestures, syntax, poem.

Thea and I: secret Theater.

Mineness Yoursness

It is with emotion and nostalgia that I touch Thea's soft fierce touch; she's the cat whose cat I am [*la chatte dont je suis la chatte*]. Night caresses me. I caress the night. I caress it as she would. It's a perfection, I'm covered with caresses from my hand to my soul, warm perfectly soft little caresses covering me, summoned up in the form of impersonal kindness. She acts on me. My heart opens like a flower. Why is there no soft, warm adjective made from the word well-being?

I am amidst well-beingness. It is not at all sexual. We are representatives of the kindnesses of love, it's a tenderness that craves and is nourished by tenderness. A craving for giving and for being received. The reflexive form of gratitude. The well-being hidden in doing good things. It's like when you lick your body while sleeping and you wake up marvelously rejuvenated. I feel a kindness nourishing the starving soul in my body and there springs from the touch an intoxicating gratitude, quaffs of sublimity.

Grace comes without acknowledgment.

* * *

Each day the cat crosses a new boundary. She makes a conquest of one garden after another, the space stretching out just as she wills it. This will is not hers: one need only see her spring through the first light of day with her silvery stride, the sparks flying from her silent slippers, to sense that she is obeying. How far will obedience lead her? Who's calling her? Her own mystery: is some motley angel the ideal-of-the-cat?

The same goes for all the inhabitants of this book: we obey, we go, we pass over with a single impassable bound one wall after another, and such is the entire action of this narrative. It could continue this way till death, that's what I'm trying to forget about as I write. As for my characters, they move forward and escape me the same way it happens in a book that doesn't seem to know what can never be known. Like the cat, they do what they want, and the author follows them. They take off at a gallop, headstrong, dizzyingly stubborn. I keep close track of them. I love them, I say "tu" to them, I am dazzled at their will. And when two days ago the woman said to me: stop talking about her and let me talk about myself, by the next page it was done. She was saying "I." Not that she knew much about it. But is there anybody capable of physically preventing a human cat from going off in search of herself? You think she's exploring the universe, but she is using the universe to explore herself. She's in pursuit of herself.

* * *

She says:

From an early age I had sons, daughters, I fed them, there are six of us now. As a mature woman I had my cat [*chatte*], before that I wasn't ready, you need a certain maturity to accept and respect one's inner animal. The animal in onself. And to learn not to think you have what you think you've got, and yet we six have superior appurtenances. The limit of the broad freedom that brings us together is that we do not practice sexual incest. It is only when a person is past the age of having, at the age of being, that he or she can venture into the zones where life is ancestral. In these parts one senses onself really not far from the future. The not-far is almost just behind the door.

When the door opens, we'll scoot out like cats to discover the future.

We have absolutely no knowledge of the future, yet it is much closer and more favorable to us than society. It's a question of age and maturity. People in society remain indefinitely at the age of having. This is why their greatest effort is to have things materialize in such a way that they can be put into boxes and taken, handled.

*   *   *

Last Saturday I was supposed to preside over a meeting with colleagues. There was a maddening crowd in the room, that's the only way to put it. I myself was part of the mad ones, I was really no longer myself. Otherwise, the anguishing lack of preparation that I acknowledge in myself. The discussion went slowly around in circles. People arrived and there was a universal hubbub. A colleague whispered to me that we were being asked to make statues on pediments for the university park. Ah no! I said, I want to make my sculpture free as a bird. The crowd became more and more dense. The arrival of personalities was announced. Sitting down, I was like a turtle in the forest. I got up to fulfill my hospitality obligations. I extended a hearty hello to the personalities. These ladies scarcely acknowledged me and turned their backs. My throat was so dry I nearly choked. I wanted some water. There were enormous pitchers on the table and all the glasses were dirty. What had started out well was taking a turn for the worse. I reacted violently. "Make no mistake," I said. "It's by choice that I'm a salaried worker." "Stop," said my internal angel. But I couldn't stop myself by then. "With my talents and my strengths, I could have been prime minister and head of the government," I said in spite of myself, throwing on the brakes just before king. "And the only reason I'm not is that the only thing that really counts for me is poetry," I cried. That made an impression on them one way or another.

But I hadn't meant to say that! In the intoxication of the indignity, I lost my head, I started to strut, high stepping like a Spanish dancer, and with a single bound I hopped on the back of ridicule. There I was decked out in all the worldly passions. Now I had no idea how I could avoid my anger, it had dug its little claws so deep into my stomach, it was as though I had swallowed a live eagle.

The only thing that counts for me in point of fact is love. Had I lied? Or maybe poetry is the scholarly word for love?

I was asked if I would agree to give a talk on Monday on this subject: "So what *IS* poetry?" After the words I'd uttered, I felt it was impossible to refuse. But I'm not a scholar. A talk! Punishment is never long in coming. It was time. The students were coming in, sitting down, notebooks out, pens poised. I backed up. To begin with, I said, fill out these cards for me. Docile, a young man asked: do we put down biographical data? "Yes," I said gratefully, "anything that might be of interest to me. I want to get to know you." The time to fill out the cards gave me a few seconds leeway. I left quickly. I went to one, I went to another, I knocked on all the doors, asking each person what's poetry—if any of them had heard about it, if there was a book, a dictionary, a list, a collection, I went from one niche to another holding out till the last one, which was the first one, to get to it I climbed on top of a huge tree trunk lying across the rubble. The thing looked uncrossable, but I found a passageway in between the stones and the trunk covered with a jumble of branches. I crawled along, brooding, my movements stymied by the tangled limbs I couldn't jump over. In short, I kept going. A door opened. I was at the two Marias'. Doesn't that mean anything to you? They are the first two sisters. Maria opened for me thinking that it was Maria. I saw their dwelling. You couldn't imagine anything simpler, more old-fashioned. It's nice here, I said, it's charming; the two Marias—like two hedgehogs [*hérissons*] without quills—they didn't know the answer either; you're going to have to grow some quills, I said, and as I left their little mud hut I noticed just behind their molehill an infinite jumble of bare rocks—it was better not to look over that way, it was ominous, in winter you'd be buried under all the snow, impossible to go any farther without losing your life. Coming back the same way I came I thought for a moment that I couldn't get over the mass of trunk and rocks, but I found the passageway again and I made it over the obstacle, getting back to the place where the students were waiting for me.

So what *IS* poetry? The question had stayed with me. During my journey I hadn't forgotten that they were expecting something, trustingly, without enmity.

I sat down in the circle *and I continued:* "that's the way my cat and I resolved the question of the telephone. How do we telephone one another? The need to telephone has always existed because it's a vital need to recall the mother. And all mammals bear the trace of the first telephone cord. It's our need to check that she's there, that's all: that she's alive. The mother figure. Who may also be a son a husband a lover. That's the way it is between people who share a life reciprocally: 'Are you there?' 'I'm here.' 'OK, then I can get on with my business.' 'Are you doing well? Is your life in good shape? Can I hit the road without fearing that my line will be cut off?' 'My life is in good shape. You can go.'

"But what do you do when you're a person from a race that can't talk long-distance, when you experience the need, always urgent, to verify a life? That's what my cat and I found out about: we're going to telephone each other person-to-person. In this way she comes over several times a day to give me a little phone call in the leg, briefly using her own body as telephone, to dial the number she rubs: everything OK? 'Everything's OK.' And she hangs up reassured. As for me, who can call long-distance, several times a day, to dial her number, I whistle three notes like this : : : and from the ends of the earth she appears, everything's OK. Two lives of different species that come to life through one another, through contact. To conclude," I said, "I asked myself what's poetry, and that's all I could find. For me it starts with a smallish phrase like: Everything's OK? You hardly pay it any mind. But if you do pay attention to it, then it's an entreaty of life asking about life over the phone. Yet it can't be a question without an answer, that would be terrible. You ask permission to go on living. And the permission is an order: live.

* * *

"But the strongest love is the one that is also the shortest on words. It is summed up by a touch of the hand.

"And is the poetry of poetry the mute emotion that rises out of sentences that graze one's legs with the chastity of passion in its absolute state?

"Now if I were asked 'what's poetry?' I would respond: 'the expression by my cat of chastity—but knowledge? I'll never know. No, no! No talk! Never!'"

House and Home:
Feminist Variations on a Theme

IRIS M. YOUNG

For millennia the image of Penelope sitting by the hearth and weaving, saving and preserving the home while her man roams the earth in daring adventures, has defined one of Western culture's basic ideas of womanhood. Many other cultures both historically and today equate women with home, expecting women to serve men at home and sometimes preventing them from leaving the house. If house and home mean the confinement of women for the sake of nourishing male projects, then feminists have good reason to reject home as a value. But it is difficult even for feminists to exorcise a positive valence to the idea of home. We often look forward to going home and invite others to make themselves at home. House and home are deeply ambivalent values.

In this essay I sort through this ambivalence. On the one hand, I agree with feminist critics such as Luce Irigaray and Simone de Beauvoir that the comforts and supports of house and home historically come at women's expense. Women serve, nurture, and maintain so that the bodies and souls of men and children gain confidence and expansive subjectivity to make their mark on the world. This homey role deprives women of support for their own identity and projects. Furthermore, along with several feminist critics, I question the yearning for a whole and stable identity that the idea of home often represents. On the other hand, I am not ready to toss the idea of home out of the larder of feminist values. Despite the oppressions and privileges the idea historically carries, the idea of home also carries critical liberating potential because it expresses uniquely human values. Some of these can be uncovered by exploring the meaning-making, activity most typical of women in domestic work.

Instead of following one line of argument, I aim here to weave together several thematic threads. All of them wind around meanings of subjectivity or identity. I begin by noting Martin Heidegger's equation of dwelling with the way of being that is human and note his division of dwelling into

49

moments of building and preservation. Despite his claim that these moments are equally important, Heidegger nevertheless seems to privilege building (as the worldfounding of an active subject), and I suggest that this privileging is male biased.

Luce Irigaray makes explicit the maleness of Heidegger's allegedly universal ontology. Man can build and dwell in the world in patriarchal culture, she suggests, only on the basis of the materiality and nurturance of woman. In the idea of home, "man projects onto woman the nostalgic longing for the lost wholeness of the original mother. To fix and keep hold of his identity man makes a house, puts things in it, and confines there his woman who reflects his identity to him. The price she pays for supporting his subjectivity, however, is dereliction, having no self of her own."

Before entering a critique of Simone de Beauvoir's devaluation of housework, I digress to tell the story of one bad housekeeper—my mother. The purpose of this gesture is not only to commemorate but also to describe in concrete terms how disciplinary standards of orderly housework and PTA motherhood continue to oppress women, especially single mothers.

Like Irigaray, Beauvoir describes women's existence as deprived of active subjectivity because their activity concentrates on serving and supporting men in the home. Unlike Irigaray, however, Beauvoir materializes this account by reflecting on the sexual division of labor. Because she accepts a dichotomy between immanence and transcendence and identifies all of women's domestic labor with immanence, however, Beauvoir misses the creatively human aspects of women's traditional household work in activities I call preservation.

That aspect of dwelling which Heidegger devalues thus provides a turning point for revaluing home. Preservation makes and remakes home as a support for personal identity without accumulation, certainty, or fixity. Although preservation, a typically feminine activity, is traditionally devalued at least in Western conceptions of history and identity, it has crucial human value.

I next challenge a group of feminist texts whose writers all reject the idea of home as inappropriately totalizing and imperialist. Essays by Biddy Martin and Chandra Mohanty, Teresa de Lauretis, and Bonnie Honig all argue that longing for home expresses an oppressive search for certainty and attachment to privilege. Although I accept much of their analysis, I question the wholesale rejection of an ideal of home for feminism. Although values of home do indeed signal privilege today, analysis of those values and commitment to their democratic enactment for all can have enormous critical political potential in today's world. In addition to preservation, those values include safety, individuation, and privacy.

Dwelling and Building

Dwelling, says Martin Heidegger, is man's mode of being. Habitual human activity reveals things as meaningful, and through dwelling among the meaningful things people have a place for themselves. Dwelling and building, Heidegger says, stand in a circular relation. Humans attain to dwelling only by means of building. We dwell by making the places and things that structure and house our activities. These places and things establish relations among each other, between themselves and dwellers, and between dwellers and the surrounding environment. But we only build on the basis of already dwelling as the beings whose mode of being is to let things be, to think, and to reveal them.[1]

Building has two aspects, according to Heidegger: cultivating and constructing. One mode of building consists in cherishing, protecting, preserving, and caring for, whose paradigm is agriculture, the cultivation of the soil. "Building in the sense of preserving and nurturing is not making anything" (BDT, 147). Thus to remain, to stay in place, is an important meaning of dwelling. "To dwell, to be set at peace, means to remain at peace within the free, the preserve, the free sphere that safeguards each thing in its nature. The fundamental character of dwelling is this sparing and preserving" (BDT, 149).

After introducing this duality of building, as preservation and construction, Heidegger's text leaves preservation behind to focus on construction. A curious abandonment, in light of the above claim that preservation is fundamental to dwelling. To describe the human mode of being in the world, Heidegger dwells on the heroic moment of place through creative activity that gathers the environment into a meaningful presence.

We can dwell only in a place. Edifices enclose areas with walls and link areas by planes, thus creating locations. Walls, roofs, columns, stairs, fences, bridges, towers, roads, and squares found the human world by making place.[2] Through building, man establishes a world and his place in the world and, according to Heidegger, establishes himself as somebody, with an identity and history. People inhabit the world by erecting material supports for their routines and rituals and then see the specificity of their lives reflected in the environment, the materiality of things gathered together with historical meaning.[3]

If building in this way is basic to the emergence of subjectivity, to dwelling in the world with identity and history, then it would appear that only men are subjects. On the whole, women do not build.

Even today, when women have moved into so many typically male activities, building houses and other structures remains largely a male activity in most parts of the world. In building industries, a woman with a hard hat is still a rare sight. Nowhere in the world do women participate in the building trades in more than very small numbers.[4] Perhaps even more significantly, men dominate the ranks of those who make building decisions—corporate boards of directors, architects, planners, and engineers. Even in some of the most egalitarian households, the work of building and structural maintenance falls most often to men.

In many traditional societies of Africa and Asia, women were the home builders. But peasants all over the world have migrated to cities and towns because capitalism and environmental destruction have made it nearly impossible in many places to live off the land in traditional ways. Many rural and urban development projects include programs where people build the houses in which they will live. Despite the fact that poorer households in developing countries are very often headed by women, they rarely participate in these house-building projects. Either they do not have title to land on which to build because of male biases in property laws, or the development project has simply assumed that men are more natural builders and thus have designed construction projects with men in mind. Frequently women's income and assets are so low that they cannot qualify for the credit necessary to participate in building projects.[5]

If building establishes a world, if building is the means by which a person emerges as a subject who dwells in that world, then not to build is a deprivation. Those excluded from building, who do not think of themselves as builders, perhaps have a more limited relation to the world, which they do not think of themselves as founding. Those who build dwell in the world in a different way from those who occupy the structures already built, and from those who preserve what is constructed. If building establishes a world, then it is still very much a man's world.

Women as a group are still largely excluded from the activities that erect structures to gather and reveal a meaningful world. It will be women's world as much as men's only when women participate as much in their design and founding. But the male bias of building also appears in the devaluation of that other aspect of building that Heidegger discusses, preservation, a devaluation to which his own philosophy tends. For a distinction between constructing and preserving, as two aspects of building and dwelling, is implicitly gendered. Later I will pick up the thread of this concept of preservation, to argue that much of the unnoticed labor of women is this basic activity of meaning maintenance. First we shall further explore the masculinism implicit in a philosophy of existence that takes building as world founding, by way of a bridge from Heidegger to his feminist follower and critic, Luce Irigaray.

Building, says, Heidegger, gathers together dispersed surroundings that have no center apart from the artifice around which they are oriented. The house in the woods gives to the trees and lakes a placement. The bridge across the river gathers the shores, revealing a nexus of relationships, a context. But man's building, Heidegger points out, occurs on the foundation of already dwelling. Man is enveloped by being, finds himself as already having been at home in nature, which building reveals as already surrounding. This revealing of the world itself depends on a prior ground that sustains and nurtures.

With such a move Heidegger believes himself to be sublating modern Western philosophy, and its specifically technological orientation. Descartes and those who come after him have the hubris to think of man as self-originating, the thinking subject as the master and representor of being. They have forgotten the humility of the ancients, who understand better the placement of mortals in a nature on which they depend, whose thoughtful tending and preserving is the lot of mortals. Man builds for the sake of dwelling, to make himself at home in respect to the prior elements that envelop and nourish him, which his building gathers and reveals.

Woman as Nostalgic Home

Luce Irigaray names the gendering already present in Heidegger's worlding of the world: Man builds for the sake of dwelling, to make himself at home, on the basis of Woman as already always positioned as the enveloping nurturing presence of nature. For man, woman is always mother, from whose dark womb he emerges to build solid structures in the light of day, with whose light he returns to look in the caverns with the speculum. In lovemaking he seeks to return to the enclosing warmth of the original union with the mother. The patriarchal gender system allows man a subjectivity that depends on woman's objectification and dereliction; he has a home at the expense of her homelessness, as she serves as the ground on which he builds.

Everyone is born in loss. Ejected from the dark comfort of the mother's body, we are thrown into a world without walls, with no foundation to our fragile and open-ended existence. Speaking mortals must come to terms with this separation from the mother, to find and form meaning and identity for ourselves, without foundation or certainty. In patriarchal culture, according to Irigaray, the gender system of masculinity and femininity makes it possible for man to come to term with this loss by never really dealing with it; instead, he attempts to return to the lost home of the womb by means of woman.

Man deals with the loss by building, in order that he may recover his dwelling. He seeks to make himself a home to stand in for the lost home. Through building he gathers the amorphous and fluid elements into solid structure. Through projecting outward he makes objective works where he can see himself reflected. He makes and affirms himself as subject through building and making. In this objectifying self-reflection woman serves as material both on which to stand and out of which to build, and women likewise serve as a primary object for reflecting himself, his mirror.

> Man's love is teleological. It aims for a target outside them. It moves to-ward the outside and the constitution, on the outside, within that which is outside themselves, of a home. Outside of the self. The tension, the intention, aims for a dwelling, a thing, a production. Which also serves men as a third part and stake.
>
> To *inhabit is* the fundamental trait of man's being. Even if this trait remains unconscious, unfulfilled, especially in its ethical dimension, man is forever searching for, building, creating homes for himself everywhere: caves, huts, women, cities, language, concepts, theory, and so on.[6]

Building is for the sake of dwelling, gathering together natural material and element into a determinate place. In the patriarchal gender scheme, woman serves as the construction material (*ESD*, 103–7) and as the place within which man dwells. His self-affirming subjectivity is possible because she supports and complements his existence as both an origin of his creativity and the product in which he can see himself reflected. She serves as the material envelope and container of his existence. "She is assigned to be place without occupying place. Through her, place would be set up for man's use but not hers. Her jouissance is meant to 'resemble' the flow of whatever is in the place that she is when she contains, contains herself" (*ESD*, 52).

The form of man's self-affirmation in this gender system is nostalgia, a longing for the return to a lost home. Man puts woman in her place, so that he can return to the original maternal home. Nostalgia is this recurrent desire for return, which is unsatisfiable because the loss is separation, birth, mortality, itself. Nostalgia is a flight from having to come to terms with this loss, by means of constant search for a symbolic substitute for lost home. Man yearns nostalgically for an original union with the mother within safe walls of warmth. In women men look nostalgically to return to their own lost home; thus they fail to face women as subjects with their own identities and need of covering,

> He arrests his growth and repeats, endlessly, searching for the moment when the separation of memory and forgetting was lost to him. But, the

more he repeats, the more he surrounds himself with envelopes, containers, "houses" which prevent him from finding either the other or himself. His nostalgia for a first and last dwelling prevents him from meeting and living with the other. (*ESD,* 142)

Man seeks nostalgically to return to the lost home by making buildings and putting things in them that will substitute for that original home. He creates property, things he owns and controls. But because the property doesn't satisfy the longing for lost home, he is launched on an acquisitive quest for more property. In this acquisitive economy women serve as raw materials, caretakers, and goods themselves to be traded. Her role is to be the home by being at home. Her being home gives him comfort and allows him to open on the expanse of the world to build and create. For her, however, the placement is an imprisonment.

Centuries will perhaps have been needed for man to interpret the meaning of his work(s): the endless construction of a number of substitutes for his parental home. From the depths of the earth to the highest skies? Again and again, taking from the feminine the issue or textures of spatiality. In exchange—but it isn't a real one—he buys her a house, even shuts her up in it, places limits on her that are the opposite of the unlimited site in which he unwillingly situates her. He contains or envelops her with walls while enveloping himself and his things in her flesh. The nature of these envelopes is not the same: on the one hand, invisibly alive, but with barely visible limits; on the other, visibly limiting or sheltering, but at the risk of being prison like or murderous if the threshold is not left open. (*ESD,* 11)

Because woman functions for man as the ground of his subjectivity, she has no support for her own self. She is derelict. She too must deal with the same loss as he, with the abandonment of mortality, radical freedom, and groundlessness, and the expulsion from warmth and security of the mother's body. By means of her, man makes for himself a home to substitute for this loss. He creates by holding her as his muse, he rests by having her serve his needs at home. Her only comfort is to try to derive her satisfaction from being in the home, the Other. She tries to take her subjectivity from her being-for-him. She tries to envelop herself with decoration. She covers herself with jewelry, makeup, clothing, in the attempt to make an envelope, to give herself a place. But in the end she is left homeless, derelict, with no room of her own, because he makes room for himself by using her as his envelope.

If building establishes a world, if building is the means by which a person emerges as a subject who dwells in that world, then not to build is a deprivation. In the patriarchal gender system, men are the builders and women the nurturers of builders and the ornaments placed within their creations. As homeless themselves, women are deprived of the chance to be subjects for themselves. Language, says Heidegger, is the house of being. Men not only build material shelters, temples, bridges to gather the environment into a place. Masculine subjects are also the founders of civilization itself, those who name things and construct the theories and epics in which their meanings are preserved over generations.[7] According to Irigaray, woman's place in language is a sign of her dereliction, of her inability to attain to the position of subject for herself.

The question for postmodern living is whether an end to such exploitation requires rejecting entirely the project of supporting identity and subjectivity embodied in the patriarchal ideology of home. The feminist writers with whom I engage later answer this question affirmatively. Although I accept many of their reasons for leaving home, I wish to explore another possibility. Is it possible to retain an idea of home as supporting the individual subjectivity of the person, where the subject is understood as fluid, partial, shifting, and in relations of reciprocal support with others? This is the direction in which I find Irigaray pointing to an alternative to the desire for fixed identity that historically imprisons women.

Interlude: My Mother's Story

The dream of a house in the suburbs became my mother's nightmare. My daddy left our Flushing apartment each morning in one of his three slightly different grey flannel suits and took the subway to midtown Manhattan. An aspiring novelist turned insurance underwriter, he was moving slowly but steadily up the corporate ladder. I imagined his office as Dagwood's, and his boss as Mr. Dithers.

My sister and I tripped out to school each morning, in the horrid saddle shoes our mommy made us wear, and she stayed home with the little baby boy. A perfect picture of '50s family bliss, with one flaw: my mother didn't clean the house.

Our two-bedroom apartment was always dirty, cluttered, things all over the floors and piled on surfaces, clothes strewn around the bedroom, dust in the corners, in the rugs, on the bookcases: the kitchen stove wore cooked-on food. I never invited my friends into my house. If they came to the door and peered in I told them we were getting ready to move. Mostly my friends did not care, because we played in the alleys and hallways, and not in each other's houses.

My mother spent her days at home reading books, taking a correspondence course in Russian, filling papers with codes and calculations. She seemed to me an inscrutable intellectual. But she also played with us: authors, rummy, twenty-questions. With gusto and sang and sang, teaching us hymns and old army songs. Sometimes on a Saturday she hauled out the oils and sat her little girls down to model, and then let us make our own oil paintings. From my mommy I learned to value books and song and art and games and to think that housework is not important.

It was 1958. My mother had to stay home with her children even though she had worked happily in a Manhattan magazine office before we were born, even though she spoke three languages and had a master's degree. I was mortified then by her weirdness, sitting in her chair reading and writing, instead of cooking and cleaning and ironing and mending like a real mom. Later, after she died in 1978, I read her refusal to do housework as passive resistance.

Like most of the Joneses (well, more likely the Cohens) on our block, my mommy and daddy dreamed of owning a house in the suburbs. They dragged us three kids all over the state of New Jersey looking at model homes in new developments. Back in Flushing, they poured over house plan sketches, looked at paint samples, calculated mortgage costs. Finally we settled on one of the many mid-Jersey developments built on filled-in wetlands (called swamps at that time). From the four models available my parents chose the mid-priced split-level. My sister and I chose the blue for our room and my three-year-old brother pointed to the green patch on the sample chart. Many Sundays we drove the more than hour-long trip to watch the progress of the house: foundation, frame, walls, grass.

Finally we moved. This was happiness. We were the Cleavers. We bought a Ping-Pong table for the game room. My sister and I went careening on the streets on our bikes. Then my daddy died—quickly, quietly, of a brain tumor.

My mother was devastated. She relied on us for what comfort there could be in this wasteland of strangers in four types of model homes. At first the neighbors were solicitous, bringing over covered dishes, then they withdrew. The folks at church were more helpful, offering rides to the insurance office or church. My mommy drank, but never on Sunday morning. My sister and I went to school sad, my brother stayed home with our mother, who had less reason than ever to clean the house. We were not poor once the insurance and social security money came, just messy.

But one spring day a uniformed man came into my class and called my name. He escorted me to a police car where my brother and sister were already waiting. Without explanation, they drove us to a teen-reform home. No word from or about our mommy, where she was, why we were being taken away.

Slowly I learned or inferred that she had been thrown in jail for child neglect. Daughters do not always defend their mothers accused of crimes. Being one to please authorities, and at eleven wanting to be knowing and adult, I believe that I told stories to confirm their self-righteousness, of how I did most of the cooking and how my mother did not keep house.

A woman alone with her children in this development of perfectly new squeaky-clean suburban houses. She is traumatized by grief and the neighbors look from behind their shutters, people talk about the disheveled way she arrives at church, her eyes red from crying. Do they help this family, needy not for food or clothes, but for support in a very hard time? A woman alone with her children is no longer a whole family, deserving like others of respectful distance. From my mother's point of view there was no difference between child-welfare agents and police. A woman alone with her children is liable to punishment, including the worst of all for her: having her children taken from her.

Neglect. The primary evidence of neglect was drinking and a messy house. We ate well enough, had clean enough clothes, and a mother's steady love, given the way she gave it: playing Ping-Pong, telling Bible stories, playing twenty questions. We were a family in need of support, but we children were not neglected.

After two months we were reunited, moved back to our gray split-level. My sister and I rode our bikes on the street again, played kickball and croquet with the neighbor kids. My mother was determined to prove she could manage a household by suburban standards, so she did what she thought she had to—called an agency for live-in maids.

One day a thin fourteen-year-old black girl arrived at the door, fresh from North Carolina. We gave her my brother's room and he moved in with my mommy. I felt a strange affinity with this shy and frightened person, who sobbed so quietly in her room. She was not prepared for the work of housekeeping. She and I worked together to prepare the packaged macaroni and cheese. We sorted laundry, silently sitting across from each other, for she did not know whose things were whose. We hardly talked; she told me the barest facts about her life. I see her standing on the landing in a cotton summer dress, a Cinderella figure holding a broom and wistfully sweeping. She quit within two weeks, and the house was not any cleaner.

So we glided through the summer, playing punch ball and tag with the kids in the terrace. My mother went to the city frequently to look for work. In August she took us out to buy three pairs of new shoes, for my brother would start kindergarten. School began, my mother was off to work. My twelve-year-old life seemed rosy enough.

Until one day in early fall I came home from school to find a police sign nailed to my door. A fire. A smoldering ember in my mother's slipper chair had ignited and sent out flames, the neighbors had summoned the fire department. I used their phone to call a family friend to come and get us kids—I wasn't going to any reform school again. There was not much damage to the house, they had caught the fire early, but when breaking in to douse it they had seen the papers strewn about and dust on the floor and beer cans. My mother was arrested again.

We lived with those family friends for a year. Every three months a box of clothes arrived for us from the Department of Social Services—I loved the discovery of what they thought we ought to be wearing. After they let my mommy out of jail and rehab we visited her every couple of months in an impersonal office for an hour or so. She hugged us and cried and told us of her job in the city and the new cleaning lady, Odessa. As I plummeted into adolescence and my brother entered his seventh year, there was a crisis in our foster home: our foster father died suddenly of pneumonia. Headed now only by a woman, our foster family instantly became a bad environment for us; they shipped us back to my mother without warning. Her family reunited again, my mother wasted no time packing up and moving us all back to the safe indifference of New York City.

Waves of grief rolled up from my gut when, ten years after my mother died, I saw the movie *Housekeeping*.

Historicity, Preservation, and Identity

Beauvoir on Housework

Simone de Beauvoir's *The Second Sex* still stands as one of the most important works documenting women's oppression, because it describes the typical life and dilemmas of women so graphically. One cannot read Beauvoir's descriptions of domestic labor without appreciating how endless the work is, how oppressive.

> Such work has a negative basis: cleaning is getting rid of dirt, tidying up is eliminating disorder. And under impoverished conditions no satisfaction is possible; the hovel remains a hovel in spite of women's sweat and tears: "nothing in the world can make it pretty." Legions of women have only this endless struggle without victory over the dirt—and for even the most privileged the victory is never final.
>
> Few tasks are more like the torture of Sisyphus than housework, with its endless repetition. The clean becomes soiled, the soiled is made clean, over and over, day after day. The housewife wears herself out marking time: she makes nothing, simply perpetuates the present.[8]

Beauvoir's account of the oppressions of domestic work fits in the frame of her general account of women's situation as confined to immanence, whereas man exists as transcendence.

> The fact is that every human existence involves transcendence and immanence at the same time: to go forward, each existence must be maintained, for it to expand toward the future it must integrate the past, and while intercommunicating with others it would find self-confirmation. These two elements—maintenance and progression—are implied in any living activity, and for man marriage permits precisely a happy synthesis of the two, In his occupation and in his political life he encounters change and progress, he senses his extension through time and the universe: and when he is tired of such roaming, he gets himself a home, where his wife takes care of his furnishings and children and guards the things of the past that she keeps in store. But she has no other job than to maintain and provide for life in pure unvarying generality, she perpetuates the species without change, she ensures the even rhythm of the days and the continuity of the home, seeing to it that the doors are locked. (430)

In the existentialist framework Beauvoir uses, transcendence is the expression of individual subjectivity. The subject expresses and realizes his individuality through taking on projects—building a house, organizing a strike, writing a book, winning a battle. These projects, which may be individual or collective, are determinate and particular contributions to the world of human affairs. Transcendence also expresses a mode of temporality. The living subject is future oriented; the future is open with possibility, which generates anxiety at the same time as its openness and possibility restructure the meaning of the present, and the past human existence is historical in this framework, in that it is structured by creative deed and always must be structured by future deeds.

In Beauvoir's scheme, immanence expresses the movement of life rather than history. Life is necessary and very demanding. Without getting food and shelter and caring for the sick and saving babies from harm there is no possibility for transcendence and history. The activities of sustaining life, however, according to Beauvoir, cannot be expressions of individuality. They are anonymous and general, as the species is general. Thus if a person's existence consists entirely or largely of activities of sustaining life, then she or he cannot be an individual subject. Women's work is largely confined to life maintenance for the sake of supporting the transcending individual projects of men and children. As in Irigaray's account, for Beauvoir, man's subjectivity draws on the material support of women's work, and this work deprives her of a subjectivity of her own.

The temporality of immanence is cyclical, repetitive. As the movement of life it moves in species time unpunctuated by events of individual meaning. The cycles go around, from spring to summer to fall to winter, from birth to death and birth to death. Beauvoir describes the activity of housework as living out this cyclical time, a time with no future and no goals.

Beauvoir has an entirely negative valuation of what she constructs as woman's situation, a negative valuation of the activity of giving meaning to and maintaining home. She is surely right that much of what we call housework is drudgery, necessary but tedious, and also right that a life confined to such activity is slavery. But such a completely negative valuation flies in the face of the experience of many women, who devote themselves to care for house and children as a meaningful human project. If Irigaray is correct, of course, many women pour their soul into the house because they have no other envelope for the self. But it seems too dismissive of women's own voices to deny entirely the value many give to "homemaking." Following Irigaray, we can reconstruct core values from the silenced meanings of traditional female activity. Because she relies on the dichotomy of transcendence and immanence to conceptualize women's oppression, Beauvoir misses the historical and individualizing character of some of the activity associated with the traditional feminine role, which in the above quotation she calls "guarding the things of the past that she keeps in store." Giving meaning to individual lives through the arrangement and preservation of things is an intrinsically valuable and irreplaceable aspect of homemaking.

Homemaking

Beauvoir is surely right that the bare acts of cleaning bathrooms, sweeping floors, and changing diapers are merely instrumental; though necessary, they cannot be invested with creativity or individuality. She is wrong, however, to reduce all or even most domestic work to immanence. Not all homemaking is housework. To understand the difference we need to reconsider the idea of home and its relation to a person's sense of identity. Home enacts a specific mode of subjectivity, and historicity that is distinct both from the creative-destructive idea of transcendence and from the ahistorical repetition of immanence.

D. J. Van Lennep suggests that we can learn what it means to inhabit a space as "home" by thinking about forms of shelter that are not home; he suggests that we consider why a hotel room is not a home. A hotel room has all the comforts one needs—heat, hot water, a comfortable bed, food, and drink a phone call away. Why, then, does one not feel at home in a hotel room? Because there is nothing of one's self, one's life habits and history that one sees displayed around the room. The arrangement is anonymous and neutral, for anyone and one no one in particular.[9]

A home, however, is personal in a visible, spatial sense. No matter how small a room or apartment, the home displays the things among which a person lives, that support his or her life activities and reflect in matter

the events and values of his or her life. There are two levels in the process of the materialization of identity in the home: (1) my belongings are
arranged in space as an extension of my bodily habits and as support for
my routines, and (2) many of the things in the home, as well as the space itself, carry sedimented personal meaning as retainers of personal narrative.

(1) Home is the space where I keep and use the material belongings of
my life. They are mine—or ours, when I live together with others—because
I/we have chosen or made them, and they thus reflect my needs and tastes.
Or they have found their way into my home as inheritance or gifts or perhaps even by accident, but then I have appropriated them. The home is not
simply the things, however, but their arrangement in space in a way that
supports the body habits and routines of those who dwell there. The arrangement of furniture in space provides pathways for habits—the reading
lamp placed just here, the television just here, the particular spices on the
rack placed just so in relation to this person's taste and cooking habits.
Dwelling, says Lennep,

> is the continuous unfolding of ourselves in space because it is our unbro
> ken relation with things surrounding us. It is human existence itself which
> constitutes space. We simply cannot do otherwise. The things which sur
> round us present themselves in a quality of space which we ourselves are
> as those who live in space. The pronoun "my" in the expression "my room"
> does not express my possession of it, but precisely a relation between me
> and the room, which means that my spatial existence has come about.[10]

Edward Casey carries this insight further in his idea of the body forming
"habit memories" in the process of coming to dwell in a place. One comes
to feel settled at home in a place through the process of interaction between
the living body's movement to enact aims and purposes and the material
things among which such activities occur. The things and their arrangement bear witness to the sedimentation of lives lived there. The home is an
extension of and mirror for the living body in its everyday activity. This is
the first sense in which home is the materialization of identity.

> But more than comfort is at issue in the elective affinity between houses
> and bodies: *our very identity is at stake.* For we tend to identify ourselves
> by and with the places in which we reside. Since a significant part of our
> personal identity depends on our exact bodily configuration, it is only to
> be expected that dwelling places, themselves physical in structure, will re
> semble our own material bodies in certain quite basic respect.[11]

(2) The process of sedimentation through which physical surroundings
become home as an extension and reflection of routines also deposits

meaning onto things. Material things and spaces themselves become layered with meaning and personal value as the material markers of events and relationship that make the narrative of a person or group. The meaningful things in my home often have stories, or they are characters and props in stories. I was a little boy in Japan and I picked out that statuette on my own. Those gashes in the top of the chest show the time I got mad at my mother and went at the chest with a pair of scissors. There's our son's room, still with the trophies he won and the books he read in high school. The things among which I live acquired their meaning through events and travels of my life, layered through stories and the wordless memories of smells, rhythms, and interactions. Their value is priceless: often worthless even on the yard sale market, the arrangement of these things in rooms is what I would mourn with the deepest grief if they were destroyed by fire or theft.

The activities of homemaking thus give material support to the identity of those whose home it is. Personal identity in this sense is not at all fixed, but always in process. We are not the same from one moment to the next, one day to the next, one year to the next because we dwell in the flux of interaction and history. We are not the same from one day to the next because our selves are constituted by differing relations with others. Home as the materialization of identity does not fix identity, but anchors it in physical being that makes a continuity between past and present. Without such anchoring of ourselves in things, we are, literally, lost.

Preservation

Homemaking consists in the activities of endowing things with living meaning, arranging them in space in order to facilitate the life activities of those to whom they belong, and preserving them, along with their meaning. Things are made or chosen for the house—furniture, pictures, draperies. Traditionally and today women furnish and decorate houses more than men. Often a home reflects a woman's taste and sensibility. Often it's the style and image she projects of herself and her family. The decor of a poor or modest home usually reflects this meaning-giving impulse as much as the homes of more wealthy people—she bought fabric for the window curtains that she made by hand, she painted or covered the chairs.

That is the photograph of my grandmother, who died before I was born, and it hung over the piano in every apartment and house we lived in while I was growing up: when my mother died it was the first thing I took home. The history embodied in the meaningful things of the home is often intergenerational. Traditionally women are the primary preservers of family as well as individual histories. Women trace the family lines and keep safe the trinkets, china cups, jewelry, pins, and photos of the departed ancestors, ready to tell stories about each of them. I am suggesting that a main dimension for understanding home is time and history.

Beauvoir, like Sartre, tends to associate historicity with futurity. So she considers the oppression of women to consist in our being inhibited from the creative activity of bringing new things into being.

> The male is called upon for action, his vocation is to produce, fight, create, progress, to transcend himself toward the totality of the universe and the infinity of the future. But marriage does not invite the woman to transcend herself with him—it confines her to immanence, shuts her up within the circle of herself. (448)

This focus on futurity, on the unique moment when the human actor brings something new into the world, makes Beauvoir ignore the specifically human value of activities that, as she puts it, guard the things of the past and keep them in store. She implicitly collapses the activities that consist in preserving the living meanings of past history into her category of immanence. This conflation prevents her from seeing the world-making meaning in domestic work. The particular human meanings enacted in the historicality of human existence depend as much on the projection of a past as of a future.

Earlier I cited Heidegger's claim that building has a dual aspect: constructing and preserving. But even his discussion of the correlation of dwelling with building drops the thread of preservation and concentrates on the creative moment of constructing. It is time to pick up the threads of preservation in order to understand the activities of homemaking. Traditional female domestic activity, which many women continue today, partly consists in preserving the objects and meanings of a home.

Homemaking consists in the activities of endowing things with living meaning, arranging them in space in order to facilitate the life of those to whom they belong, and preserving them, along with their meaning. Dwelling in the world means we are located among objects, artifacts, rituals, and practices that configure who we are in our particularity. Meaningful historical works that embody the particular spirit of a person or a people must be protected from the constant threat of elemental disorganization. They must be cleaned, dusted, repaired, and restored; the stories of their founding and continued meaningful use must be told and retold, interpreted and reinterpreted. They must also be protected from the careless neglect or accidental damage caused by those who dwell among and use them, often hardly noticing their meaning as support for their lives. The work of preservation entails not only keeping the physical objects of particular people intact, but renewing their meaning in their lives. Thus preservation involves preparing and staging commemorations and celebrations, where those who dwell together among the things tell and retell stories of their particular lives and give and receive gifts that add to the dwelling world. The important work of preservation also involves teaching the children the meanings of things among which one dwells, teaching the children the stories, practices, and celebrations that keep the particular meanings alive. The preservation of the things among which one dwells gives people a context for their lives, individuates their histories, gives them items to use in making new projects, and makes them comfortable. When things and works are maintained against destruction, but not in the context of life activity, they become museum pieces.

The temporality of preservation is distinct from that of construction. As a founding construction, making is a rupture in the continuity of history. But recurrence is the temporality of preservation. Over and over the things must be dusted and cleaned. Over and over the special objects must be arranged after a move. Over and over the dirt from winter snows must be swept away from the temples and statues, the twigs and leaves removed, the winter cracks repaired. The stories must be told and retold to each new generation to keep a living, meaningful history.

It would be a mistake, however, to conceive of the identity supported through this preservation of meaning in things as fixed. There are no fixed identities, events, or interactions, and the material changes of age and environment make lives fluid and shifting. The activities of preservation give some enclosing fabric to this ever-changing subject by knitting together today and yesterday, integrating the new events and relationships into the narrative of a life, the biography of a person, a family, a people.

Preserving the meaningful identity of a household or family by means of the loving care of its mementos is simply a different order of activity from washing the unhealthy bacteria out of the bathroom. As Beauvoir rightly says, the latter is general, the abstract maintenance of species life. The former, however, is specific and individuated: the homemaker acts to preserve the particular meaning that these objects have in the lives of these particular people. The confusion between these acts and the level of immanence is perhaps understandable, because so many activities of domestic work are both general and particular simultaneously. The homemaker dusts the pieces in order to keep away the molds and dirt that might annoy her sinuses, but at the same time she keeps present to herself and those with whom she lives the moments in their lives or those of their forebears that the objects remember. She prepares the sauce that physically nourishes her children according to her mother's recipe, but at the same time she keeps alive an old cuisine in a new country.

Thus the activity of preservation should be distinguished from the nostalgia accompanying fantasies of a lost home from which the subject is separated and to which he seeks to return. Preservation entails remembrance, which is quite different from nostalgia. Where nostalgia can be constructed as a longing flight from the ambiguities and disappointments of everyday life, remembrance faces the open negativity of the future by knitting a steady confidence in the pains and joys of the past retained in the things among which one dwells. Nostalgic longing is always for an elsewhere. Remembrance is the affirmation of what brought us here.[12]

We should not romanticize this activity. Preservation is ambiguous; it can be either conservative or reinterpretive. The same material things sometimes carry the valences of unique personal identity and status privilege. By using my grandmother's china I both carry the material memory of childhood dinners and display the class position of my family history. I spoke once to a woman committed to restoring and preserving her grandmother's Victorian southwestern ranch house, fully mindful of her grandmother's passive participation in the displacement of Native Americans from the land. The house has the history whether she chooses to live in it or not. The moral and political question for her is how she constructs her own identity and tells the stories of her family to her children. Homemaking consists in preserving the things and their meaning as anchor to shifting personal and group identity. But the narratives of the history of what brought us here are not fixed, and part of the creative and moral task of preservation is to reconstruct the connection of the past to the present in light of new events, relationships, and political understandings.

Given the cruelties of the histories of persons and peoples, remembrance and preservation often consist in the renewal of grief or rage. A Jewish survivor of the Holocaust keeps safe the small and tattered mementos of her long-dead parents. A city debates whether to demolish or preserve the two-hundred-year-old slave auction block that once stood in its center; after much political struggle in which many African Americans, among others, demand its preservation, the city decides to leave it as a painful memorial of slavery. Some of the meaning preserved in things that anchor identity can be summed in the words *never again*.

Preservation of the history that supports a person's identity by means of caring for and arranging things in space is the activity of homemaking still carried out primarily by women in the West and in many other cultures as well. Such homemaking is not done exclusively by women, but to the degree that women more than men attend more to family and community ties in everyday life, the activities of preservation tend to be gender specific. Through these same activities, moreover, as I have already begun to indicate, the identity of groups and peoples is preserved. Especially in this late modern world where public administration and corporate standardization tend to drain individualized meaning from politics, schooling, and work, home and neighborhood retain meaningful importance as primary bearers of cultural identity and differentiation. For many migrants who wish to succeed in their new land, for example, their home is the primary place for the expression of cultural identity and continuity with their native lands.[13]

In many premodern or non-Western societies, as I pointed out earlier, home is not confined to houses. Often the spaces of village squares, meeting halls, or mountaintops are more the home of the people in a group than are their individual shelters. The activities of preservation of the meaningful things that constitute home are important here as public acts of the group: maintaining collective spaces, guarding and caring for statues and monuments. For some traditional societies this preservative work is highly regarded, the responsibility of priests and elders. Modern Western societies also perform such public acts of preservation, but they are less often noticed or valued.

Such collective preservative activities continue today in the interstices of modern urban societies in the activities of civic clubs, neighborhood organizations, and religious institutions. When cities commemorate buildings as historic landmarks and stage periodic historically tinged festivals, they are also often performing the self-sustaining actions of preservation. These projects of keeping the meaning of past events and characters by maintaining material thus are not confined to things with positive feeling. In modern Western societies these public activities of preservation are also often coded as feminine, the devalued responsibility of "preservation ladies" who drink tea and look through moldy records, and often it is women in fact who seek to maintain or recover, interpret, and reinterpret the historical meaning of places.[14]

Beauvoir is right to link her account of women's oppression with domestic work, but not entirely for the reasons she has. A sexual division of labor that removes women from participation in society's most valued and creative activities excludes women from access to power and resources and confines women primarily to domestic work is indeed a source of oppression. Much of what is typically women's work, however, is at least as fundamentally world making and meaning giving as typically men's work. Especially modern, future-oriented societies devalue this work, but at the same time they depend on its continued performance for the nurturance of their subjectivity and their sense of historical continuity. We should not romanticize this activity. Like the other aspects of home that I have discussed, preservation is ambiguous; it can be both conservative and reinterpretive, rigid and fluid. To the extent that it falls to women to perform this work for men and children, just as they perform the work of cooking and washing for them, without men's reciprocation, then women continue to serve as material for the subjectivities of men without receiving like support for themselves. Equality for women, then, requires revaluation of the private and public work of the preservation of meaningful things and degendering these activities.

Contemporary Feminist Rejection of Home

I have been arguing that the value of home is ambiguous, and that feminists should try to disengage a positive from an oppressive meaning of home. If women are expected to confine themselves to the house and serve as selfless nurturers and as those who automatically expand their domestic tasks when economic retrenchment rebounds on families,[15] then house and home remain oppressive patriarchal values. To the extent that both men and women seek in their homes and in the women who make them a lost unity and undisturbed comfort, moreover, the idea of home fuels a wrongful escapism. Values of homemaking, however, underlie the affirmation of personal and cultural identity, which requires material expression in meaningful objects arranged in a space that must be preserved.

A chain of recent interlinked essays elaborates an argument that feminists should reject any affirmation of the value of home. Biddy Martin and Chandra Mohanty launched this discussion in their reading of Minnie Bruce Pratt's reflections on growing up as a privileged white woman in the American South.[16] Teresa de Lauretis then commented on Martin and Mohanty, enlarging their insights about the connection between home and identity.[17] Most recently Bonnie Honig criticizes what she perceives as a privileged position of withdrawal from politics that the idea of home affords, and she enlarges de Lauretis's ideas about decentered identity and feminist politics.[18]

All these essays express a deep distrust of the idea of home for feminist politics and conclude that we should give up a longing for home. Although I agree with their critiques, in this section I argue that whereas politics should not succumb to a longing for comfort and unity, the material values of home can nevertheless provide leverage for radical social critique. Following bell hooks, I shall suggest that *home* can have a political meaning as a site of dignity and resistance. To the extent that having home is currently a privilege, I argue, the values of home should be democratized rather than rejected.

All of these writers suspect a tendency they perceive among feminists to seek a home in a sisterhood with women. Home is a concept and desire that expresses a bounded and secure identity. Home is where a person can be "herself"; one is "at home" when she feels that she is with others who understand her in her particularity. The longing for home is just this longing for a settled, safe, affirmative, and bounded identity. Thus, home is often a metaphor for a mutually affirming, exclusive community defined by gender, class, or race.[19]

Feminist analysis reveals that this feeling of having a home as a bounded identity is a matter of privilege. Recall Irigaray's claim: man's ability to have a home, to return to his original identity, is achieved by means of the dereliction of woman as she provides the material nurturance of the selfsame identity and the envelope that gives him his sense of boundary. In the feminist texts I am exploring here, the privilege of home the writers refer to is less a specifically gender privilege and more a class and race privilege. Martin and Mohanty interpret Pratt's text as revealing how the sense of security and comfort that Pratt experienced as a child was predicated on the exclusion of blacks and lower-class whites at the same time that they were invisibly present—as workers producing the comforts of home. Bonnie Honig argues that the sense of home as a place where one is confident who one is and can fall back on a sense of integrity depends on a vast institutional structure that allows such a luxury of withdrawal, safety, and reflection for some at the expense of many others who lose out in the global transfer of benefits. Home here is constructed in opposition to the uncertainties and dangers of streets and foreign territories where various riffraff hang out in less-than-homey conditions.

> "Being home" refers to the place where one lives within familiar, safe, protected boundaries, "not being home" is a matter of realizing that home was an illusion of coherence and safety based on the exclusion of specific histories of oppression and resistance, the repression of differences, even within oneself.[20]

The women writers we are examining all conclude from these considerations that feminist politics should reject the idea of home. In giving up the idea of home, feminism is consistently postcolonial, exposing the illusion of a coherent stable self or a unified movement of women. A more honest and open attitude toward the world recognizes the plural identities of each of us and a politics that recognizes and affirms differences that cannot draw safe borders for the self.

> When the alternatives would seem to be either the enclosing, encircling, constraining circle of home, or nowhere go, the risk is enormous. The assumption of, or desire for, another safe place like "home" is challenged by the realization that "unity"—interpersonal as well as political—is itself necessarily fragmentary, itself that which is struggled for, chosen, and hence unstable by definition; it is not based on "sameness," and there is no perfect fit.[21]

According to de Lauretis, feminism must make a shift in historical consciousness that entails

> a dis-placement and self-displacement: leaving or giving up a place that is safe, that is "home"—physically, emotionally, linguistically, epistemologically—for another place that is unknown and risky, that is not only emotionally but conceptually other; a place of discourse from which speaking and thinking are at best tentative, uncertain, unguaranteed.[22]

Bonnie Honig argues specifically against the use of "home" as a means of withdrawing from politics into a place of more certain principle and integrity. Feminist politics should be prepared to face dilemmas to which there are no simple responses. Longing for home is the effort to retreat into a solid unified identity at the expense of those projected and excluded as other.

> The dream of home is dangerous, particularly in postcolonial setting, because it animates and exacerbates the inability of constituted subjects or nations,—to accept their own internal divisions, and it engenders zealotry, the will to bring the dream of unitariness or home into being. It leads the subject to project its internal differences onto external others and then to rage against them for standing in the way of its dream—both at home and elsewhere.[23]

Martin and Mohanty, de Lauretis, and Honig are right to criticize the bourgeois-dominative meaning of home, and earlier sections of this essay have explicated why. They are also right to fear the nostalgic seductions of home as a fantasy of wholeness and certainty. Through a reading of Irigaray, I have also elaborated on this claim. They are right, finally, to suggest that the attempt to protect the personal from the political through boundaries of home more likely protects privilege from self-consciousness, and that the personal identities embodied in home inevitably have political implications. I have also explored this undecidable difference between the personal and the political in preserving the meaning of things. These writers make persuasive analyses of the depoliticizing, essentialist, and exploitative implications that the idea of home often carries.

While agreeing with much of this critique, I have also argued that home carries a core positive meaning as the material anchor for a sense of agency and a shifting and fluid identity. This concept of home does not oppose the personal and the political, but instead describes conditions that make the political possible. The identity-supporting material of home can be sources of resistance as well as privilege. To the extent that home functions today as a privilege, I will argue later, the proper response is not to reject home, but to extend its positive values to everyone.

bell hooks expresses a positive meaning of *home* for feminism. She agrees with Martin and Mohanty, de Lauretis, and Honig that *home* is associated with safety and the making, of identity. She gives a positive and political meaning, however, to these functions of *home*. Appealing to the historic experience of African American women, she argues that *homeplace* is the site of resistance to dominating and exploiting social structures. The ability to resist dominant social structures requires a space beyond the full reach of those structures, where different, more humane social relations can be lived and imagined. In hooks's view, homeplace uniquely provides such safe visionary space. The mutual caring and meaningful specificity provided by homeplace, moreover, enables the development of a sense of self-worth and humanity partially autonomous from dominating, exploiting, commercial, or bureaucratic social structures. Thus, hooks agrees with the feminist critics of *home* that home is a site of identity, whereas they criticize a search for pregiven, whole, and apolitical identity. However, hooks finds homeplace to be the site for a self-conscious constructed identity as a political project of criticism and transformation of unjust institutions and practices.

> Historically, African American people believed that the construction of a homeplace, however, fragile and tenuous (the slave hut, the wooden shack), had a radical political dimension. Despite the brutal reality of racial apartheid, of domination, one's homeplace was the one site where one could freely confront the issue of humanization, where one could resist.[24]

Thus, hooks reverses the claim that having "home" is a matter of privilege. "Home" is a more universal value in her vision, one that the oppressed in particular can and have used as a vehicle for developing resistance to oppression. As long as there is a minimal freedom of homeplace, there is a place to assemble apart from the privileged and talk of organizing; there is a place to preserve the specific culture of the oppressed people. The personal sense of identity supported in the site and things of a homeplace thus enables political agency.

hooks emphasizes this political value of homeplace as the place of the preservation of the history and culture of a people, in the face of colonizing forces of the larger society. This project of preservation and remembrance, I have argued above, is very different from the nostalgic longing for home that Martin and Mohanty, de Lauretis, and Honig rightly suspect. Preservation and remembrance are historical. Colonized people can project an alternative future partly on the basis of a place beyond dominance that is preserved in everyday life; hooks herself seeks in her essay to remember the African American mothers and grandmothers who have preserved generations of homeplace and distinct African American cultural meanings in stories, foods, songs, and artifacts.

> I want to remember these black women today. The act of remembrance is a conscious gesture honoring their struggle, their effort to keep something for their own. I want us to respect and understand that this effort has been and continues to be a radically subversive political gesture. For those who dominate and oppress us benefit most when we have nothing to give our own, when they have so taken from us our dignity, our humanness that we have nothing left, no "homeplace" where we can recover ourselves.[25]

Home as a Critical Value

The criticisms of the idea of home I have reviewed dwell primarily on a temptation to reject or reconstruct conflict and social difference by creating safe spaces in politics. Nationalism is an important and dangerous manifestation of this temptation, in romanticizing "homeland." The positive idea of home I have advocated is attached to a particular locale as an extension and expression of bodily routines. Nationalism attempts to project such a local feeling of belonging onto a huge territory and "imagined community" of millions,[26] and in so doing creates rigid distinctions between "us" and "them" and suppresses the differences within "us." Other attempts to project an ideal of home onto large political units are just as damaging. A useful response to such idealizations of politics as a search for home, however, is to emphasize the radical potential of values that attend to the concrete localized experience of home and the existential meaning of being deprived of that experience.

Having the stability and comfort of concrete home is certainly a privilege. Many millions of people in the world today do not have sufficient space of their own to live by themselves or with others in peace. They do not have the time or space to preserve much of the history and culture of their family and community, though only refugees and the most desperately destitute are unable to try. With upwards of fifty million refugees and other homeless people in the world, that deprivation is serious indeed. Even if people have minimal shelter of their own, moreover, they need a certain level of material comfort in their home for it to serve as a place of identity—construction and the development of the spirit of resistance that hooks discusses. In this way, having a home is indeed today having a privilege.

The appropriate response to this fact of privilege is not to reject the values of home, but instead to claim those values for everyone. Feminists should criticize the nostalgic use of home that offers a permanent respite from politics and conflict and which continues to require of women that they make men and children comfortable. But at the same time, feminist politics calls for conceptualizing the positive values of home and criticizing a global society that is unable or unwilling to extend those values to everyone. There are at least four normative values of home that should be thought of as minimally accessible to all people. These stand as regulative ideals by which societies should be criticized.

(1) Safety—Everyone needs a place where they can go to be safe. Ideally, home means a safe place, where one can retreat from the dangers and hassles of collective life. It is too much to ask, perhaps even in the ideal, that everyone can be safe anywhere. The potential for violence and conflict cannot be eradicated from the world. But it is not too much to ask that everyone have a home in which they can feel physically safe and secure.

Today we are frighteningly, horribly far from this simple goal. For too many women and children, their houses do not enclose them safely, but threaten them with violence from the men who live there with them. Too many poor peasants and barrio dwellers in the world cannot sleep peacefully in their homes without fear that paramilitary squads will rouse them, rape them, shoot them, or carry them away in the dark. If anything is a basic need and a basic liberty, it is personal safety and a place to be safe. Yet ensuring such safety at home is an arduous and complex matter, one that seems too daunting for the will of the late twentieth century. We must be ashamed of a world in which safety at home is a privilege and express outrage at any stated or implied suggestion that such a need and liberty is too expensive for any society to meet.

(2) Individuation—A person without a home is quite literally deprived of individual existence.[27] However minimal, home is an extension of the person's body, the space that he or she takes up, and performs the basic activities of life—eating, sleeping, bathing, making love. These need not all be done in the same place or behind closed doors, in a house. But the individual is not allowed to be if she does not have places to live and to perform the activities of life, with basic routine and security. As I have already outlined in the concept of homemaking, moreover, people's existences entail having some space of their own in which they array around them the things that belong to them, that reflect their particular identity back to them in a material mirror. Thus it is basic to the idea of home to have a certain meaning of ownership, not as private property in exchangeable goods, but in the sense of meaningful use and reuse for life. Even the monk has a cell of his own in the collective life of the monastery; even in crowded families with little space there is usually an effort to allocate each person a cor-

ner of his own where he can sleep and put the things he calls his own. Where this is not possible it nevertheless remains as an ideal.[28]

(3) Connected with the value of individuation is privacy. A person does not have a place of her own and things of her own if anyone can have access to them. To own a space is to have autonomy over admission to the space and its contents. Some feminists doubt the value of privacy, because they associate this idea with the "private sphere" to which women have been historically confined. But there are crucial differences between the two concepts. Privacy refers to the autonomy and control a person has to allow or not allow access to her person, information about her, and the things that are meaningfully associated with her person. The traditional "private sphere," on the other hand, confines some persons to certain realm of activity and excludes them from others. As a value, privacy says nothing about opportunities for the person to engage in activity. It only says that whatever her social activities, a person should have control over access to her living space, her meaningful things, and information about herself.[29]

Feminists have been suspicious of a value of privacy also because traditional law has sometimes appealed to a right of privacy to justify not interfering with autocratic male power in the family. Because of a supposed right of privacy, the law should turn a blind eye to marital rape or battering. But perhaps the most important defense against this legitimation of patriarchal power is an insistence that privacy is a value for individuals, not simply or primarily for households. Anita Allen argues that if we insist on privacy as a value for all persons as individuals, then the extent to which women deserve privacy at home and elsewhere, and do not have it, becomes apparent: The appeal to privacy as a value thus enables social criticism.[30]

Some might claim that appeal to a value of privacy is ethnocentric, because the idea of privacy is a Western idea. Scholars disagree on the question of whether non-Western societies both historically and today have held a value of privacy. My cursory reading of that literature leads me to conclude that there is often, if not always, a form of respect for the physical person of another and for some kind of spaces associated with the person. In stratified societies, such respect may be restricted to those in the upper strata. This does not mean that such a value does not exist in the society, but rather that it is held as a privilege. I am arguing here that certain values associated with home, among them control over access to one's person and personal space, be made available everyone: to the degree that non-Western and premodern societies, as well as modern societies, do not democratize privacy, then I am indeed criticizing them.

(4) The final value of *home* that should be available to everyone I have already explicated at length in an earlier section: preservation. Home is the site of the construction and reconstruction of one's self. Crucial to that pro-

cess is the activity of safeguarding the meaningful things in which one sees the stories of one's self embodied and rituals of remembrance that reiterate those stories. I have argued that preservation in this sense is an important aspect of both individual and collective identity.

Home is a complex ideal. I have argued with an ambiguous connection to identity and subjectivity. I agree with those critics of home who see it as a nostalgic longing for an impossible security and comfort, a longing bought at the expense of women and of those constructed as others, strangers, not-home, in order to secure this fantasy of a unified identity. But I have also argued that the idea of home and the practices of homemaking support personal and collective identity in a more fluid and material sense, and that recognizing this value entails also recognizing the creative value to the often unnoticed work that many women do. Despite the real dangers of romanticizing home, there are also dangers in turning our backs on home.

PART II

Enactments between Existentialism and Psychoanalysis

Splitting the Subject:
The Interval between
Immanence and Transcendence

GAIL WEISS

In her classic essay, "Throwing Like a Girl," Iris Young offers a critical analysis of the work of two existential phenomenologists, Erwin Straus and Maurice Merleau-Ponty.[1] More specifically, Young reveals the inadequacies in both Straus's and Merleau-Ponty's accounts of embodiment, insofar as both they and other thinkers have failed "to describe the modalities, meaning, and implications of the difference between 'masculine' and 'feminine' body comportment and movement."[2] Although Straus acknowledges differences between girls and boys in styles of throwing, he seeks to explain these differences biologically. The differences noted by Straus include a girl's tendency to isolate her forearm and to use it alone to throw the ball, leaving the rest of the body relatively immobile. The boy, however, is more likely to make use of his whole body in preparing for and executing the throw. For the girl, the outcome of this process is that "the ball is released without force, speed, or accurate aim," whereas, for the boy, "the ball leaves the hand with considerable acceleration; it moves toward its goal in a long flat curve."[3]

Young does not dispute Straus's findings of significant differences between boys' and girls' throwing styles, but she does take issue with his explanation for them. Indeed, Young readily agrees that such differences between throwing styles for boys and girls do exist, although clearly there are many girls who do throw "like boys" and a (smaller) number of boys who do throw "like girls."[4] Moreover, Young notes that with respect to physical goal-oriented activity, many other stylistic differences between boys and girls can be found. Whether the task at hand involves throwing, carrying, sitting, or bending and lifting, in each case the observation is similar; namely, boys tend to be much more effective in maximizing their bodily potential in executing physical tasks than are girls.

Although post-Beauvoirian feminists have long been concerned about reifying a "masculine" norm as a goal for women, insofar as it seems inevitably to lead to a further devaluing of whatever gets identified by contrast as "the feminine," Young, Straus, and others clearly imply that the "masculine" style of throwing, carrying, and bending and lifting is preferable to the "feminine" one.[5] Though Young never makes the claim outright, she does imply throughout her essay that the "masculine" style is, indeed, the one that girls as well as boys should be encouraged to emulate because of the psychological as well as physiological advantages that come from utilizing one's whole body while engaged in a particular task. Greater confidence in oneself and one's bodily capabilities, a more accurate understanding of one's physical potential, and a sense of openness to and readiness for the demands of a given situation are positive experiences that both accompany and continue to encourage the development of one's bodily abilities. And yet, although we may readily agree that it is much better to maximize rather than to minimize one's bodily potential, *both* Young and Straus fail to dwell on the *consequences* of this greater valuation of what they describe as "masculine" bodily comportment for both boys and girls.

For Young, living as a woman in contemporary Western industrial patriarchal society involves living a tension between transcendence and immanence, a tension that is reflected in the contradictory modalities that comprise "feminine" bodily comportment. Rejecting Straus's essentialist appeal to an innate (and rather mysterious) "feminine attitude" as the cause of gender differences in throwing styles, Young argues that it is the clash between how girls experience their own bodies and how society experiences and views their bodies that is responsible for many girls' lack of confidence in their bodies, restricted bodily movements, and anxiety about taking bodily "risks" in the performance of new physical tasks.

Working from a Sartrian/Beauvoirian understanding of transcendence as a sense of openness to future projects as an existence for itself and immanence as a sense of rootedness to the past stemming from one's objectification as a being for others, Young agrees with Beauvoir that the young girl is societally regarded as more immanent than transcendent and that this is not the case for the young boy. In particular, Young focuses on the ways in which society has typically discouraged young girls from developing their full bodily potential by exaggerating both the threat of physical injury that could come from increased exertion and the danger of appearing "unfeminine" in the performance of physical tasks.

For instance, whereas the young boy is often encouraged to engage in "rough-and-tumble" play, the young girl in a similar situation may just as easily be warned not to get her clothes (especially dress) dirty. And, while the skinned knees and torn trousers of the young boy are often viewed as a "badge of honor" that results not only in peer approval and acceptance but also in the tolerant indulgence of parents proud to have such an active boy, the young girl's skinned knees and torn trousers (or dress) often result in disapproval from her more "feminine" peers if not from parents who, if the behavior occurs in an "unsuitable" context, may be slightly ashamed of their "tomboy." Moreover, the source of this disapproval is often twofold: not only does the girl fail at the project of "being a girl," but she also fails equally to achieve the status of the boy.[6]

Young claims that it is the *self-referred* quality of "feminine" bodily comportment that gives rise to its contradictory modalities. That is, it is because young girls are socialized to focus so heavily on their bodies, to treat their bodies as objects to be "pruned," "shaped," "molded," and "decorated" that they move with "ambiguous transcendence," "inhibited intentionality," and "discontinuous unity."[7] According to Young:

> The three contradictory modalities of feminine bodily existence—ambiguous transcendence, inhibited intentionality, and discontinuous unity—have their root . . . in the fact that for feminine existence the body frequently is both subject and object for itself at the same time and in reference to the same act. Feminine bodily existence is frequently not a pure presence to the world because it is referred onto *itself* as well as onto possibilities in the world.[8]

Intertwining Beauvoir's recognition that transcendence is societally associated with males and immanence with females with Merleau-Ponty's radical understanding of the body as a transcendent subject of perception, Young is able to combat Merleau-Ponty's "gender-blind" account of the body with Beauvoir's emphasis on the bodily consequences of gendered social practices, and she is also able to use Merleau-Ponty's understanding of the body as transcendent as a corrective to Beauvoir's more negative (and traditional) view of the body as immanent. And yet, Young still remains trapped within the confines of the hierarchical transcendence/immanence distinction itself and this is why I find her "explanation" of the contradictory modalities of "feminine" bodily existence in terms of the latter's self-referred character ultimately so unsatisfying. For, in the end, what Young is suggesting is that self-referral is an immanent move that threatens one's transcendent activity because it disrupts the flow of one's action and concentrates one's attention explicitly upon one's body rather than on the task to be performed. This, in turn, "inhibits" one's intentionality and leads to discontinuities in one's bodily movements. But does explicit reference to one's body while one is engaged in an action necessarily take away from the "transcendence" of one's intentional activity? And, by implying that this is the case, doesn't Young end up in the unpalatable situation of supporting an entire patriarchal philosophical tradition that seeks to render the body and its contribution to everyday experience invisible?

The problems that give rise to the contradictory modalities of "feminine" bodily existence, as I see it, are not tied to the latter's self-reference as it is described by Young, but rather have to do with what I would call the "socially referred" character of bodily existence for many women (and many men). For there are many tasks that require paying close attention to one's body prior to (and even while) acting, and thus self-reference alone does not seem to mark out the specific contradictions that Young identifies with "feminine" as opposed to "masculine" bodily existence.[9] Moreover, I would resist viewing the socially referred character of bodily existence as inherently negative or as leading inevitably to immanence. This is because, I would argue, all of our (men's as well as women's) actions have a socially referred character insofar as they arise in response to a social situation.

In particular, I am maintaining that the contradictory modalities of "feminine" bodily existence identified by Young occur not because women focus on their bodies before and during their action, transforming their bodies into objects in the process, but because many women mediate their own relationship with their bodies by seeing their bodies as they are seen by others and worrying about what they and these (largely invisible) others are seeing as they are acting. In fact, Young herself notes that for a particular woman experiencing these contradictory bodily modalities "the source of this objectified bodily existence is in the attitude of others regarding her," yet she quickly moves on from this observation to focus upon how "the woman herself often actively takes up her body as a mere thing."[10] In shifting the focus so quickly from the individual woman to the attitudes of others that motivate her objectified relationship to her body, and then back to the consequences of this objectification for the individual woman, Young deflects attention away from what she calls the source of the objectification, namely, societal attitudes towards women, and inadvertently reinforces an interpretation of these contradictory bodily modalities as an individual woman's (rather than societal) "problem."

What makes the social reference of "feminine" bodily existence so problematic, is that the imaginary perspective of these often imaginary others can come to dominate and even supersede a woman's own experience of her bodily capabilities so that the latter becomes conflated with the former much as the child's spectral image in the mirror stage comes to dominate and take priority over the child's kinesthetic experience of her/his body. And, just as Lacan emphasizes the alienating aspect of this identificatory move that both boys and girls undergo in the formation of the (bodily) ego, we can speak in this situation of another form of bodily alienation whose ground is already laid by the earlier one that occurs in the mirror stage. Here, we have a kind of "doubling" of the Lacanian mirror, a doubling in which I am watching this imaginary other watching me. To call this "self-reference" does not acknowledge or do justice to the very real effects of this imaginary other on my action. To call it "social reference" carries with it a parallel danger, namely that the agent of the action can be rendered invisible altogether, a fate that Irigaray fears has become reality for the "specular woman" who is the source but never the author of all (philosophical) speculation.[11]

Despite the dangers inherent in attributing the contradictory modalities of "feminine" bodily existence to its socially referred character, I do feel that this displacement of the "self" onto the "social" realm that both supports and constructs the self is necessary and illuminating not only in accounting for what differentiates "feminine" bodily existence from "masculine" bodily existence (insofar as different types of social reference are operative in each) but also in accounting for what differentiates "black" bodily existence from "white" bodily existence, and "Jewish" bodily existence from "Catholic" or "Muslim" bodily existence, to give but a few examples. In addition, appealing to the particular kind of social reference that contextualizes an individual's movements, comportment, and action in a given situation also avoids identifying social reference with either immanence or transcendence and encourages a focus on the *type* of social reference operative rather than the *fact* of social reference itself.

Social reference, like self-reference, can just as easily increase as decrease confidence in one's bodily abilities and potentialities. It can indeed give rise to the contradictory bodily modalities described by Young when it sets limits to, rather than encourages, the full development of bodily motility and spatiality. Realizing the crucial (and usually invisible) role that social reference plays in mediating our relationships with our bodies allows us to recognize why it is so difficult to eliminate the contradictory modalities discussed by Young. For doing so successfully must be much more than a cognitive process; indeed, it involves a radical modification of our body images and, therefore, of our corporeal styles. Moreover, pointing to the socially referred character of our bodily comportment enables us to see why it would be overly simplistic to view bodily habit alone as responsible for the body's resistance to change. Instead of continuing to focus, as so many feminists have done, on the need for women to change their relationship to their bodies to a more loving and accepting one (a project that may paradoxically, from Young's perspective, encourage women to accept rather than challenge their bodily "limitations"), an emphasis on the socially referred character of all types of bodily existence reveals the need for societal change in the way "feminine" bodily existence is identified and differentiated from "masculine" bodily existence in the first place. This latter project Young herself undertakes in three other essays on female embodiment that follow "Throwing Like a Girl," namely, "Breasted Experience," "Pregnant Embodiment," and "Women Recovering Their Clothes." [12]

Throughout Young's inquiry into the varying meanings of female embodiment expressed through throwing styles, fascination with clothes, pregnancy, and female breasted experience, the notion of the "split subject" is continually evoked, though it is never named as such. In "Throwing Like a Girl," Young describes the ways in which the female subject is split between contradictory bodily modalities, between a confident "I can" and a diffident "perhaps I cannot." Here, the "splitting" of the subject is understood negatively by Young insofar as it is responsible for many women's unwillingness to maximize their bodily potentialities. Moreover, Young's description of the "self-referred" character of "feminine" bodily existence also suggests that the reference to the self both prior to and during one's action "splits" the subject by breaking up the fluidity and unity of one's action, creating an alienated, objectified perspective on that action. Specifically, Young understands the "splitting" of the subject as involving the creation of an artificial separation between a transcendent subjectivity and an objective, immanent body.

> This objectified bodily existence accounts for the self-consciousness of the feminine relation to her body and resulting distance she takes from her body. As human, she is a transcendence and subjectivity, and cannot live herself as mere bodily object. Thus, to the degree that she does live herself as mere body, she cannot be in unity with herself, but must take a distance from and exist in discontinuity with her body. The objectifying regard that "keeps her in her place" can also account for the spatial modality of being positioned and for why women frequently tend not to move openly, keeping their limbs closed around themselves. To open her body in free, active open extension and bold outward-directedness is for a woman to invite objectification. [13]

Young's final point in this passage is crucial, for she suggests that the price of refusing to objectify (and monitor) one's own body may be that others do so instead. On this account, self-objectification and contradictory bodily modalities may very well turn out to be worth the risks entailed (i.e., self-alienation, failure to utilize bodily capabilities to the utmost, etc.) insofar as they anticipate and attempt to preclude societal objectification, which is all too often a first step toward more violent forms of bodily aggression (e.g., sexual assault). The "split subject," then, arises in response to a patriarchal social system in which women internalize and respond to the (imaginary and real) responses of (imaginary and real) others to their bodies before, during, and after their action. Overcoming the "splitting" of the subject will therefore involve overcoming the inequities that permeate a patriarchal society in which women continually find themselves subject to the invisible and omnipresent male gaze.

At this point, it may seem as if, for Young at least, the "splitting" of the subject is always a negative phenomenon, especially for women, inevitably resulting in contradictory bodily modalities and self-objectification. Indeed, Young is not the only feminist theorist to address the dangers inherent in this type of self-fragmentation. In her essay "On Psychological Oppression," Sandra Bartky defines fragmentation as "the splitting of the whole person into parts of a person which, in stereotyping, may take the form of a war between a 'true' and 'false' self—or, in sexual objectification, the form of *an often coerced and degrading identification of a person with her body . . .*" [14] For both Bartky and Young, then, the "splitting," or fragmentation, of the subject can be seen as undermining the integrity and agency of the self.

To feel humiliated when one is receiving unwanted attention directed at one's body is understandable in a society in which bodies are a constant source of ridicule and embarrassment. Every week in the aisles of the grocery store, magazine headlines "shout" at women (and increasingly, men) with bold urgency about ways to improve our sagging, overweight, aging bodies. Alternately mocking and beguiling, these "miracle stories" of dramatic weight loss and complete bodily transformation beckon, at one time or another, to the most skeptical among us, if only for a phantasmatic moment as we glance at the accompanying (and inevitable) pictures that give testimony to the reality of what can be accomplished if only one is "willing" (read financially able) to try. [15] Yet, I am not convinced that the experience of objectification or even self-objectification is sufficient to bring about psychological oppression. Nor does fragmentation, or the "splitting," of the subject seem to be inevitably a negative phenomenon. If, for instance, we are being singled out for our intelligence alone, would this form of objectification (and reduction) be viewed as humiliating and oppressive? Some might claim that having attention drawn to one's intelligence is not even an instance of objectification. But why not? Objectification is indeed a "dirty word" in our society, and many feminists (myself included) have rebelled against Sartre's understanding of being-for-others as always involving objectification. My question is, are there ways of understanding both fragmentation and objectification that are nonoppressive or even self-affirming? Addressing this question is especially crucial if we are to understand the impact that the experiences of fragmentation and objectification have on the development and significance of the body image.

Interestingly enough, it is Young, in her essay "Pregnant Embodiment:

Subjectivity and Alienation," who offers an example of a *positive, non-alienating* experience of the "splitting" of the subject in pregnancy. This example is also illuminating because of the noticeable changes in the body image that accompany and reinforce the feelings of being a "split" subject. Moreover, in this essay Young clearly differentiates her position from that of,

> existential phenomenologists of the body [who] usually assume a distinction between transcendence and immanence as two modes of bodily being. They assume that insofar as I adopt an active relation to the world, I am not aware of my body for its own sake. In the successful enactment of my aims and projects, my body is a transparent medium. For several of these thinkers, awareness of my body as weighted material, as physical, occurs only or primarily when my instrumental relation to the world breaks down, in fatigue or illness. . . . Being brought to awareness of my body for its own sake, these thinkers assume, entails estrangement and objectification. . . . Thus the dichotomy of subject and object appears anew in the conceptualization of the body itself. These thinkers tend to assume that awareness of my body in its weight, massiveness, and balance is always an alienated objectification of my body, in which I am not my body and my body imprisons me. They also tend to assume that such awareness of my body must cut me off from the enactment of my projects; I cannot be attending to the physicality of my body and using it as the means to the accomplishment of my aims.[16]

According to Young, pregnancy offers a paradigmatic example of "being thrown into awareness of one's body." In pregnancy, she notes, "contrary to the mutually exclusive categorization between transcendence and immanence that underlies some theories, the awareness of my body in its bulk and weight does not impede the accomplishing of my aims."[17] To become aware of my body, especially during the second and third trimesters of pregnancy, is to become aware of the movements of another body inside my body, and this is one of the reasons why the pregnant woman comes to experience herself as a "split" subject. Young argues, moreover, that

> [t]he pregnant subject . . . is decentered, split, or doubled in several ways. She experiences her body as herself and not herself. Its inner movements belong to another being, yet they are not other, because her body boundaries shift and because her bodily self-location is focused on her trunk in addition to her head. This split subject appears in the eroticism of pregnancy, in which the woman can experience an innocent narcissism fed by recollection of her repressed experience of her own mother's body. Pregnant existence entails, finally, a unique temporality of process and growth in which the woman can experience herself as split between past and future.[18]

Ultimately, for Young, the "splittings" described here can and should be positive bodily experiences for the pregnant woman. Nonetheless, Young also maintains that

> [t]he integrity of my body is undermined in pregnancy not only by this externality of the inside, but also by the fact that the boundaries of my body are themselves in flux. In pregnancy I literally do not have a firm sense of where my body ends and the world begins. My automatic body habits become dislodged; the continuity between my customary body and my body at this moment is broken. In pregnancy my prepregnant body image does not entirely leave my movements and expectations, yet it is with the pregnant body that I must move. This is another instance of the doubling of the pregnant subject.[19]

When Young states in this passage that pregnancy undermines bodily integrity, I am led to question what she (and I) mean by bodily integrity in the first place. In the context of this discussion, bodily integrity seems to refer to a more unified, bounded experience of the body and the corresponding presence of a unitary, clearly defined body image. *The Random House Dictionary of the English Language* provides three definitions of integrity: "1. soundness of and adherence to moral principle and character; uprightness; honesty; 2. the state of being whole, entire, or undiminished; 3. a sound, unimpaired, or perfect condition."[20] In everyday usage of the term integrity, these three alternative definitions are often conflated, with the moral connotation predominating. Although Young's use of the term bodily integrity is appealing to me insofar as it subverts the identification of the moral connotation of integrity with the mind, I also find it rather problematic because the expression itself appeals to notions of wholeness and closure that historically have constituted a regulative norm for bodily experience. Young herself is critical of the dominant model of health which "assumes that the normal, healthy body is unchanging." "Health" she elaborates,

> is associated with stability, equilibrium, a steady state. Only a minority of persons, however, namely adult men who are not yet old, experience their health as a state in which there is no regular or noticeable change in body condition. For them a noticeable change in their bodily state usually does signal a disruption or dysfunction. Regular, noticeable, sometimes extreme change in bodily condition, on the other hand, is an aspect of the normal bodily functioning of adult women. Change is also a central aspect of the bodily existence of healthy children and healthy old people, as well as some of the so-called disabled. Yet medical conceptualization implicitly uses this unchanging adult male body as the standard of all health.[21]

Thinking back to my own pregnancies, my changing bodily experiences did not so much undermine as *resignify* bodily integrity; newly emerging bodily rhythms, the temporality Young identifies with process and growth, gave both consistency and insistency to even the most unsettling and disruptive aspects of my pregnant existence. What was surprising for me was that this alternative sense of bodily integrity was realized and even reinforced, rather than diminished, *through* (not in spite of) the continual changes I was experiencing in my body. Fluidity and expansiveness, rather than the myths of wholeness and closure (which I don't believe any of us, male or female, ever truly experience) were the tangible signs of this newly discovered bodily integrity. Paradoxically, I would argue that it was precisely through experiencing the "splittings" that Young describes above, that I first discovered what it means to have a sense of bodily integrity. This is not to say that pregnancy is the only way to achieve the kind of bodily integrity I am talking about here. Rather, what I would argue is that bodily integrity is *created* through developing a greater sensitivity to one's bodily changes, capacities, movements, and gestures, whether these latter involve the more noticeable changes of pregnancy, childbirth, and lactation or the daily changes that *all* bodies continually undergo. On this account, it is not the "splitting" of the subject that undermines bodily integrity, but rather the denial of the co-existence of disparate sensations and movements that threatens the consistency of bodily existence, a consistency that is based, more often than not and in true Heraclitean fashion, upon incomparable and even inconsistent bodily experiences.

Contemporary societal "splittings" of the pregnant subject's maternity from her sexuality, on the other hand, *do* seem to me to be serious threats to the bodily integrity of the pregnant woman. For in denying that pregnant existence is simultaneously sexual existence, our society seeks to restrict the meaning of both sexuality and the pregnant body to opposite, mutually exclusive poles of existence, not to be occupied by the same person at the same point in time. As Young notes,

> [t]here was a time when the pregnant woman stood as a symbol of stately and sexual beauty. While pregnancy remains an object of fascination, our own culture harshly separates pregnancy from sexuality. The dominant culture defines feminine beauty as slim and shapely. The pregnant woman is often not looked upon as sexually active or desirable, even though her own desires and sensitivity may have increased.[22]

Paradoxically, for Young, this denial of the sexuality of the pregnant woman may afford her a greater degree of freedom from sexual objectification by others. Regarded societally as the "expectant mother," she may find it problematic that for others her sexuality is denied, "split off" from her current pregnant existence, yet this may also provide her with a welcome "break" from unwanted sexual attention. Nonetheless, what Young doesn't go on to add is that the pregnant woman may now find herself to be the focus of a different kind of attention that can be quite as disturbing and invasive as the sexual attention she may have experienced formerly. Neither her breasts nor her buttocks, but her abdomen is now subject to the penetrating stare of the other. From the abdomen, the usual trajectory of the other's gaze moves to the ring finger on her left hand to "verify" the "legitimacy" of her pregnancy. Depending on whether or not the wedding ring is present, the other's gaze may move on to the pregnant woman's eyes to signal social acceptance and personal approval or be averted altogether in a gesture of dismissal and disrespect.

In the essay "Women Recovering Our Clothes," Young marks, in yet another register, the split between seeing myself and seeing myself being seen, and she fantasizes about the possibility of splitting the former experience away from the latter one. Turning to critical analyses offered by psychoanalytic feminist film theorists that reveal the narrative construction of identity played out in contemporary images of women's clothes, a construction that is always facilitated by the "voyeuristic gaze of the other," Young confronts a dilemma:

> It's all true, I guess; at least I cannot deny it: In clothes I seek to find the approval of the transcending male gaze; in clothing I seek to transform myself into a bewitching object that will capture his desire and identity. When I leaf through magazines and catalogs I take my pleasure from imagining myself perfected and beautiful and sexual for the absent or mirrored male gaze. I take pleasure in these images of female bodies in their clothes because my own gaze occupies the position of the male gaze insofar as I am a subject at all. I will not deny it, but it leaves a hollowness in me. If I simply affirm this, I must admit that for me there is no subjectivity that is not his, that there is no specifically female pleasure I take in clothes.[23]

Can a woman experience narcissistic pleasure in looking at, fantasizing about, and wearing clothes that is not mediated by an omnipresent male gaze and phallic desire? In addition, can narcissism itself be resignified so that its connotations of immaturity, self-absorption, and petty vanity are superseded by the three foci of Young's own analysis, namely, touch, bonding, and fantasy? Last, but not least, what role do clothes and clothing images play in the development of the body image?

In her discussion of the erotic, communal, and imaginative possibilities offered to women by clothes, Young succeeds in giving voice to a nonphallic, specular pleasure that refuses to be circumscribed by the omnivorous male gaze. Following Irigaray, Young claims that "touch immerses the subject in fluid continuity with the object, and for the touching subject the object touched reciprocates the touching, blurring the border between self and other." [24] "By touch" she adds,

> I do mean that specific sense of skin on matter, fingers on texture. But I also mean an orientation to sensuality as such that includes all senses. Thus we might conceive a mode of vision, for example, that is less a gaze, distanced from and mastering its object, but an immersion in light and color. Sensing as touching is within, experiencing what touches it as ambiguous, continuous, but nevertheless differentiated. [25]

Not only is Young expanding the parameters of touch to incorporate a vision that is immersed in, rather than distant from, its object, but she is also seeking to discover, like Merleau-Ponty, that which is "untouchable" within our tactile experience, that which cannot be reduced to, or superseded by, a dialectic between self and other. In a passage written in May 1960, Merleau-Ponty explores the meaning of tactility and visibility through the phenomenon of specularity, which underlies them both. Here he suggests that the fissure (*écart*) between touching and being touched, seeing and being seen, actually produces (rather than undermines) a strong sense of self. "The flesh," he notes,

> *is a mirror phenomenon* and the mirror is an extension of my relation with my body. . . . To touch oneself, to see oneself, is to obtain . . . a specular extract of oneself. I.e. fission of appearance and Being—a fission that already takes place in the touch (duality of the touching and the touched) and which, with the mirror (Narcissus) is only a more profound adhesion to Self. [26]

Without the duality of touching and being touched, seeing and being seen, Merleau-Ponty implies, narcissism would itself become an impossibility. And, although all narcissism may indeed be mediated by the presence and perspective of others, this need not mean that the specular confirmation offered by the mirror is reducible to how we are seen by these others. Nor, as Young subtly points out, need we experience the perspective of others through the alienating model of the voyeuristic gaze.

In "Women Recovering Our Clothes," Young describes a nonantagonistic, mutually affirming relationship between women that can be achieved through such banal narcissistic experiences as trying on clothes *together,* looking, perhaps, in the same dressing room mirror, sharing the possibility of self-transformation in the process.

There they chat to one another about their lives and self-images as they try on outfits. . . . Women buy often enough on these expeditions, but often they walk out of the store after an hour of dressing up with no parcels at all; the pleasure was in the choosing, trying, and talking, a mundane shared fantasy.[27]

For Young, the untouchable nonrealm invoked by Merleau-Ponty, a non-realm that is neither consciousness nor the unconscious, is itself a site of fantasy. "Clothing images," Young asserts, "are not always the authoritative mirror that tells who's the fairest of them all, but the entrance to a wonderland of characters and situations."[28] By focusing in on the lack of coincidence between touching and being touched, and, more specifically, on the imaginative possibilities that arise in the gap between touching (oneself and others through) clothes and being touched by them, Young seeks liberating fantasies for women that are nonvoyeuristic and nonoppressive, fantasies that allow us to revalue the mundane narcissistic pleasures of "dressing up," of wearing a favorite outfit, of window shopping with friends.

In her final essay on female embodiment, "Breasted Experience," Young leads us further away from a purely narcissistic interpretation of being concerned with one's appearance by concentrating on the need for an expansion of *societal* imagination. She argues here that society must endeavor to create positive images of the one-breasted woman, images that would offer an alternative to the current practice of hiding mastectomy (another type of "splitting" of the subject) through surgical implants and/or breast "reconstructions."

Before moving on to consider Young's description of female breasted experience and how it affects our body images, let us examine more closely what she has to say about fantasy. Contrary to Judith Butler's emphasis upon the *morphological imaginary,* a phrase that itself highlights the materiality of this traditionally immaterial (in both senses of the word) domain, Young seems to accept the classic equation of fantasy with that which is unreal or desubstantialized even while she argues for the important role that fantasy plays in women's lives.[29]

Part of the pleasure of clothes for many of us consists of allowing ourselves to fantasize with images of women in clothes, and in desiring to become an image, unreal, to enter an intransitive, playful utopia. There are ways of looking at oneself in the mirror that do not appraise oneself before the objectifying gaze, but rather desubstantialize oneself, turn oneself into a picture, an image, an unreal identity. In such fantasy we do not seek to be somebody else. Fantasizing is not wishing, hoping, or planning; it has no future. The clothing image provides the image of situations without any situatedness; there is an infinite before and after; thus the images are open at both ends to an indefinite multitude of possible transformations.[30]

I am troubled by the way in which the body disappears altogether in this description of both fantasy and the phantasmatic image. To claim, as Young does, that "the clothing image provides the image of situations without any situatedness" implies that the clothing image is itself disembodied, a phantom that frees us from our own corporeality. Once again, and despite earlier arguments to the contrary, it seems as if Young is accepting a more immanent view of the body, as if the body is a material prison that our fantasies can allow us to escape. In contrast, what I would emphasize is that when I am trying on clothes before the mirror, the clothing images that I create and fantasize about, are images of my clothed *body*. Furthermore, I would argue, the self-transformations I explore through these fantasies offer so much narcissistic pleasure precisely because they are not unreal or desubstantialized, but rather, because they are materialized through my body and because they hold out the possibility of *resituating* myself within my existing situation.

Reinforcing her disembodied view of fantasy, images, and the imaginary, Young goes on to identify women's fantasies of themselves and other women in clothes with aesthetic freedom, "the freedom to play with shape and color on the body, to don various styles and looks, and through them exhibit and imagine unreal possibilities." "Women," she adds,

> often actively indulge in theatrical imagining, which is largely closed to the everyday lives of men or which they live vicariously through the clothes of women. Such female imagination has liberating possibilities because it subverts, unsettles the order to respectable, functional rationality in a world where that rationality supports domination. The unreal that wells up through imagination always creates the space for a negation of what is, and thus the possibility of alternatives.[31]

There are several problems with this account of what Young calls "female imagination" that are brought to the fore in this particular passage.[32] First of all, Young not only tacitly sets up the body as an adversary to be overcome through aesthetic freedom, which will allow us to "exhibit and imagine unreal possibilities," but she also suggests that "female imagination" is at odds with "respectable, functional rationality," inadvertently supporting, rather than subverting, traditional stereotypes about women's "inherent" irrationality. If this "irrational" (at least from the standpoint of rationality) female imagination "creates the space for a negation of what is," how are we to understand this space and the alternatives it is supposed to offer if we are ourselves "desubstantialized," turned "into a picture, an image, an unreal identity"? That is, how can self-transformation (much less social transformation) be realized in such a nonmaterial fashion?

In "Breasted Experience," by contrast, Young does present a more *corporeal* fantasy of the new possibilities that can and should be made available to women who have had a breast removed. Rather than attempt to deny (as many physicians and concerned friends and family have done) that a woman's breasts are central to her bodily existence, Young maintains that "for many women, if not all, breasts are an important component of body self-image; a woman may love them or dislike them, but she is rarely neutral." [33] Just as Beauvoir, in *The Second Sex*, points out the contradictions that permeate the "many-faced myth" of Woman, so too, Young explores the contradictions that constitute the "breast ideal":

> What matters is the look of them, how they measure up before the normalizing gaze. There is one perfect shape and proportion for breasts: round, sitting high on the chest, large but not bulbous, with the look of firmness. The norm is contradictory, of course. If breasts are large, their weight will tend to pull them down; if they are large and round, they will tend to be floppy rather than firm. In its image of the solid object *this norm suppresses the fleshy materiality of breasts,* this least muscular, softest body part. [34]

The bra, Young argues, aids in the dematerializing normalization of women's breasts, both by "lifting and curving the breasts to approximate the one and only breast ideal" and by hiding the presence of the nipples, those "no-no's," that "show the breasts to be active and independent zones of sensitivity and eroticism." [35]

Plastic surgery also facilitates the realization of patriarchal culture's phantasmatic breast ideal, not only through breast reconstructions after mastectomy, but also through the increasingly popular surgical procedures of breast reduction, breast augmentation, and breast "lifts." For women with the money and desire to undergo the necessary (and extremely painful) medical procedures, the "perfect breasts" may indeed seem to be a practical option; however, many of the women who do undergo these operations are not prepared for the long-term bodily effects, which can include inability to lactate and nurse a baby, lack of sensitivity in the breasts, infections, bruising, and recurrent pain. [36]

Women who lack the money for cosmetic surgery but who nonetheless desire "perfect breasts" can try any number of physical regimens and/or can mail away for special apparatuses advertised in the grocery store magazines, all of which promise to transform the breasts one is (and, they imply, ought to be) ashamed of into objects of pride. It is patriarchal culture, Young asserts, that "constructs breasts as objects, the correlate of the objectifying male gaze." [37] Not only the breasts, but also abdomens, buttocks, thighs, calves, upper arms, and other body parts are often isolated and subjected to rigorous disciplinary practices, presented as forms of "body maintenance," in order to allow the body to approximate its particular gendered ideal.[38] In the end, Young implies, the possibility of distinguishing between a female and a social imaginary is obliterated because "there is little choice of what body to value; the normalized body is reinforced by the transformative possibilities of medical technology. Why wouldn't a woman 'choose' perfect breasts when the opportunity is there?" [39]

Young finds breast enlargement to be, on the whole, more problematic from a feminist standpoint than breast reduction. This is because the latter operation is often done to decrease back pain and/or to allow women to participate comfortably in everyday physical activities. By implication, Young suggests that breast augmentation lacks these more "worthy" motivations and that the women who undergo it transform their own breasts into commodities that they (literally) purchase in order to achieve the phallocentric breast ideal.

And yet, what Young doesn't acknowledge is that breast reduction is as problematic as breast enlargement as far as sexual objectification is concerned. Both the woman whose breasts are perceived to be (by herself as well as others) "too small" and the one whose breasts are viewed as "too large" suffer enormously for these bodily "inadequacies." Although the attainment of the "perfect breasts" through plastic surgery or some other nonmedical means may seem to play into sexual objectification, these operations may just as often appear to the women who undergo them as ways of *relieving* sexual objectification, that is, ways of drawing attention away from their breasts through their "normalization." [40]

Breast loss, according to Young, is indeed a trauma not only because of the split the surgeon's knife creates in the body, but also because of the corresponding (and usually less expected) rupture experienced in one's self and body image. Precisely because the breasts are identified by phallocratic society as the *visible* site of a woman's sexuality, the loss of a breast is societally interpreted as a corresponding loss in sexuality.[41] Moreover, the socially referred character that we earlier discussed in relation to women's bodily experiences all but guarantees that individual women who have undergone mastectomies will internalize the societal notion that one's sexuality and sexual appeal are diminished with the removal of one's breast.

Phallocentric perceptions regarding the desexualizing character of mastectomy are internalized not only by heterosexual women, but also by many lesbians as well. Although "Cathy," a woman who offers a personal account of the effect of her mastectomy on her life in Wendy Chapkis's book, *Beauty Secrets: Women and the Politics of Appearance,* attributes the extensive support she received after her operation to her lesbian community, she expresses her lover's and her own fears about the effect the mastectomy would have on her sexuality.[42] Not surprisingly, Cathy discovers "that straight people were much more threatened by me with one breast than were lesbians. Men in particular seem threatened by 'unwhole' women." [43] Her surgeon, in fact, was very upset by her decision not to get implants or wear a prosthesis. "The oddest thing about this conversation," Cathy notes,

> was that there was nothing I could say to silence him. He gently told me that he had seen "many a marriage flounder on the shoals of a mastectomy." If I said "I don't need this discussion because I am a lesbian" it would sound as if lesbians don't care about how they look. I felt totally trapped listening to him go on and on.[44]

As far as Cathy is concerned, the primary motivation for buying a prosthesis is "to keep people from being threatened by anyone looking physically different." [45] And, she pragmatically points out, this is hardly a good enough reason to go out and spend the six or seven hundred dollars necessary to own one. Nonetheless, Cathy also acknowledges that

> [c]onstantly confronting sexism is exhausting. You can't do it non-stop. So you make compromises. But I make compromises to make myself comfortable, not other people. It is either their reactions or my feelings. I'm not willing to try to make other people less uncomfortable with the fact that I have had cancer and have one breast. Why the hell should I take care of them? I'm the one whose feelings should be protected.[46]

A photograph that appears in the middle of Cathy's story shows a naked woman with one breast, arms outstretched to the sunny sky above, head back soaking in the rays and warmth of the sun. She appears relaxed, triumphant, and joyful, and where the scar marking her "missing" breast would be, an undulating garland of flowers appears. "Deena," the woman photographed, is the very picture of confident sensuality and contentment, and she best illustrates, I think, the positive body images that Iris Young would like to see realized for all one- (and two-) breasted women. We are not made privy to Deena's story; we do not know how she has managed to overcome the substantial cultural obstacles that prevent so many women from loving themselves, being loved, and loving others with one breast. We also do not know if her confidence and contentment will stay with her throughout her life as she deals with the inevitable responses of others to what our culture regards as her "unfortunate tragedy." Nonetheless, what makes Deena such a powerful and riveting figure is her proud affirmation of her one-breasted body, an affirmation that is achieved in and through the splitting of her breast from her body, a splitting that allows rather than denies her new bodily possibilities. In this photograph, Deena lives out what for many of us is a utopian fantasy. In her erotic embodiment of this fantasy, Deena alters the morphology of our own imaginaries, and thereby expands the power and range of our body images.

Together, Iris Young's four essays on embodiment are landmark contributions to feminist phenomenology. These essays open up a rich terrain completely ignored by Paul Schilder, Maurice Merleau-Ponty, and others who have explored the development and significance of the body image. What Young succeeds in demonstrating, above all, is that there is no such thing as *the* body image, though she accomplishes this in a much different way than Schilder, who provocatively argues that each of us possesses an infinite number of body images.[47] For what Young emphasizes is that it is always *her* or *his* body image that we are talking about, fantasizing about, and altering through our bodily discourse with one another. Throughout these essays, Young lovingly engenders the body image, embracing its fluidity, multiple possibilities, and resistance to constricting cultural forces. What Young amply demonstrates is that the "splitting" of the subject through contradictory bodily modalities, pregnancy, the inevitable disparity between seeing myself and being seen, and mastectomy is unable to negate our bodily possibilities once and for all; rather, depending on our own responses to these experiences, it may even enhance them.

Simone de Beauvoir:
Disrupting the Metonymy of Gender

DEBRA B. BERGOFFEN

Today's feminists are reassessing their relationship to Simone de Beauvoir. We no longer dismiss her as a masculinist in women's dress and no longer assume that her philosophical currency is tied to the viability of Sartre's. Returning to Beauvoir for contemporary rather than merely historical insights, we are led to ask whether we have adequately mined the possibilities of her thought. The answer to this question depends on whether or not we confine Beauvoir's thinking to the existential, humanist, and Marxist domains; for if we insist on confining Beauvoir to these territories, we will not gauge the full possibilities of her thinking.

As I read Beauvoir, I find her saying something to us precisely at those points where her thinking exceeds the familiar categories by which she is usually assessed. Contemporary feminist thought is increasingly attentive to questions of the body, desire, and the other. It is concerned with the politics of representation and the possibilities of an ethics of the "we." Beauvoir's thought, directed by the concept of ambiguity, anticipates many of the questions currently circulating in the feminist field. Blurring the line between the self and the other, the body and the flesh, the active and the passive, the concept of ambiguity exposes the fault lines of patriarchy. This becomes especially clear if we focus on the question of gender.

Beauvoir's critique of patriarchy is several pronged. First, it accuses patriarchy of barring women from their status as subjects; second, it finds patriarchy guilty of distorting the meanings of subjectivity per se for both men and women; and third, it puts patriarchy on trial for obfuscating the ethical dimensions of the erotic event. Beauvoir's first accusation is familiar and by now noncontroversial. Designating woman as the inessential other is immoral. Beauvoir's second and third accusations, however, are neither familiar nor well understood. Deciphering them will be the business of this essay.

Ambiguity

The thesis of ambiguity is basic to Beauvoir's thought. It provides her with an alternative reading of Husserl's thesis of intentionality. It commits Beauvoir to an understanding of subjectivity that refuses to bifurcate the meanings of transcendence and immanence. It shades the difference between the subjective and the intersubjective. It detects the fluidity between the body and the flesh. Ultimately, it leads Beauvoir to the category of the erotic and to a reformulation of the ethical question of the "we." The path from the thought of ambiguity to the idea of the erotic is cut by the concept of the lived body.

The idea of the lived body is fundamental to phenomenology and existentialism. According to this idea the human body is neither a biological given nor an historical construct. It is neither identical with nor completely severable from consciousness. It can neither be divorced from nor reduced to its materiality. As lived, the human body is both a habituated reality—a reality formed through the cultivation of habits and amenable to the regimens of habituation—and a spontaneous reality—a reality that breaks through its material and cultural codings in unexpected and disruptive ways. As lived, the human body is ambiguous.

In Beauvoir's hands, Husserl's ideas of habit and style and the existential/ phenomenological idea of the lived body produced the idea of gender. Deploying the concepts of habit, style, and bodily intentionality, Beauvoir discovered that "One is not born, one becomes a woman." In this discovery, she articulated the distinction between sex and gender. As she exposed the ways in which gendering was analogous to boot camp, a way of stylizing the bodies of girls and boys through the imposition of fashion, manners, roles and postures, Beauvoir also discovered that though the habituation of the body that produces gender is historical and cultural, it is not unnatural. Our male-female gender system takes its cues from bodily materialities.

Phenomenologically, all bodies may be said to be the same insofar as they are "the radiation of a subjectivity" and "the instrument" through which we engage the world.[1] The phenomenological body, however, is also and necessarily a sexed body. It is a male, penised body or a female, breasted, menstruating body. It is (as an adolescent and mature adult) a stronger man's body or a weaker woman's body. Attending to the sexed body undermines the idea of a phenomenologically neutral body. It does not, however, undermine the phenomenological idea of embodiment. Rather, it leads us to ask whether sexual differences affect the ways in which we experience our subjectivity and whether sexually different bodies engage the world differently. Beauvoir, working with the idea of the sexed phenomenological body, determines that the penised body is experienced as less mysterious and more controllable than the menstruating body. She finds that the boy's body gives earlier and stronger signals of subjectivity and the ability to engage the world.

Patriarchy takes its cues from the sexed phenomenological body. It, like phenomenology, identifies the body as the instrument of subjectivity and identifies subjectivity with engagement in the world. But, Beauvoir notes, patriarchy rejects the idea of a phenomenologically neutral body in order to declare that sexual differences embody crucial phenomenological distinctions. It identifies the man's body as the proper instrument of world engagement and the legitimate mark of subjectivity. Gendering practices enact this patriarchal judgment. Boys are encouraged to engage the world. They are expected to take risks, climb trees, get dirty, and compete. Girls are withdrawn from the world. The girl, Beauvoir writes:

> is dressed in inconvenient and frilly clothes of which she has to be careful, her hair is done up in fancy style, she is given rules of deportment: Stand up straight, don't walk like a duck; to develop grace she must repress her spontaneous movements; she is told not to act like a would-be boy, she is forbidden violent exercises, she is not allowed to fight. In brief, she is pressed to become, like her elders a servant and an idol.[2]

If at age five or six boys' and girls' bodies are equally vulnerable to the vicissitudes of world engagement, gendering practices, anticipating the coming strength differential between men and women and exaggerating the advantages of the penis and its early signals of subjectivity, gives boys and girls different images of their bodies and its competencies. Groomed by these practices and informed by these images, the boy comes to live the fullness of his phenomenological body, while the girl loses her body's phenomenological bearings. The boy's body is confirmed in its instrumentality and assured of its ability to negotiate the world. It realizes itself as the embodiment of subjectivity. The girl's body, confined to safe spaces and closed in upon itself, loses its sense of instrumentality. As she is taught to question her ability to engage the world, the girl comes to experience her body as inadequate. It becomes a suitable home for the inessential other.

Contemporary feminists challenge Beauvoir's formulation of gender on several fronts. Some object to the ways in which she seems to naturalize sex and accept its givenness. Some object to the ways in which she seems to valorize the male body and deprecate the female body. Some object to the ways in which she seems to embrace the idea of Woman rather than attending to the differences among women. Many of these objections are well taken. They do not, however, get to the whole story. They can, in fact, be misleading if we take them to indicate that Beauvoir accepted the nature culture divide; was taken in by the patriarchal figures of the male and female body; or was ignorant of the differentiating powers of race, class, and culture. For if Beauvoir often leaves the question of sex unproblematized, if she tends to see the male body as marked by transcendence and the female body as marked by immanence, if she tends to become abstract and speak of Woman rather than women, she is neither committed to the binary distinction between nature and culture, nor blinded by the myths of patriarchy, nor seduced by the abstractions of philosophy.

Beauvoir is committed to deciphering the particular concrete phenomenon called woman. This commitment leads her to the body. For it is as bodied *particular* individuals that women become woman, *concrete* instantiations of particular cultural ideals. Coming to the body with her eyes phenomenologically trained, she refuses to see it as a biological given. Instead, she sees the body somewhat as Freud saw human instinct. Lying on the cusp between the natural and the historical, it is a demand on the mind for work. Gender is the product of that work. It is helpful in this regard to refer to the phenomenological notion of constitution and to think of the sexed body as an event or a series of family events neither random nor chaotic but not yet schematic. As eventing, the body is inventing its bodily schema. As eventing, the body is soliciting its style. Gendering practices respond to the call of the eventing body by providing it with a stabilizing set of schematizing images.

Beauvoir seemed to understand that though severing gender from sex (insisting on the nature-culture split) would provide the strongest possible case for the argument against patriarchy, the price for this argument would be an inability to account for the pervasiveness of woman's position as the inessential other. Refusing to pay this price, she adopted the more complicated (and often misunderstood) view that the patriarchal gender system though perverse and immoral, is not arbitrary. Its resilience and resistance to change is not merely a tribute to the power of myths and the sedimentations of habit, it is also attributable to the fact that gender refers to the materially given eventing body, and uses this reference to pass itself off as an immutable givenness. That is, having succeeded in limiting the expression of sexuality to its codifications, patriarchy insists that its schematization of sexuality is the inevitable expression of sex. Thus gender, a response to the call of the eventing body, passes itself off as an effect of the demands of an originally schematized body.

Developing this complex concept of gender, Beauvoir determined that we needed to see it as constructed, but not as constructed ex nihilo. The "natural" body gender identified as its own is not the materially given flesh. It is a boundary body that is also in some sense produced. As a boundary body, the phenomenological body lies somewhere between the flows of the flesh and the body object. It is a family of events not yet stabilized in a determined schema. As the eventing of the flesh, it is grounded in materiality. As a family of events tending toward a style, it is a production. To understand the gender body reference and to appreciate the ways in which this reference does and does not refer to an originally given materiality, we need to understand gender as a metonymic system—an economy of part-whole substitutions that satisfies our desire for identity, clarity, and distinction.

Beauvoir herself did not formulate the sex gender distinction in this way; but the ways in which she insists on the idea of ambiguity, the ways in which she shows gender to be following the hints of biology, and the ways in which she undermines the idea that the hints of biology legitimate patriarchal gender lead us to formulate the sex gender relationship as both contingent and inevitable. The trick is to discriminate between the contingencies and the inevitabilities and to see how we are tricked by their intertwining. Thinking of gender as a metonymic strategy we see the desires at work in this trickery and are able to catch the trickster at work.

If we attend to the work of psychoanalysts, we discover that the metonymic move that produces gender recalls us to an original psychic position; for psychoanalysts tell us that we begin psychic life libidinally attached to part objects. The breast is the original loved object. The penis is an object of infantile desire. It takes work to see the breast as a part of a whole loved object, the mother, and work to abandon the fetish of the penis. Analysts tell us that healthy human beings do this work. They outgrow their attachment to the part object and adopt a preference for the whole object. But when considering the question of gender (the system that gives us the whole objects Man and Woman), it would do well to remember Freud's warnings about our reluctance to give up our original love objects and accept libidinal substitutes. The substitute, Freud said, is never as satisfying as the original. We accept it only so long as it recalls us to the original and only so long as the satisfaction captures our desire. Mature identities and desires are fragile. Regression remains a constant feature of psychic life. The wife may be the mother. The gendered woman may be a womb. The gendered man a penis.

Lacan becomes suspicious of the psychoanalytic account of our move from the part to the whole object on encountering the Marquis de Sade's *Juliette*. He reflects on rule of reciprocity that governs *Juliette*:

> Lend me that part of your body that will give me a moment of satisfaction and, if you care to, use for your pleasure that part of my body that appeals to you.[3]

He takes up Sade's suggestion that the part object has a pull on us that is independent of its relationship to the whole. However mature and normal we may appear, we may not outgrow the preference for the part. The analysts' account of the maturation process may be too infected with the idea of progress—too optimistic.

Lacan does not develop the implications of this continued lure of the part object, though he does indicate that it is packed with ethical import. If, however, we bring the issue of our part object desire to Lacan's account of the mirror stage, we are able to see the ways in which gendering allows us to simultaneously meet the demands of maturity—love the whole object— and satisfy the nostalgia for the original part object—construct the whole on the model of the part. Considered chronologically, the mirror stage is the infant's first attempt at identifying itself with a whole object. In this sense it is progressive and developmentally essential. Considered retrospectively, however, the mirror stage is the infant's first refusal of its lived ambiguity—a refusal of its being as a (w)hole object. (A (w)hole object is a reality whose wholeness depends upon and revolves around an empty center, a lack that propels its desire and grounds its being. (W)hole objects are notorious for their refusal to acknowledge the lack and for their insistence that they are complete, full, and whole.) In identifying with the imago (the image of its desire) that is the prototype of the ego, the infant inaugurates the process of self-alienation.

The ego imago originates as a body image that represents the body of the infant's desire. As the child matures, this imago remains the locus of individual identity. At its origin and throughout its existence, the ego imago is a pseudo whole object, a part passing itself off as the totality of the individual's psychic reality whose function, in part, is to repress the voice of the subject—the voice that speaks for the (w)hole. It is, of course, dangerous to speak of the subject as a repressed (w)hole object when Lacan gives it to us as an absence, but it is helpful to see the ego imago as a part object masquerading as a (w)hole object; to see that the effect of this masquerade is to mistake the part for the (w)hole; and to see this metonymic move as embedded in our psychic lives. For once we see the ego as a part object and once we acknowledge the fit between ego and gender identity, we are prepared to see that gender, like the ego, may be a part object and that what we currently identify as (w)hole objects—patriarchally gendered men and women—are actually part objects passing for wholes.

Put together, Freud's account of the fragility of libidinal substitutions, Lacan's suspicions regarding the persistence of the part object economy, the mirror stage's account of the alienations of the ego, and Beauvoir's account of bad faith as nostalgia, suggest that the same desires at work building the fortress ego and luring us to the "Sadean" part object economy are also at work solidifying patriarchal gender. Following this sugges-tion, we see that an adequate critique of gender will have to attend to the desires at play in the metonymic-imaginary game. Working from this insight we discover that to adequately understand gender, we must see it as a sys-tem of metonymy where a part of an ambiguously given (w)hole is singled out as definitive and where the lived ambiguity of the material reality is "forgotten" as the definitive part assumes a privileged position and takes up its representative and repressive function.

We are taught to desire whole (as distinct from (w)hole) objects. Want-ing ourselves to be objects of desire, we want to be whole objects ourselves. As the infant flees its experience of fragmentation, the adult evades its ex-perience of ambiguity. The infant is lured to the reflected imago from two directions. First it images the desired (m)other. Second it is an image of in-strumental competency. Given the lure of the mirror, the infant experiences its earliest embodiment as lack. It reads its original experience of embodi-ment through the lens of the later imago to call it fragmented and uncoor-dinated rather than exuberant and polymorphous. The adult, orienting it-self around the legacy of the imago, reads its experience of the ambiguous body through the lens of the ego to call it threatening rather than exhila-rating. Given our ego-imago position, our desire is directed toward impos-sible whole objects. That is, rejecting the insufficiency of the part object, we desire the integrity of the part object. We want whole objects that mimic the definitiveness of part objects. We do not want the unbounded open-ness of the (w)hole. We want wholes that are instrumental. The solution? Pseudo whole objects—coordinated collections of parts (therefore wholes) with discrete identities (therefore parts). Psyches constructed as egos. Bod-ies defined by gender.

Beauvoir's discussions of the ways in which body part objects become the definitive marks of gendered bodies are instructive here. Directed by the concept of ambiguity, Beauvoir notes the ways in which our diversely sexed bodies invite us to experience ourselves differently. She insists, however, on distinguishing the invitations of the body from the demands of patriarchy. Though Beauvoir will ultimately argue that the economies and myths of pa-triarchy establish the male body as privileged, her analysis of embodiment suggests that the body with the penis has certain advantages.

According to Beauvoir, children first experience their bodies as a myste-rious otherness and a threat.[4] The boy's experience of bodily alienation, however, is overridden by the penis; for the penis shows him how to trans-form the body from a site of alien otherness to an opportunity for self-affirmation. In experiencing himself as a specifically sexed body, the boy experiences his penis as his double and in this doubling begins to experi-ment with his potential for self-agency—transcendence. He can, as in urinating games, for example, use his penis to transform a natural process into a subjective project.[5] Lacking a penis, the girl has no visible body sign of transcendence. Her sexed body appears marked by immanence—passivity. Whereas the boy's sexual marking invites him to "take charge" of his body, the girl's sexed body presents itself as "out of control." Menstrual cycles do not respond to her commands. Opaque and apparently at the call of the species, the girl's sexual marking invites her to see herself as a being for others whose being is defined by its being-for-the-other.[6]

To adequately understand the importance Beauvoir assigns to the penis, we need to see that for her the task of becoming a subject engages the processes of self-objectification and alienation.[7] In reflections that bear the marks of Hegel and Marx and that allude to Lacan's account of the mirror stage, Beauvoir tells us that though it is true that self-objectification is a mode of alienation, it is also true that self-objectification and alienation are modes of transcendence that are crucial for the formation of the subject. In finding myself objectified in the world I discover that I can be/become what I am not. I discover that I can alienate myself from my current way of being. I discover the agency of my becoming. Alienation and subjectivity are not simple opposites.

We are each faced with the same task—the task of becoming a subject. We are not, however, given the same tools. The boy's body gives him a ready double. He can alienate himself in his penis, see himself as other, appropriate this otherness to himself. The girl's body makes no such offering. Unable to alienate herself in a part of herself, her whole body must become the site of her self-alienation and retrieval. Given a more complex and dangerous task, patriarchal structures compound the girl's difficulties. More than not having a penis to sign her transcendence, patriarchy codes her womb, ovaries, and uterus as signs of immanence. Following the invitations of sexual difference, patriarchy identifies the male body with the alienations of subjectivity and the female body with the alienations from subjectivity. Taking up the strategies of the imaginary, patriarchy invokes the strategies of metonymy to produce gendered bodies. Men will become Man the penis/phallus subject. Women will become Woman the womb/inessential other.

Were the penis an unambiguous sign of transcendence and the womb a clear mark of immanence, we might be able to establish a justifiable link between sex and patriarchal gender. Beauvoir notes, however, that though the penis offers itself an as alienating double and though its erections and ejections gives boys/men bodily signs of their existential transcendence, the penis is not always erect. Its ejections are not always within the boy's/man's control. Patriarchy "forgets" the ambiguities of the penis. It does not count its flaccidness, its wet dreams, or its "uncontrollable" urges as marks of immanence. Further, though it may be true that woman's "out of control" menstrual flow may be seen as signs of immanence, it is also the case that these flows, as signatures of the birthing body, are marks of transcendence — signs of an openness to the future and the other. Again patriarchy is forgetful. Instead of registering the ambiguities of the female body it erases all marks of its transcendence.

There are many ways in which Beauvoir's descriptions, intended to expose the pretensions of gender, fall prey to the myths of femininity. For example, though she is willing to allow the boy to transform the natural process of urinating into a project of subjectivity, she is not willing to consider the natural process of childbirth as amenable to inscriptions of subjectivity. Getting beyond these difficulties, however, we see that the point of Beauvoir's critique is to establish that in transforming hints of the ambiguous body into mandates of the gendered body, patriarchy strips the female body of its transcendent possibilities to render it immanent, and erases the immanent realities of the male body to render it transcendent. The differently ambiguously sexed immanent *and* transcendent bodies of men and women become the distinctively gendered transcendent *or* immanent bodies of man and woman.

Beauvoir invokes the category of bad faith to account for this gendered bifurcation of transcendence and immanence. Gender is to our sexed embodiment as the role of the waiter is to the existential self. Unlike Sartre, however, who sees bad faith as an inescapable ontological response to the anxieties of freedom, Beauvoir sees bad faith as a contingent historical response to the lost securities of childhood.[8] Patriarchal gender is one of the bad faith ways in which our anxieties are allayed and our nostalgias are satisfied. Men gendered as Man are saved from the anxiety of recognizing the Other. Figured as the absolute (impossible) subject, they are permitted to live out the desire to be God. Women gendered as Woman are saved from the anxiety of exercising their freedom. Figured as the eternal child, they are permitted to live out the nostalgia to be merged with the (m)other. A perfect, if immoral fit. For if it is true that it is as the eternal child that women are exploited, it is also true that it is as the (impossible) absolute subject that men are barred from crucial dimensions of their humanity.

Beauvoir appeals to the concepts of existentialism and phenomenology to describe the metonymic moves through which gender exchanges the different ambiguously eventing male and female bodies for the distinct, stable, and stylized bodies of man and woman. Psychoanalysis provides us with alternate categories to produce the same/similar results: the (w)hole object is exchanged for a whole object under the guidance of the imago, part object paradigm. Given these existential, phenomenological, and psychoanalytic analyses we are left to consider whether the metonymic strategy is a necessary feature of the human condition. We are left wondering if our current gender economies are inevitable. We are left with the thought that the feminist project may be utopian.

Considering the insights of *The Ethics of Ambiguity, The Second Sex,* and psychoanalysis, we at least know this: given gender's references to the first part objects of our desire and given our affinity for metonymic substitutions, exposing the immoralities and mythologies of patriarchal gender will have little practical effect so long as the metonymic desires of the ego imago go unchallenged. Though it surely is important to remember the ambiguities of the lived body, including the ambiguity of the supposedly unambiguous part designated to represent the whole, it is also important to remember that it is not forgetfulness per se, but the desires of forgetfulness that ground the patriarchal gender system. Appealing to the truths of the ambiguous body will not undo the perversions of gender. As a matter of desire, it is a question of finding a desire that contests the desires of metonymy, clarity, and identity. It is a matter of attending to the desires of the erotic.

The Erotic

Patriarchy's attitude toward the erotic is complex and contradictory. On the one hand it romanticizes the erotic. As romanticized the erotic reinforces patriarchal gender roles. Prince Charming, the most dashing, handsome, and masculine man, will sweep Cinderella, the most beautiful, unappreciated, and feminine woman, off her feet. His love will make her valuable. His power (he is a prince) will compliment her fragility (she has the smallest feet in the kingdom). Her joyful dependency (so different from the misery of her subjection to the power of her stepmother and stepsisters) will justify his autonomy. They will live happily ever after.

On the other hand, patriarchy trivializes the erotic. Acknowledging its power to disrupt the mythical link between love, marriage, and the happy ending, patriarchy limits the force of the erotic to the instant and ultimately allows it to count for nothing. As in the enormously popular *The Bridges of Madison County,* the erotic is allowed to momentarily expose the lie of the "happily ever after" but not to critique it. The diversion of the erotic is no match for the tranquility and responsibilities of the "real" world. *The Bridges of Madison County* serves patriarchy well, for if it shows us that there is no romantic "happily ever after" for the mother, it asks us to imagine one for her children. The disruptive erotic has no future.

Giving us the choice between the romanticized or the trivialized erotic (which amounts to no choice at all because choosing either commits us to depriving the erotic of its significant disruptive function and dissuades us from investigating the erotic for what it might reveal about our desire) patriarchy allows the erotic one other signification—perversity. Here the truth of the erotic prevails, but under the sign of negation. Now the truth of the disruptive power of the erotic is acknowledged but expelled from the domain of the proper. This is the truth of sin. The meaning of the desire to transgress the boundaries of the gendered body is simultaneously acknowledged as a challenge to the fixities of these boundaries and outlawed as immoral and pornographic.

Beauvoir alerts us to the significance of the erotic by suggesting that we understand it as an event (in Lyotard's sense of the term),[9] which depends on the ambiguity of the fleshed body for its being and which carries within it the paradigm of an ethic of generosity that contests the prevailing laws of recognition. Though patriarchy insists that "opposites attract" and that it is as metonymically gendered that man and woman are passionately drawn to each other, Beauvoir recalls the link between the erotic, delirium, and excess to suggest that it is the ambiguous body, the body that escapes the regimes of gendered embodiment that ignites our passion. Inviting us to attend to the writings of the Marquis de Sade, Beauvoir invites us to see that the erotic event speaks of the passions of transgression and that these passions reveal and are sustained by the vulnerable, ambiguously, and differently fleshed body.

The ethical moment of the erotic is fragile. It is the moment in which I assume my vulnerability, accept your otherness, and offer you the gift of the flesh. Making this offer, I live the unique active passivity of my ambiguity. As the gift of the flesh I ask for nothing, not even reciprocity. Beauvoir is under no illusions. This gift, often accepted, is rarely allowed to circulate. It is more often than not taken up in rituals of exchange. If passion disrupts gender, gender reasserts its reign over passion—until the next eruption.

The price of evading the ethic of the erotic event is the forfeiture of the fullness of our passion. We trade the risks of the erotic for the securities of gender. Secure in her feminine passivity, Woman cannot *offer* herself as a gift to her lover, she can only allow herself to be taken; she cannot *assume* the risks and vulnerabilities of the generous body, she can only *be* vulnerable. Secure in his masculine autonomy, Man cannot allow himself to be taken by another. He cannot allow himself to become vulnerable. Erotic passion cares little for our gendered priorities. In revealing the ambiguities of our bodies and the vulnerabilities of our flesh, the erotic event dramatizes the precarious ground of the gendered body—hence gender's vigilance.

The gendered body lures us to violence. Like the fortress ego, its boundaries must be defended. Man will demand recognition. Woman will require protection. The erotic body decouples the patriarchal link between risk and violence. It introduces us to the link between risk and generosity. In unveiling the vulnerability of my flesh, I ask you to recognize me as your other.

I know that the combination of alterity and vulnerability can be lethal. I take the chance. I opt for the value of generosity. Challenging the patriarchal order that teaches me, as woman, (1) to degrade the experience of the flesh and (2) to experience myself as degraded insofar as I acknowledge myself as flesh, I take up the dignity of the flesh in the hope of luring you, as man, from your deceptive privileges and autonomous satisfactions.[10]

Open to the erotic, taken up by the erotic event, the flesh is transformed from the body as object for the other's look to the wild-bodied gift. It becomes the site where "in the midst of carnal fever [men and women are] a consenting, a voluntary gift, an activity; they live out in their several fashions the strange ambiguity of existence made body."[11] As the desires of nostalgia lure us to the stringent, metonymic patriarchal body, the desires of the erotic reveal the strange and severally fashioned fleshed body. As the desires of nostalgia situate us in an order of demand, exploitation, and violence, the desires of the erotic open us to an economy of spontaneous recognition and generous giftings. Beauvoir does not suggest that the excesses of the erotic can either be tamed or stabilized. But instead of labeling them transgressions that are tolerated reluctantly if at all, she sees them as transgressions that carry within them a paradigm for an alterative understanding of the other, the couple, the "we," and the world.[12]

Though Beauvoir asks us to link her name with Sartre's, the ways in which her interrogation of ambiguity leads her to the flesh, the erotic event, and the idea of an erotic intentionality that supplements/contests instrumental intentionalities leads us to the name of Merleau-Ponty. The affinities between (1) Beauvoir's analyses of the erotic and Merleau-Ponty's attention to the flesh; (2) Beauvoir's discussions of the warm world of the erotic and Merleau-Ponty's discussions of the intertwining and enfolding; and (3) Beauvoir's revelation of the active-passive, subject-object transgressions of the erotic and Merleau-Ponty's phenomenology of the double sensation, are striking. If we tap the resources of Merleau-Ponty's phenomenology for Beauvoir's discussions the erotic, we are led to formulate an ethic of the erotic that teaches us to see alienation, violence, and the flight from the flesh, whether it be via the mirror stage or through the metonymies of gender, as a particular mode of subjectivity rather than as a universal paradigm for the subject.

If we read *The Second Sex* from back to front, that is, if we bring its later discussions of the erotic to its earlier explanations of women's place in patriarchy, we discover that thinking through the erotic alerts us to the nuances of woman's inessential otherness. Beauvoir opens *The Second Sex* by providing us with three possible explanations for women's complicity in their exploitation:

Thus woman may fail to lay claim to the status of subject because she lacks definite resources, because she feels the necessary bond that ties her to man regardless of reciprocity, and because she is often very well pleased with her role as the other.[13]

As lacking definite resources, woman defers to patriarchal demands out of economic necessity. As well pleased with her role as the inessential other she is guilty of bad faith. As feeling the necessary bond that ties her to man regardless of reciprocity, however, woman may be seen as speaking for the ethic of generosity etched in the erotic event. In valuing the bond more than reciprocity, woman is not so much a victim of exploitation as a voice for an alternative set of values. Here the value of the bond is not the value of the master slave relationship but the value of the erotic couple where the demands of reciprocity are subordinated to the generosities of gifting.

It is important to be clear here lest we mistake the erotic paradigm of generous gifting for the model of the erotic bond offered by patriarchy. Patriarchy also asks us (women) to value the bond. It also asks us (women) to forego the requirements of reciprocity. It praises our (women's) generosity and accepts our (women's) offerings as gifts. Within patriarchy this ethic of the erotic, when and if it is recognized, is registered as a feminine ethic—appropriate for women only and confined to the private sphere. Taking my cue from Beauvoir, I am proposing that the values embodied in the erotic event be taken as feminist values—values that speak the ambiguities of variously fashioned fleshed bodies and contest the metonymies of gender. As feminist, these values are neither confined to the private sphere nor only for women.

In attending to the phenomenon of the erotic, Beauvoir disrupts the distinction between the private and the public, the event and the paradigm, transcendence and immanence, transgression and affirmation, the I and the other. She leads us to suspect that insisting on these divisions and in erasing the marks of our ambiguity, patriarchy is intent on maintaining an antihuman social order. She shows us that in teaching us to approach the erotic as a temporary upsurge that only fleetingly disturbs things and in insisting that the erotic disturbance, as an irrational impulse, ultimately counts for nothing, patriarchy is protecting itself from the fundamental challenge of the erotic event. For once we see that the spontaneous dynamic of the erotic is an event that offers us the paradigms of the gift and generosity; and once we discover the ways in which these paradigms free the meaning of risk from its patriarchal associations with violence and death, we understand that far from being an erratic moment that changes nothing, the erotic is the event that changes everything—or at least could change everything if we gave it the attention it deserves. This is not to say that thinking through the disruptions of the erotic can, by itself, create the conditions of a just society, but rather to say that I do not think a just community can come into being if the ethical import of the erotic event is not brought to bear on the realities of social, political, and ethical life.

PART III

*Emancipating
Phenomenology*

Love and the Labor of the Negative:
Irigaray and Hegel

MORNY JOY

Her [woman's] interest is centred on the universal and remains alien to the
particularity of desire; whereas in the husband these two sides are separated;
and since he possesses as a citizen the self-conscious power of universality, he
thereby acquires the right of desire and, at the same time, preserves his freedom in regard to it.

— G. W. F. Hegel, *Phenomenology of Spirit*

For woman, therefore, the universal comes down to practical labor within the
horizon of the universal delimited by man. Deprived of a relationship to the
singularity of love, woman is also deprived of the possibility of a universal for
herself. Love, for her, amounts to a duty—not a right—establishing her role
within humankind where she appears as man's servant.

— Luce Irigaray, *I Love to You*

Throughout the work of Luce Irigaray, the thought of Hegel has resonated
with recurring intensity that reaches its culmination in her work *I Love to
You* (1996). From her early reflections on the situation of Antigone and the
master/slave relation[1] to her final revision of the dynamics of recognition,
Irigaray engages with Hegel's increasingly conservative and ultimately inconsistent treatment of women.[2]

The motifs of difference and negativity stimulate Irigaray's explorations.
In contrast to Hegel, where negativity (as a necessary movement of the dialectic) will be integrated in the interests of a final mode of self-consciousness
or universality,[3] Irigaray seeks to transform radically this triumphalistic procedure. Her desire is to rescue negativity from its employment as a device
that artificially introduces alienation in the service of a higher (yet equally
suspicious) unity. To achieve this, the dialectic process and its concomitant
moment of recognition will be renegotiated. Then women, no longer abstract and disembodied ciphers in a system not of their own devising, can
become both instigators and partners in a revised model that incorporates

113

a positive mode of sexual difference.[4] Women will also attain a form of universality in their own right, a prerogative that Hegel denied them.[5]

This acknowledgment of sexual difference does not imply simply an acceptance of the irreducibility of the other and its resistance to preordained categories (though it involves this). It is, rather, an acknowledgment that women will no longer conform to definitions of femininity that do not respect a woman's integrity and her responsibility for her own becoming. No one else can determine exactly what the exact components of each particular mode of becoming woman should be—though there is a generalized admonition from Irigaray that each woman should seek the perfection of her gender.[6] This, however, is not an innate identity but that form of universality which, within a Hegelian dispensation, acknowledges that the final stage of individuality can be expressed as a reaffirmation of the primary abstract formula at a personalized level.

> Being born a woman requires a culture particular to this sex and this gender, which it is important for the woman to realize without renouncing her natural identity. She should not comply with a model of identity imposed on her by anyone, neither her parents, her lover, her children, the State, religion or culture in general. . . . She should, quite the contrary, gather herself within herself in order to accomplish her gender's perfection for herself, for the man she loves, for her children, but equally for civil society, for the world of culture, for a definition of the universal corresponding to reality.[7]

Elsewhere in *I Love to You* Irigaray will refer to this process by such other expressions as women need "to be true to their gender" or their "natural identity." These are indeed suspicious phrases that are in need of careful examination—for initially there would appear to be an unproblematized appeal to the traditional modes of sex/gender and nature/culture. Yet, given Irigaray's earlier deconstructive mimetics of Western philosophy and psychoanalysis, as well as her morphological depiction of the body, it is difficult to believe that she is adopting a naive biologism that has its own gender-specific modes of behavior. This would merely reinstate conventional essentialist categories of womanhood. Instead, Irigaray recommends conscious appropriation, cognizant of historical and cultural influences on the construction of identity, but with a distinct twist. For Irigaray, there has to be, on the part of women, a deliberate claiming of a birthright and a conscious cultivation of a particular orientation. This does not involve specific idealized qualities but certain activities that affirm and give expression to women's desires and subjectivity. This, for Irigaray, is the only way to dislodge the entrenched symbolic system and its phallic values, which privilege masculinity. Thus, it is at once a complex, intricate, and dangerous task that Irigaray undertakes. For, in one sense, she wants to keep in play the deconstructive dismantling of any abstract binaries, especially that of nature/culture. At the same time, she poses a nonessentialistic alternative with a definite strategy for its attainment. Negativity will remain, but rather than being a confrontational element, it will now imply a stage of self-analysis and critical appropriation that has distinctive implications for both women and men. As Irigaray states, "the negative can mean access to the other of sexual difference and thereby become happiness without being annihilating in the process." [8]

For Irigaray, a relationship between a woman and a man will now involve moving beyond the undifferentiated state of the couple as it existed within Hegel's privatized domestic realm. "We need to establish an ethics of the couple, a place, a bond, where the two halves of the natural and spiritual world can be and change." [9] And though the ideal that Irigaray promotes is a love relationship between women and men, it is not to be confused with a facile fusion of romantic sensibilities. For Irigaray such hackneyed conventions simply feed into an absorption that obliterates necessary distinctions. Instead, "Love is the redemption of the flesh through the transfiguration of desire *for* the other . . . into desire *with* the other" [10] Thus, Irigaray's understanding of love presupposes a movement away from Hegel's final appreciation of desire and love, which denied women full participation in its realization.

> Love, as Hegel writes of it, is therefore not possible on the part of a woman. . . . She must love man and child as generic representations of the human species dominated by the male gender. . . . In other words, a woman's love is defined as familial and civil duty. She has no right to singular love nor to love for herself. She is thus unable to love but is to be subjugated to love and reproduction. [11]

Irigaray's model of love does not indicate a return to the ethical proprieties of old that reinforced reproductive rights and duties. It is, in contrast, a labor of love that will permit an affirmative recognition that enhances life, rather than imposing sacrifice or death on women by precluding their access to self-determination. Irigaray states, "Hegel knew nothing of negative like that." [12]

It is this move endorsing a felicitous meeting of female and male genders that marks a distinct development in her work. Indeed, since *An Ethics of Sexual Difference* (1993), Irigaray has been preoccupied with establishing a right order of relationship, of ethics, between men and women. It is this emphasis that becomes the focal point of much of Irigaray's later work.

If sexual difference is to be overcome is it not imperative first of all to find a sexual ethics? If one day we are to be one must we not now be two? Otherwise we fall back into some formal and empty (male) one, back into hierarchies we are familiar with, or into a nostalgia for returning back into the womb where the other is nothing but an encompassing source of food and shelter.[13]

The question is, however, whether Irigaray, in her engagement with Hegel in order to reformulate the terms of the dialectic, unnecessarily employs similar universalizing strategies that can have limiting prescriptive consequences.

In her analyses of Hegel, Irigaray detects two principal problems with reference to women. One is the denial of the free subjective expression of undistorted desire or pleasure.[14] The second is the exclusion of women from the development of history (i.e., an objective identity in the public world).[15] The rectification of these two separate but interrelated issues, that of a specifically female identity and manifestation of desire—which will find its vindication in her redepiction of recognition—and that of social/public rights for women are regarded as prerequisites for right relationship. To achieve this, since *An Ethics of Sexual Difference,* Irigaray has advocated the establishment of civil rights, specific to women, to help to promote their individual and collective identity. Irigaray explains this modification of her previous strategy in *Je, Tu, Nous: Toward a Culture of Difference:*

Since 1970 I have regularly worked with women or groups of women who belong to liberation movements, and in these I've observed problems or impasses that can't be resolved except through the establishment of an equitable legal system for both sexes.[16]

Such a statement is a prelude to Irigaray's declaration that women's recent admission to the public forum has not been without its difficulties. She decries the unilateral promotion of equality, fearing that this is just another reduction of women to the level of sameness—that is, identification with the male standards and privileges that feature in a democratic society.

The rights women have gained in the last few years are for the most part rights that enable them to slip into men's skin, to take on the so-called male identity. These rights do not solve the problems of their rights and duties as women towards themselves, their children, other women, men and society.[17]

It is not, however, as if Irigaray is against rights, but she believes that equivalent relations between the sexes can be established only if there are specific collective civil and legal rights to protect women's specific sexual identity. When asked to identify these rights Irigaray has defined the principal ones as follows:

1. The right to *human dignity,* which means:
   a) Stopping the commercial use of their bodies and images.
   b) Valid representations of themselves in actions, words, and images in all public places.
   c) Stopping the exploitation of motherhood, a functional part of womanhood, by civil and religious powers.
2. The right to *human identity,* that is:
   a) The legal encodification of *virginity* (or physical and moral integrity) as a component of female identity that is not reducible to money, and not cash-convertible by the family, the State, or religious bodies in any way.[18]

Irigaray's emphasis on such rights is intended to protect certain conditions that will ensure for women both the public and private space and liberty to be faithful to herself. Her recommendations proclaim the need for such guarantees to be safeguarded by a civil code.[19] These material prerequisites then allow women to undertake the necessary task of the discernment and shaping of their desires that are no longer denied nor captive to alien directives.

This strategy is helpful in appreciating Irigaray's rebuttal of Beauvoir's famous dictum "one is not born, but rather becomes, a woman."[20] Irigaray recasts Beauvoir's prescription for overcoming negativity. In fact, in contrast to de Beauvoir, Irigaray states: "It's not as Simone de Beauvoir said: one is not born, but rather becomes a woman (through culture), but rather: I am born a woman, but I must still become this woman that I am by nature."[21]

Yet, it is this "becoming" woman, with its seemingly contrary impulses of a pluralistic, open-ended trajectory and, at the same time, a deliberate appropriation of definite attitudes and structures of a given gendered nature, that marks a problematic aspect of Irigaray's work.[22] Although it may not be a repetition of the nature/culture paradox that Joan Scott has detected at the heart of the modernist feminist movement, whereby women alternately appeal to and contest cultural notions of equality.[23] Irigaray certainly appropriates the nature/culture and difference/equality debate on terms that complicate, rather than resolve, the issue. This has lead to extremely diverse evaluations of her work.

The Question of Gender

Perhaps the most problematic issue is that of gender. Irigaray proposes a complex resolution to the question of the nature of sexual difference, which she has stated is the crucial question for our age.[24] This is amplified in *I Love to You:*

> I belong to the universal in recognizing that I am a woman. This woman's
> singularity is in having a particular genealogy and history. But belonging
> to a gender represents a universal that exists prior to me. I have to accom-
> plish it in relation to my particular destiny.[25]

This final attainment of universality is an intricate and discriminating task that needs to be undertaken by each woman. A vital component is an acknowledgment of an efficacious female heritage—which encompasses a positive dynamic in mother/daughter relationships whereby a woman's identity is not confined to maternity—that she has portrayed in detail else-where.[26] But, more importantly, by introducing a deliberate challenge to the nature/culture configuration, Irigaray aims to counteract prevailing im-posed stereotypes. For Irigaray, a woman needs to cultivate a distinct iden-tity. Rather than a passive acquiescence, however, this involves an accep-tance of the fact of being born a woman, as well as a fidelity to her body and her genealogy. A conscious intentionality is thus required.

This process is delineated by Irigaray according to a dialectical pattern that mirrors Hegel. It moves from a generic universal of physiological definition, by way of particular cultural differentiations (protected by the civil code), to the attainment of a distinct individuality. This unique iden-tity, as in Hegel, involves a complex reintegration of the component parts that in its comprehensiveness becomes a refined mode of universality. But for Irigaray there is a change from the repressive Hegelian implications for women. As Irigaray states, "The universal [universality]—if this term can be used here—consists in the fulfillment of life and not in submission to death, as Hegel would have it."[27] This achievement also entails, as it does for Hegel, a spiritual task—but again with an alteration. For Irigaray, there is no totalization or absolute transcendence. The reign of spirit is not equated with the estrangements of a disembodied ideal or an illusion of completion. Instead, the spiritual aspect is promoted as involving an enlivening energy that animates and renews but neither suppresses nor exhausts life. "There will be no definitive 'negation of negation.' Man being irreducible to woman and woman to man, there no longer exists any absolute spirit nor one final-ity of being."[28]

Irigaray's reformulation of the dialectic, however, does not avoid the positing of certain requirements with regard to the gendered situations of both women and men. But again, this does not imply either innate traits nor obligatory ideals to which women must conform. Instead, Irigaray rec-ommends a deliberate cultivation of appropriate cultural mediations, specific to her own circumstances, that are conducive to a woman's own consolidation of subjective and objective consciousness. In this sense, Irigaray endorses a concrete universality, specific to our historical period.

> This woman I am has to realize the female as universal in the self and for the self as far as she is able during the period of History in which she finds herself and given the familial, cultural, or political contingencies she has to overcome.[29]

Given this contextualization, Irigaray cannot be labeled either an essentialist or a constructivist according to the way that these terms are usually employed. This is because she does not view culture as determinative; yet she allows it a conscious constitutive role. In her most recent work, however, she is not a stranger to the notion of the universal statements, specifically with reference to her amendments of Hegelian protocols. Naomi Schor, in her article, "French Feminism Is a Universalism," is helpful in situating Irigaray's employment of the universal. She states,

> What is certain is that whereas in American feminist theory there has been a tendency to extrapolate from the falseness of phallocentric universalism the notion that all universals are false, in French feminist theory the universal remains, despite all its misappropriations, a valorized category to be rethought and refashioned. Though French feminists reject the imperialistic universalization of masculine particularity, like so many French intellectuals they remain wedded to the concept of the universal.[30]

Warning against the conflation of essentialism and universalism, Schor continues by recognizing that if, as Irigaray affirms, philosophy is the mark of the universal[31] and that this universal is not transhistorical,[32] then Irigaray, as a late-twentieth-century woman, perceives her task as one of inscribing for this age "the mark of gender onto the alleged neutrality of the universal handed down by the Enlightenment and post-Enlightenment philosophers."[33] Yet it is evident that, in her promotion of a universal mode that respects sexual difference—the contours of which have yet to be established[34]—Irigaray nonetheless does endorse some absolutes. Firstly, there is the primacy of sexual over other modes of difference, such as race for which she has been taken to task.[35] This stance is a provocative and contentious one in that she does not acknowledge the importance of the intersections of race, class, and gender that prevail in many discussions of North American feminist theorists.[36] Irigaray also depicts the Western heritage as monolithic in its misogynistic principles and practices. Finally, Irigaray promotes the idealization of the heterosexual couple as the mode of relationship whereby universality can also be attained. "An encounter between a woman and a man may reach a dimension of universality if it takes place with each being faithful to their gender." [37] It is assertions such as this that render her recent work controversial. [38]

The Return of the Couple

In Irigaray's depiction of the relationship between the two sexes, there is the insistence on two distinct gendered universals. [39] The task of each is to realize, both separately and together, the fullness of life in civic and personal domains that is expressed in the currency of universality. This restructuring, however, does not entail an externalized alienation from oneself, but internal differentiation.

> I thus differentiate myself within myself through the facts of my being a particular individual and of my belonging to a gender. This process enables me to make a pact with a person of the other gender without the mediation of the object. [40]

Yet this development also frees the relationship of men and women from the demands of the family to which it was consigned by Hegel. [41] Thus, when Irigaray articulates her alternative vision of a new love relationship between the two genders, it comes as something of a surprise that she chooses to endorse a heterosexual form.

> Love is accomplished by two, without dividing roles between the beloved and the lover, between objectival and animal passivity on the one hand, and generally conscious and valorous activity on the other. Woman and man remain two in love. Watching over and creating the universe is their primary task, and it remains so. [42]

Irigaray is adamant in wishing to retain an opposite (though not opposing) gender as the irreducible token of otherness. [43] She also posits the moment of recognition as the vindication of heterosexual love. Such a recasting of recognition respects the irreducibility of the other, while allowing what Irigaray describes as "a positive access—neither instinctual nor drive-related—to the other." [44]

This interactive mode constitutes a recognition that requires the labor of the negative, [45] where negativity now implies an acceptance of one's limitations, rather than an alien threat to be subjugated. "With this recognition, I mark you, I mark myself with incompleteness, with the negative. Neither you nor I are the whole nor the same, the principle of totalization." [46] It is love thus enacted—with attentiveness, with generosity, with a form of intransitivity—that Irigaray denotes by the phrase "I love to you." [47] Irigaray's passionate refutation and reformulation of Hegel is devoted to a proclamation of life and love and a new dimension of the spirit in History.

> We need to realize History—or at least continue it—as the salvation of humanity comprised of men and women. That is our task. In accomplishing it, we are working for History's development by bringing about more justice, truth and humanity in the world. This is the task for our time. . . . It is a task for everyone. No one is beyond it, and it makes no one naturally a master or slave, rich or poor. [48]

Irigaray's engendered revision supplants the former ritualized rivalry between the sexes by permitting both parties separate access to self-consciousness. Irigaray thus introduces an alternate route to absolute or universal consciousness of *Geist*/spirit. Hegel was often taken to task for his arcane abstractions in this regard, particularly with reference to the reconciliation of subjective and objective spirit. Irigaray has no patience for these abstruse meanderings, for she does not see them connected in any intimate way with issues of flesh and blood human beings. In contrast, Irigaray's revision situates an ultimate realization of spirit as embodied in the actual physical embrace of male and female. As she proclaims, "The wedding between man and woman realizes the reign of spirit. Without it, there is no spirit." [49]

Evaluation

Although it is easy to concur with Irigaray's observation that without sexual difference there would be no life on earth, it is not so simple a matter to agree with her assertion that this difference is an essential element for the realization of spirit. Firstly, in her reworking, if each sex undertakes its own differentiation, there would no longer seem to be a need for an encounter with an external mode of otherness. Secondly, if each sex is now freed from its duty to procreate, must the dominant sex-specific genital categorization still exert control in such a decisive way? Irigaray seems insistent on this point, and such inflexibility would seem to mar her otherwise exuberant challenge to traditional feminine categorizations. In fact Irigaray would seem to be advocating two inconsistent agenda, which has been remarked on by other commentators. [50] One is the dismantling, in the name of multiplicity, of the univocal arrangements that have permeated Western traditions. At the same time, there is the endorsement of definite sex-specific identities that need to be observed to enable this plurality to flourish.

Perhaps Irigaray's insistence on the strict division of gender reflects her continued challenge to the rigid psychoanalytic categories that still prevail. As Elizabeth Grosz observes, this task has informed all her work, particularly with regard to the need to establish a feminine symbolic.[51] And indeed, in this regard, Irigaray posits gender as a mode of refashioning the Oedipal scenario. For although Irigaray does not develop it as an alternative mode of symbolic castration, she suggests the introduction of gender as a third term. As Irigaray states, "All we need to do is become our gender in order to get away from an undifferentiated relation with the mother." [52] In her estimation, gender's strategic interventions could remove the posited irrevocable decision between psychosis and the prohibition of incest that sustains the Freudian paternal model as it has informed our psychic and symbolic itinerary. Irigaray thus challenges the pervasive Oedipal script with its endorsement of female lack as determinative of women's exclusion from ethical maturity and culture and their incapacity to dispute this designation.

It is the magnitude of the task that Irigaray has undertaken that must be appreciated, whatever the reservations are regarding her tactics. In Irigaray's view, throughout history, women have been sacrificed. From Antigone's silencing, entombed by the father's addiction to war and conquest, to the slave deprived of the right to life and liberty, to finally the wife and mother deprived of lifeblood as her substance is consumed by reproductive and marital duties, the scenario is similar. Hegel's interpretations in his various works have provided graphic illustrations for Irigaray's declamation of women's fate. She wishes to rescue women from the sacrifice of their "sexed identity to a universal defined by man with death as its master." [53]

Nevertheless, it remains difficult to appreciate why Irigaray retains the Hegelian system (even if revised for her program). It is not as if Hegel's dialectic, especially with its fascination for the contrivances of *Geist,* has wide appeal or application today. It may well be, however, that his totalizing maneuvers epitomize both the material and spiritual machinations that have conspired to prevent women from attaining their full potential as human beings. In response, Irigaray indeed wants women to be able to undertake the risk of consciousness and to realize a form of universality, though with far different applications from those envisaged by Hegel. This is particularly so with regard to the supreme manifestation of *Geist,* or spirit, which had both potent philosophical and religious associations for Hegel. Hegel's Absolute Spirit or Consciousness that figures as the consummation of the *Phenomenology of Spirit,* although not necessarily identical with the transcendent God of Christianity, nonetheless intimates a spirit at work in the world that fosters the reconciliation of the competing interests

of subjectivity and objectivity. But this *deus ex machina* of absolute consciousness, as both an artificial and abstract contrivance, is invoked by
Hegel as a heuristic principle to justify the social, ethical, and religious determinations that he deemed indispensable for humankind. Irigaray effectively takes issue with this disembodied, all-encompassing, conflict-driven
model that condenses human desire.

Conclusion

Thus, whereas Hegel vindicated the freedom and rationality of modern
man, Irigaray disputes and disrupts their distortions of desire by her appeal
to carnal love. Whereas Hegel extols the virtues of family life and rec-
ommends the restriction of women to secondary status, Irigaray rhapso-
dizes about the spiritual transformation that a truly independent and self-
possessed woman can effect in male/female relationships. Irigaray's spirit,
in contrast to Hegel's, is indeed one of this world. The infinite is now manifest in the finite not just because God is incarnate, but because both male
and female, in their sexualized embodiment, disclose their inherent divinity, as well as celebrate their infinite capacity for love.[54]

Irigaray's spiritual vision is indeed an impassioned plea for a revolution
in the traditional interactions of the sexes. The question persists, however,
as to whether Irigaray's own ethically based solution depends too much on
an idealization of the couple and on a determination that a bilateral sexual
difference is of prime importance. The need for women's rejection of patriarchal formulas of identity, originally proposed as a not-yet-expressed
mode sexual difference,[55] transmutes in the course of Irigaray's work into
a formal separation of the sexes that, as in Hegel, leads to regulative pronouncements regarding their proper mode of relations. Could it be said
that Hegelian megalomania remains insidious, even perverse, in its attrac-
tions? By succumbing to its enchantment Irigaray could be said to confine,
if not compromise, the ideal of self-realization and social transformation
for woman that lies at the heart of her project. Or is Irigaray cognizant not
only of the irresolvable conflict inherent in the nature/culture, difference/
equality split as it has haunted the modernist project of feminism,[56] but
also, from a deconstructive perspective, of their inevitable mutual implication?[57] To this end, Irigaray has elected, albeit deliberately and not without generating further anomalies, to espouse a platform that seeks the best
of both worlds.

"The Sum of What She Is Saying": Bringing Essentials Back to the Body

HELEN A. FIELDING

Consciously or unconsciously, [man] thinks of himself as a machine: a sexuality of drives, an energy governed by tensions and discharges, in good or bad
working order, and so on. Something capable of uniting the different drives
has been forgotten. . . . Who or what can move us out of mere survival except
a return to the bodily-fleshly values that have never yet come to full flower?[1]

The devaluation of the body is part of a larger epochal move to reduce experience and to reproduce the world, according to the cognitive, the linguistic, the signified. It is not that the body is ignored; indeed, it has come under
even more intense scrutiny. But in this age that is characterized by a pro-
pensity to rationalize and systematize all areas of our existence, the more
the body comes into focus, the more our understanding of embodiment re-
cedes. To conclude as does Foucault, however, that any attempts to explore
embodied existence would only contribute further to the production of sys-
tematized bodies, does not allow for how descriptions of our embodied experiences can help us understand the dangers of the systematizing itself.

Feminist theorists have not been unaware of this paradox. But the pro-
pensity to remain at the cognitive or linguistic level is so strong that even
important attempts to rethink the Cartesian mind/body dualism tend to reproduce the body as an object, constituted through cultural, social, psychic,
and political discourses. The problem is that embodiment describes the
ways in which a body-subject intertwines with the world perceptively, socio-
affectively, and through motility. These aspects of embodiment, although
dependent upon having a tangible corporeal presence, are ultimately relational rather than open to objectification, which is the mode of exploration
to which we are drawn. Although the difficulty in thinking the body in terms
of embodiment is epochal, I also think it is linked to a continued reluctance
on the part of feminists to take up the body in any way that could imply an
essential biologism that ties social potential to so-called biological realities.
This means that in much feminist discourse, embodiment is avoided, leaving

the Cartesian dualism unchallenged. And when the body is taken up, it is too often presented in its objectlike aspect. For example, Elizabeth Grosz points out that feminist campaigns against sexual harassment and rape and for access to abortion are often presented in terms of women as subjects protecting their inert objectlike bodies.[2] In much poststructuralist theory, although this dualism is expressly challenged, it is done so through a focus on the significatory and symbolic aspects of the body providing yet another way of avoiding an essentialist incarnation of the feminine body. Although these explorations are important, they do not open up our understanding of the body as lived. What I am arguing is that between the materialist emphasis on the body as a stable and tangible reality that precedes the discursive and a poststructuralist exploration of the body as socially and culturally inscribed or engendered lies a significant gap. This gap can be filled by a phenomenological approach to embodied experience.

Rather than simply describing what such a phenomenological approach would entail, I want to (re)turn to a conceptual site of debate, one that by many accounts has been exhausted and should be put aside—that of essences. I think, however, that we have only begun to understand the significance of this concept and that it is too early to abandon all discussion. Indeed, I want to argue that one way to understand experience according to our interaction with the phenomena themselves is through Merleau-Ponty's understanding of essences as embodied. As I shall later show, an essence explored as embodied allows us to describe aspects of embodiment that exceed the cognitive that, as neither reified nor static, are made present "as a certain absence."[3] For example, exploring embodied essences helps us to reflect upon the materiality of the body, upon its inherent sinuosity,[4] as well as upon the ways that the body moves into its environs and takes them up. An exploration of corporeal experience helps us to describe essences that will show us what it is to live our bodies as systematicity, and perhaps how to move out of this machinelike tendency. Importantly, then, it is not yet time to put aside discussions of essence; what is needed is a rethinking of essence in its relation to corporeal experience.

I am not arguing that essences are not often associated with the body in feminist theory. Indeed, when feminists speak of essence and essentialism, what has generally been thought to be at question is the body and its status as a ground for feminism; but in recent refigurings of essence and essentialism, feminists have been able to maneuver around the problem of an essence of the body without refusing essence altogether.[5] At issue is a discussion of essence in terms of the body, which means attributing something substantive that inheres in the body making it that which it is, such as "Woman." This kind of formal essence is unchanging and universal, suggesting that there are attributes or aspects of the feminine that are shared by women across class, culture, race, ethnicity, and ability and without which women would not exist as women. Such universal essences are problematic for feminism because, for one, they have been used repeatedly as a justification for denying women significant power over their own lives. Such a perspective takes historical conditions as biological necessities. Second, when drawn upon for feminist projects, essential needs or qualities have, in the past, usually been identified by women who are privileged enough to have access to the modes of communication that allow them to establish the goals of feminism. These needs are by no means recognized as important by or for all women. Third, a growing body of academic studies conducted by feminist scholars in various fields provides strong evidence against such sharply defined shared traits. What this means is that in general, descriptions of formal essences cannot achieve the universality to which they aspire. At the same time, there is some kind of essential gathering of women's experiences, at however local the level, that defines and supports feminist projects. Such a gathering, however, seems to be more dependent upon historical, political, and cultural necessity than some kind of formal essence.

It is not, however, an understanding of the formal essence, to which I want to return. Rather, I am concerned with attempts to deal with this dilemma by rethinking essence discursively. Teresa de Lauretis, for example, claims that most feminists are not guilty of *real* essentialism, but only of *nominal* essentialism. Drawing on Locke's division of essence, she explains that a real essence is the "intrinsic nature" of the "thing-in-itself . . . on which all the sensible properties depend," but a nominal essence is merely conceptual; it is the properties or qualities that are ascribed to something without which it would not be that thing.[6] She argues, as most feminists would agree, that if gender is not innate but rather a sociocultural and historical construction, then "the 'essence' of woman that is described in the writings of many so-called essentialists is not the *real essence*" but rather the *nominal* one. Understood as nominal, then, an essence is more like the qualities and properties that feminists "define, envisage, or enact for themselves."[7] In other words, essences are not really grounded in the body but in language. Naomi Schor concurs with this assessment, arguing that there is wide agreement that "real essentialism inheres in language" and not in the body. Indeed, for her, the extreme antiessentialist constructionist approach does not seem to appreciate that language itself is essentialist in the way that it necessarily categorizes and groups things together.[8] This means that in the naming nature of language itself can be found the formal essentialist qualities that feminists have criticized, but that ultimately seem necessary for offering feminism its voice.

Just as the ground of essence shifts from the body to language in these debates, so too is such a linguistic shift often initiated with regard to experience, in that experience is reduced not simply to its expression in language, but more pointedly to its discursive production. The significance of such a shift is that it entails the assertion that there is nothing substantial or substantive that grounds experience, meaning for Diana Fuss that it, like essence, provides "a rather shaky ground" on which to base claims for women as a group. By warning that "we need to be extremely wary of the temptation to make substantive claims on the basis of the so-called 'authority' of our experiences," she dispenses with the notion that experience has any reference to the female body, to processes that "may seem to be real, immediate and directly knowable."[9] Bodily experiences are not only socially mediated, but there is nothing that underlies or intertwines with that mediation.[10]

Similarly, Joan Scott argues that feminists need to focus not on some conception of experience as authentic, but rather on "the discursive nature of 'experience' and on the politics of its construction."[11] Because experience is "always already" an interpretation, that is, an experience is itself formed by the particularities of the background of the experiencer as well as the society she lives in, it always stands itself in "need of interpretation."

In drawing attention to the shift of essence and experience from the body to language, I am not trying to argue in favor of an unmediated access to a bodily experience that defines the specificity of our individual and collective lives as women. Our experiences are, of course, shaped by language, by the discursive, by the social. At the same time, if we only consider experience from the perspective of language, then we will learn nothing about the aspects of embodiment that exceed language. This is not to indulge in individualism. Indeed, I agree with Gayatri Spivak's assertion that the feminist slogan, "the personal is political," has become, in what she calls this *personalist* culture, reduced to "*only* the personal is political."[12] Rather, in turning to essence and experience in terms of embodiment, we may be able to learn more about the significance of what it is to be embodied in this epoch.

I think that the paradoxically logical way in which the debate over experience and essentialism has proceeded in the work of Fuss, Scott, Schor, and others is due to the way that the question itself has been posed. In short, it is much easier to remain at the discursive level and much more difficult to take up the body in a way that is not reifying. But these debates leave us with the choice of an essence situated in the body as being substantive, or of essence inhering in language as conceptual. Whereas both options can be understood as being open to change, neither helps us to learn about embodiment. Although these theorists have certainly challenged a mind/body split, they assert that rationality is infused by desire, by the psyche, in other words, by the body, and ultimately their works only tell us more about language. For its part, the question of essences in feminist theory is, accordingly, discussed representationally; by representation I mean that essences are thematized, defined, and categorized, a process that tends to shut down complexity to a rearticulable and unambiguous meaning. This is not the language of poetry, which gathers the nonrepresentational in its multiplicity and ambiguity. It is rather the language of advertising or of signposts, which refers yet again to other signs and codings but has lost its referential ties to corporeal existence. An opportunity to explore essences in a way that would help us to learn more about embodiment is missed. To rethink the question, we must once again explore the concept of essence in terms related to the body that cannot be rendered representationally; we must leave aside these accepted and institutionalized understandings.

It is not accidental that both essence and experience have been collapsed into the discursive. Although they would seem to be diametrically opposed, the one suggesting something immutable and the other something centered in our ongoing interaction with the world, I want to show how both concepts are, in fact, linked not only in the ways they have been collapsed into the discursive but also in how they can help to lead us on a path towards a better understanding of what it is to be embodied. For this move, I turn to Merleau-Ponty, for whom we come to learn about the body not by focusing on the body as object, but rather by living it, because "experience of one's own body runs counter to the reflective procedure which detaches subject and object from each other . . . [giving] us only the thought about the body, or the body as an idea. . . ." [13] What this means for Merleau-Ponty is that if we focus our attention on the body, we learn only about its objectlike nature. If we take this assertion further, then focusing our attention on the body might also show us how the body is taken up in representation or in language. What such a study does not open up for us, however, is embodied nature, which, as Merleau-Ponty shows us, can be best explored when we shift our focus from the body as an object to the ways that the embodied subject interacts with the world. For example, my movements are not commanded by a consciousness that orders the transport of my body from one place to the next through representations of that movement. I am borne towards the friend I see across the street. I rush to meet her, enveloping her in my embrace. Merleau-Ponty shows us that "A movement is learned when the body has understood it, that is, when it has incorporated it into its 'world,' and to move one's body is to aim at things through it; it is to allow oneself to respond to [the things'] call, which is made upon it independently of any representations." [14] Movement, then, is solicited by the world without the mediation of representation. My body is not an object, an "in itself" (*en soi*) in space and time; rather my body inhabits space and time. It literally *in-corp-orates* the world into bodily structures, capacities, and habits, and not as a series of representations. Indeed, the body has an intrinsic sinuosity that defies representation, but is also, in this age of representation, too easily suppressed.[15] Our bodies have this amazing ability to move into and along uneven and rugged surfaces, leaping, bending, turning, and inclining. This sinuosity is neither encouraged nor shown up in the angular lines of paved roads, smooth floors, even stairways, and square buildings that we generally inhabit. Shifting our attention to embodied experiences allows the body's intrinsic essences to emerge. Importantly, experience is not that which links up or which comes midway between mind and body as argued by Grosz.[16] This interpretation of experience adheres to the commonly held misunderstanding of Merleau-Ponty's phenomenology as centered on consciousness. The difference I am trying to articulate is subtle but important. Although I argue that corporeal experience can, to some extent, be cognitively accessed, this does not mean that it can be exhausted by the cognitive, nor that it must necessarily be cognitively processed. Rather, what this implies is that experience can be thoughtfully reflected upon. This reflection upon our corporeal experiences may yield an understanding of corporeal essences, and hence embodiment.

The distinction I want to introduce through the work of Merleau-Ponty is between the body as object and the corporeal subject. By taking up the body as the body-subject, the body is considered in terms of the ways in which it opens out onto and into the world, the ways in which the corporeal subject interacts with others and with her environment. Although Merleau-Ponty's work implies a direct critique of Cartesian dualism, this critique is best explained as the subordination of the body's three regions of perception, motility, and socioaffective relations to the cognitive.[17] For Merleau-Ponty, the cognitive is still a separate region. What is different is that it overlaps with the other regions in much the same way that sight, as a distinctive sense, still overlaps with hearing or with touch. For example, being nearsighted, if I take off my glasses, I find it more difficult to hear the person with whom I am conversing. In sedimenting my perceptual structures, listening to an other has involved visually perceiving and intertwining with her corporeal presence.

Just as the regions of the body-subject overlap and spread into one another, the body has an amazing capacity to move into a situation and to take it up—what Grosz refers to as the body's "organic openness to cultural completion."[18] But the capacities and structures of the body that allow for such openness also provide the possibility for rethinking essences corporeally. Thus, in order to consider what it is about the body that exceeds representation, I have turned to Merleau-Ponty's distinctive use and meaning of *essence,* or what he also refers to in his later work as *ideality,*[19] terms that if understood as embodied rather than as cognitive will help us to understand better the significance of corporeal experience.

Importantly, because essence as ideality cannot be reduced to the discursive, nor to the representational, it is not something that unchangeably exists. Rather, it is a manner or a style of being, the *"sosein* and not the *sein."*[20] Dionne Brand, in her short essay "Seeing," provides a description of such an essence: "The eye has citizenship and possessions. Else what makes me recognize Sherona's right hand at the beginning of the trajectory of her body reach across her face rapidly while her left plants itself on her left hip and her lips thin themselves on some precise word, the whole move describing her politics, her affirmation, her insistence and her don't-take-shit-from-nobody attitude?"[21] In this description, Brand illuminates her own picture, a perception from the experience of making a "film about women in [her] community."[22] In the frame of her perception, she sees Sherona's bodily being as "the sum of what she is saying." Brand's eye intertwines with Sherona in her embodied essence; Brand's cinematographer, however, zooms in on the woman's face, "filling the screen with it until all other gestures are absent." The white cinematographer, Brand elucidates, is investigating the color, the texture of the black woman's skin. He focuses on her face as the reflection of her soul, a reflection that can only serve as an inferior mirror of the same, of the white European male, a "faciality" that abhors otherness, and seeks sameness in the face, the body being subordinated to this one colonized surface.[23]

The cinematographer's eye, Brand writes, is the eye that possesses. It is the eye that reads, regulates, categorizes, and disposes of. It is the eye that if left alone "will fall back on itself, on things it knows," and the seeing of this eye is the way we tend to relate to others in this age. Brand, however, describes the embodied essence of Sherona, because she is not reading this woman representationally.

Brand's description is the embodied essence or ideality that Merleau-Ponty illuminates. Like the poststructuralists who succeeded him, Merleau-Ponty is critical of the move in Western philosophy to search for essence as something immutable without which the thing itself could not exist. He views this search for a formal discursive essence as an abstraction of contextual existence. According to Merleau-Ponty, there are indeed essences, but they adhere to "a domain of history and of geography."[24] Essence for Merleau-Ponty is an embodied, lived essence that cannot endure outside of space and time. For example, it would be impossible for a painter of this age to paint like Vermeer, to capture the essence and style of Vermeer's paintings, for "one cannot spontaneously paint like Vermeer after centuries of other painting have gone by and the meaning of the problem of painting itself has changed." [25]

In order to discern a formal essence, it would be necessary to achieve absolute distance from that which was being studied. In this manner, un-covering an essence would be to know what something would be from all different perspectives outside of time or history; such a feat would be im-possible to achieve because, within the realm of our experiences, it would be impossible to even anticipate all perspectives. Such an understanding of essence would assume that essences can be cognitively represented.

But, because an embodied essence cannot be severed from space and time, we may conclude that it is not that we are bodily in space or time; that would imply an absolute presence that can be sensorially accessed. Rather, temporality and spatiality extend beyond and are behind the visible present. We carry with us corporeally our individual and collective corporeal histo-ries that intertwine "in depth, in hiding" [*en profondeur, en cachette*] in a way that defies the cognitive representational way of seeing that attempts to render all things visible through the use of signs, images, and figures. [26] This does not mean that an essence is restricted to its geographical and tem-poral position, making it inaccessible for others. Nor does this mean that essences are fully there and just made unreachable by their spatioltempo-rality or embodiment. Rather, they are ontologically changeable and open textured because they are the same as embodiment. An essence, then, or more specifically for our purposes what Merleau-Ponty interchangeably calls an "ideality" of the body, can never be extracted from a situation and surveyed from above. For this reason a painter from our current age could not simply study Vermeer's paintings and replicate their essence.

This is, of course, what is happening with the cinematographer in Dionne Brand's perception. The camera surveys Sherona from above. It is a tight aerial view with a close frame that narrows to the woman's face, to the color, the texture of her skin, reducing the complexity of her embodied ges-tures that gather together her lived experiences corporeally. That is, he eliminates her embodied essence. This framing choice arises out of a his-tory of filming practices, a history that cannot be separated from the ten-dency to reduce this woman to a representational image. That is to say, the cinematographer is incapable of capturing her embodied essence, not be-cause of the medium of film that he uses, but because he does not allow that which is Sherona to emerge, to be captured by his lens. Brand, however, as a political activist, as well as a poet, filmmaker, and writer, who writes that for her politics and poetry cannot be separated, does not reduce this woman she knows to a representational image. This is not to say that she does not bring her own history and sociopolitical consciousness to this encounter; engaging with the other is not to leave a part of ourselves behind. Rather, she is engaging with Sherona in order to bring out that which is the bodily expression of that aspect or essence that she knows this woman to be through their friendship, although such an essence could never be exhaustive.

Essences emerge through the interplay of chiasmic relations. A chiasm is an intertwining (*l'entrelacs*) between two subjects (or two entities) that allows each to come into a relation with the other whereby each maintains its independence even as the interdependence of the two provides for the emergence of something new.[27] It is a simultaneous holding and being held that cannot be described as a possession because the subjects will always remain separate in their own depths.[28] In another shot that Brand sets up, a woman, Leleti, reads a lesbian love poem to a woman off camera to whom the poem is addressed.[29] In this framing, the viewer can see neither the woman to whom the poem is being addressed, nor Leleti's eyes as she reads the poem. In this framing, the chiasm is implied through the words of the poem, presumably through Leleti's voice and through her bodily comportment, angled as it is off frame. The cinematographer is sure that Brand has made a mistake in calling this shot because his eye has not been addressed. On one level he understands the mechanics of the chiasm. But, it is in actually engaging with the other and with the world that corporeal essences emerge. Alternatively, encountering others and the world representationally allows us to draw on our familiar, ordered, and rationalized consciousness; we do not have to deal with situations or with others in the contingency and fullness of the present. Still, despite this tendency, what Merleau-Ponty shows us is that the "environment of brute existence and essence" is one that we cannot leave. In this world we inhabit, we cannot abstract facts or ideas as distinct and separate systems. An embodied essence or ideality, as exactly that which is not of cognition, that cannot be represented, grants to the body "its axes, its depth, its dimensions."[30]

Essence is found in the folding over of my body upon the world; my body does not simply exist, perform, enact as an independent entity. It is the nature of the embodied subject to move into and to be taken up by the world around her. Essences emerge through this intertwining, in the space between. They are enacted, but always and only in relation to the world and to others. An ideality of the body is not the same as ideas taken from the realm of the natural sciences involving mathematical equations and facts. Rather, this ideality, which has a carnal presence only because it is taken up in the body-subject, cannot at the same time be removed from the carnal itself and transcribed into the cognitive realm. For this reason, it cannot transcend culture or history. As a capacity, "ideality" is always open to refinement and modification. It is the capacity or skill to be with things and others generally (*ideal*-ity), but with a generality that can never be finished or closed.

Merleau-Ponty writes that Proust, in his exploration of musical ideas, understood the intertwining of the flesh and the idea. The expression of love that is manifest to Swann in "the little phrase" is communicated to everyone who hears it, although they probably would not recognize it cognitively.[31] Nor would those who heard this music be able to experience this expression of love when only observing others in love. The music itself holds the idea of love, but this idea can never be separated from the carnality, the sensibility of the music itself. This does not mean that the carnal idea has an existence only when the music is played. Rather, it has a latent existence in the body that is ready to be evoked, to shine forth; such are "our notions of light, of sound, of perspective, of bodily desire." [32]

In short, if we try to capture an essence as an idea in order to possess it, then it will no longer be an idea. Perhaps it is more accurate to say, then, that we are possessed by the ideas themselves, just as Proust's violinist is possessed by the musical ideas of the little phrase and "must snatch up his bow and race to catch them as they came." [33] Because the body is not an idea itself, it can lend to ideas a carnality that bears them forth as idealities. Because of this intertwining, an essence or ideality cannot merely exist as an abstract characteristic of the embodied subject; nor can it be simply imposed upon her. What Merleau-Ponty shows us is that an essence can only be evoked because it resonates with our carnal being. Essence, as an ideality of the body, is "the texture of style . . . elaborated within the thickness of being." [34] What this means is that embodied essences are enacted in their specificity only within the corporeal existence of an embodied, situated, living, moving, perceiving, affective subject. Essences can only then come into being through being enacted in relation to others and the world.

Artists, Proust tells us, know this when they evoke in others the theme they have found, "shewing us what richness, what variety lies hidden, unknown to us, in that great black impenetrable night, . . . of our soul." The artwork itself presents the idea in a way that is not simply cognitively recognized but can also be bodily understood. Swann's profound response to the little phrase occurs in the presence of the music being played, even as the ideas leave an echo that can later be cognitively reflected upon. As the body lends itself to the idealities, they in turn reveal something about the materiality of the body itself, its inherent sinuosity, contingency, and openness. Idealities or essences are inherent to corporeal being because the body is neither a thing, nor an idea, but is rather "the measurant of the things." [35] Because essences are the invisible of the visible that inhabit us corporeally without being reducible to the cognitive, they cannot be laid out representationally; they can only emerge from depth in the specificity of the indeterminate.

To consider the subject as embodied phenomenologically, then, is to consider the subject not simply in terms of her psyche, but also in terms of the ways she perceives, moves in the world, and engages in socioaffective relations. What is important to Merleau-Ponty's understanding of the body is that it has an amazing capacity to move into and embody its environs. When I type, I do not think representationally that the letters that form this word must be replicated by the representations of the letters on the keyboard. Rather, my fingers respond to the general existence of the words and thoughts that flow bodily through my fingers.

Accordingly, for Merleau-Ponty, "each 'visual structure' eventually provides itself with a mobile essence." [36] As we perceive and habituate ourselves within the world, the structures of the world that we perceive become an essential understanding of how we move and relate. In this way, the tendency to understand our bodies as surfaces—*literally as surfaces*—is a result of observing bodies on television screens and on billboards as surfaces of outer adornment, as well as of thinking our bodies as the surfaces of skin, bones, and flesh revealed to us in diagrams and medical accounts. Finally, even the ways that the North American urban environment tends to solicit the body's motility is in terms of the cognitive. City streets are navigated; we read traffic signals, street names, and building signs and plan out often according to maps the journey we shall take. Moreover, the smooth straight surfaces of roads and sidewalks encourage our bodies to move similarly in smooth and straight lines that demand limited corporeal extension.

Unfortunately, this visual representational structure becomes incorporated into the generality of our being. As we literally bodily move in a straightforward way, our capacities to think differently, creatively, and more openly are also more liable to become similarly confined. An essence as ideality, then, does not necessarily evoke a profound response that opens up the possibility of a multiplicity of corporeal expression, as Proust elaborates. Taken further, an exploration of corporeal experience helps us to reflect upon essences that will show us what it is to live our bodies as systematicity, and perhaps how to move out of it.

Embodied essences are found at the joints, the hollows that are not inside us but that connect us, so that we are not isolated within cultural and historical zones. Essences are shared both culturally, in, for example, the particular cultural expressions of being in love, and individually, in the particular way that love will manifest itself for me. Our lived experiences will offer themselves to ideas that will flow back into our daily existence, a vortex that connects both our individual bodily experiences with their communicable and communal sharing. Thus the attempts of this epoch to go beneath the skin, to flatten the body's depths on the operating table, the anatomical chart, or the screen or through "depth structures" of psycho-analysis or linguistics distort, and they appear to extract the ideality of existence that cannot be detached from life and represented cognitively "to be spread out on display under the gaze." [37] Idealities of the body can neither be thought of nor understood apart from the lived body.

Reconsidering essence as an ideality of the body shows a way of opening up embodied experience to description. The theoretical response that some poststructuralist feminists make to the problem of essence, to equate an understanding of essence as embodied with essence as a formal quality or attribute of the body, simply separates essence from corporeal experience while linking it with experience as discursive. The next step is to conclude that essence in feminism *is* discursive, that it is not an unchanging formal essence, but rather the product of particular discourses. This move allows feminists to retain a concept of essence while dismissing embodied essences, which most feminists understand as formal essences that describe natural and unchangeable feminine qualities.

Fuss, for example, concludes that essences are, in fact, socially constructed because they are rooted in the discursive, in social practices. Similarly, the claim that everything is constructed is ultimately deemed an essentialist move because the implication of "everything" and "always" implies essentialism. In this gesture, essence and construction are collapsed into one another.[38] But such a move can only be made if essence, like the discursive, is reduced to the cognitive level. Although this conclusion is not logically wrong, it is also not helpful for understanding embodied being. Of course, the root problem with this denial of essence as corporeal lies in the denial of the primordial body.

What is significant about accepting a primordial body is that it is to acknowledge that there are capacities particular to the body that cannot be thought at the cognitive level, that are distinct from, but are not outside, social construction. Although the tendency in this age is to process everything inwardly through the intellect and hence the discursive, to be corporeally in touch is to be directed outward. Merleau-Ponty writes, "to touch *oneself,* to see *oneself* . . . is not to apprehend oneself as an ob-ject, it is to be open to oneself, destined to oneself . . .—Nor, therefore, is it to reach *oneself,* it is on the contrary to escape *oneself,* to be ignorant of *oneself,* the self in question is by divergence (*d'écart*), is *Unverborgenheit of the Verborgen* as such, which consequently does not cease to be hidden or latent." [39] The corporeal self is the opening out from that which is latent or hidden in depth. It is not an interiority but rather it is that which supports the subject's relations with the world. Whereas a poststructuralist emphasis on the discursive and on signification shows to some extent the extraordinary ability of the body to "be constructed," at the same time it does not open up an understanding of the body other than that of a materiality that is subjected to cultural inscription, or even evolvement, making it impossible to formulate essence in any other terms than the discursive. What cannot be captured in the poststructuralist understanding of the corporeal is the prediscursive body. The prediscursive body is not a natural body that is outside of, or absolutely unmediated by, the social. Indeed, the very prefix *pre* already defines this body in relation to the discursive. At the same time, for the prediscursive body, the discursive is merely on the horizon.

To say, then, that embodied essences are primarily prediscursive is not to say that we cannot capture something of the inexhaustibility of our corporeal existence in language. Indeed, all bodily regions are interconnected. But it does mean that embodiment cannot be exhausted by or reduced to the cognitive. Rather, attending to the corporeal regions of perception, motility, and sociality can open up and significantly inform our cognitive processes. What we need is to think according to the body.

In approaching this issue of how to bring bodily essences into language, for thought does indeed rely upon language, we must return first to our critique of the formal discursive essence; importantly, we cannot initiate a search for formal essences, a search for that which is pure, observed from an aerial or distanced vantage, and represented discursively. Yet, in seeking to describe embodied essences, we are not seeking the measure of pure existence, a fusion with the things that is completely immune to the mediation of language and social relations.

As Merleau-Ponty shows us, these two extreme positions are both types of "positivisms." Trusting absolutely in the coincidence of speech with the world, or absolutely distrusting the ability of speech to touch the world is, in fact, to be ignorant of the mediating role that language plays. According to these two forms of positivism, philosophy is either reduced to the plane of a formal or discursive "ideality" or else to the "sole plane of existence." In the one case, the purpose of philosophy is to achieve an "infinite distance" from the world and in the other an "absolute proximity," or identification; but the result of both is the same, which is to ignore our embodied interrelations with others and with the world itself.[40]

Merleau-Ponty is arguing against a semiology where language becomes completely self-referential with no relation between it and the things themselves—as "if there existed nothing but things said."[41] Nor does language play the role of pure coincidence. This means that an essence, as neither coincidence nor fusion, as an ideality of the body, can "emigrate" not, so to speak, from one body to the next, but rather it can be taken up into "another less heavy, more transparent body." In being taken up in this way by language, an essence does not become completely freed from the conditions of existence but is rather "emancipated." [42] Ideality thus animates speech; it is a shining forth, an openness between speech and the body. Just as there is a reversibility between the visible and vision, touching and the touched, as well as the visible and the tangible, so too there is a reversibility between language and the world, between speech and that which it signifies.

Because we are corporeal, then, meaning does not come to us only, or even primarily, through language. We are first perceptual, motor, and socioaffective beings. We learn to move as embodied, to perceive the world, and to engage with others according to the particular ways that the world manifests itself in this epoch. Thus, for example, I have a particular embodied essence of movement that will reflect the cognitive emphasis of this age. The straight lines of buildings and roads, the flat surfaces I walk on, the chairs that I sit in for hours on end reflect a cognitively thought-out, corporeally efficient existence. This particular embodied essence is actually produced by the emphasis on the cognitive, but it is taken up corporeally. To describe the ways in which my body moves into these straight lines, along these flat surfaces, is to describe, not exhaustively, some aspect of this essence. My embodying of this corporeal essence is not, therefore, an individual experience and hence has political implications. Indeed, Dionne Brand's essay illuminates that the struggle against the embodiment of this cognitive essence is a political act, because this essence makes it too easy to read the other representationally and not to engage with her in the particularity of her embodied existence. Moreover, describing corporeal essences is a way of gathering shared traits that are indeed historically and culturally formed, and yet also grounded in an essential embodiment.

An important way to learn more about embodiment is to return to experience, not experience as discursive, but the embodied nature of our experience that will help to show up this dangerous tendency to systematicity. Feminists would do well not to dismiss experience so quickly as an ideological and discursive construct; that would be to reduce it to the cognitive and representational forgetting its grounding in embodied lived experience. Rather, we need to turn to experience to understand where we actually are in order to better understand how to effect change.

Making the Phenomenological Reduction Experientially Real

MONIKA LANGER

I will examine the significance of Merleau-Ponty's attempt to make the phenomenological reduction experientially real in one of his best early essays, "Cézanne's Doubt." I will also turn to the work of Emily Carr, one of Canada's greatest painters. Through a phenomenological description of her artworks, I hope to encourage more feminists to consider Merleau-Ponty's philosophy and to further his philosophical concepts in a way that is meaningful for feminism. Feminists have repeatedly emphasized that reflection and knowledge are rooted in a prereflective realm that is the lived world of concretely situated, bodily beings. The grounding of reflection and knowledge in concrete, prereflective bodily experience is the essence of Merleau-Ponty's method of phenomenological reduction. Feminists have long practiced such a method. The question is how best to theorize it and how to describe the realm that it opens. Merleau-Ponty offers the most explicit, detailed attempt to provide a theoretical framework for the practice of phenomenological reduction thus understood. The insights and shortcomings of that attempt prove useful for feminist theorizing.

Especially insightful is Merleau-Ponty's insistence on the inadequacy of the traditional "either/or" logic and its resultant categorizations. Instead, he advocates a multifaceted approach to phenomena and a willingness to entertain ideas traditionally deemed incomprehensible. He is highly critical of "operational" thinking—a thinking that dichotomizes, decontextualizes, reifies, and manipulates phenomena. Such thinking separates nature from humans and regards meaning as springing solely from the latter. Merleau-Ponty stresses the need to subvert this interiorization of meaning and to reestablish the bonds between humans and the (so-called) natural world. He recognizes that this can be accomplished only if prereflective experiences of integration are reawakened. Unfortunately, Merleau-Ponty is oblivious to issues of gender and tends to transform masculine modes of perception into allegedly universal structures of experience. However, this tendency can

138

remind feminists that a corresponding gynocentric universalism is equally unsatisfactory. For feminists concerned to eschew universalistic assertions, "Cézanne's Doubt" is especially significant. It stresses the individuality of a particular painter in illustrating crucial claims couched in more universalistic terms in *Phenomenology of Perception.* It is instructive to refer to the latter to appreciate the extent of Merleau-Ponty's ingenuity in this essay.

In *Phenomenology of Perception,* published in the same year (1945), Merleau-Ponty calls for and undertakes a phenomenological reawakening of our direct experience of the world, upon which the entire universe of science rests.[1] His "Preface" points out that this reawakening requires a phenomenological reduction and that it involves seeing the "world as strange and paradoxical."[2] Merleau-Ponty says that philosophy (meaning phenomenology) must place our relationship with the world "once more before our eyes"; and that "true philosophy consists in relearning to look at the world."[3] He adds that philosophy, "like art, [is] the act of bringing [a] truth into being"; and that in its task of revealing the world and reason as mysterious, phenomenology is characterized by "the same kind of attentiveness and wonder, the same demand for awareness," and the same desire to "seize" emergent meaning as are the paintings of Cézanne.[4]

Significantly, the final page of the "Preface" thus invokes Cézanne, and the very last page of *Phenomenology of Perception* reiterates the importance of seeing and the interrelatedness of philosophy with other endeavors (such as painting): "Whether it is a question of things or of historical situations, philosophy has no other function than to teach us to see them clearly once more and . . . it comes into being by destroying itself as separate philosophy."[5] As Merleau-Ponty interprets him, Cézanne practiced the phenomenological reduction artistically. By focusing on him in the essay "Cézanne's Doubt," Merleau-Ponty hopes to "awaken the experiences which will make [the] idea [of phenomenological reduction] take root" in us.[6] We have, effectively, a double phenomenological reduction in this essay: Merleau-Ponty's phenomenological reduction, practiced philosophically, brings to light Cézanne's phenomenological reduction, practiced artistically. This doubling not only elicits experiences that suspend our operational thinking, but also prompts us to reflect philosophically on that experiential awakening.

In the essay, Merleau-Ponty notes that creating and expressing an idea is not enough. I suggest that the idea of phenomenological reduction that emerges from the notoriously difficult *Phenomenology of Perception* is insufficient to bring about the requisite experiential shift away from an operationalized world. However, it prepares us philosophically to appreciate the nature of this experiential shift, which the essay is designed to induce. Merleau-Ponty's description of the phenomenological reduction in

Phenomenology of Perception proceeds in large measure via a sustained critique of Cartesian philosophy. A full appreciation of Cézanne's artistic practice of phenomenological reduction presupposes a philosophical comprehension of that critique. Because the scope of this paper precludes a recapitulation of Merleau-Ponty's critique, I shall likewise consider it a given, tacit counterpoint for the themes developed in "Cézanne's Doubt."

Descartes' doubt was a purely scientific, methodological one. It involved the mistrust and bracketing of sensibility and of the so-called external world and the reduction to an abstract, allegedly inner, realm of innate ideas declared to be an indubitably certain foundation for science.[7] Cézanne's doubt, on the other hand, was a lifelong, concrete, experiential doubt that permeated his entire existence. Cézanne bracketed the common sense and scientific attitudes to the world and, in wonder, drew attention to the sensible, prereflective, primordial world underlying science. Cézanne's doubt effected a reduction "to the root of things beneath the imposed order of humanity;" so as "to make *visible* how the world *touches* us" and to express its structure "as an emerging organism."[8]

Whereas Descartes insisted on rigid dichotomies (mind/body, reason/sensibility, self/world) and deductive logic, Cézanne steadfastly refused to entertain such dichotomies. He preferred to suspend "the already constituted reason in which 'cultured men' [such as Descartes] are content to shut themselves."[9] Yet Cézanne's doubt did not imply a rejection of reason. Rather, it cultivated the kind of rationality described in Merleau-Ponty's "Preface" to *Phenomenology of Perception*—a rationality in which, mysteriously and miraculously, "perspectives blend, perceptions confirm each other, a meaning emerges."[10] This type of reason does not preclude paradoxes; indeed it abounds in them.

Merleau-Ponty paradoxically focuses on a past, dead painter and his art in order to bring us "closer to present and living reality."[11] By employing this paradoxical approach, he alerts us to the inadequacy of our traditional categorizations—past/present, dead/living, painter/philosopher, art/reality. He notes that his phenomenology seeks "to make [human knowledge] as sensible as the sensible, to recover the consciousness of rationality. This experience of rationality is . . . rediscovered when it is made to appear against the background of non-human nature."[12] It is precisely "the base of inhuman nature" that Cézanne tried to capture on canvas.[13] Through phenomenological description, Merleau-Ponty endeavors to render present to us Cézanne's experience of "germinating" with this "inhuman nature."

Merleau-Ponty's description of Cézanne does not offer any sustained and "concrete" examination of the paintings themselves. One might argue that this renders his approach abstract and makes the description phenomenologically unsound. In *Art Line Thought,* Samuel Mallin claims Merleau-Ponty failed to "take individual artworks seriously enough" and instead relied on the writings of artists and others. Mallin says this error largely accounts for Merleau-Ponty's "remaining entrapped and befuddled by metaphysics." [14] Mallin notes the same flaw is found in ourselves and our entire epoch. He suggests Merleau-Ponty's writings on Cézanne "flow from a contact with the artworks" and that "Merleau-Ponty's most genuine effect has been to return us phenomenologically to what the works show. . . . We have learnt through his example that there is so much more in a Cézanne painting than in any of the artist's or historian's comments about it." [15]

In his "Preface" to *Phenomenology of Perception,* Merleau-Ponty points out that unlike the essences of idealistic philosophy, those that the phenomenological reduction brings to light inhere firmly in existence and must be approached from all angles simultaneously. Just as Cézanne painted everything on his canvas simultaneously, Merleau-Ponty approaches Cézanne from all angles at once—the biographical, psychoanalytic, historical, and aesthetic. He shows us how Cézanne's heredity, environment, social conditions, and creative transformation of all these factors, made him into the person and painter he became.

To make his case, Merleau-Ponty contrasts Cézanne with Leonardo da Vinci. Whereas the former was concerned with the "lived perspective" and the "primordial world" underlying the sciences, da Vinci was fascinated with the sciences and geometric perspective. To his friends and frequently to himself, Cézanne seemed to be caught in immanence—his painting seemed to be merely a product of his schizoid temperament or an accident of his optical makeup. Da Vinci, however, seemed to be absolutely detached from any conditions and to exist as utter transcendence—"a monster of pure freedom." [16] Merleau-Ponty attempts to show that Cézanne and da Vinci both existed as paradoxes of immanence and transcendence—that is, as concrete freedoms. Just as da Vinci was neither cut loose from nor determined by the conditions of his life, but creatively expressed these, so Cézanne, too, was not determined by his circumstances but, rather, creatively took them up and expressed them in his work.

Da Vinci was, to use an anachronistic reference, a profoundly Cartesian artist. His fascination with science and his meticulous anatomical drawings of plants, animals, and human beings are well known. Precision, clarity, and distinctness characterize these anatomical studies. The lines out-line entities, simultaneously defining the particular being and excluding other beings. Meaning is suctioned out of (so-called) nature into the human being. Restricting one's attention to specific pieces of reality removed from their organic context helps to change nature into a separate, defined thing, as

Neil Evernden notes.[17] Citing J. H. van den Berg, he suggests that da Vinci's *Mona Lisa* painting epitomizes this transformation: "The famous enigmatic smile reveals a realm of privacy which we can glimpse but never know or possess, and the true individual is born. But the individual is created by pulling significance inward, and nature retreats outward as the thing we know as landscape."[18]

In Cézanne's paintings we have a reversal of this dichotomizing, reifying approach to nature. As Merleau-Ponty points out, Cézanne gives up "the contour of an object conceived as a line encircling the object" and—in his famous paintings of apples for example—indicates multiple outlines instead. These effectively "unfreeze" the objects and restore their endless emergent meanings as they intermingle. In his paintings of *Mount Saint Victor,* we literally see the mountain shatter as an inert entity and come-into-being as a vibrating play of colors. By the same token, Cézanne paints "a face 'as an object' "—thus overturning the interiorization of significance and reintegrating the human into nature.[19]

Merleau-Ponty describes how Cézanne artistically practiced a phenomenological reduction that, in principle, could never be complete. His stated aim was to make art and nature "the same" in portraying the spontaneous formation of the "primordial world" in "primordial perception." In this endless endeavor to express "the continual rebirth of existence," his only guide was "the immediate impression of nature," without benefit of enclosing outlines or pictorial arrangements. He was also fully aware that the act of painting inevitably involves interpretation, so that the genesis of the perceptual world that he struggled to depict was always already an interpreted genesis of an artistically perceived world. Cézanne said of himself that he "wrote in painting," and he sought to express the world's "infinite Logos" by installing himself in that realm of "primordial experience" where reflection and vision are inseparably intertwined.[20]

At this prereflective level of lived experience, immanence and transcendence are mutually implicatory and paradoxically transposable. Intentionality here miraculously both inheres in and transcends "the lived object" being painted. In the painter's experience, the perceptual world wants—indeed, demands—to be painted, and the painter simply expresses what it wants to say. "The landscape thinks itself in me," Cézanne said, "and I am its consciousness.[21] From the standpoint of common sense or of science, such a claim is dismissed as ridiculous or, at best, as mystical obfuscation. However, from a phenomenological perspective Cézanne's assertion communicates an important existential truth, which a painter is particularly prone to experience. In "Eye and Mind" Merleau-Ponty undertakes a more detailed phenomenological investigation of this paradoxical truth: that the world and the human perceiver are so intertwined prereflectively that any

relegation of intentionality to one term alone profoundly distorts the phenomenon.[22] "Cézanne's Doubt" provides a significant step towards the later
treatment of this wonderful intertwining of ourselves and the world. In
daily life, as in art, meaning comes into being through coexistence with the
perceived; and this prepersonal creativity provides the basis for the personal, or explicit, creativity of the artist.

Merleau-Ponty highlights Cézanne's individuality as a person and as an
artist. He endeavors to show how, paradoxically, this uniqueness is precisely what gives Cézanne's paintings their power to speak to us and to
draw us out of our reified perceptions. Unfortunately, however, Merleau-
Ponty assumes that not only the artist par excellence—Cézanne—but "the
artist" as such is a male. Thus, he says, "The artist launches his work just
as a man [un homme] once launched the first word. . . . An artist's creations, like a man's [l'homme] free decisions, impose on [the] given a figu-
rative sense which did not pre-exist them."[23] This implicit sexism stems
from Merleau-Ponty's sociotemporal situation, and it is tempting to dismiss it. To do so is to underestimate its significance and the importance of
creating ways to render Merleau-Ponty's concepts more relevant for wom-
en's experiences of embodiment. Emily Carr's work is particularly fruitful
for this latter project.

Emily Carr is widely recognized as one of Canada's greatest painters.
Much of what Merleau-Ponty says of Cézanne can be said equally well of
Carr. I suggest that ultimately the latter's paintings are better able to express "the base of inhuman nature" than are those of Cézanne.[24] Carr herself did not consider her womanhood crucial to her art, and I am not claiming that her gender rendered her closer to "nature" and enabled her to
effect the phenomenological reduction more successfully. Rather, I will try
to demonstrate that Carr's artworks are exceptionally helpful for feminists
who are interested in developing Merleau-Ponty's philosophical concepts
so that they better reflect women's experiences.

Emily Carr (1871–1945) studied art in San Francisco, in England, and in
Paris. She thought highly of Cézanne, and in a 1930 lecture entitled "Fresh
Seeing," she praises him as "the great Frenchman who did so much . . . to
open the way, to change our vision" from conventional to "Creative Art."[25]
Like Cézanne, she felt herself to be different and was regarded as eccentric.
For the most part, her artworks were met with indifference or rejection,
and throughout her life she experienced intense self-doubt, isolation, and
loneliness. She is best known today for her marvelous paintings of West
Coast forests and *Haida* cultural artifacts.

It is fashionable nowadays to devalue artists' comments about their works
by arguing that artists have no privileged access to their works' meaning (a
line frequently taken by advocates of deconstruction). Alternatively, it is of-

ten claimed that artists' writings merely offer conscious, rational explanations of their works, and that such explanations serve to obscure the concrete particularity of the works themselves. Although there is some truth in both critiques, they are misleading as generalizations. Artists do not inevitably have a better understanding of their works' meaning. Yet sometimes their sense of it is more insightful and provides an invaluable access to their artworks. Similarly, although some artists' writings provide conscious, rational explanations, the writings of other artists—such as Carr—often explicitly reject such an approach. Hence, it behooves us neither to shun artists' writings nor to invoke them as substitutes for their artworks. I will present both Carr's own comments on art and my phenomenological assessment of her artworks.

Like Cézanne, Carr practiced an artistic phenomenological reduction that bracketed conventional modes of perception in favor of what she called "fresh" or "pure seeing." She explained that "you must dig way down into your subject, and into yourself. And in your struggle to accomplish it, the usual aspect of the thing may have to be cast aside." [26] Fresh seeing is a seeing that, "disconnecting [objects] from all practical and human associations," tries "to get a little nearer to the reality of the thing." [27] The "creative" artist must dig "right down to the base of things" and "feel [their] very nature." [28] In portraying this primordial world, the painter pulls meaning "forth into visibility" and experiences a paradoxical transposition of intentionality to that world: "It is by expressing the felt nature of the thing, then, that the artist becomes the mouthpiece of the universe. . . ." [29]

"Artists talk in paint," says Carr. [30] The meaning to be conveyed does not exist anywhere ready-made. Rather, it emerges from the intertwining of artist and perceptual world, as she points out: "Nor can I find the things I want to say in the art books. They do not seem to be in them, but out in the woods and down deep in myself." [31] In her journals, Carr describes this paradoxical intertwining of pure seeing and the visible: "There is a sea of sallal and bracken, waving, surging, rolling towards you. . . . Perfectly ordered disorder designed with a helter-skelter magnificence. . . . From the bowels of the earth rushes again the great green ocean of growth. The air calls to it. The light calls to it. The moisture. It hears them. . . . It is life itself, strong, bursting life . . . life speaking to life." [32] There can be no question of explaining Carr's paintings, for as she said, "How could anyone do that?" [33] Instead, I shall draw attention to a few of her best-known pieces to illustrate some of her observations about painting, before proceeding to consider two in more detail.

A Rushing Sea of Undergrowth splendidly illustrates the passage just cited. We literally see "the great green ocean of growth" rushing "from the bowels of the earth." We sense that Carr has indeed dug "right down to the base of things," felt their nature, and enabled the primordial world to "speak itself" via her paints. Her canvas palpably conveys the "polylogue" among vegetation, air, sky, light, and moisture. The "base of inhuman nature" depicted here defies both the mechanistic conception of nature as meaningless bits of matter in motion and the conventional conception of nature as gentle brooks, pastoral meadows, fields of grain, or orchards (or baskets) of fruit—the sort of human "inhuman nature" that Cézanne's canvases tend to suggest. Carr's painting portrays nature here as an emerging organism structuring itself spontaneously, devoid of any "pre-fabricated" human significations (to the extent that that is possible).

In one of Carr's most remarkable paintings, *Forest, B.C.,* she portrays waves of light, of air, and of vegetationlike clouds flowing through an oval opening and a passage created by a "corridor" of trees. The trees are topped with undulating, sun-flecked greenery and are traversed by a mysterious blue "curtain" suggestive simultaneously of skies and water. This painting shows the intermingling of nature's elements and evokes experiences of sexual union, birthing, and more generally, of "life itself, strong, bursting life." In *Abstract Tree Forms,* Carr has stripped away all "the forms of representation" so as to reveal the primordial world as a luminous, vibrant flow of life in "perfectly ordered disorder," prior to any imposition of human categorizations (to the extent that it is humanly possible to perceive and convey this "inhuman" primordial world).[34] In her somewhat less abstract, untitled, painting of three tufted treetops swaying in a swirling sky, we can almost feel palpably the trees' invitation to join their dance and, paradoxically, to mingle with "inhuman nature." Carr wrote in a 1936 journal entry: "Those woods . . .—a solidity full of air and space—moving, joyous, alive, quivering with light, springing, singing paens of praise, throbbingly awake. Oh, to be so at one with the whole that it is *you* springing and *you* singing."[35]

It should not be concluded that Carr shunned the portrayal of human constructions. She was one of the first non-Natives who recognized the splendor of the *Haida* cultural artifacts and endeavored to convey it to others through her own art. In her famous watercolor *Great Eagle,* a gently shimmering, almost kaleidoscopic background throws into relief the majestic eagle. In the painting *Big Raven,* the carved raven seems to palpably rise out of swirling, curling, "flames" of vegetation flanked by trees, a mountain, and shafts of light descending from a domelike sky. We have here a superbly executed intermingling of the "inhuman" and the "human" orders—an interplay of "nature" and "culture" such that meaning emerges from this very interplay. The same is true of Carr's painting *Zunoqua of the Cat Village,* in which cats seem to swim in the flamelike green-blue sea of vegetation behind the carved Zunoqua. Natives' houses are buffeted about by the "awful force" of surging vegetation, while additional cats peer out of the distant, flowing-swaying trees. What better intermingling could one imagine than this powerful "embracing" of vegetal, animal, and "cultural" orders?

Carr's work is very fruitful for feminists interested in furthering Merleau-Ponty's philosophical concepts in ways that speak to women's experiences. Jeffner Allen has argued that "sinuosity is . . . a mode of being that founds women's specific experience of being-in-the-world [and] . . . enables the emergence of a positive women-identified sensibility and feminist experience." [36] Allen does not mention Merleau-Ponty; however, her notion of sinuosity furthers Merleau-Ponty's critique of Cartesian concepts. The sinuous inherently resists disembodiment, atomization, regularization, geometrization, and categorization. It is not straight, even, circular, or symmetrical. To a Cartesian, the sinuous tends to look disorderly, clumsy, incomplete, and even ugly. Though apparently unaware of Allen's discussion of sinuosity, Samuel Mallin has noted that regularization pervades our epoch, putting us out of touch with "the sinuous line of nature." [37] While concentrating on the sinuosity revealed by certain sculptures, Mallin comments that "a painting that helped us encounter once more the intrinsic sinuosity of trees or nature" would have "immense ontological importance." [38] In my view, Emily Carr's paintings superbly reveal precisely that sinuosity. They thus counter Cartesian concepts and contribute to women's specific experiences of embodiment. As Allen has suggested, the curved and sinewy character of women's bodies expresses a fundamental sinuosity. Further, women are forced "to turn aside from the rigidity of the upright" if they are to be faithful to themselves and other women. [39] Their relationships and the patterns of their lives tend to be winding: "Through insinuation we perceive the sinuosity of women's lives as a curving, winding, turning, folding out of and into itself." [40] This sinuosity echoes that of nature. In revealing the latter, Carr's paintings speak to women's experiences.

The intrinsic sinuosity of trees and of other constituents of nature emerges especially well in some of the paintings I discussed earlier. *Forest, B.C.* implicitly invites us to enter the oval opening created in its foreground through the inclining of two gigantic trees towards each other. The intermingling of colors in their enormous stems results in a shimmering brownish, reddish, bluish, greenish, yellowish sensuousness that suggests their woodiness as a living substantiality, rather than an immobile mass. The curving lines that convey the inclining of the two trunks towards one another are repeated at the base of the tree on the right. This time, the curvatures are heightened by shadings, so that these curving lines reveal the sinewy nature of the stem. The trees emerging beyond the oval opening echo the colors and curves of the foreground tree on the right; so that the various trunks seem to flow into each other without losing their own particularity. They coax us to let our eyes yield to the sinuous play of these stems, which seem to caress each other. This palpable intermingling is further strengthened by the undulating, vegetationlike clouds and flowing treetops overhead. As our eyes follow the waves of air, of light, and of foliage flowing from tree to tree, we find ourselves completely unable to separate these elements or isolate tree from tree. Instead, we experience the fundamental sinuosity of the natural world.

That intrinsic sinuosity is even more pronounced in *Abstract Tree Forms,* where luminous multicolored flows intermingle in profusion. Here it is impossible to delimit individual trees or to determine just what is trunk and what is branches or foliage. The painting prompts us to abandon our Cartesian conception, which reduces trees to bits of scenery or to parts of an "ecosystem" whose aliveness is described in scientifically observable processes. Such a perspective distorts the life force of trees—the vitality that defies calculation and prediction. *Abstract Tree Forms* portrays that very vitality through flowing, swirling, billowing bands of vibrant colors. The colors themselves seem to vibrate and shimmer as they modulate into other colors. If we set aside our conceptions and let ourselves be drawn visually into the multihued flowing bands, we experience a corresponding deconstriction of our entire bodily being. Feeling ourselves intermingle with the flows of intermingling colors, we become aware of that essential sinuosity that we share with the trees.

Carr's painting of three tufted treetops celebrates nature's sinuosity by portraying the "dancing" of trees amidst a swirling sky. This time, the trees are discernible in their particularity while simultaneously emerging as inseparable from each other and from the sky. Once again, copious curving lines and modulating colors create this effect. Even the tree trunks are slightly curved, and the pronounced curvatures of the foliage convey a profound sense of vitality. There are neither definite outlines nor solid blocks of color here, for these would impart a feeling of immobility and separation. Instead, the greenish, bluish, brownish, yellowish hues provide undulating outlines, such that the trees themselves seem to vibrate and sway in unison. The tufted tops of the three foreground trees are so windswept that they seem to sweep the sky, and the sky's swirling lines accentuate the swaying, sweeping movement of the trees. The movements of sky and trees intermingle as the sky appropriates the greenish, brownish, yellowish hues of the trees, while the latter incorporate the bluish hues of the sky. The result is a joyous, sinuous reconnection of earth and sky, signifying the overcoming of long-standing Cartesian dualisms between the "physical" and "mental" spheres.

The palpable linking of earth and sky is even more apparent in Carr's *Big Raven* painting, where shafts of light literally connect the "lower" and "upper" realms. In the painting of three tufted treetops, we are left to imagine the ground from which the trees emerge, for that ground lies beyond the painting's bottom border. In *Big Raven* the vegetation, trees, and carved raven visibly emerge from the hilly land and share the colors of the sky. The brightly colored mountain in the background draws our attention to the multihued shafts of light linking all these elements. Once again, sinuosity is paramount: curved lines predominate throughout the painting and become particularly pronounced in the swirling, flamelike vegetation surrounding the carved raven. These sinuous lines express nature's intrinsic vitality and hence, the inadequacy of "operational" thinking concerning nature. As for the raven, it seems to spring from the land itself, and its coloring splendidly blends the colors of the hilly land, the flamelike undergrowth, the trees, the mountain, and the sky. The raven therefore seems to belong to this "natural" world as surely as do the other elements. *Big Raven* thus subverts our traditional tendency to dichotomize "nature" and "culture," "reality" and "art," or the "inhuman" and the "human."

Zunoqua of the Cat Village similarly overturns our expectations regarding "nature" and "culture." Steeped in Cartesian thinking, we generally divide "nature" from "culture" and accord priority to the latter. "Nature" has come to signify quantifiable matter for manipulation and control as "resources" in the interests of "culture." If we bracket these assumptions and immerse ourselves visually in this remarkable painting, our sensuous experience will prompt us to revise our thinking about "nature" and "culture." As we allow our vision free rein, we feel ourselves buffeted and tossed about by the raging sea of undergrowth. The turbulent waves of vegetation are filled with wild-eyed cats and mysterious sea monsters. These fearful waves surge towards two wooden houses and, on impact, become flamelike tongues that threaten to demolish them. The flowing, curving lines of this sealike undergrowth, and of the background trees, express the tremendous vitality of nature as a force that cannot be quantified or controlled. Indeed, culture in the form of human habitations here appears utterly vulnerable to the sway of nature.

The carved figure of Zunoqua in the foreground does not reestablish the supremacy of culture over nature. Both the houses and Zunoqua seem literally rooted in the surging undergrowth and inseparable from it. The sinuous lines of Zunoqua suggest that she is of a piece with nature: the snakes on her head seem to slither down towards the turbulent undergrowth below, while the deep curves of her eyes and mouth reflect the curves of the cat-filled waves and the background trees. The play of light enlivens Zunoqua's face, and the coloring that she shares with some of the cats and the tree trunks emphasizes her participation in nature's vitality. Overall, this painting encourages us to experience the fundamental aliveness of nature and the inseparability of culture from nature. Further, the buffeting of the houses by the undergrowth prompts us to recognize that all our constructions—including our cherished intellectualizations—depend on what Merleau-Ponty describes as the prepersonal realm of bodily experience.

Earlier, I said that sinuosity intrinsically resists disembodiment, atomization, regularization, geometrization, and categorization. Consequently, it tends to appear disorderly to the Cartesian viewer. These crucial aspects of sinuosity are especially evident in *Zunoqua of the Cat Village*. The greenish, yellowish, bluish, whitish colors of the surging undergrowth and swaying trees convey an immediate, undeniable sensuousness and fluidity. As they flow into one another and intermingle, these colors show an incredible lushness that utterly precludes any disembodiment. They shimmer, ripple, billow, stream, and whip along in sinuous lines that are inherently irreducible to divisible components. The vegetation in the foreground rolls away from Zunoqua to the right over fearsome sea monsters. Meanwhile, the immediate background swings in an arc from right to left to right, and is filled with cats madly swimming in several directions away from the two houses. Back of this, the undergrowth undulates and the most prominent trees sway against each other in opposite directions. These sinuous, irregular movements cannot be categorized or contained. From a Cartesian point of view, the effect is one of complete chaos. Yet if we put that perspective in abeyance, we perceive a vital rhythm in this unruly intertwining of vegetation, animals, and human constructions. So immersed in vegetation are Zunoqua, the animals, and the houses, that isolation of any one of these elements is inconceivable. Together they create a sensuous whole that splendidly conveys characteristics of lived experience—rather than a reconstruction that seeks to tailor such experience to fit preestablished concepts.

In *A Rushing Sea of Undergrowth,* there is not a single straight line. Majestically rolling waves of undergrowth sweep us visually into the painting at the bottom of the canvas and carry our gaze upwards through further undergrowth and trees to the sky. Color, lighting, and line combine to manifest nature's marvelous vitality. A massive, dark-green wave of vegetation curves across the lower section and visibly gathers itself together. The play of sunlight throughout its breadth emphasizes the vastness and power of this vegetal wave, which is about to hurl itself forward. Ahead of it, luminous, lighter-green waves of undergrowth rear up and roll towards the trees. These trees rise from an even more stunningly luminous undergrowth in which we can catch glimpses of the tree roots and the underlying soil. Here, the sun-drenched undergrowth positively quivers with life as it sweeps this way and that way with the wind. Above it, the fir trees sway, their branches curving concavely or convexly. Although these trees are roughly triangular in shape, they preclude geometrization, for each apparent triangle bends—some dramatically, others only slightly. A white mist, which is detectable behind the most distant trees, enables us to perceive nature's life-giving air and moisture.

Although all the trees in this painting have their own particular shape and color, none is divorceable from the others. Each overlaps with others, and several also incline towards others. Even the gigantic tree spanning the left top half of the canvas is only seemingly isolated from the rest. In fact, it overlaps with the most distant trees and bends towards them. Nor are the trees separable from the undergrowth and the sky. Each tree trunk is firmly embedded in the undergrowth, and the foliage of each tree has a bluish hue that links it sensuously to the sky. Neither sky nor undergrowth is circumscribable; for both extend beyond the borders of the canvas. There are tree trunks that reach the top of the canvas without their foliage—which must lie beyond it. Conversely, the undergrowth rushes up from below the bottom of the canvas. Once again, there can be no question of disembodiment or atomization here. The rolling, green waves of undergrowth are so lush and so patently sensuous that they rule out any abstraction—and the same is true of the fir trees. The sinuous lines of both thwart any attempt to reduce them to a summation of smaller units. This painting prompts us to let go of the common conception of nature by reawakening our sensuous experience. To bring about such a shift, *A Rushing Sea of Undergrowth* reverses the usual figure/background structure. Commonly, we consider undergrowth to be inconsequential and disposable—in fact, we generally fail to notice it at all. Here the undergrowth acts as figure, rather than background, and as such, it dominates the bottom half of the painting. As our vision moves upwards to the trees, these become "figure" too, while the sky serves as background. This reversal of the figure/background structure prepares us to experience the profound vitality of even the most ignored aspect of nature.

Carr's focus on nature is particularly important for those interested in Merleau-Ponty's philosophy, given that Merleau-Ponty pays astonishingly little attention to nature in his writings. Unlike our usual cultural constructions, nature is inherently vital and sinuous. By participating visually in this utterly un-Cartesian nature through Carr's canvases, we become aware of our own intrinsic sinuosity. Prereflectively, we thus dislodge the Cartesian approach to the world and ourselves. Carr's artworks illustrate splendidly the main points that Merleau-Ponty makes about "relearning to look at the world" in "Cézanne's Doubt." In both Carr and Merleau-Ponty, there is a profound attentiveness to, and revalorization of, prereflective experience. Both insist on the corporeal, sensuous nature of that experience and regard it as the ineradicable source of knowledge. Both note the inadequacy of traditional approaches and categorizations, and emphasize the need to put those in abeyance. Instead they favor fresh ways of seeing our fundamental inherence in, and dynamic relationship with, the perceptual world. Both underline the situatedness, and the lived perspectivity, of that seeing. Both seek to reawaken our concrete, prereflective, sensuous experience of integration with the world. Neither is suggesting that lived perspectivity condemns humans to separatism or isolationist individualism. The charge of separatism/individualism itself arises from an abstract "either/or," "all or nothing" stance that Merleau-Ponty consistently exposes as fallacious. Such a stance claims that either we all see identically the same world, or we are condemned to monadic existences. Instead, Merleau-Ponty and Carr invite us to celebrate the fact that—contrary to the traditional categorizations—inherence, situatedness, perspectivity, difference, plurality, intermingling, dialogue, and communication with the world all belong together.

Feminists have long insisted on the importance of attending to and revalorizing prereflective bodily experience as the actual ground for reflection and knowledge. They have criticized the traditional "either/or" logic and the "operational" thinking of the dominant scientific paradigm. They have deplored its dualistic, hierarchical approach to nature, and have indicated how that essentially Cartesian approach makes for the simultaneous exploitation of nature and women. They have sought to show up the destructiveness and inadequacy of traditional categorizations. They have practiced a phenomenological reduction that puts those categorizations in abeyance and attends to concrete experiential evidence. All this harmonizes with similar themes in Merleau-Ponty's philosophy. I hope that my development of Merleau-Ponty's concepts through Emily Carr's artworks will encourage more feminists to consider Merleau-Ponty's philosophy and to further it in fruitful ways.

PART IV

Creative Collaborations

Disappropriations:
Luce Irigaray and Sarah Kofman

PENELOPE DEUTSCHER

One runs . . . a greater danger of madness with repetition, even the deconstructive repetition with which I work, than with "original invention." . . . My
"mimetic" or "hysterical" writing runs the risk of madness, not only because
the authors I write on are just about all mad, but because this method leads
one to a permanent disappropriation.

> —Sarah Kofman, "Apprendre aux hommes
> à tenir parole—portrait de Sarah Kofman"

Appropriations

In his reading of Rousseau in *Of Grammatology,* Derrida makes a distinction between what Rousseau's work ostensibly "declares" and what it actually "describes." [1] There are, reminds Robert Bernasconi in the wake of
Paul de Man, occasional passages where Derrida seems to introduce an
"ethical overtone of deceit," speaking as if Rousseau chooses to remain
blind to what his texts really describe.[2] In *Blindness and Insight,* Paul de
Man argues against "those critics" who "pretend" to have a superior access to what Rousseau "really did" mean to say.[3] Does Derrida suppose he
has access to what Rousseau did not intend his text to "declare"?

Or is it de Man who returns to the language of the author's intentions?
Claiming that Rousseau is in control of the unstable elements in his work,
de Man reinstates the language about the author's consciousness that he
also undermines. He locates in Rousseau's work examples of what he terms
"controlled contradiction." [4] Controlled contradictions are those that are
part of, rather than disruptive to, an author's theoretical schema. For example, rather than being paralyzed by difficulties in his argument, Rousseau
sometimes discusses or draws philosophical inferences from those difficulties (*Allegories,* 229).[5]

It is with no small fascination that one witnesses a parallel debate between

155

Luce Irigaray and Sarah Kofman in their readings of Freud. In *The Enigma of Woman,* Kofman defends Freud against Irigaray's interpretation:

> Luce Irigaray was the first to draw attention to the phallocratic character of [Freud's "Femininity"]. I shall arrive at a similar conclusion while offering a quite different reading, one that emphasizes the complexity of the Freudian undertaking.[6]

Kofman acknowledges that she and Irigaray offer complementary interpretations of Freud's phallocentrism. According to Kofman, however, Irigaray mistranslates Freud, renders his work simplistic, undoes the order of his argumentation, cites him in a misleading fashion, and selectively cites that which reinforces her argument, while suppressing that which does not. Above all, Irigaray underestimates the complexity of Freud's work.

How does Kofman manage to so distance herself from Irigaray's reading of Freud whilst also agreeing with it? She presents herself as a reader who is better prepared than Irigaray to appreciate Freud's complexity. The author in question—Rousseau or Freud—contains a "deconstructible" level to their work, de Man and Kofman agree. But this demonstrates the complexity of Rousseau's and Freud's thought. This complexity has not been appreciated, indeed, it has been appropriated; by those who seek to read the author's text against the author's declarations. Thus, de Man and Kofman appear, unexpectedly, as apologists for Rousseau and Freud against deconstructive interpretations of those authors (from Derrida and Irigaray) *with which they also accord.*

When de Man and Kofman locate "complexity" in Rousseau's and Freud's texts, this gesture collapses into the language about the author's intentions they also resist. Kofman proposes that "the double appeal to poetry in 'Femininity' has to be interpreted as part of a *strategy*" (*Enigma,* 103; my emphasis). Freud's modesty, says Kofman, is "feigned and tactical" (*Enigma,* 104); "Freud only pretends to be giving way to the specialists (specialists in female sexuality, in this case) whose 'truths' he exhibits the better to criticize or deconstruct them" (*Enigma,* 104). Freud is engaged in a complex project of presenting the reader with distinctions so as to complicate those distinctions. He risks being misread as a self-contradictory author who undermines distinctions to which he also appeals. He risks the arrival of a deconstructive critic at the scene of his text who sifts out one refrain as the "declared level," another as the inconsistent "described level," thereby thinking to have turned Freud's own text against himself. This is how Kofman represents the arrival of Luce Irigaray at the scene of Freud's text:

[Freud] risks being misunderstood, being criticized (as Luce Irigaray has not failed to do) for holding onto the old words *masculine* and *feminine* in their most traditional, most metaphysical sense at the very point where he is attempting to reevaluate them, at the moment when he is seriously complicating the conventional schema that identifies masculine with *active* and feminine with *passive*. (*Enigma,* 115)

The positions taken by de Man and Kofman make surprising property claims concerning deconstructive activity and the boundaries between Irigaray and Freud, Derrida and Rousseau. Irigaray and Derrida are taken to be mistakenly attributing deconstructive activity to "themselves" rather than to Rousseau and Freud, and so to be misappropriating the latter's textual complexity. According to de Man and Kofman, it is by failing to appreciate the extent to which these authors are already deconstructive that Derrida and Irigaray take themselves to be deconstructing the texts of Rousseau and Freud.[7]

The debate, then, is partly about the status of deconstruction. If a deconstructive reading demonstrates that a text is more complicated than its explicit "declared" level suggests, for de Man and Kofman the object in question (Rousseau or Freud) is therefore more complicated than is usually thought. In this way, Sarah Kofman is led into proprietal issues: Does Irigaray misappropriate Freud's complexity? A debate about the status of deconstructive readings converts into the implicit return to concepts of "proper" boundaries between author, text, and critic. For Kofman, Irigaray has preyed upon Freud, inappropriately attributing to her own reading the level of complexity found in Freud's text, which should be recognized as belonging to "Freud."[8]

Disappropriations

I shall later argue that Kofman's best work acutely calls into question just such issues of intellectual property rights and renders all the more questionable her arguments against Irigaray. Working towards that argument, I shall first make some comments about Kofman's response to Irigaray. When Kofman accuses Irigaray of a misappropriation of Freud's complexity, the most obvious response is to wonder at the level of disappropriation the (critical) self Kofman engages in through her own reading of Freud. When, in *The Enigma of Woman*, Kofman ingeniously demonstrates the complexity of "Freud," she displaces onto the figure of Freud the complex reading she has effected. Kofman's defense of Freud contra Irigaray suggests in turn Kofman's willful disappropriation of her own complexity. If a deconstructive reading of Freud can lead to an insistence on the complexity of Freud, *or* can lead to the deconstructive critic understanding his or her work as an intervention into the text, then why does Kofman so downplay the extent to which she has intervened into Freud's work?

Having attributed the complexity of Freud's text to "Freud," Kofman is in a position to present herself as a critic who (merely) mimics or repeats the Freudian text, rather than making a more critical intervention into that text. Because (disappropriating herself) she attributes her reading of Freud to "Freud," she is able to identify her interpretation as (merely) repeating the deconstructive complexity of "Freud." In an interview, she acknowledges the risk of this practice: disappropriation of herself in favor of Freud.[9] Elsewhere, Kofman does avow that her project is to repeat Freud *while very lightly displacing his text.*[10] Kofman's project, then, is not to "merely" repeat Freud—even were "mere" repetition possible. Yet she is at pains to downplay the level of textual intervention she makes into the Freudian corpus.

The comparison with Irigaray throws into relief the curiousness of Kofman's role. Kofman and Irigaray concur in their demonstration of Freud's phallocentrism. But Irigaray has no investment in downplaying her level of (feminist) intervention, and we must ask, why does Kofman? Irigaray's is an explicitly political project to subvert phallocentric accounts of women. This renders all the more stark the oddness of Kofman's *identification* with Freud in the context of a parallel and assiduous analysis of phallocentrism. Luce Irigaray's work has been much analyzed and debated by critics. The juxtaposition of her work with that of Sarah Kofman is intended to open debate on the lesser-known Kofman. I shall pursue the relationship between feminist intervention and identification, and between modes of appropriation and disappropriation, in the work of both philosophers.

Kofman and Irigaray

Kofman died in 1994, the author of a huge and little-interpreted corpus. In more than twenty works, she had explored phallocentric renderings of femininity in the history of philosophy, arguing that they are symptomatic of blind spots and weaknesses in philosophical systems. Only a few English translations of Kofman's work appeared during her lifetime, and she was best known to Anglophone audiences for *The Enigma of Woman,* which appeared in English concurrently with Irigaray's *Speculum of the Other Woman* in 1985. Though Kofman's book is highly critical of Irigaray's project, there are considerable parallels between the interpretations Irigaray and Kofman offer of Freud in these works.[11] Both argue that his account of sexual difference excludes concepts of femininity as radically other and is riddled with textual instability, contradiction, inconsistency, and blind spots. Both, with varying degrees of irony, get Freud on the couch, locating Freud's desire to seduce the daughter, or his fear of looking directly at the mother, or analyzing his theory of penis envy as Freud's own fetish solution.

If Irigaray fared far better than Kofman in terms of the progress of English translations and immeasurably better in terms of the progress of Anglophone commentary on her work, Kofman's book was from the first well known and well received, favorably compared with Irigaray's reading of Freud: "more detailed, more scholarly," suggested Gayatri Spivak, "more sophisticated in its methodology, and perhaps more perceptive." [12] But in comparison to Irigaray's work, it could be said that Kofman's work did not get a footing among feminist readers.

Kofman had shared Irigaray's vigilance in analyzing phallocentric projections of femininity in the work of figures such as Nietzsche, Freud, Hegel, Plato, Kant, and Rousseau. But Irigaray's work is infinitely easier to identify as a feminist intervention. Like Irigaray, Kofman exposed femininity as the blind spot of great works of the history of philosophy. But unlike Irigaray, she did not attempt to disrupt those texts by generating alternative figures of the feminine or by refiguring sexual difference. What, then, was the point of her project? Her criticisms of Irigaray's reading of Freud are confusing and telling in this regard. As Monique Schneider asked of Kofman, was it a matter of defending Freud against Irigaray's accusation of misogyny? [13] Clearly not—Kofman's reading is in close proximity with that of Irigaray. What then are the politics of Kofman's readings, and can her work be seen as a feminist enactment of philosophy?

If it is Irigaray's politics of textual intervention that most allows us to distinguish the style of her work from that of Kofman, the tone Kofman takes to Irigaray has served her badly. Kofman appears, and presents herself, as she who repeats the text, she who charts its phallocentrism, but not she who makes her subversive intervention. From this perspective, it is telling that Kofman identifies a deconstructive reading—her own style of deconstructive reading—as repetition of a text ("Apprendre," 7). Isn't deconstruction usually thought of as making an intervention into the text, not redoubling a text (*Grammatology,* 158)? This is the depiction to be found in *Sexual Subversions,* for example:

> In opposition to Freud's containment of women in men's self-reflecting representations. . . . Irigaray attempts a feminist deconstruction of psychoanalysis. Her project is both to undo the phallocentric constriction of women as men's others and to create a means by which women's specificity may figure in discourse in autonomous terms.[14]

Kofman appears, by contrast, to be a theorist who analyzes the containment of women in men's self-reflecting representations in texts in the history of philosophy, while not attempting to undo those representations.

Although Kofman goes to extraordinary lengths to discount the originality of her work, specifically distinguishing her methodology from that of "original invention" ("Apprendre," 7), it is wrong to relegate her to the ranks of commentators whose brief is to repeat faithfully. Moreover, Kofman's original and critical interventions may be located at the heart of her maverick project of identification with phallocentric philosophers. Irigaray and Kofman both engage in projects of mimesis with the philosophers they interpret, and Kofman's project of mimesis renders questionable the metaphorics of intellectual property she draws upon to criticize Irigaray. Nevertheless, by comparing the little-known Kofman style of mimesis with the much-discussed Irigarayan politics of mimesis, we are better able to identify the strange interventions practiced by Kofman.

Reappropriation

Much has been written about Irigaray and her projects of mimesis. In order to evoke concepts of femininity excluded from culture and theory, she mimics conventional concepts of femininity so as to displace them:

> One must assume the feminine role deliberately. Which means already to convert a form of subordination into an affirmation, and thus to begin to thwart it . . . To play with mimesis is thus, for a woman, to try to recover the place of her exploitation by discourse, without allowing herself to be simply reduced to it. It means to resubmit herself . . . to ideas about herself, that are elaborated in/by a masculine logic, but so as to make "visible," by an effect of playful repetition, what was supposed to remain invisible.[15]

Debate has turned on whether this is a prudent project. Some critics have suggested that Irigaray's repetition of conventional tropes of femininity simply reinforce those tropes. As Margaret Whitford points out, "It is this deliberate mimetic assumption of male metaphors, male images of the feminine which has led to accusations of essentialism and logocentrism" (*Irigaray*, 71). But Whitford also points out that "one cannot alter symbolic meanings by *fiat;* one cannot simply step outside phallogocentrism"(*Irigaray*, 70). What tools are at Irigaray's disposal to "thwart the feminine role"? Irigaray cannot simply invent new feminine roles out of thin air, and for this reason she returns to many of the conventional associations of femininity, such as matter, the bodily, the maternal, fluidity, and formless-

ness. To do so deliberately is a different project, she argues, from being subordinated to conventional representations of femininity: it is an affirmative
and subversive resistance. Woman is not reducible to those roles if she is
deliberately mimicking them. Women's excess to a conventional feminine
mimicry is underlined by their ability to undertake playful repetition. Furthermore, Irigaray argues that the dependence of masculine identity on
femininity-as-other is culturally invisible. Therefore, she claims that a subversive function is served by a mimesis of conventional femininity. For
women to mimic femininity deliberately is a means of demonstrating that
women are always mimicking femininity: they are always produced and
producing themselves in accordance with conventional tropes of femininity. To render this visible is, by Irigaray's argument, subversive because it
demonstrates that women, by the very fact of their mimicry, always necessarily resist or exceed their role as other to masculinity. Therefore, *playing*
with mimesis, suggests Irigaray:

> also means "to unveil" the fact that, if women are such good mimics, is be-
> cause they are not simply resorbed in this function. *They also remain else-
> where:* another case of the persistence of "matter". . . . [I]f women can play
> with mimesis, it is because they are capable of bringing new nourishment
> to its operation. Because they have always nourished this operation? (*This
> Sex,* 76)

The outlines of this project of displacing mimesis are less abstract when
seen in the context of a specific intervention into a philosophical account of
femininity. The first section in Irigaray's work on Nietzsche, *Marine Lover,*
reiterates her project of mimicry and the steps laid out in interviews from
which the above comments are drawn. Irigaray reconstructs the figure of
femininity such as she takes it to operate in the Nietzschean corpus. In a
project of mimesis, we see Irigaray adopt the voice of the feminine as she
has reconstructed it, in order to interrogate and resist Nietzsche. Adopting
this voice, we see Irigaray claim of the Nietzschean figures of women that
they are cut to reflect desirable images of a masculine self. Says Irigaray as
the feminine speaker, addressing herself to Nietzsche:

> Either you seize hold of me or you throw me away, but always according
> to your whim of the moment. I am good or bad according to your latest
> good or evil. Muse or fallen angel to suit the needs of your most recent
> notion.[16]

Says the feminine speaker to Nietzsche, "Doesn't your gaze reduce me to
your images or illusions" (*Marine,* 31)? And the trope of mimicry is introduced: where in "Power of Discourse" we are told that women "are such

good mimics," (*This Sex*, 76); in *Marine Lover* the feminine speaker asks, "Is this not the worst reversal of all, to make me mimic your mirages" (*Marine*, 31)? Irigaray, therefore, uses feminine mimicry to articulate the mimic's excess to that enactment of femininity. Embodying the voice of the mimic, Irigaray embodies the voice of she who is the remainder to her own performance of masculine mirages of femininity. In using the phrase, "to make me mimic your mirages," a voice is inserted of she who is more than her mimicry. Irigaray tries to reinsert and then expand on this concept of the feminine who can be seen as "remainder." A familiar gesture is Irigaray's use of the concept of "reduction." If the feminine is represented as other-to-the-masculine, the representation is limited and reductive. Stating, therefore, that the feminine has been "reduced" to this role, Irigaray is able to embody the voice of the feminine who could be understood as "having been" reduced.

The gesture is less straightforward than it seems. Rather than supposing there is a coherent identity to a true femininity underneath false phallocentric distortions, Irigaray asks, If women mimic, are shaped and shape themselves, could we not suppose that all of the possibilities for women are not exhausted in these shapings? As a device, she attempts to speak as the feminine exceeding these shapings within a Nietzschean text. This is not asserting a truth to the feminine.

Given that women are asked to "reflect" desirable images, Irigaray uses the concept of a mirror to underscore the concept of women exceeding these reflections. There must, she proposes, be a material element to the mirror out of which is constituted a reflecting surface. Again, Irigaray attempts to speak "as" or from the position of this "material" element, in a resistance to the Nietzschean references to femininity:

> You had fashioned me into a mirror but . . . I have washed off your masks and make up, scrubbed away your multicolored projections and designs, stripped off your veils and wraps. (*Marine*, 4)

Irigaray's embodiment of the feminine, for example of the "me" who has been "made to mimic" or the "me" who scrubs away the projections, is not an attempt to suggest that there is some sort of locatable, authentic feminine identity distinct from Nietzschean tropes for women. Rather, Irigaray would have it that the Nietzschean tropes themselves serve as an indirect affirmation of excess or remainder to those tropes. It is in this sense that Irigaray both occupies and resists Nietzsche. Nietzsche's requirement of mimicry from women affirms that they must exceed the mimicry in question. This is a statement about the logic of Nietzsche's demand, not about some "truth" to women's identity. In occupying the speaking voice of the feminine "me," Irigaray speaks, not from the place of feminine truth but from the place of excess opened up by Nietzsche's demand. Thus, one sees the connection between Irigaray's assertion that there is a phallocentric demand for feminine mimicry and her attempt to deliberately mimic the feminine by assuming a "suppressed" feminine voice.

So, it is through (re)appropriating this voice that Irigaray resists Nietzsche by asserting that what is required within the Nietzschean corpus is a feminine that reflects desirable images of masculinity:

> Of course it's true that she can send you back the melancholy effects of your self-marriage. But isn't this a strange love you are preaching: love for a looking glass eternally set opposite you. (*Marine,* 32–33)

She suggests that this demand reflects an economy of sameness also seen in the Nietzschean concept of eternal recurrence. Thus, Irigaray suggests to Nietzsche, "For you pleasure is the return of the same" (*Marine,* 10). Therefore he suppresses concepts of sexual difference, and Irigaray accordingly cautions Nietzsche about the need to affirm relations with a feminine other in terms of difference:

> Your dawn harbors degeneracy and decline if you . . . refuse to wed that other (woman) as a stranger. (*Marine,* 61)

Nietzsche fails to relate to the feminine as strange, other, nonrelational. This failure is not mitigated by the Nietzschean images of femininity in terms of enigma and distance. Like Kofman, Irigaray takes the trope of "distance" to amount to a desire to keep the feminine at a distance, rather than engaging with women in terms of sexual difference.

This leads to an indictment of expressions of otherness in Nietzsche's work in general. Nietzsche does speak of his requirement for a worthy enemy and a good friend and of the ideal of two subjects who heighten each other's forces in their encounter. This might seem to be a positive affirmation of alterity: of the encounter between two equal but different selves. But, says Irigaray, "your search for a rival who can match up to you, . . . the urge to fight on equal terms" is not this another manifestation of the hope that "someone *like yourself* turns up . . . someone other, and yet like, a faithful mirror" (*Marine,* 66; my emphasis). Here Irigaray challenges the status of the other with whom Nietzsche wants to engage. Nietzsche expresses the need for engagement with the worthy other. Still, his ideal is not, she suggests, an encounter with the other as foreign, strange, but as "like myself"—thus not really other but same. Just as the role of the feminine is to serve as mirror to the (masculine) self, Irigaray suggests that in general, ideals of alterity, of encounters between different selves, which Nietzsche paints in the glorious terms of the friend as worthy enemy, is really, again, no more than the desire for a mirror. The other, suggests Irigaray, in the Nietzschean corpus "has no role except as counterweight or balance arm between you and yourself" (*Marine*, 73).

Adopting the voice of the Nietzschean feminine, Irigaray converts the voice into one that would resist the demands made on her by Nietzsche and who would promote an ethos of the encounter between sexually different subjects. Asks this voice, "Why are we not, the one for the other, a resource of life and air?" (*Marine*, 31). For such an encounter to take place, the feminine voice converted into voice of resistance admonishes, "You will hear nothing of women as long [as] you are bending them thus to your will . . . you will never have pleasure (jouir) in woman . . . If you insist to making her a stage in your process" (*Marine*, 39).

This, then, is an exemplary instance of Irigaray's project of mimesis. She draws on her own diagnosis that woman is being asked to play the role of man's other, to locate a rhetorical point of excess to the performance. Personifying that voice of a feminine identity who performs for Nietzsche, Irigaray evokes the performer's resistance:

> I shall escape a mask custom-made to beguile you. For smothering myself in such vain show repels me. (*Marine*, 59)

> I am no longer the lining to your coat, your—faithful—understudy. (*Marine*, 4)

Irigaray identifies with and mimics the feminine voice as it is evoked in Nietzsche's work. But the project is clearly feminist and political. It resists the phallocentric casting of femininity and does so according to a politics that would articulate resistance while avoiding assertions about the truth of the feminine.

Appropriate Readings

Kofman never commented on Irigaray's interpretation of Nietzsche. Her criticisms of Irigaray are directed at the possibility that the latter overly stabilizes Freud's network of thoughts into a solidified line, so as to expose its phallocentrism. Irigaray is trying too hard to catch Freud out, excessively foregrounding one tendency in Freud's texts as the real meaning of the text and underemphasizing Freud's textual heterogeneity. Irigaray's reading, therefore, fails to reconstruct the complex, unstable lines of Freudian argument concerning femininity, because her critique depends on a preliminary work of exaggerated textual stabilization. What is odd is that Kofman's commitment to emphasizing Freud's plural voices outweighs her considerable points of agreement with Irigaray.

To interrogate the political impetus of Kofman's readings, one must therefore interrogate the stakes of her insistence on textual heterogeneity. For Kofman, textual heterogeneity is the inescapable mark of the fact that the philosopher writes in the ambivalent play between systematicity, and what she designates as his or her sexual positioning, rationality, and the philosopher's drives, instincts, body, passions:

> Even in a philosophical text, a so-called rational and systematic text, independent of all empirical and pathological subjectivity, and therefore of sexuality, it isn't possible to separate the text from the sexual positioning of its author.[17]

An appropriate reading of a philosophical text attends to its necessary expression of passion and desire, ambivalent identifications and ambivalent claims, textual levels that produce unstable and inconsistent texts. Though Irigaray is acutely attentive to Freud's inconstancies, inconsistencies, passions, and desires, Kofman's concern is that Irigaray can only locate these in a mode of reading *against the grain of the text*. Kofman places the emphasis on the fact the grain of a text is multiple and ambivalent and is therefore unimpressed with the idea that reading Freud's multiple voices is inevitably to read against Freud.

To what danger is Irigaray supposed to have succumbed by supposing she is reading Freud *against* Freud? Perhaps the manner of her unveiling of Freud's impropriety—his inconsistent voices—reinforces the idea that the proper text would be stable, consistent, not ridden with contradictory desires. When Irigaray takes herself to be reading "against Freud," exposing what she takes to be his underbelly, she underemphasizes the way in which all texts are heterogeneous, multiple, dehiscent. For Kofman, the politics of emphasizing the heterogeneity of all philosophical texts is crucial and must accompany the exposure of Freud's phallocentrism.

I have asked what the politics are of this emphasis of his textual complexity. If not clearly feminist, is it at least a subversive enactment of philosophy? Should Kofman's work be interpreted as a project of subversion of philosophy? Yes, suggests Ann Smock, because of Kofman's demonstration of how "the greatest thinkers are led all unknowingly by the very drives and instincts from which they believe their thought to be utterly independent."[18] In the words of Kofman,

> Haven't we . . . always known that a writer writes with their blood? Hasn't an entire tradition opposed philosophy to literature under the pretext that the former is produced independently of the life of the philosopher?[19]

Kofman's intervention into the history of philosophy is to expose its unspoken debts to the embodiment, the life of the philosopher. If Comte manages to construct an early positivist system, she argues, it is in interconnection with his repression of the feminine. Rousseau's political philosophy, which relegates women to a private sphere crucial to the good operation of the public sphere, is not disconnected from his sexual economy in which there is a desire both to idolize women and to keep them at a distance. And, according to Kofman, Kant's sexual economy inaugurates his ethics.[20]

About one-third of Kofman's corpus consists of critical readings directed at a series of philosophers who might pretend that their theory transcends or offers some escape from the domain of the body and the passions, such as Comte and Kant. Kofman attempts to subvert the pretensions of these philosophers through readings that constitute an overall claim that no philosophical position can be divorced from its sexual economy.[21] As Kofman explains the genesis of her project:

> I came to the conclusion . . . on the basis of my work on Auguste Comte, that there is no philosophical thought which is separable from a certain sexual position. I then undertook the same kind of interpretation of Kant and Rousseau . . . in *Le Respect de femmes*. ("Interview," 12)

We have seen that the series of Kant, Comte, Rousseau, and others consists of those who might hope, through the device of philosophy, to divorce themselves from their sexual economy. What then of her readings of Derrida, Freud, and Nietzsche? These figures do not represent to Kofman philosophers with such pretensions. Kofman particularly figures these three as avowing the association between life, body, and text, and a theorization of life and body as text.

For example, she presents us with the Freud, who "compares the great social productions of art, religion, and philosophy to the neuroses . . . establish[ing] relations of one-to-one correspondence between the different social productions and the different mental illnesses which echo them. . . . [T]he totality of productions are but different dialects of a single language: that of the unconscious. . . . Art, religion, and philosophy . . . are social solutions that spare the artist, the religious man, and the philosopher the corresponding neurosis from which he was 'not far removed.' "[22] In other words, Freud is not committed to a life/work dichotomy, and indeed, agrees that systematic philosophy has parallels with paranoiac psychic structures.

The stakes of reading the philosopher's work in terms of his sexual economy must be different in the context of figures such as Freud and Nietzsche, who do not disavow such a connection. How then should we interpret Kofman's philosophical project in relation to such figures? In *Camera Obscura* and elsewhere Kofman also accuses Nietzsche of sharing a sexual economy that can be likened to that of Rousseau, a castration anxiety in which one desires, but fears to look upon, the woman (mother).[23] Kofman locates phallocentrism in Nietzsche's work as in that of Rousseau. And as before, her suspicion is that phallocentric representations of women indicate more general weak spots in the philosopher's argument. Nietzsche's antimetaphysical position is that no truth remains a truth without its veil; there are, in other words, no truths behind veils. However, Kofman reads Nietzsche's position on women as symptomatic of a possible return of conventional concepts of truth. Thus the importance of the Baubô chapter in *Nietzsche et la scène philosophique,* in which Kofman interrogates Nietzsche's figures of women.[24] Her aim is not to denounce misogyny as such, but to interrogate the presence of fetishism in Nietzsche's textual, sexual economy. A fetishist economy, she argues, indicates a reemergence of a metaphysical concept of truth in Nietzsche's work.

However literally we wish to take the suggestion that Comte, Rousseau, and others are paranoiac, melancholic, and fetishist, Kofman's readings are intended as subversive. Traditional metaphysical philosophy has the pretension to be free of neurosis, psychosis, and perversion. But, argues Kofman, such domains articulate themselves in the philosopher's position on women. And, more strongly still, perhaps the metaphysics can't be articulated without the position on women and the feminine ("Interview," 13–14).

It's because of their expression of the drives of the body that Kofman argues that texts are complex and heterogeneous, riddled with multiple lines. It may well be in the interests of a feminist approach to the history of philosophy to hold out for a textual reading of a given philosopher in these terms. Philosophy that avows the debt to the body may not be a transparently feminist enactment of philosophy, but its importance can be seen in Kofman's demonstration that the denial of that debt tends to be accompanied by an overt marginalization of femininity in that same text.

What is remarkable is that Kofman makes these points through an occupation of the works of Freud and Nietzsche, which both resists their accounts of femininity while affirming and identifying with their analyses of the philosopher's debt to the body. In constructing her own critical persona, Kofman leaves fluid the boundaries between it and the Freudian and Nietzschean critical personae. Again, the politics of this methodology remain ambiguous. Why identify with figures whose phallocentrism one has criticized?

Kofman on Nietzsche

Comparing the readings of Irigaray and Kofman of Freud and Nietzsche, one more clearly dislodges the nature of Kofman's reading as subversive intervention. Although Kofman did not respond to Irigaray's interpretation of Nietzsche, an exchange between their interventions into Nietzsche can be staged. One major difference between Irigaray and Kofman in their readings of Freud is that whereas Irigaray attempts a subversion of Freud's phallocentrism, Kofman's critical intervention into Freud's work is synthesized with her identification with Freud. Where Irigaray identifies with the feminine appropriated by Nietzsche, Kofman identifies with Nietzsche himself. Irigaray reappropriates the Nietzschean feminine so as to personify it in resistant fashion. Yet Kofman disappropriates herself in favor of a personification of Nietzsche. I turn, then, to Kofman's last major work, the most dramatically identificatory of her projects on Nietzsche.

In 1992 and 1993, Kofman published *Explosion I* and *II*, a 770-page monument to, and occupation of, Nietzsche's *Ecce Homo*. With this long project, Kofman concludes that she has become one of Nietzsche's children (*Explosion II*, 371). She has, she declares, followed Nietzsche step by step, and so she asks:

> Has one properly understood Nietzsche? . . . at any rate, one will have loved him, one will have been with him symbiotically to the point of being confused with him. (*Explosion II*, 371)

From her earliest work on Nietzsche, in the first pages of *Nietzsche and Metaphor*, Kofman had asked what it would mean to be faithful to Nietzsche.[25] As Duncan Large writes in introducing that work, "Her aim is to give a 'faithfully' Nietzschean reading of Nietzsche."[26] It is the issue of fidelity that is particularly foreign to the Irigarayan project of textual occupation. And on first glance, Kofman will seem to have been assiduously faithful throughout her career to Nietzsche, returning to him repeatedly in commentary (in *Nietzsche and Metaphor, Nietzsche et la scène philosophique, Le mépris des juifs,* and the two *Explosion* volumes) and in the style of that commentary: a study of Nietzsche and his account of metaphor; a study of Nietzsche on "the philosophers" ; a defense of Nietzsche against charges of anti-Semitism, the monument to *Ecce Homo*. Yet the bemused reception by certain critics of *Nietzsche and Metaphor* alone should alert us to the misleading nature of Kofman's fidelity, because it is precisely on the grounds of infidelity that critics tend to tax Kofman. In the most agitated of these readings, for example, one critic accuses Kofman precisely of everything from inaccurate citation of Nietzsche, mistranslation, omission of passages that contradict her own argument, and even of "what Nietzsche would have called interpretive 'dishonesty'" by translating words misleadingly so that they further her own exegesis, leaving interpretations untrue to Nietzsche's images.[27] As we hear the Sarah Kofman as painted by Richard Weisberg, I think of the figure of Luce Irigaray as scathingly painted by Sarah Kofman: that poor translator, selective citer, and so forth. How resoundingly Kofman speaks in the name of the standards of faithful citation and translation, while thwarting and undermining those standards as well. Kofman's work speaks and acts under the sign of fidelity while constituting the challenge to that sign.

Kofman may espouse fidelity to Freud, but who does she think "Freud" is? If one turns to *The Enigma of Woman,* in which Kofman, stinging on the subject of Irigaray's "inappropriate" appropriation of Freud, speaks in the name of fidelity to Freud, we find, not conventional faithful commentary on Freud, but a Freud very lightly synthesized with Nietzsche. For example, Freud, Kofman suggests, may well consider that the enigma of femininity is a masculine concern, but he need not be condemned on this basis.

> One might interpret that gesture, indeed, in a Nietzschean sense: to speak of a riddle of femininity and to try to solve that riddle are a strictly masculine enterprise; women are not concerned with Truth, they are profoundly skeptical; they know perfectly well that there is no such thing as "truth." (*Enigma,* 104–5)

Furthermore, if we turn back again to the early Nietzschean works, we find a Nietzsche becoming Freud. Kofman discusses metaphor in terms of Freudian concepts of repression (*Metaphor,* 35) and sublimation (*Metaphor,* 169 n. 16) and claims that Nietzsche's discussion of dreams is "very close to Freud's" (*Metaphor,* 170 n. 17). She discusses the Nietzschean concept of benefiting from fictions in terms of the Freudian concept of benefiting from illness, and in discussing the forgetting of metaphor, Kofman will declare, "Freudian concepts are essential here" (*Metaphor,* 76, 157 n. 13). In *Nietzsche et la scène philosophique,* Kofman asks if Nietzsche's notion of fetishism is not close to that of Freud (*Nietzsche,* 176). "Well before Freud," we are told, "many passages in Freud do invoke the notion of castration" (*Nietzsche,* 176). Noticeably, Kofman tends to invoke the parallel with Freud to defend Nietzsche—or vice versa—against certain otherwise inevitable accusations. Above we have seen that it is Freud's proximity to Nietzsche that suggests we should not "condemn" him for his positing of the enigma of woman as a masculine preoccupation. In *Nietzsche et la scène philosophique,* we see the reverse gesture operate in favor of Nietzsche:

> Let us not then rush headlong to "decide" this question and pronounce Nietzsche "misogynist." Rather we must weave a cloth from both theological perversion and the veils whose reality one cannot or will not see, a

reality which one has a reason to hide. Freud, himself, taught that women invented cloth, by which this dissimulation operates. And Freud, again, called attention to the importance of clothes for fetishism, especially the undergarments of a beloved woman. (*Nietzsche,* 180)

Kofman's interweaving of texts and corpuses can involve anything from rendering Nietzsche and Freud parallel or interchangeable figures, locating points at which they concur or differ, locating apparently echoing concepts, proposing how Nietzsche might respond to Freud, or offering a "psycho-analytic" interpretation of Nietzsche.

The most regular technique used by Kofman is this cross-fertilization of material by Freud, Nietzsche, and also Derrida. When interpreting Nietzsche, Kofman cannot refrain from her references to Freud. Her work on Freud is marked by her tenacious fidelity to Nietzsche. The constant in Kofman's work is not fidelity but the refusal to treat philosophical corpuses as homogenous, stable or self-enclosed entities. Kofman plays with a deployment of authors amidst each other. Where Kofman is tenaciously faithful to Freud, she is tenaciously faithful to the multiple Freudian voices she locates. Kofman will not read Freud without unleashing multiple Freudian voices against each other, will not read Freud without unleashing Nietzsche amongst Freudian concepts, and will not read Nietzsche without synthesis with Freud.

Turning to *Explosion I* and *II,* on the one hand we are confronted with a work of grandiose fidelity to Nietzsche. Yet the work is a monument not to Nietzsche but to an appropriation of Nietzsche for the purposes of cross-fertilization: with literary figures (Nerval, Hoffman), with philosophers (Plato, Rousseau), with Freud and Derrida, with paintings by Bosch, with Nietzsche's letters throughout his life from early childhood onwards, and so on. True to the cross-fertilization with Freud, the *Explosion* volumes conclude with a reference to the death of Nietzsche's little brother, the proposal that the death corresponded to Nietzsche's death wish, an interpretation of a dream recounted by Nietzsche, the relationship this may have had with his madness. Perhaps the missing brother is the missing counterpart Nietzsche craved, suggests Kofman. Thus Kofman's reading of Nietzsche concludes again with a "becoming-Freud" on the part of Kofman. As she says herself, reading Freud, she has read him with a Nietzschean ear; while reading Nietzsche, she reads him with a Freudian ear:

Perhaps this is what constitutes the specificity of my reading: at the closest proximity to Nietzsche I cross-fertilise and lightly displace him thanks to my Freudian ear. (*Explosion II,* 372)

While Kofman rarely discussed her methodology, she does so at the conclusion of *Explosion II*. Freud and Nietzsche, she explains, have been for her

the two rival "geniuses" I always needed to hold together so that neither held sway definitively over the other nor over "me." Endlessly playing the one and the other and the one against the other in "me" I prevent both from having the upper hand. (*Explosion II*, 372)

These comments clarify the stakes of Kofman's light displacement of Nietzsche and Freud. Kofman's readings are a styling of self whose purpose is to break down the concept of the unified critical self. Kofman reads Nietzsche and Freud in a becoming-Nietzsche-and-Freud, acquiring Freudian and Nietzschean "ears," to use one of her metaphors, or becoming their "child," to use another.

So, despite the mask of faithful reader adopted by Kofman when she criticizes Irigaray, Kofman and Irigaray can be distinguished not in terms of fidelity versus intervention and appropriation, but in terms of their different variations on intervention and appropriation. Irigaray isolates, occupies, and implodes so as to reappropriate the Nietzschean account of the feminine. For Kofman, by contrast, the stakes are whether, in an engagement with a particular text, both she and the text alter in the encounter. For example, she explains that she never offered a reading of Heidegger precisely because she never changed nor was changed by Heidegger in her engagement with him ("Apprendre," 7). By contrast, her own summary of her reading of Nietzsche is precisely that in a symbiosis with him, she and Nietzsche ceaselessly cross-fertilized each other. Notice the depersonalized voice she uses to declare in reference to herself, "One has been symbiotically united with him, to the point of being confusable with him, one has been continuously cross-fertilised by him while trying also, a little, to cross-fertilise him in return" (*Explosion II*, 371).

No Propriety: Kofman and Irigaray

Where Irigaray's project is the identification with and appropriation of the Nietzschean feminine, Kofman's project is an identification with Nietzsche that calls into question the boundaries between Freud, Nietzsche, and Kofman. When Kofman reads Nietzsche, are there entirely discrete boundaries between the two? When Kofman reads Nietzsche and Freud, will not Kofman become partly Nietzsche, partly Freud? Is Kofman not partly a composite of all she has read? Is Kofman not a company or corporation of "three+n authors, what Derrida jokingly calls a "sarl"?[28] Her autobiography, she declares, would be no more than an assemblage of citations of diverse authors ("Apprendre," 7). Where, then, are the boundaries between Kofman and Nietzsche? When Kofman reads Nietzsche, is Nietzsche not then going to become partly Freud; the Freud of Kofman's reading? Speaking in the name of fidelity, Kofman breaks down the boundaries between the different figures to whom one would be faithful. Kofman's work of apparent fidelity is a work of appropriation and intervention, which far from respecting the proper boundaries of texts, calls into question the possibility of proper boundaries.

Kofman so destabilizes the concept of the unified critical self "Kofman" that she declares herself to be a composite of Freud, Nietzsche, and other figures she has identified with and about whom she has written. She does not hesitate to disappropriate herself in the sense of seeing herself as no "more" than the figures of which she is a composite. She also does not hesitate to disappropriate herself by attributing to the philosophers she analyzes the textual complexity she locates. Yet she is so severe with Irigaray for her appropriation of Freud's textual complexity to herself. It might seem as if, according to Kofman's practice of disappropriation, the devaluation of Irigarayan "appropriation" is only to be expected. What is unusual in this context is Kofman's adherence to an ethos of the property of the critical self. We see this adherence in the very notion that Freud's complexity has been appropriated by Irigaray. Kofman destabilizes the integrity of one critical self "Kofman," all the while affirming the integrity of the critical self "Freud." We do not see this affirmation where Kofman directly discusses Freud, for where she does we are presented with a complex, polyvocal, and textually self-conflicting Freud. But where we see the challenge to Irigaray in the name of demarcating "who" is doing the deconstructing, we do see a reinvocation of boundary lines between texts, the deconstructor and deconstructed, reader and author. And it is Kofman's work that allows us to question her own invocation of these boundary lines.

Although Kofman is sometimes thought of as the mere commentator or the overly faithful reader, her corpus stages an extremely complex styling of critical personae and intertextuality. In reading "Freud," "Nietzsche," and so forth, Kofman becomes Freud or Nietzsche. This is disappropriation, but not simply so, for the figures in whose names she disappropriates herself are figures already become Kofman, sometimes on grand scale, as in *Explosion I* and *II*. The concept of appropriation implies critical boundaries between appropriator and the appropriated object, between reader and text read, between deconstructor and deconstructed, between Nietzsche, Freud, Kofman, and/or Irigaray, and it is precisely these boundaries that are challenged by Kofman.

The criticisms of Derrida and Irigaray by Paul de Man and Kofman are erroneous in suggesting the possibility of neat boundaries between the work a text does "alone" and the intervention rendered by a deconstructive reading. They are also surprising, because they are made by critics whose work challenges these boundaries. But, from another perspective, the criticisms aptly summarize the Derridean and Irigarayan projects. Of course these projects are appropriations of the texts in question. What is at stake in deconstructive reading—and in all reading—is appropriation: the failure to secure proper boundaries between text and reader. Reading, one identifies, attributes to the reader what is found in the text, or attributes to the text what one reads into to it. One alters, incorporating fragments of voice, tone, persona, standpoint, perspective. Reader and text alter each other in the disappropriation of the reader and the appropriation of the text. To suppose that Derrida and Irigaray have *mis*appropriated Nietzsche and Freud is to presuppose that we can keep an entirely secure grip on the differences between Rousseau and Derrida's reading of Rousseau, Freud, and Irigaray's reading of Freud—and that Derrida and Irigaray should have kept such a grip. The fact that reading is always appropriation renders far more unstable than the criticisms directed at Derrida and Irigaray would suggest from the category of a misappropriative reading.

I have shifted the discussion from the question of the ethical reading (in terms of which Kofman challenged Irigaray) to the question of the political reading (in terms of which Kofman herself has been challenged). Kofman challenges Irigaray for not keeping the boundaries between "Freud" and "Irigaray" distinct. But it is Kofman who takes as her project a deliberate blurring of the boundaries between "Freud" and "Kofman." The politics of Irigaray's reading practice are very clear. Irigaray's is an identifiably feminist reading that resists the tropes for women to be found in theorists such as Nietzsche and Freud. By comparison, the politics of Kofman's reading practice have appeared less clear. Although both theorists analyze the phallocentrism of Freud and Nietzsche, the reader is left wondering if Kofman's relationship to Nietzsche and Freud is more conservative than that of Irigaray. Irigaray is inserting a definitive, markedly parrying voice into Freud's and Nietzsche's texts, and above all, is attempting to embody the feminine foreclosed by Nietzsche and Freud. We are quite clear about what Irigaray is doing. What is Kofman doing? Not only does she seem to halt her analysis of phallocentrism, not attempting a project of resistance, but at times she merges with Nietzsche and Freud to the point where she ostensibly loses her grip on herself. What is subversive about the project is its destabilization of the ideals of textual control, homogeneity and systematicity, rationalism, and rational transcendence of the drives, which philosophers have traditionally taken to be most dear.

Certainly, it is disturbing that the subtle differences from Irigaray on the issue of whether Freud's complexity should be understood as "part" of his textual heterogeneity are taken by Kofman to be more pressing than their shared demonstration of Freud's phallocentrism. One strategy for clarifying Kofman's contribution, I am suggesting, is to ask what she offers to our evaluation of Irigaray's interventions into the history of philosophy. Interpretation of Kofman's work is at an early stage. An assessment of its value should direct attention to the weight that it attributes to the issue of emphasizing the heterogeneity and sexual position of a philosophical text, the absence of the unified voice of any philosopher, and the lack of firm borders between texts. Because Kofman's relationship to feminism was ambivalent, this makes all the more difficult the assessment of her work as "feminist enactment of philosophy." One course to follow is to ask how we might usefully reconsider Irigaray's work through the lens of Kofman's looking glasses.

Irigaray and Propriety

Irigaray occupies philosophical texts so as to resist and subvert those texts. For all that she occupies, appropriates, mimics, and embodies a given philosophical voice such as that of Freud and Nietzsche, one can immediately identify her resistance to their philosophical texts. One might say that this is precisely the strength of the work: that it allows for the insertion of the resistant feminine voice, without compromising the integrity of that voice in relation to the text. The strength of Irigaray's political project, her feminist enactment of philosophy, is that she has found a means to navigate her way so intimately through the texts she would resist, without compromising herself. It is also important that Irigaray's practice of mimicry does not presuppose safe boundaries between the femininity mimicked and the femininity that Irigaray takes to be resistant. She does not attempt to evoke some concept of femininity sanitized of all phallocentric connotations. Irigaray understands full well that the project of articulating a resistant, hypothetical, foreclosed femininity cannot be entirely pure of the phallocentric images of femininity it would resist. Her attempt to achieve the former through a mimicking, appropriating occupation of the latter acknowledges this.

I have suggested that Irigaray renders deliberately unstable the boundaries between her resistant, mimicking femininity and the conventional femininity it mimics. Nevertheless, the following suggestion might have come from Kofman. In reading Irigaray, are we still left too confident of the stable boundaries between "Nietzsche," "Freud," and "Irigaray?" To what extent is Irigaray prepared to acknowledge the risk of "becoming" Freud, "becoming Nietzsche," the fact of herself as the *sarl?* There is an inevitable identificatory/compromising/transformative mimicry in all writing, and it may be that Kofman's writing renders this more successfully explicit. From this perspective, Irigaray's playful occupation of Freud might even be too safe. Is Irigaray supposing in her methodology that her politics of overt, resistant intervention does safeguard her from identification, disappropriation, hysteria? Could Irigaray learn from Kofman's attempt to avow the indeterminacy of these boundaries? In Kofman's work, disappropriation is complexly interwoven with appropriation. Kofman's becoming-Nietzsche will always incorporate the textual work of asserting a Nietzsche already become Kofman. She might be lost in a disconcerting ambiguity of borderlines with Nietzsche, a disappropriation of self. But we might conclude that in Irigaray's occupation of Nietzsche, the identity of the latter is not sufficiently put into question.

I would add Kofman to a genre of feminist philosophers who have dislodged phallocentric philosophers' debts to their figurings of the feminine, but who have avoided the strategy of refiguring the feminine in favor of the strategy of refiguring philosophy. Where mind/body and reason/emotion oppositions have been too complicit with gender symbolism, Lloyd and Gatens have avoided the strategy of refiguring gender symbolism in favor of a strategy that demonstrates the proximity of philosophical reason with the emotions and passions, and of mind with body. Where philosophical argument has been considered autonomous of its metaphorical content and has therefore not seriously considered its own deployment of gendered metaphors, Le Doeuff has argued for a refiguring of metaphor with a more significant component of philosophical argument than is often acknowledged.[29] These are all feminist enactments of philosophy. But to understand them as such, one needs to recall the implicit sexual symbolism that accompanies each of these dualisms because it may not always be clear at first glance why revaluing the proximity of mind with body, reason with the passions, and argument with metaphor are feminist gestures. Kofman's strategy of demonstrating that philosophical reason is in close proximity with the sexual positioning of the philosopher in question is a parallel gesture. To understand this is a feminist enactment by a French philosopher, one needs to return to Kofman's own position that philosophy's denial that its major figures enact their sexual positions leads to the failure to recognize how these figures philosophically stage the feminine.

To recognize this staging, Kofman has argued that we need to read philosophical texts for their heterogeneity, the interplay of reasoned argument and sexual positioning. This leads Kofman to question, if erroneously, feminist theorists she believes downplay this heterogeneity. Irigaray is considered to be one such candidate, although Irigaray's own deconstructive and psychoanalytic readings of philosophers render this a surprising accusation. Nevertheless, Kofman believes that the way in which Irigaray reads Freud downplays the constant presence of diverse textual refrains in philosophical texts. For Kofman, Irigaray reinforces the idea that Freud's text is aberrant, that it may be "exposed" or "unveiled" for containing submerged textual elements that may be thrown back at the text to defeat it. As Schneider recounts the objection, Irigaray has too much taken the tone of exposing Freud *in flagrante delicto* ("Le regard," 40). The difference between Kofman's and Irigaray's positions on Freud usefully demonstrates the overriding importance Kofman wishes to give the recognition of the plural elements and heterogeneity of all philosophical texts, the multiple forces at work in them. Only through such an approach, she suggests, will we read these texts for their sexual positionings. But here is Kofman's curious suggestion. Only if the reader (Kofman) is prepared to risk greater identification and blurring with the author in question (Freud, Nietzsche) than does Irigaray, and an avowal of and engagement with that identification, will she be in a position to read adequately for the philosopher's textual heterogeneity.

Ecce Mulier? Disappropriation and Appropriation

What is striking in the careers of both Kofman and Irigaray is the way in which both philosophers moved toward an implosion of their own tropes of appropriation and disappropriation in relation to the philosophers they analyze. Kofman's reading of Nietzsche in the *Explosion* volumes is a stupendous blowup of the identities of Kofman, Nietzsche, and the figures with whom Nietzsche identifies. Kofman so reads the thematic of identification *into* Nietzsche: Nietzsche would be primarily, for Kofman, that author who repeatedly identifies with imaginary genealogies and heredities, with figures such as Socrates, Christ, Napoleon, Schopenhauer, and Wagner. That is Nietzsche, but it is also very much Kofman's Nietzsche. At the end of *Explosion II,* Kofman declares that Freud and Nietzsche have been for her what Wagner and Schopenhauer were for Nietzsche: identificatory figures. Nietzsche is to Kofman then what Wagner was to Schopenhauer, and Kofman aligns herself as the child of Nietzsche. Appropriation and disappropriation break down here. Kofman disappropriates by naming herself the child. Yet, Kofman has had to so appropriate in constructing the primarily identificatory Nietzsche (Nietzsche-as-Kofman) in favor of whom she disappropriates herself, rendering *Explosion* a 780-page work of disappropriation-appropriation.

Consider against this backdrop the movement in Irigaray's work from *Marine Lover* to the short, disturbing piece "Ecce Mulier." In *Marine Lover,* Irigaray reappropriates figures of femininity from Nietzsche's work so as to cast the voice of resistance and excess within the Nietzschean corpus. However, in "Ecce Mulier," Irigaray identifies not with the appropriated feminine in Nietzsche's works, but with Nietzsche himself. In this sense, "Ecce Mulier" must be the Irigarayan piece closest as a project to Kofman's identificatory, disappropriative stylings of self.

Identifying with the Nietzsche of *Ecce Homo,* Irigaray presents herself as a singular figure who respires fresh air, who indicts decadence, the "falsely democratic," and the journalistic culture, who unveils a horizon for a humanity to whom she brings "strange new truths." The style of the piece repeats the isolated, impassioned, earnest, self-conviction of Nietzsche:

> Many reproach me for not teaching them something. This does not stop them from announcing to me, in the months that follow, that they have discovered love, given birth, written a book, or produced some work of art. But the connection between these events and our meeting is rarely drawn. Nevertheless, some do draw it. Otherwise, I would doubt it myself. . . . Listening to me might leave anyone who has already lost the path of their becoming with empty hands and stomach. But it can be a light for those who walk in the path of fidelity to themselves.[30]

Irigaray repeats, as deliberate stylistic evocations of Nietzsche, a series of references from *Ecce Homo* and from his last letters: the isolation and sense of received ill-treatment, the confiding tone that recounts certain slights, the comparison of the reception of their work in different European countries. Irigaray's bitterness at her reception in French circles equals Nietzsche's bitterness at his reception in German circles. She repeats his excitement about Italy, the trope of one's words being perfectly ripened fruit. She repeats the description of the mixed genealogy inherited from her mother and father, and the description of a fantastic genealogy: Irigaray's Italian heritage equaling Nietzsche's Polish heritage.

Ecce Homo provokes projects of identificatory disappropriation from both Kofman and Irigaray. Yet I think that it produces from Kofman her most-successful project, from Irigaray her least-promising direction. I suggested that, in an initial comparison between the early work of Kofman and Irigaray, Kofman appears to make little intervention, and it is Irigaray who is the more political reader. One can defend Kofman against the criticism that she merely is repeating, identifying. I have argued that her intervention lies in the complexity of her identification with figures such as Nietzsche who she has already mediated, displaced, cross-fertilized, appropriated. Kofman's self-proclaimed disappropriation occurs only in favor of figures ("Nietzsche," "Freud") she has always already appropriated. It is the cleverness, difficulty, and complexity of that work that is highlighted, I think, when Irigaray turns from identifying with the feminine to a simplistic identification with "Nietzsche."

Beyond her analyses of tropes of women and femininity in the history of philosophy, Kofman's work also bears a particular value in playing out breakdown of boundaries between text and reader. I have suggested that this staging of the "becoming-Nietzsche-and-Freud" of Kofman and the "becoming-Kofman" of Nietzsche and Freud should be seen as a particular virtuosity of Kofman's work. This is the alternative to seeing that breakdown as weakness or fault. Kofman's work is not a failure to sustain boundaries, it is a staging of the inevitability of that failure. Kofman's work makes the failure interesting: interesting to track and analyze. Admittedly, this is an interventionist reading of Kofman. One can read Kofman as failing in her renditions of Freud, Nietzsche, and others. There will always be commentators alert to the slightest interpretative inconsistency ready to offer that reading. But reading Kofman as having staged a "becoming what we read," and "it becoming us," is a plausible interpretation. It is, furthermore, a more generative reading than the interpretation that would see Kofman as the mere acolyte of Derrida and Nietzsche.

Are Irigaray's politics too indebted to a Freud presumed very neatly "Freud" and an Irigaray clearly demarcated from Freud, an "Irigaray" who subverts him? Are the boundaries of each too safely secured in Irigaray's work? It is the very risk of Kofman's project that suggests this. To return, then, to Irigaray's becoming-Nietzsche in "Ecce Mulier," I am suggesting that the reading highlights the strength of Kofman's work. In "Ecce Mulier," Irigaray also avows becoming that which she resists, reads, engages in: the figure of Nietzsche. But "Ecce Mulier" fails to challenge the status of the Nietzsche whom Irigaray would become. In Kofman's work, disappropriation is complexly interwoven with appropriation. Kofman's becoming-Nietzsche will always incorporate the textual work of asserting a Nietzsche already become Kofman. In Irigaray's "becoming-Nietzsche," a staging of disappropriation occurs in favor of a "Nietzsche" whose identity is, I suggest, too secure.

Becoming-Imperceptible as a Mode of Self-Presentation: A Feminist Model Drawn from a Deleuzian Line of Flight

TAMSIN LORRAINE

For centuries, stereotypical notions of femininity have supported the confinement of women to a more restricted social role than that of men. Despite the fluctuations in such stereotypes in different times and places, the result has been to define womanhood in a way that was painfully oppressive to many of the women to whom these stereotypes were supposed to apply. The question of how feminists can or should affirm their identities as women as well as their political solidarity with other feminists and yet avoid subjecting one another to oppressive definitions of womanhood is yet to be resolved. Part of the dilemma relates to how we define ourselves as human beings. One dominant norm of what it means to be human is that of a rational, autonomous individual with the clearly defined goals and desires of someone with a coherent, unified sense of self that remains constant over time.[1] Some feminists have argued for a political strategy premised upon sexual difference rather than a fight for equality because they object to promoting women as candidates for attaining a human ideal of mainstream culture that they believe to be inherently masculinist (as well as racist and classist).[2] They claim that the masculinist ideal valorizes self-sufficiency and independence at the expense of the "feminine" traits of nurturing connection and open acknowledgment of interdependence. It is not surprising that many feminists have turned away from theories about human nature that define it in terms of a set of fixed attributes in favor of theoretical notions of human existence that characterize it as an ambiguous, open-ended project of temporal becoming.[3] Psychoanalysis has provided feminists interested in sexual difference with a particularly attractive version of a theory that depicts human beings in terms of an undecidable project of becoming,

179

due to its attempts to account for the formative period of early childhood development as well as for the role of the sexed body in human existence.[4]

In this essay I address the dilemma of fighting for the acknowledgment and acceptance of women as fully human as a problem of self-presentation: how can we evade the reifying categories that stifle human creativity at the same time that we don't disappear as subjects in our own right struggling for social and political recognition? How do we present ourselves in all our differences in terms that defy containment in fixed categories and yet prevent the loss of visibility that thwarting categorization can entail? And how can the new forms of self-presentation we develop affirm our connections with one another and the world without effacing our specificity as individuals? In the first section of this paper, I present the critique of the Lacanian version of Freudian subjectivity given by Gilles Deleuze and Félix Guattari in *Anti-Oedipus,* and in the second, I explore the concepts of the "between," a deterritorializing line of flight, and becoming-imperceptible, created by Deleuze, sometimes in collaboration with Guattari, in order to develop an alternative model of subjectivity that might address this problem. It will be my contention that the work of Deleuze, as well as of Deleuze and Guattari, provide a fruitful resource for feminist conceptions of the self with exciting implications.[5]

A Lacanian model of subjectivity suggests that human subjects are a problematic intertwining of contingent and often conflicting social identities assumed at the level of imaginary identifications involving a morphology of the body (that is, an ongoing materialization of the body in the specific forms it takes), as well as at the level of conscious thought. This model captures some of the ambiguity of an existence lived on neither side of a mind/body dualism in interdependent relationship to others, and yet it still gives priority to the subject who would become self-sufficiently whole and master his connections to the world. Deleuze and Guattari's emphasis on flows, energies, movements, and capacities, rather than a subject acting upon a world, present a compelling alternative. Deleuze's work, along with his collaborative work with Guattari, develops a series of concepts that provide another perspective upon ourselves and our relations to the world and others. Their perspective emphasizes the myriad connections of self to world and the transformative interactions that are an inevitable part of such connections.

Deleuze and Guattari are both wary of becoming entrapped in any one conceptual framework and deliberately move from one model to the next. Any one system of thought, on their view, rigidifies into a set of binary oppositions that close off possible connections, thereby disallowing the becomings of vital living. For Deleuze and Guattari, concepts are created to provide new perspectives rather than to pronounce upon an already existing reality. And yet for the purposes of this paper I will develop one model along my own peculiar line of flight—a model that speaks to my own need to challenge traditional boundaries between self and world and self and others. It is my hope that this model will be read as an experiment designed to initiate further experiments in self-presentation rather than as a description to be measured against the "truth" about human existence.

The model I explore here develops a vocabulary for presenting oneself in a way that minimizes the gap between self and world instead of assuming the self as the privileged anchor of a subject/object split. This self could be compared to an area of geographical terrain encompassed by the larger environment that surrounds it with no necessity for maintaining clear-cut distinctions between what is self and what is not-self. A self, a conversation, a book, on this model can be seen as a configuration of random and aleatory elements converging to form one location with its own peculiar topology, strata, and atmosphere. The contours of this self suggest a rich sense of connectedness, a kind of inevitable and mutually informing contact with surrounding terrain and the arbitrariness of any one way of staking out one's boundaries. Such an image evokes a three-dimensional, multiply overdetermined sense of a self submerged in a world. A self that becomes part of a terrain rather than acting upon it. The interconnections of such a self and its world reach out in all directions and cannot be reduced to any one linear chain of cause and effect. Instead, it is a multiplicity among multiplicities, the various lines of which present distinct possibilities for movements of becoming. This model problematizes dichotomies of active/passive and agent/object and evokes an image of collaboration of self and world, a singular coming together of multiple lines in which the specific location and shape of the self is impossible to pin down to any one point. It evokes an open-ended and embodied involvement with the world that is never completely articulable and that is always moving in uncanny directions. Rather than the insertion of a subject into a world that is other to it, this model suggests that living is a collaborative encounter and that the most interesting encounters are those that occur beyond the reach of any kind of mastery. Such a model could be both personally empowering as well as politically effective as an alternative to the model for self-presentation assumed in identity politics.

Mapping the terrain of such a self involves attentiveness to the intricate convergence of multiple singularities that defy any imposition of a preconceived grid. The writer who would map such terrain must engage in a process of becoming-imperceptible; instead of locating herself vis-à-vis her subject matter, she must follow the lines of flight that run through herself and the multiplicities of which she is a part. This entails betraying any recognizable positioning and ignoring conventional boundaries in order to follow the moving lines of this terrain. Developing a vocabulary for mapping imperceptible becomings could enable an alternative approach to characterizing the singularities of local terrains without sacrificing the power of self-presentation. Writing as a becoming-imperceptible is thus, on the reading I will give here, not about relinquishing the desire for visibility and political empowerment, but is rather about an alternative model for achieving visibility.

Writing that is a becoming-imperceptible articulates a process of transformative encounters. It attempts to, as it were, get behind the scenes of self-presentation and map some part of the all-encompassing process of temporal becoming out of which a recognizable self emerges. This mapping refuses a deterministic account of the origins of self and instead lays out a terrain of the self that opens out onto surrounding territory. It suggests new ways of understanding the interconnections of self and world while retaining the specificity of the self's local terrain. Visibility, on this model, is predicated not upon maintaining a gap between the self and the world, but rather upon attentiveness to shifts in terrain. A becoming-imperceptible that is mapped challenges traditional demarcations between self and other without sacrificing the distinctive features of specific encounters. Mapping refuses both reductionistic categories of self-presentation as well as the failure of self-presentation. A self whose vitality emerges from behind-the-scene encounters is a self immersed in a world of which it is an integral part. It is a self that both affects and is affected by a vast range of heterogeneous multiplicities, a self who is formed and informing, a collaborative result involved in further collaboration.

In the next section I present Deleuze and Guattari's challenge to the psychoanalytic conception of desire and explore a model of subjectivity premised upon productive desire rather than lack. Although the Lacanian model problematizes the conception of self-sufficient autonomy as the ideal norm for human selfhood, Deleuze and Guattari criticize this model for interpreting all desire in terms of the limited constraints of the Oedipal triangle. Assuming all desire to be Oedipal in nature turns out to entail the presentation of a self whose contact with dynamic becoming is filtered through gender-inflected structures. Their own model will turn out to be less concerned with self-identity—gender-inflected or not—and more concerned with productive connections of multiple kinds with a nonhuman as well as human world-in-process.

The Lacking Subject and Productive Desire

According to Lacan's account of (masculine) subjectivity, taking up a position as a speaking subject requires clear-cut distinctions between oneself as subject and one's objects. Human subjects emerge from corporeal entanglement with the mother and develop selves with definite corporeal and conceptual boundaries. This occurs first when the infant layers up a "fictional" ego through a series of imaginary identifications with images that assure pleasurable maternal contact. The subject further emerges out of this state of confused boundaries by taking up a position as a speaking subject from which he can represent his desire for maternal contact with words. Representations of the pleasurable maternal contact that would satisfy the subject's desire undergoes transformation as the subject substitutes socially appropriate objects of desire for the original one. The phallus as the master signifier of desire authorizes concepts, representations, and formalizations of language that prescribe an economy of subjectivity premised upon "castration." That is, the desire for connection and continuity with one's origins, which is really a desire for connection and participation with life processes extending beyond oneself, is reduced to the desire for an object one lacks. To reconnect with one's origins is translated into possession of the maternal body, and only those who have the phallus are entitled to such possession.

Deleuze and Guattari argue that to conceive of desire as a yearning to fill in that lack that would make a subject whole is to diminish and overlook the creative connections that desire is capable of producing. They insist that the unconscious is not a theatre where a self is staged and performed as the Oedipal drama of mommy/daddy/child, but a factory or production machine. To construe it as the theatre of an Oedipal drama is to vastly impoverish the possibilities it produces for us. Instead of referring unconscious desire to what is lacking in the subject in terms of the Oedipal triangle, they posit an immanent notion of the unconscious, one that insists upon its productive nature.[6] The fluid connections of unconscious processes produce syntheses according to immanent flows of desire. The symbolic systems of society provide a wide range of names that become attached to the various zones of intensity (or, in more Freudian terms, libidinal surges of desire) of an individual. These names only converge onto the limited cast of characters of the Oedipal drama in societies with a specific form of social production that could have been otherwise. The unconscious doesn't unravel into delirium (for example, in schizophrenia) through daddy/mommy, but through races, tribes and continents, history, and geography—identifications drawn from the entire social field rather than merely from the familial drama. The model of subjectivity that Deleuze and Guattari present in *Anti-Oedipus* insists upon viewing human beings as formed by and participating in processes of material production that are heterogeneous to the perceptions and conceptions of an Oedipal subject.[7]

Schizoanalysis is a practice by which an individual, or group of individuals, can rework their participation in social processes of subjectification. Like psychoanalysis, schizoanalysis reads aspects of conscious experience as symptoms of unconscious (or in more Deleuze-Guattarian terminology, *molecular*) processes and attempts to alleviate alienation from oneself, others, and life itself by symbolizing manifest indications of the unconscious that allow for greater integration of these processes into conscious awareness. Unlike psychoanalysis, schizoanalysis draws upon a wide range of disparate vocabularies to symbolize presently imperceptible processes. It also assumes that all life processes have molecular elements mostly imperceptible to us, whose configurations into larger aggregates are constantly changing. Human existence is but a part of this larger process. Rather than investigating the unconscious for secrets waiting to be revealed according to an Oedipal frame of interpretation, schizoanalysis assumes that the unconscious is productive. Symbolization of unconscious processes according to experiments in meaning created as desire unfolds, create new possibilities in living rather than reveal ones that have always been there. Insofar as schizoanalysis engages a transformation of an individual or group that has reverberating effects throughout the social field, it is a practice with revolutionary potential.

Like psychoanalysis, schizoanalysis does not take the conscious subject we think of as fully human for granted. A sentient, language-speaking individual with self-conscious awareness is the effect of a complicated process. Deleuze and Guattari's descriptions of this process emphasizes the continuity of human processes of production with other processes of production. On their view, all of life (which includes inanimate as well as animate objects) is a ceaseless flux of singularities that become organized into various forms that could always have been otherwise. Because human life is always implicated with "larger" productive processes, understanding human subjectivity requires theorizing human life in its ongoing implication with all of life.

Psychoanalysis refers the submerged background out of which our thoughts and actions emerge to the monotone account of an Oedipal drama. But the unconscious in which Deleuze and Guattari are interested is not the unconscious whose symptoms can be explained in reference to an already-established framework of interpretation. Deleuze and Guattari advocate what they call "deterritorialization" from the norm by attending to points of destabilization in existing patterns of organization. This process is analogous to schizoanalysis and entails attentiveness to the here and now in a way that brings the "body" into play and challenges the traditional mind/body dualisms of Western thought. Deleuze and Guattari would have you use caution in your deterritorialization by mapping the process—pay attention to where you are! Meticulously map your relation to the forms of organization in which you find yourself and see where you might free a line of flight. Following a line of flight entails pursuing the connections created in the unfolding of a desire interested only in the intensity of its own flow.

Making a map entails experimenting with the connections one can make. "The map does not reproduce an unconscious closed in upon itself; it constructs the unconscious." [8] It fosters connections among different areas of life and the removal of blockages both within as well as among individuals in dynamic interaction with a world.

Deleuze and Guattari's refusal to remain with a psychoanalytic account of desire prompts them to explore an exciting range of possibilities in deterritorialization. Psychoanalysis can lead one to believe that the only route to destructuring overly constrictive forms of subjectivity in order to stimulate richer integrations of libidinal drive is through pursuing the secret of Oedipalized desire. According to Deleuze and Guattari's critique, psychoanalytic theory preserves the bounded self of the cultural norm by filtering connections to the world through the Oedipal schema. Although one could argue that psychoanalysis revives connection with the world by challenging the notion that the self has nonproblematic boundaries, it still tightly controls any ruptures in those boundaries. That is, according to the Lacanian model, although I might not be the unified, coherent self I want to present myself as, I have no choice but to attempt to obtain the objects of desire that I believe—if only unconsciously—would make me the self I pretend and want so much to be.

Deleuze experiments with forms of self-presentation that insist neither upon staving off a world from which the self must remain distinct, nor on comparing the self to a totalized identity it can never achieve. Although Lacanian psychoanalysis chooses to view the lack of the subject with respect to a totalized ideal as the inevitable tragedy of the human condition, Deleuze chooses to present himself as never lacking. Instead of remaining focused on a personal self maintaining itself in a world that always threatens to overwhelm it, Deleuze focuses on the multiple productive connections each individual has with her or his surroundings. This renders the conception of a self-identical self highly problematic; productive desire inevitably entails dynamic interaction with a world in continual transformation. This self, rather than having a perspective upon and apart from the world of temporal becoming, is part of a process of dynamic differentiation. It is the contention of this paper that Deleuze begins to provide a new model of subjectivity that would enable a form of self-presentation premised upon such dynamic interaction.

Returning to the metaphor of self as geographical terrain, it becomes apparent that dynamic contact with one's surroundings and shifting boundaries do not necessarily entail annihilation of the self. Subject/object distinctions are problematized; with uncertain boundaries (between one part of the land and another, between earth and sky, between the creatures living in one area and those of another), no one term of any dichotomy can be privileged as the originating agent, and no one dichotomy can be abstracted from the process in which its terms are immersed. And yet Deleuze provides a vocabulary for mapping the contours of the self's terrain. It is not shifting boundaries that threaten this self, but the failure to map its transformations. To extend the metaphor, we might compare the self to a line of movement in an ecosystem. By focusing on lines of movement rather than abstracting originating points for that movement out of the processes of which they are a part, Deleuze creates concepts that allow us to map, and thereby render perceptible, a self that is always in flux.

It turns out to be part of Deleuze's self-presentation that he is and thinks and writes only in collaboration and never as what we might call an autonomous individual. He contests any assumption of unified identity and chooses instead to emphasize the becomings of which subjects are only the effects. In the next section, I will further explore the process of rendering dynamic becoming perceptible in the context of a model of self-presentation by examining Deleuze's notion of writing—or mapping—as a form of becoming-imperceptible.

Becoming-Imperceptible and Self-Presentation

In *Dialogues* Deleuze characterizes both *Dialogues* itself, his work, his work process, and his collaborative effort with Guattari.[9] *Dialogues* was meant to be an interview. Instead, it became a collaboration between Deleuze and Claire Parnet in which neither's contribution was clearly marked. In the English preface to *Dialogues,* Deleuze says about the book that emerged that

> (W)hat mattered was not the points—Félix, Claire Parnet, me and many others, who functioned simply as temporary, transitory and evanescent points of subjectivation—but the collection of bifurcating, divergent and muddled lines which constituted this book as a multiplicity and which passed between the points, carrying them along without ever going from the one to the other. Hence, the first plan for a conversation between two people, in which one asked questions and the other replied, no longer had any value. The divisions had to rest on the growing dimensions of the multiplicity, according to becomings which were unattributable to individuals, since they could not be immersed in it without changing qualitatively. (*Dialogues,* ix–xzz)

This description of the making of the book captures aspects of the writing process that are typically ignored. First, Deleuze chooses to emphasize the *between* of a collaborative process rather than label the origin and ownership of the ideas making up the content of the book. Second, Deleuze emphasizes the aleatory nature of this coming together of a collection of lines rather than the mastery manifested by any individual vis-à-vis these lines.

In *Dialogues,* Deleuze calls himself an empiricist and says that empiricism is linked to a logic of multiplicities. Every "thing" is a multiplicity and is made up of a set of lines (*Dialogues,* vii). One extracts concepts corresponding to multiplicities by mapping the lines that make up a multiplicity. These lines are "true becomings." Becomings are not unities. They are not subjects of a history. They cannot be captured through a process of representation that would trace an event's origin from out of a historical context; instead, they happen behind one's back. Deleuze suggests that it is in such becomings that the real stuff of life occurs—the happenings that lead to encounters with others, novelty, creativity, and the singularity of existence when it just is rather than when it conforms to a preconceived schema.

> Movement always happens behind the thinker's back, or in the moment when he blinks. . . . We think too much in terms of history, whether personal or universal. Becomings belong to geography, they are orientations, directions, entries. (*Dialogues,* 1–2).

Mapping contextualizes by providing the texture of the lay of the land; instead of tracing out a historical sequence, it provides a cartography that can be pursued in any number of ways. To say that *Dialogues* is a multiplicity is to say that the book emerged neither from Deleuze as author or interviewee, nor from Claire Parnet as interviewer, nor from Guattari or the various thinkers affecting Deleuze and Guattari's work. We could talk about Deleuze and Parnet as subjects of distinct histories and give an account of how they came together in the writing of this book. But this would miss what for Deleuze is the crucial point: the book grew along lines that cannot be reduced to such a history. The becomings that make up the book are unattributable to individuals and cannot be accounted for by giving a history of its various factors construed as coherent unities with past and future effects. This does not, however, render the lines of the book any less real. Books, as well as selves and other "things," can be thought of as unities with histories, or they can be thought of as multiplicities with lines of becoming that connect with the lines of other multiplicities in unpredictable ways. To think and write in terms of recognizable unities is to close off movement along lines of flight; it is to conform to a code of dominant utterances (*Dialogues,* 74). Instead of responding to subtle shifts in terrain, such thinking conforms to an already established conceptual grid and so cannot introduce genuine novelty. Texts composed in order to cohere into a closed system don't foster multiple connections with the world; lines of flight adhere to no already established structure and instead give priority to following out the intensities of new connections. To think and write in terms of becoming is "to release from becoming that that will not permit itself to be fixed in a term" (*Dialogues,* 75). This kind of thinking challenges any preconceptions by bringing one up against that which forces a kind of thinking which is also a creating.[10]

Deleuze thinks that traditional philosophy impedes and even prevents thinking. Emphasizing the centers of totalization and points of subjectivation of multiplicities, be they books, people, or thoughts, prevents the "transmutation of fluxes, through which life escapes from the resentment of persons, societies and reigns" (*Dialogues,* 50). He deliberately contrasts his own approach to that of traditional philosophy (which he claims to be "shot through with the project of becoming the official language of a pure State" [*Dialogues,* 13]). For Deleuze, the aim of writing is to follow out, rather than stop, the lines that make up multiplicities, even if this means running the risk of becoming unintelligible or unrecognizable.

> Still way beyond a woman-becoming, a Negro-becoming, an animal-becoming, etc., beyond a minority-becoming, there is the final enterprise of the becoming-imperceptible. Oh no, a writer cannot wish to be "known," recognized. . . . Writing has no other end than to lose one's face, to jump over or pierce through the wall, to plane down the wall very patiently. (*Dialogues,* 45)

Perception involves resemblance and similarity. To be visible, a becoming must already be perceivable, and to be perceivable means that it will be perceived as being like something else. Becomings are imperceptible. In the third chapter of *Difference and Repetition,* Deleuze claims philosophy's image of thought is based on a model of recognition. This model assumes a coherence of both subject and object and a correspondence between the two. Subject and object are both taken to be unities, and these unities are determined through resemblance and analogy. Deleuze argues that the philosophical doctrine of faculties assumes this model of recognition and in so doing assumes the unity of a thinking subject and thus the convergence of various faculties upon a coherent object. Plato's theory of the forms created a representational image of thought that subordinated difference to identity and resemblance; the "truth" of thinking was measured against the original ideals of the forms.[11] Kant continued in this tradition when he posited the "I think" as the most general principle of representation; it is when each faculty "locates its given as identical to that of another" that the faculties are related in the "I think" of the subjective unity of a consciousness with a recognizable object as its correlate.[12]

Recognition, for Kant, entails relating our faculties through a harmonious accord brought about in the convergence of the faculties upon an object that each faculty takes as identical to the object of the other faculties. "[I]t is the *same* object that can be seen, remembered, imagined, conceived, and so on." Common sense is "the supposed identity of the subject that functions as the foundation of our faculties, as the principle that unites them in this harmonious accord" (*Sensation,* 30). For Deleuze, conceiving of thought in terms of recognition curtails its creative force. Harmonious accord of the faculties can only be achieved in terms of agreement on the identity of their respective objects. To assume that it is only such objects that are real is to subordinate difference to identity. What is thinkable or perceivable is what is recognizable; what is recognizable is that which can be referred to what is the same.

> Following lines of becomings might indicate a different story. Something in the world forces us to think. This something is an object not of recognition but of a fundamental *encounter*. . . . It may be grasped in a range of affective tones: wonder, love, hatred, suffering. In whichever tone, its primary characteristic is that it can only be sensed. In this sense it is opposed to recognition. (*What Is?* 139).

Insofar as an object is unrecognizable, it is imperceptible. The object of an encounter cannot be recognized, Deleuze argues, because one's sensibility can recognize only that which can be apprehended by the other faculties as well, in the context of a coherent object upon which the faculties converge (*What Is?* 140). The assumption that the various faculties of a self will converge in recognizing an object suggests that "the form of identity in objects relies upon a ground in the unity of a thinking subject, of which all the other faculties must be modalities" (*What Is?* 133). In a discussion of Platonic reminiscence, Deleuze states that sensibility in the presence of the imperceptible "finds itself before its own limit . . . and raises itself to the level of a transcendental exercise" (*What Is?* 140). Thinking that is forced to grasp "that which can only be thought" unhinges the faculties and breaks with common sense (*What Is?* 141).

> Rather than all the faculties converging and contributing to a common project of recognising an object, we see divergent projects in which, with regard to what concerns it essentially, each faculty is in the presence of that which is its "own." Discord of the faculties, chain of force and fuse along which each confronts its limit, receiving from (or communicating to) the other only a violence which brings it face to face with its own element, as though with its disappearance or its perfection. (*What Is?* 141)

Kant's project delineates multiple forms that common sense can take. The faculty of understanding dominates logical common sense, reason dominates moral common sense, whereas "various faculties enter into an accord which is no longer determined by any one of them" in the case of aesthetic common sense.[13] That there can be more than one form of common sense suggests that there can be more than one way that one's faculties converge upon an object. This suggests that the form of thought is not as uniform as the model of recognition might indicate. Furthermore, Deleuze argues that Kant's notion of the sublime provides an example of faculties in a discordant harmony in which "there is . . . something which is communicated from one faculty to another" without forming a common sense.[14] Against an image of thought that posits it as a passive process of representation,

> Deleuze defends a conception of thought as something to which we are provoked precisely by those phenomena we do not recognize, or by forces from outside our habitual range of experience. Only by abandoning the banal model of recognition in favor of something closer to the Kantian sublime is it possible to conceive of thought as an essentially creative activity: thought as the creation of concepts, where concepts themselves are understood as existing only in immediate relations with forces and intensities outside thought. ("Anti-Platonism," 145)

What Deleuze calls a "superior," "transcendental" empiricism would explore that which cannot be grasped from the point of view of common sense by exploring the point at which each faculty is brought to:

> the extreme point of its dissolution, at which it falls prey to triple violence: the violence of that which forces it to be exercised, of that which it is forced to grasp and which it alone is able to grasp, yet also that of the ungraspable (from the point of view of its empirical exercise). (*Difference*, 143)

Objects apprehended according to the dictates of common sense may evoke nothing new—no creative thinking, for example. But life always eludes common sense. It is the violence of an aleatory encounter that brings a particular faculty to its own specific limit, thus rendering the communication among faculties necessary for achieving a harmonious convergence upon an object either difficult or impossible. Without such a convergence, no empirical object can emerge, and yet, Deleuze suggests, it is precisely such violent encounters that make up the terrain of actual living.

A Deleuzian doctrine of the faculties would require determining what element carries the faculties to their respective limits.

This element is intensity, understood as pure difference in itself, as that which is at once both imperceptible for empirical sensibility which grasps intensity only already covered or mediated by the quality to which it gives rise, and at the same time that which can be perceived only from the point of view of a transcendental sensibility which apprehends it immediately in the encounter. (*Difference*, 144)

Here Deleuze approaches talking about the unsayable—that part of experience which cannot be talked about because it is singular, the part of experience—no matter how ordinary or mundane that experience may be— that eludes any description we may try to give it. For Deleuze, thought has to deal with this difference rather than proffer the model of recognition as an image of thought because it is only due to "an original violence inflicted upon thought" that thought is awakened:

[T]here is only involuntary thought, aroused but constrained within thought, and all the more absolutely necessary for being born, illegitimately, of fortuitousness in the world. (*Difference*, 139)

For Deleuze, it would seem that we are brought to a thinking that goes beyond a dogmatic image of thought by something imperceptible about our experience—something that we encounter, that we experience, that we immediately apprehend, and yet do not perceive. Such encounters, if pursued, challenge the unity of the self and the unity of an object presented to a self. Focusing on the element of difference involves both an intensity of experience as well as violence and the dissolution of one's faculties. One is precisely not a unified self attending to a unified object when one grasps this intensive element. This element is instead that which brings each faculty to its limit. Transcendental empiricism would explore the limits of each faculty in pursuit of the behind-the-scene encounters that provoke vital living and thinking.

To write in a way that follows out this kind of thinking is to refuse a dogmatic image of thought—that is, to refuse an image of thought based on a model of recognition where everything is referred to a self. But what would an imageless thinking be? To write, for Deleuze, should be a becoming-imperceptible where you allow lines of flight to release you both from the central reference of a self as well as the organizing focus of coherent objects. Instead, one allows a kind of violence to occur that follows intensities and flows without worrying where they come from or what their histories might be.

To write has no other function: to be a flux which combines with other fluxes—all the minority-becomings of the world. A flux is something intensive, instantaneous and mutant—between a creation and a destruction. It is only when a flux is deterritorialized that it succeeds in making its conjunction with other fluxes, which deterritorialize it in their turn, and vice versa. (*Dialogues,* 50)

Following out the lines of flight of a multiplicity involves delirium and betrayal. On such lines of flight one no longer has a past or future; one betrays the fixed and established powers of the earth that try to hold one back, and one turns one's face away from God who turns his face away from humanity. "It is in this double turning-away, in the divergence of faces, that the line of flight—that is, the deterritorialization of man—is traced." Thus, one "goes off the rails," betrays one's commonsense notions of oneself, one's place in society or history, one's relationship to people and things, and becomes demonic (*Dialogues,* 40). A writer jumps across intervals and "makes one multiplicity pass into another." She refuses traditional boundaries and her utterance "is the product of an assemblage—which is always collective, which brings into play within us and outside us populations, multiplicities, territories, becomings, affects, events." Her proper name "does not designate a subject, but something that happens, at least between two terms that are not subjects, but agents, elements" (*Dialogues,* 51). She is, in an important sense, impersonal. Although the lines that make her up form a singular multiplicity, none of these lines have a history. And each line presents the possibility of a line of flight that both escapes the limits of any commonsense understanding of personal boundedness and transmutates into other multiplicities.

As writers that are becoming-imperceptible, we are not unified subjects with histories, but nomads following lines of flight, traitors to established practices with neither past nor future. We map geographies of intensities in a desert bereft of traditional landmarks and yet full of becomings and encounters with the imperceptible. We are no one self with an interior and exterior but are ourselves inventions of assemblages that in turn invent (*Dialogues,* 51).

Deleuze's conception of the self and of writing suggests that living and writing are inevitably collaborative processes that are reduced to the acts of individuals only by discounting living lines of flight among multiplicities. His overtly collaborative work with Guattari is therefore a natural extension of his project. His way of presenting the collaborative process between them suggests the obvious parallels to be made between one self as a multiplicity and the multiplicity formed through the collaboration of two selves.

We were only two, but what was important for us was less our working together than this strange fact of working between the two of us. We stopped being "author." And these "between-the-twos" referred back to other people, who were different on one side from on the other. The desert expanded, but in so doing became more populous. This had nothing to do with a school, with processes of recognition, but much to do with encounters. And all these stories of becomings, of nuptials against nature, of a parallel evolution, of bilingualism, of theft of thoughts, were what I had with Félix. (*Dialogues,* 17).

Deleuze neither denies nor denigrates his part in this process of collaboration, and yet the place that he finds for himself in it is not predicated upon having to claim or own any particular part of the work. He may present himself as becoming-imperceptible in his writing, but his writing maps this process by attending to the terrain of its occurrence. The encounters of this becoming-imperceptible are part of this terrain. The writing produced from this mapping results in a collaborative effort in which two selves become one multiplicity with neither self losing its specificity in the process.

Intensities, flows, affects that we cannot name, are all part of our experience—an elusive part that we may attempt to express or ignore as trivial. Vocabulary for the emotions and for kinesthetic experience is crude and inadequate. And yet many of us feel that what we can talk about in words is often inadequate to our reality. A writer—or at least the kind of writer Deleuze is interested in—is a becoming-imperceptible and becoming-imperceptible arises through encounter. It is through a thinking that doesn't refer itself to an image and a writing that is a line of flight that the becomings of encounters can manifest. The characterization Deleuze gives of the book *Dialogues* works as well for thinking and the "between" of ideas, writing and the "between" of becoming-imperceptible, and living and the "between" of conversations with people. In all three forms of life, Deleuze creates a vocabulary that minimizes the role of anything that one might call a starting or ending point in order to focus on the moment of contact or interaction between and among ideas, events, and people. In the process, he puts commonsense notions about ideas, events, and people into question.

Self-presentation, according to such a model, could indicate the multiple connections of women with the world without confining them to any one image of womanhood. On a terrain marked by gender warfare, I will have some relationship to the cultural stereotypes imposed upon me. This relationship will shift given the terrain of my specific situation. Mapping the contours of my terrain allows me to present myself to others in terms of the connections I have created and want to create. Because I present myself in terms of my engagements with the world, rather than in terms of an identity I maintain as the self-same, my boundaries can shift without the risk of self-annihilation. As long as the category of "woman" is a part of the terrain, it will be part of my self-mapping; alliances can shift without changing that this category is still a feature of the terrain I share with others.

Focusing on the moment and the place where something happens shocks our sensibilities and suggests new lines of flight. This suggests alternative understandings of events and things. A self as a desert populated with flora and fauna. A writing that is not an enunciation, but a becoming-imperceptible. A conversation that is not about the people involved, but about the zigzag of ideas that takes place. Emphasizing contact and contiguity, lines among heterogeneous elements, suggests that the stuff of life, whatever is, can be understood in ways other than that of subject, object, and predicate. Instead of subordinating a description to a focal point anchored in a substratum— that which remains the same despite any changes—Deleuze attempts descriptions that focus on the moment of contact and so shift and mutate to follow points of living movement into a line of flight. This necessitates a conceptual shift in our thinking. It requires a kind of movement that can be both liberating and disorienting. It involves a process of deterritorialization that can bring us both exhilarating highs as well as terrifying risks.

PART V

Resistance, Flight, Creation

Between the Visible and the Articulable: Matter, Interpellation, and Resistance in Foucault's DISCIPLINE AND PUNISH

EWA PLONOWSKA ZIAREK

Neither a social historian nor a philosopher, Foucault is most frequently associated with the historical genealogies of the types of knowledge and power embodied in various institutional practices—for instance, the development of the penal system, medicine, psychiatry, the birth of the asylum—and with the consequences of these practices for the historical constitution of bodies and subjectivities.[1] Although Foucault's account of power relations functioning beyond the state control—for instance, the procedures of discipline, docility, and surveillance—has been very influential in feminist analyses of the normalization of the sexed and racial bodies in contemporary cultural practices such as consumerism, fashion, diet, fitness regimes, cosmetic surgery, or reproductive technologies,[2] feminist critics of Foucault have consistently raised objections that this approach to power seems to evacuate psychic space and to eliminate the possibility of agency. From the early anthology *Feminism and Foucault: Reflections on Resistance* to the 1996 collection *Feminist Interpretations of Foucault,* the feminist engagements with Foucault expose the paradoxical achievements of his genealogical critique occurring at the expense of its practical ethos.[3] Although Foucault frequently proclaims that the ethos of his work is to write the history of the present so that we can experiment with different ways of becoming, such an ethos seems to be realized merely in a negative way: the Foucauldian histories of sexuality and the penal system demonstrate time and again the insufficiency of the liberal projects of liberations.[4] Lois McNay sums up this dilemma rather nicely when she points out that "despite Foucault's assertions about the immanence of resistance to any system of power, this idea remains theoretically underdeveloped, and, in practice, Foucault's historical studies give the impression that the body presents no material resistance to the operations of power."[5] Or, as Francis Bartkowski argues, what is missing in Foucault's articulation of "power-knowledge-

197

pleasure" is the "fourth term of resistance."[6] Although resistance is affirmed theoretically as the necessary outcome of power conceived in terms of the relation between forces, the historical genealogy of docile individuals threatens to eliminate it as a practical possibility.[7]

Building on the work of Wendy Brown, Judith Butler, Susan Hekman, and Jana Sawicki, who in different ways have explored the possibilities of resistance and freedom in Foucault's work,[8] I argue that these possibilities are located in Foucault's notion of the causality of power and in his concept of the split, dispersed subject. Without a clear articulation of the causality and subjectivity in Foucault's work, we might end up, as Judith Butler warns us, with the unacknowledged personification of power itself, with a blind displacement of power into the emptied position of the political or ethical agent.[9] Even worse, as the reception of Foucault exclusively in terms of subjection aptly shows, his work can be dissociated from its Nietzschean legacy and reduced to utilitarian functionalism—that is, to the very notion of causality that Foucault, following Nietzsche, takes as the main target of his genealogical critique in *Discipline and Punish*. In order to raise the intertwined questions of causality, subjectivity, and resistance, I turn to Gilles Deleuze, who provides one of the most provocative, and, from the feminist point of view, one of the most productive interpretations of the "profound Nietzscheanism" in Foucault's work. By taking Deleuze's interpretation of power and causality as my point of departure, I show that, for Foucault, the conditions of resistance to the disciplinary regime emerge from the radicalization of finitude and the dispersion of the subject. In order to understand Foucault's claim that resistance occurs at the level of the bodies, I then propose to rethink the historical constitution of embodiment as an event of materialization.

I.

Despite the significant differences in the arguments about the "usefulness" of Foucault's theory of power for feminism,[10] what is characteristic about the majority of feminist discussions of Foucault is either a lack of explicit reflection on the causality of power or the assumption that the operation of power is characterized by a continuity of causes and effects, as if causes could manifest themselves in their effects without reserve, for instance, disciplinary power could be actualized in the modern docile individual.[11] On the basis of such a notion of causality attributed to historical formations, Nancy Hartsock, for instance, writes that in Foucault's theory "things move, rather than people, a world in which subjects become obliterated or, rather, recreated as passive subjects."[12]

Insofar as it perpetuates the notion of the subject as a passive receptacle or an effect of the historical formations, this reception of Foucault, I argue, is deeply implicated in the utilitarianism Foucault takes as one of the targets of his genealogical critique. The often-unacknowledged debt to utilitarianism in Foucault criticism is nowhere more apparent than in the concept of causality ascribed to "historical formations." As early as "The Discourse on Language," Foucault has warned his readers that what is at stake in historical genealogy is not "consciousness and continuity (with their correlative problems of liberty and causality)" but events and series. As he writes, "If it is true that these discursive, discontinuous series have their regularity . . . it is clearly no longer possible to establish mechanically causal links or an ideal necessity among their constitutive elements" (*DL,* 231). Foucault follows here rather closely Nietzsche's critique of utility in *On Genealogy of Morals.* In his reflection on the genealogical method, Nietzsche deplores the naïveté of seeking the origin of punishment in its utility. Nietzsche finds "the calculus of utility" deeply problematic because it focuses exclusively on the reactive forces and forgets the endless transformations of things toward new ends in the context of changing relations of power:

> One had always believed that to understand the demonstrable purpose, the utility of a thing, a form, or an institution, was also to understand the reason why it originated. . . . Thus one also imagined that punishment was devised for punishing. But purposes and utilities are only *signs* that a will to power has become master of something less powerful and imposed upon it the character of a function; and the entire history of a "thing," an organ, a custom can in this way be a continuous sign-chain of ever new interpretations . . . whose causes do not even have to be related to one another but, on the contrary, in some cases succeed and alternate with one another in a purely chance fashion. . . . The form is fluid, but the "meaning" is even more so.[13]

As Foucault aptly sums up Nietzsche's critique, it is "wrong to follow the English tendency in describing the history of morality in terms of linear development—in reducing its entire history and genesis to an exclusive concern for utility" (*NGH,* 139).

In contrast to this Nietzschean insistence on the discontinuity of cause and utility in the genealogy of morals, utilitarianism, let us recall, in its instrumental conception of the social Good and the utility of pleasure aims to control social relations through the manipulation of causes. The organizing principle of utilitarian morality, as Nietzsche reminds us, is "calculating prudence." By ascribing a proper function even to human waste, Jeremy Bentham's project of panopticon is one of the paradigmatic examples of how the utilitarian notion of causality eliminates contingency for the sake of efficiency and calculability. As Jacques-Alain Miller notes, utilitarian functionalism, based on the logical homology of visibility, law, and language, enables the continuous derivation of causes and effects and the calculation of means and ends: "This utilitarian concept of the world is based on a simple belief: nothing is without its effect. That is, every thing uses or serves another thing . . . and any effect can be fitted into the hierarchy vis-à-vis its relationship to a result." [14] If we substitute in the above quotation "historical formations" for "causes" and "docile individuals" for "effects" we might get a general schema of the predominant Anglo-American criticism of Foucault, which Joan Copjec calls "historicist": "the social system of representation is conceived as lawful, regulatory, and on this account the cause of the subject, which the former subsumes as one of its effects. The subject is assumed to be virtually there in the social and to come into being by actually wanting what social laws want it to want." [15]

In order to clarify the status of the subject and the causality of power in Foucault's genealogical critique of utilitarianism, and thus to move beyond a certain impasse in the reception of Foucault, I would like to recall Gilles Deleuze's reading of *Discipline and Punish*. What I find most remarkable in his interpretation is his diagnosis of the disjunction at the very center of the historical formation—a rift between the forms of visibility and the forms of signification. Unlike utilitarianism's insistence on the homology of language and visibility, Foucault, Deleuze argues, discovers in *Discipline and Punish* the disjunction between prison and law, and, on the basis of this disjunction, theorizes the "irrational" rift in "historical formation" itself. Building on his earlier distinction of "discursive formations" and "nondiscursive practices" in *Archeology of Knowledge*,[16] Foucault gives in the figure of panopticism a positive articulation of "the non-discursive" as a form of visibility, that is, the historically variable constructions of space, which determine specific modes of perception, practice, and normalizing judgment. It is important to stress that the figure of panopticism serves the double duty, as it were, referring on the one hand to the network of power relations (the diagram of forces) and to the particular form of its realization, that is, to the form of visibility, on the other. The overcoming of utilitarian functionalism and causality in *Discipline and Punish* is thus achieved not only by situating the social utility of pleasure in the context of the disciplinary technologies of bodies—technologies, which for Foucault function as a modern mutation of Nietzsche's "ascetic ideal"—but, even more so, by the discovery of the noncoincidence between the forms of visibility and the forms of discourse at the center of disciplinary formation.

As an immanent cause, the disciplinary power is neither visible nor discursive. It is on the level of its actualization in the historical formation that it constitutes historically specific "art of space," and a form of discourse. In the case of the disciplinary society, it constitutes the architectural panopticon as a form of visibility and delinquency as a new form of articulation. As Foucault repeatedly argues, the disciplinary organization of visibility and the discourse of the penal law do not have the same genealogy, nor the same object of punishment, nor the same form. Deleuze evokes Foucault's earlier study of Magritte's famous painting, "This is not a pipe," to underscore the heterogeneity between the prison form and the law-form, as if visibility and discourse constituted two different semiotic systems: "prison as the visibility of crime does not derive from penal law as a form of expression but evolves from something completely different, which is 'disciplinary' not judicial; while penal law, for its part, produces its statements of 'delinquency' independently of prison as though it were always led to say, in a certain way, that this *is not* a prison." [17]

By replacing an earlier mode of visibility, which Foucault defines as a "society of spectacle," disciplines invent new, analytical, and useful spaces modeled on the precise partitioning and distribution characteristic of the town afflicted with plague: "In organizing 'cells,' 'places' and ranks, the disciplines create complex spaces that are at once architectural, functional and hierarchical . . . they mark places and indicate values; they guarantee the obedience of individuals but also a better economy of time and gesture" (*DP,* 148). Characterized by precise location and distribution of bodies and objects, by the calculation of presences and absences, by permanent visibility and functionality, the organization of disciplinary spaces parallels and responds to the emergence of population control as a political problem. That is why Foucault defines disciplinary organization of spaces as an antinomadic and anticollective technique, transforming what is perceived as "confused, useless or dangerous multitudes into ordered multiplicities" (*DP,* 148).

If disciplinary power establishes a new mode of visibility through the reversal of spectacle, its discursive actualization is even more complex because it proceeds through the inversion rather than replacement of the law. Indeed, as Peg Birmingham suggests, "these two heterogeneous but inseparable views (juridical and disciplinary) of power together characterize modern political life." [18] The inversion of the law is nowhere more evident than in a redefinition of the right to punish at the turn of the eighteenth and nineteenth century. Within the disciplinary regime, the function of punishment is expressed on the one hand as a deprivation of liberty and on the other hand as the rehabilitation of individuals. The right to punish has thus a "double foundation—juridico-economic on the one hand, technico-disciplinary on the other" (*DP,* 233). The deprivation of the right of liberty gives the punishment its contractual/economical form, akin, as Foucault argues after Nietzsche, to the negative wage system through which the criminal pays his debt to society. Yet, when the function of punishment is redefined as the rehabilitation of the offender, then it no longer deprives the juridical subject of its right but instead aims to transform the very nature of the criminal—its content is delinquency, that is, conscience, morality, or, simply, the whole existence.

Whereas the juridical form of law denotes formal equality and symmetrical contractual obligations, delinquency excludes such reciprocity and institutes in its place asymmetries of domination and the hierarchical classification of isolated individuals. Thus, the disciplinary power institutes a new mode of articulation by "parasitically" usurping the juridical form for the expression of a new content (delinquency) that is not only incompatible with the law but functions as a "counter-law" (*DP*, 224). The parasitical inversion of the law means that formal equality of justice is given the "content" of disciplinary subjection. What we encounter in *Discipline and Punish* is not only a disjunction between visibility and articulation but also a rift within discourse itself, that is, the noncoincidence of the institutionalized content (delinquency as a pathological mode of being) and the juridical forms (the democratic forms of exchange and contract). These rifts are both the condition of the actualization of power within the historical formation and the possibility of resistance, and, thus, of the emergence of a different configuration of forces.

For Deleuze what brings the forms of visibility and discourse into contact and enables their mutual capture and combinations in various types of knowledge is the Foucauldian concept of power as "an immanent dispersed cause." Even though Deleuze stresses the immanence of the cause (power relation) in the socio-historical field, he presupposes neither continuity or nor calculability of causes and effects. The realization of cause (power) within the institutional framework and within specific formations of knowledge accomplishes on the one hand an integration of force relations that otherwise remain abstract, unstable (almost virtual, Deleuze says), and without form. In Foucault's words, the forms and "concatenations" of power seek to "arrest" the movement of "these unbalanced, heterogeneous, unstable, and tense force relations" (*HS*, 93). Yet, on the other hand, this process of integration is also a differentiation into the visible and articulable forms of knowledge. In other words, cause can be realized only by splitting and doubling the form of its realization:

> Things can be realized only through doubling or dissociation . . . *it is here that the two forms of realization diverge or become differentiated*: a form of expression and a form of content, a discursive and non-discursive form, the form of the visible and the form of the articulable. . . . Between the visible and the articulable a gap or disjunction opens up . . . where the informal diagram (of forces) is swallowed up and becomes embodied instead in two different directions that are necessarily divergent and irreducible (*F*, 38).

What emerges from Deleuze's reading of Foucault is the contrast between forces (potentiality) and forms of power/knowledge (the actualized power relations), evocative, despite Deleuze's protests to the contrary, of the Nietzschean inflection of Heidegger's distinction between Being and beings. In this sense, as Maurice Blanchot remarks, the actualization of power proceeds not only through the doubling of visible and articulable form but also through the withdrawal of force that in itself is neither visible nor articulable. This excess or withdrawal of force from the visible and articulable forms that it produces and in which it is actualized constitutes a certain outside of the historical formation. Forces, as Foucault puts it, constitute "moving substrate" of the states of power—substrate that are never accessible in themselves but constitute "power's condition of possibility" (*HS,* 93). For Foucault, this outside is a condition not only of resistance but also of the emergence of a new configuration of power. Thus, although it is correct to say that in the disciplinary society power relations dominate the entire social field, it is necessary to add that the withdrawal of force constitutes an outside of that field as the possibility of social transformation. As Deleuze puts it, "the thought of the outside is a thought of resistance" (*F,* 90).

In the end, I would like to suggest briefly certain parallels between Deleuze's and Blanchot's concept of the outside as the irreducible residue of social formation and Judith Butler's notion of "the psychic remainder" in her recent study of the psychic life of power. It seems to me that the withdrawal of force in the process of its historical realization indeed leaves the reminder on the level of subject formation. Thus, although it is important to stress that the outside of the historical formation does not have a psychic status, the withdrawal of force does explain why historically constituted subjects can, in Butler's words, be "nevertheless haunted by inassimilable remainder, a melancholia that marks the limits of subjectivation." [19] To put it differently, there can be a limit to subjectivation only because the social "life of power" itself is marked and redoubled by what cannot be assimilated in the process of its actualization.

II.

What interests me in particular are the consequences of the split between the visible and the articulable for the historical constitution of bodies. Although feminist critics from Susan Bordo, Sandra Bartky, and Elizabeth Grosz to Judith Butler have found the political investment of the body by power relations to be one of the most productive aspects of Foucault's work, few have attempted to problematize such "investment" in the context of the possible disjunction between visible and articulable bodies. Foucault himself sometimes gives his critics ample reasons for ignoring this difference, when, for instance, in "Nietzsche, Genealogy, History" he generalizes the effects of power in terms of "inscription" so that the body can indeed be defined as "the inscribed surface of events," "totally imprinted by history" (*NGH*, 148). Indebted to Nietzsche's "physiological investigation" of the origin of morality in the body inscribed by pain, Foucault's understanding of power changes the very notion of bodily subjection: the subjection of the body "is not only obtained by instruments of violence or ideology; it can also be direct, physical, pitting force against force, bearing on material elements and yet without involving violence." [20] Neither violence (acting through the destruction of a body) nor ideology (acting on the level of consciousness) disciplinary power establishes within bodies a specific relation of force.

By accepting this analogy between political investment and inscription, Butler argues that the historical actualization of power is inseparable from the discursive forming of matter, which she calls "the process of materialization:" "here the body is not an independent materiality that is invested by power relations external to it, but it is that for which materialization and investiture are coextensive." [21] Yet, although it is true that for Foucault power relations are not external to bodies, this does not mean that the process of materialization is thus coextensive with "discursive intelligibility." We need to inquire about different modalities of materialization—a question Butler herself poses but does not pursue in terms of Foucault's work: "We need to ask," Butler writes, "whether there are *modalities* of materialization—as Aristotle suggests, and Althusser is quick to cite." [22] If we juxtapose *Discipline and Punish* and *The History of Sexuality,* volume I, we might distinguish two such modalities, implied by the difference between visible and discursive bodies, corresponding, however imperfectly, to the deployment of disciplines and the deployment of sexuality. Consider, for instance, that in contrast to the discourse-sex-power alignment in the first volume of *The History of Sexuality,* an alignment that culminates in the intensification of pleasure and in the incitement to discourse, Foucault makes clear that the disciplinary regime acting on the body is not concerned with the signification of the body (putting the body into language), but with its form of visibility—with "anatomo-chronological schema of behavior." In stressing what was new about the political investments characteristic of the projects of docility in the eighteenth century, Foucault remarks that "it was not or no longer *the signifying elements* of behavior or the language of the body, but the economy, the efficiency of movements . . . ; constrain bears upon *the forces rather than upon the signs*" (*DP,* 137; emphases mine). The target of disciplinary power is not the sign or the signifier but the force and the functionality of the body.

As the juxtaposition of *The History of Sexuality* and *Discipline and Punish* suggests, within the regime of biopower the process of materialization proceeds in two different but interrelated ways: through disciplinary forms of visibility, aiming at the regulation of the productive forces of the body, and through putting of sex into discourse, enabling the organization of power over life. As Foucault writes:

> Starting in the seventeenth century, this power over life evolved in two basic forms. . . . One of these poles . . . centered on the body as machine: its disciplining . . . all this was ensured by the procedures of power that characterized the *disciplines: an anatomo-politics of the human body.* The second, formed somewhat later, focused on the species body, the body imbued with the mechanics of life and serving as the basis of biological process. . . . Their supervision was effected through an entire series of interventions and *regulatory controls; a biopolitics of the population* (*HS*, 139).

The difficulty of this passage is that it sets up two types of contrasts. In a more obvious way, Foucault talks here about two poles of regulation: the individual bodies on the one hand and population on the other hand. Although Foucault claims in *The History of Sexuality* that it is the deployment of sexuality that mediates between the individual bodies and population, in *Discipline and Punish* disciplines, characterized as antinomadic techniques, also perform such a mediatory function. Consequently, what this passage implies is not only the contrast between individual and collective bodies as the two targets of power but also a disjunction between two types of materialization: the docile, disciplined body and the discursive, sexed body.

Foucault's description of disciplined body recalls Nietzsche's diagnosis of the embodiment of the ascetic ideal—the will to nothingness culminating in the mortification of the body—in training of docile individuals.[23] Rather than functioning as "an incitement to discourse" and intensification of pleasure, the specific forms of visibility—the isolated bodies fixed in cellular space and subjected to continuous observation and evaluation of their performance—invest the productivity of the body. These techniques make possible "the meticulous control of the operations of the body," by imposing uninterrupted coercion on "processes of activity rather than its result" (*DP*, 137). Drawing on this model of disciplinary power, feminist cultural critics have analyzed the contemporary technologies of the normalization of women's bodies ranging from fashion, diet, fitness regimes to plastic surgery and reproductive technologies. As Susan Bordo suggests, the disciplinary ascetic ideal manifests itself in popular feminine culture as an infinitely "malleable," perfectible "plastic body"—a body divided into "target zones," each submitted to different regimes of exercise, makeup, or corrective surgery.²⁴ Even though these modalities of regulation seem not to be directly concerned with the productivity of the female body, it might be worth recalling, as Hilary Radner argues, that the rise of the new disciplinary regimes occurs at the moment when "the majority of U.S. women worked outside the home." ²⁵

Although for Foucault the forms of discourse in the nineteenth century instill in sexed bodies the specific "management of life forces" through the hysterization of women's bodies, sexualization of childhood, psychiatrization of perversions, and socialization of reproduction, the forms of visibility materialize bodies according to the relation between the increased normalization and the diminished political force—a relation, which in itself is neither visible nor articulable:

> Discipline increases the forces of the body (in economic terms of utility) and diminishes these same forces (in political terms of obedience). In short, it dissociates power from the body; on the one hand, it turns it into an "aptitude," a "capacity," which it seeks to increase; on the other hand, it reverses the course of energy, the power that might result from it, and turns it into a relation of strict subjection. . . . Let us say that the disciplinary coercion establishes in the body the constricting link between an increased aptitude and an increased domination (*DP,* 138).

As this passage suggests, the body for Foucault is not a neutral surface inscribed by history, but the materialized relation of forces. While the discursive materialization of sexed bodies establishes a new set of relations between power and pleasure, history and life, and thus gives power access to "the life of the body and the life of species" (*HS,* 146), the disciplinary modality of materialization establishes a correlation between the normalization of the body and its political submission. In contrast to the eroticization of the apparatus of power, which, according to Judith Butler, might constitute the possibility of resistance, the reification of the bodily forces into socially useful capacities dissociates the body from its political power and eventually "reverses" its active forces into a reactive force of submission.

If we accept the hypothesis that the disjunction in the historical formation between visibility and articulation produces a rift between different modalities of materialization of bodies, as I have suggested in this essay, then we might have a better understanding of Foucault's approach to the body as "the inscribed surface of events." The fracture between different modalities of materialization allows Foucault to link the question of the body invested with the specific type of power to the notion of event, which he defines as a reversal of forces. In "The Discourse on Language" Foucault links this reversal with a dispersion of matter:

An event is neither substance, nor accident, nor quality nor process; events are not corporeal. And yet, an event is certainly not immaterial; it takes effect, becomes effect, always on the level of materiality. Events have their place . . . it occurs as an effect of, and in, material dispersion. Let us say that the philosophy of event should advance in the direction . . . of an incorporeal materialism (*DL,* 231).

As this paradoxical formulation of "incorporeal materialism" suggests, Foucault initiates here a radical rethinking of matter as the actualization of the specific relation between forces. In particular, the event of materialization precedes the distinctions between matter and form, and thus is irreducible to the corporeal as a permanently formed substance. Consequently, what is at stake in Foucault's redefinition of materialization is the possibility that bodies can undergo "the reversal of a relationship of forces" (*NGH,* 154). Such a notion of event seems at first at odds with the materialization of bodies, described in *Discipline and Punish* and *The History of Sexuality* volume I, where the actualization of the specific type of power is indeed coextensive with the fixed form of matter. However, if power is actualized in bodies according to multiple modalities, which, despite numerous interconnections, do not constitute a unified bodily form, then the process of materialization is never complete or uniform. Because of this structural incompleteness allowing for the reversal of forces, Foucault speaks of bodies as "volumes in disintegration." When considered as an event, the dispersion of matter does not entail a violent destruction of the body but opens a possibility of yet another reversal of forces, so that the intensification of pleasure and the increased productivity no longer, and not always, result in "the strict political subjection" we came to associate with docility.

Let me add that only by taking into account bodies as surfaces of events, can we make sense of what otherwise might appear as the incomprehensible contrast between docile bodies produced by the disciplinary apparatus and the body in the state of revolt, evoked in Foucault's description of prison revolts. It is important to recall at this point that the brief evocation of the prison revolts frames the entire historical project of *Discipline and Punish:* "In recent years, prison revolts have occurred throughout the world. . . . In fact, they were revolts, at the level of the body, against the very body of the prison" (*DP,* 30). As this passage suggests, Foucault is not only tracing the historical processes enabling us to understand the modes of subjection but also a possibility of resistance, understood as the reversal of forces, at the level of the bodies.

This possibility is disregarded, however, when feminist criticism ignores the multiple modalities of materialization in contemporary culture and focuses exclusively on the production of docile female bodies. As Hilary

Radner argues, a more fruitful approach to power in contemporary popular culture would focus on the disjunctions and contradictions in the production of the feminine bodies: "neither a model of cultural production
formulated in terms of penology (. . . docile body), nor in terms of sexuality (the culture of the self), is adequate to the formulation of . . . the feminine body. The feminine body is perhaps best understood as a terrain in
which these two modes of cultural production both contradict and support
each other." [26] This mode of analysis not only foregrounds ambiguities between agency and subjugation but also "offers a model of resistance that
does not fall back on some form of repressive hypothesis." [27]

III.

How can we reconcile these "revolts at the level of the bodies" with another claim of Foucault, namely, that disciplinary power reverses "the political axis of individualization"? This reversal means that in modernity individuality is no longer associated with sovereignty and privilege but with
subjection and docility: "in a disciplinary regime . . . individualization is
'descending': "as power becomes more anonymous and more functional,
those on whom it is exercised tend to be more strongly individualized"
(*DP,* 193). In this conception of the descending individuation, Foucault develops Nietzsche's diagnosis that the individuals presupposed by contract
theory are in fact produced through disciplinary training: "the right to make
promises evidently embraces and presupposes as a preparatory task that
one first *makes* men to a certain degree necessary, uniform, like among like,
regular, and consequently *calculable.*" [28] Despite the belated aestheticiza-
tion and romanticization of crime as the "right" of the great individuals, as
for instance, in the work of de Sade or De Quincey, in modern democracy
individuality ceases to be synonymous with exceptional subjects but becomes associated instead with calculability and the homogenization of the
social body.

As a way of reconciling these incompatible claims about revolt and subjection, I would like to suggest that the thesis of individualizing subjection
is a genealogical reworking of Foucault's earlier analysis of finitude in *The
Order of Things.* In "Man and his Doubles," Foucault argues that the subject formulated by modern social sciences can be described as an ambiguous
"enslaved sovereign." The crucial topos of finitude emerging in nineteenth
century postulates that the subject is determined by the historical forces of
labor, life, and language. Because these determinations appear to be not
only exterior but also anterior to the birth of the subject, they cannot be
recovered in the analysis of experience or self-knowledge. Thus, the historicity of labor, life, and language separates the modern subject from her

origin, which remains inaccessible and alien. For Foucault, the Marxist notion of alienation or the psychoanalytic theory of the unconscious are two different ways to thematize the radicality of this separation. No longer contemporaneous with what determines her, the modern subject is split between being and language, the unthought and the thought, the same and the other.

Foucault's critique of modern subjectivity, I argue, aims to radicalize both the theme of finitude and the dispersion of the subject that he inherits from modernity. Foucault claims that the modern thought of finitude and the historicity of life, labor, and language is not radical enough as it is still motivated by the reclaiming of origin as the site of the lost truth of the subject. Thus, modern historicism is grounded in the self-reflective subject aiming to recover the always already lost truth of its own past. Similarly, the discovery of the other within the subject informs the will to knowledge as the impossible conversion of "the unthought" into "the same": "more fundamentally, modern thought is advancing toward that region where man's Other must become the Same as himself." [29] Despite the discovery of the "radical spatiality of the body," history motivated by the search for origin in fact resembles a project of a metaphysician that "would seek its soul in the distant ideality of the origin" (*NGH*, 145). For Foucault, then, the critique of the origin and self-reflexivity goes hand in hand with the critique of the soul animating the historical will to knowledge. As he writes, "the historian's history finds its support outside of time and pretends to base its judgments on an apocalyptic objectivity. This is only possible, however, because of its belief in eternal truth, *the immortality of the soul*" (*NGH*, 152). No longer seeking the lost truth of the subject in the ever receding origin, Foucault's historical analysis of disciplinary biopower (in place of the historicity of labor and life) radicalizes the finitude of the subject and, in so doing, liberates "divergence" within its fictional identity: "where the soul pretends unification or self fabricates the coherent identity" (*NGH*, 145), genealogical research "introduces discontinuity into our very being as it divides our emotions, dramatizes our instincts, multiplies our body and sets it against itself" (*NGH*, 154).

Perhaps now we are in a better position to understand why Foucault calls *Discipline and Punish* a genealogical critique "of the modern soul" (*DP*, 23). In a very Nietzschean passage, Foucault argues that the appearance of the moral conscience (soul) as a new object of punishment at the beginning of the nineteenth century is but an effect produced by the new disciplinary technologies of the body:

> If the surplus of power possessed by the king gives rise to the duplication of his body, has not the surplus of power exercised on the subjected body of the condemned man given rise to another type of duplication? That of a

"non-corporal," a "soul," as Mably called it. . . . It would be wrong to say that the soul is an illusion, or an ideological effect. On the contrary, it exists, it has a reality, it is produced permanently around, on, within the body by the functioning of power that is exercised on those punished (*DP,* 29).

No other passage produced more misunderstanding in Foucault feminist criticism than the one I just cited. Lois McNay, for instance, reads this passage as a "problematic inversion of Cartesian body/soul dualism," substituting the concept of the body for the concept of person.[30] Even Judith Butler, who most rigorously defends the possibility of agency in Foucault's work, argues in *The Psychic Life of Power* that Foucault "appears to treat the subject as if it received unilaterally the effect of the Lacanian symbolic."[31] Yet, what is at stake in Foucault's critique of the soul is not the evacuation of the psyche, but rather, a radicalization of the finitude and conflict within the subject. As Foucault repeats after Nietzsche, the genealogy "makes one 'happy, unlike the metaphysicians, to posses in oneself not an immortal soul but many mortal ones.' And in which of those souls, history will not discover a forgotten identity eager to be reborn, but a complex system of distinct and multiple elements, unable to be mastered by the powers of synthesis" (*NGH,* 161).

Both Foucault and Nietzsche describe the appearance of the soul in terms of the confusion of causes and effects. Foucault claims that just as the excess of power associated with the exercise of sovereignty produces a double body of the king, so too, the excess of reactive forces associated with subjection redoubles the subjected body in the noncorporal soul, which produces "sublime self-deception" by misinterpreting subjection as freedom. As a ghostly double of the subjected body, the soul makes subjection possible by hiding it behind the appearance of "the spiritual sovereignty." Nietzsche, likewise, diagnoses the appearance of the soul in terms of a confusion of causes and effects, freedom and subjection:

> There is no "being" behind doing, effecting, becoming; "the doer" is merely a fiction added to the deed—the deed is everything. The popular mind in fact doubles the deed; when it sees the lightning flash, it is the deed of a deed: it posits the same event first as cause and then a second time as its effect. . . . The subject (or to use a more popular expression, the *soul*) has perhaps been believed in hitherto more firmly than anything else on earth because it makes possible to the majority of mortals, the weak and oppressed of every kind, the sublime self-deception that interprets weakness as freedom, and their being thus and thus as a *merit.*[32]

The invention of the soul not only unifies multiple fissures within modern subjectivity but also sustains the misrecognition of subjection as freedom. For Foucault, a similar function is performed by the speculative character of sex. Insofar as it is constructed as a fictitious unity of anatomy, sensation, instinct, and meaning, or as a principle of our secret identity, sex makes it possible to link together knowledge, liberation, and pleasure. In this sense, sex replaces the function of the soul "over the centuries it has become more important than our soul, more important almost than our life" (*HS,* 156).

Similar to the speculative function of sex, the soul imprinted on delinquency privatizes and separates illegality from social and political struggles with which it was still potentially linked at the end of the eighteenth century. In so doing, the soul, like sex, becomes the effective instrument of the management of collectivity: "on the horizon of these illegal practices . . . there emerged struggles of strictly political kind . . . a good many of them were able to turn themselves to account in overall political struggles and sometimes even to lead directly to them" (*DP,* 273–74). As a principle of subjection, the soul disarms the transgression of the law, separates it from social and political struggles, and turns it into a case of the individual pathology in need of moral reformation.

As we have seen, Foucault diagnoses in his critique of the soul a complicity between the historical will to knowledge and the formation of moral conscience. In "Nietzsche, Genealogy, History," Foucault argues that the trope of the soul, and by extension, the speculative character of sex, functions as both the principle of subjugation of individuals and the unacknowledged ascetic ideal animating the historical will to truth ("the beliefs that place the historian in the family of ascetics") (*NGH,* 158). In so doing, he suggests parallels between modern historicism grounded in the figure of the self-reflective subject and the formation of moral conscience (the soul), which, according to Nietzsche, is likewise an effect of a certain reflective turn of the reactive forces of punishment upon the subject.[33] In her reading of Hegel, Nietzsche, and Freud, Judith Butler has identified the figure of self-reflective recoil as the main trope of subjugation. Commenting on this paradoxical figure, Butler stresses "a persistent problem that emerges when we try to think of the possibility of a will that takes itself as its own object and, through the formation of that kind of reflexivity, binds itself to itself, acquires its own identity through reflexivity. . . . Is this strange posture of the will in the service of social regulation?"[34] What is then at stake in Foucault's critique of the soul is an overcoming of this subjugating reflexivity operating in both morality and history. By radicalizing the topos of finitude, by dissociating genealogy from the search for the lost origins, Foucault gives the figure of self-recoil one more turn so that it initiates its own overcoming. This is yet another sense in which his critique of the soul follows Nietzsche: "all great things bring about their own destruction through an act of self-overcoming."[35]

Foucault suggests such overcoming of reflexivity when he discusses the internalization of the observer/observed relation in the disciplinary regime: "he who is subjected to a field of visibility . . . he inscribes in himself the power relation in which he simultaneously plays both roles; he becomes the principle of his own subjection" (*DP*, 202–3). Given Foucault's reticence, we can only speculate about the effects of the radicalization of this split within the subject. For instance, what does it mean to occupy both positions—the observer and the observed—simultaneously when panopticon is defined as "a machine for dissociating the see/being seen dyad"? In addition to internalized surveillance, isn't the mechanical dissociation itself also inscribed within the subject? Does not then the subject become a dissociated dyad, split into the invisible, "unverifiable" observer and the fixed observed object who does not see? Although this series of doubling reminiscent of "Man and His Doubles" in *The Order of Things* is the condition of the actualization of surveillance, at the same time, the dissociation at the core of the subject constitutes a possibility of a psychic space very different from the soul, which, as we have seen, acts as the instrument of subjection insofar as it unifies being. In contrast to the soul, which isolates the prisoner from his fellow inmates and any form of exteriority more effectively that his cell does, the dissociation within the subject opens a relation to the outside.

What Foucault stresses in *Discipline and Punish* is not only a dissociation within the subject but also the internal conflict among different subject positions "superimposed" one upon the other:

> The correlative of penal justice may well be the offender, but the correlative *of the penitentiary apparatus is someone other;* this is a delinquent . . . representing a type of anomaly. . . . This penitentiary element introduced in turn *a third character* between the individual who is condemned by the law and the individual who carries out this law (*DP*, 254; emphases added).

If, following Judith Butler, we compare this passage to the structure of interpellation, then we have to notice that this mechanism fails to perform an essential function of interpellation; namely, it fails to institute a coherent position of an addressee.[36] This is the case because the inverted law "hails" at least two incompatible "characters" at once: the juridical subject and the pathological individual (we will come back to a third character, the subject of internalized surveillance, in a moment). Unlike a juridical subject abstracted from any particularity and defined only in reference to general rights and obligations, this other character, the delinquent, constitutes a particular, pathological life-form—"a pathological gap in human species" (*DP*, 254). Despite the mediating function of the norm, there is no continuity between the juridical abstraction and the sequence of the particulars, a stuttering proliferation of "this" ("this anomaly, this deviation, this potential danger, this illness, this form of existence" [*DP,* 255]) character-istic of delinquency. Because of this noncoincidence, the "hailed individual" is always "elsewhere," in an eccentric relation to a position he or she assumes.[37]

The eccentric relation to a subject position one assumes means that the effect of the Foucauldian interpellation cannot be described in terms of the specular (mis)recognition that Althusser deploys. One implication of such an eccentric relation is, therefore, that the discursive constitution of sub-jects cannot be reduced to an imaginary relation—and this might be the most important consequence of the rift between visibility and articulation. In place of the imaginary recognition of individual subjects in the absolute Subject, Foucault deploys the trope of the parasite to indicate the decen-tered and conflicting subjectivity behind the unity of the soul. Not only the two incompatible forms of subjectivity (the juridical subject and the delin-quent) coexist as the parasite and its host, but this parasitical symbiosis reveals retrospectively a prior split within the juridical subject—the con-tradiction between the fallen monstrous class and the transgressors of the law (*DP,* 256).

Rather than reducing the problematic of modern subjectivity to ego for-mation or to passive receptacle of power, my reading of Foucault's *Disci-pline and Punish* follows the Nietzschean "hypothesis," namely that "the assumption of one single subject is . . . unnecessary; perhaps it is just as per-missible to assume a multiplicity of subjects, whose interaction and struggle is the basis of our thought and our consciousness in general?"[38]

One consequence of stressing the disjunction between the forms of visi-bility and articulation in the materialization of bodies and the historical constitution of subjects is the possibility of resistance. Although it seems, as many feminist scholars point out, that *Discipline and Punish* precludes resistance, Foucault is very explicit that what motivates his project are prison revolts taking place in France in the early seventies. In the course of his study, he cites several other historical cases in which the contradictions in the structure of interpellation and the modes of materialization are mobi-lized for the sake of resistance. In the chapter "Illegalities and Delinquency," Foucault explicitly discusses the growing peasants' and workers' illegalities from the end of the eighteenth century to the Revolutions of 1848 and the development of the complex political dimension of these illegalities, which opposed law as an instrument of class domination: "A whole series of il-legalities was inscribed in struggles in which those struggling knew that they were confronting both the law and the class that had imposed it" (*DP,* 274). It is in this context that Foucault cites a rather minor and iso-lated case from August 1840 involving a thirteen-year-old delinquent. This incident was picked up and discussed extensively by *La Phalange* journal associated with the Fourierists, who in their antipenal polemics attempted to give the crime a positive political value. In the impudent responses to the judge, the thirteen-year-old exposes not only the law as an instrument of injustice but also the disciplinary apparatus behind it: "Confronted with discipline on the face of the law, there is illegality, which puts itself forward as a right; it is indiscipline, rather than the criminal offense, that causes the rupture" (*DP*, 290–91). This anonymous delinquent, conjured by Foucault from the pages of the workers' press, exploits the contradictions within the structure of disciplinary interpellation precisely at a point where law is inverted into counterlaw, and the juridical into the natural. He pits the delinquency against the law and the law against delinquency, by affirming "indiscipline" as a political right. We may wonder whether Foucault gives us here a concrete historical example of what he alluded to briefly at the end of "Two Lectures" as a "new form of right" mobilized in the struggle against the disciplinary power: "If one wants to look for a non-disciplinary form of power, or rather, to struggle against disciplines . . . it is not toward the ancient right of sovereignty that one should turn, but towards a possibility of a new form of right, one which must indeed be anti-disciplinarian, but at the same time liberated from the principle of sovereignty." [39]

The fact that the workers' press picked up such a minor affair is for Foucault indicative of the possibilities of resistance against the disciplinary regime. The commentaries that followed in *La Phalange,* and which Foucault cites extensively, seized upon the double "juridical-natural" reference of disciplinary interpellation and gave it one more twist. In these antipenal polemics, the immorality and pathology are removed from the discourse of nature and placed on the side of enslaving civilization whereas nature and the "instinctive development," and not law, are affirmed as "immediate liberty" and inalienable right. In referring to these polemics, Foucault is obviously not interested in the Fourierist utopia proclaiming the abolition of the social restraints for the sake of instinctual gratification; what he finds in this rather atypical for him historical example is a political strategy that manipulates fissures in modern subjectivities and in the structures of interpellation for the sake of resistance. For Foucault, *La Phalange* manages to politicize the polemics around the crime, to represent the problem of punishment as struggle—as "a rumbling from the mist of the battle-field"— rather than as a dilemma for a "humanitarian" reform. In repeating the tone of these polemics in his own study, Foucault finishes *Discipline and Punish* with a similar injunction: in the carceral city "we must hear the distant roar of the battle."

By focusing on the paradoxical causality in Foucault's work, I not only propose a more complex model of the modernization of the patriarchal power but also argue for the importance of the Foucauldian ethos of resistance for feminism. Neither a simple effect of disciplinary power nor an obstacle on the path of its realization, the multiple fissures in the materialization of bodies and in the constitution of the modern subjects are both the condition of power's actualization and the possibility of its transformation. Foucault does not offer us a simple choice between subjection and resistance. As he writes, "No one is responsible for an emergence; no one can glory in it, since it always occurs in the interstice" (*NGH*, 150). This does not mean, however, that the question of agency is immaterial for Foucault but that it has to be rethought in the context of the event understood as the emergence of a different configuration of forces. What opens the possibility of such an event—which in the case of *Discipline and Punish* would mean a rupture of the strict correlation between forces of utility and subjection—is the relation of human agency to what exceeds it, namely, to the experience of the outside. The outside in question is what is excluded in the process of actualization of power and what figures as a reservoir of the not yet realized force. For Foucault, it is the relation to the outside that opens a possibility of power's transformation and the creation of the new modes of life: new sexualities, genders, new ways of being.

Carnival:
The Novel, Wor(l)ds,
and Practicing Resistance

JANE DREXLER

Truth belongs to no one; it is realized, rather, in the realm of dialogue, where the linked utterances of the self and the other interpenetrate, yielding a truth which is fluid, ephemeral, and evanescent. Not only does it not reside with any *one*, but it is itself contextual, depending upon its temporal and spatial configuration, [and] in the interlacing of the dialogic word of the self *and* the other.

—David Danow, *The Thought of Mikhail Bakhtin*

My interest in Bakhtin's heteroglossia and Deleuze and Guattari's concept of becoming originates from my experiences within, or in many cases outside of, the dominant discourses that authorize meaning-making, knowledge-production, who can speak, and who cannot. My interest also originates from my courses, as I often, not without ambivalence, teach the "proper way" to write philosophical papers to new undergraduates—usually from diverse social and cultural positions, which have their own "proper ways" of speaking and writing—and in that way, I reinscribe the legitimacy of dominant discourses and the silencing of others. My interest involves thinking about ways to utilize dominant discourses—such as philosophical languages, languages of my home, languages of the southwestern, working-class Anglo-American—as tools for developing strategies of resistance within the discursive frameworks that circumscribe my experiences, my understandings, and my ability to speak and be heard. I want to examine to what extent one can experiment with and practice resistant strategies that move in between different ideological and discursive frameworks and integrations in order not only to conceptualize an ontology of difference and heterogeneous multiplicities, but also to develop ways of reading and acting in the concrete world.

In my attempts to think through possible strategies, I have found that Mikhail Bakhtin forms an apparently unlikely coalition with Gilles Deleuze

216

and Félix Guattari. Although these two philosophies are rarely connected, it is precisely by doing so that I am able to understand and to develop strategies for practicing the experimentations and resistances that I am calling for above. Deleuze and Guattari, I contend, develop an ontology of difference in their theory of multiplicities and becoming, an ontology that Mikhail Bakhtin recognizes to be at play in the aesthetic, and specifically, in the novel's heteroglossic styles. As I will argue, the coupling of Bakhtin's theory of the emancipatory possibilities within the discourses of the novel with Deleuze and Guattari's notions of fluidity in the theory of becoming produces an ontology of difference that can offer a strategy for actively dismantling the illusion of the totality of the powers of domination and for creatively engaging the subversions that lie in the cracks and carnivals of the dismantled social body.

Mikhail Bakhtin, a Russian social philosopher of literature in the mid-1900s, understood, firsthand, the dualistic tendencies of monologic systems and their claims for exclusive privilege and objective authority. Living in Stalinist Russia, Bakhtin experienced the oppression of monologic authority and spent the majority of his philosophic effort envisioning an alternative to this system within the novel's narrative styles, based on the fundamental notion that literature in particular and art in general reflect the societal conditions from which they originate.[1] Bakhtin theorized that within the different positions and classes of society there exist a multitude of different language systems and voices—what he termed "heteroglossia." He argued that heteroglossia is resistant to all dominant ideologies that assume they are the only voice of truth and that therefore claim to have an exclusive privilege for speaking that truth. Examining the characteristics of the novel, he determined that heteroglossia was at play in its "dialogics" and characterized its dynamic system in terms of the "carnival," a festival of "free and familiar contact." Through the carnival, he argued, the dialogic method exposes the false dichotomy of "center" and "margin" that codifies the existing power structure's claim to centrality, legitimacy, and authority, and, in doing so, serves as a site for resistant practices against the dualistic foundations of monologic discourse and society.

Bakhtin's notion of heteroglossia is often criticized by social philosophers who claim that the free and familiar contact of the carnival cannot be permanently established in society and, therefore, can never really do anything more than appease the masses and maintain the status quo.[2] However, as I will show, the critics fail to understand that the carnival cannot be thought of in terms of a traditional utopic envisioning of "the way it ought to be," but rather should be conceived in terms of an "anti-utopian utopia" that serves as a site for becoming and multiplicities, that has no beginning and no end—that is, no blueprint, no goal—but rather, ceaselessly engages in fluid experimentation while offering new glimpses of alternative systems of relations.

In *A Thousand Plateaus,* in the section called "Becoming-Intense, Becoming-Animal, Becoming-Imperceptible. . . ," Deleuze and Guattari develop a theory of multiplicities and becoming, an ontology of difference that, at the very least, challenges static conceptions of identity and sociality and exposes and practices active, creative reconfigurations of both. It should be noted in this introductory section that Deleuze and Guattari's work is seen by many feminist and other marginalized scholars to be of little use. Several critiques are based on the claims that Deleuze and Guattari further marginalize women and minorities in their theory of difference, a move that is irresponsible if not downright patriarchal.[3] In the chapter "Becoming Intense. . . ," for instance, the status of women and minorities seems to be problematic, because Deleuze and Guattari appear to require woman, for example, to cease being a woman in order to "become" woman. The result of this requirement, some feminists claim, is that, rather than including women and minorities, differences must disappear in order to become, and this erasure is unacceptable for those who, rightly, acknowledge the problems of marginalized members of society who are already forced by the dominant authority to disappear as different.

Although it is not my intention to launch into a full discussion of either the critiques or responses to them in this preliminary section, it is important to introduce some of the feminist critiques of Deleuze and Guattari and the postmodern social critiques of Bakhtin, because later in this essay, I will make use of them in order to see how Deleuze and Guattari can provide Bakhtin's heteroglossia and carnival a stronger reading in terms of anti-utopian processes of becoming and to see to what degree Bakhtin's concept of heteroglossia can offer feminists an alternate way to understand Deleuze and Guattari's theory of becoming.

Heteroglossia in the Novel

According to Bakhtin, in "Discourse in the Novel," heteroglossia refers to a "multiplicity of social voices and a wide variety of their links and interrelationships."[4] Bakhtin believes that such social voices, in their ongoing dialogues, are constantly changing. They are engaged in a process of feedback and conflict, interacting with new voices, causing more feedback and conflict, and so on. Bakhtin declares that this aspect of multiple voices and their dialogic interactions with one another is crucial to heteroglossia, in that, whether we are examining language as a whole or individual utterances, no voice is singular and unitary. Rather than positing the unitary language that suppresses all difference and produces the stability of the one voice, Bakhtin argues that language is engaged in constant interactions, processes, and changes, which he describes in terms of centripetal and centrifugal forces—those forces in an utterance that unify meaning and representation, and those that simultaneously decentralize, fragment, and multiply meanings within that utterance.[5]

In explaining "dialogics" in the novel, Bakhtin emphasizes a relationship between the reader, text, and author in that not only are multiple voices inherent in the characters of the novel, but also there are voices that the author brings with her (in terms of her own experiences, conflicts, and position in society); and, similarly, there are inner voices brought to the reading by the readers, in terms of their subject positions, the relations of power between subject positions, and the experiences that have informed their understandings of the reading. Bakhtin argues that, due to its heteroglossic and dialogic characteristics, the novel is a medium in which these social speech types are realized, even in a culture that tries to silence all but the powerful. The heteroglossic nature of society is subverted by the authoritarian suppression of difference by a system of thought that effectively maintains disembodied, objective authority. In order to bring about a change in this oppressive system, Bakhtin seeks, acknowledges, and brings into the forefront evidence of heteroglossia, silenced in society but nevertheless existent.

When Bakhtin speaks of the "novel," it is sometimes assumed that he is speaking of novels in general, that is, any book in a fictional, narrative style. This leads many to conclude that he is incorrect in making claims for the subversive qualities of heteroglossia, because there are many examples of novels whose purpose is a propagandist reinstantiation of the dominant authority. However, Bakhtin limits the label novel to express those literary forms that house heteroglossia. At first this reasoning may seem circular, because Bakhtin (1) finds characteristics of heteroglossia in the novel, but then turns around and says that (2) whatever has heteroglossia is a novel, and at the same time acknowledges that (3) some novels do not promote heteroglossia. However, this confusion can be cleared up. Bakhtin acknowledges that there are oppressive narrative literary forms. But his interest is not necessarily in making a comprehensive claim about all novels. It is, rather, in examining subversive literary texts in order to determine the characteristics that make them subversive and the possibilities that lie therein. Bakhtin finds the most subversive qualities of literature to be the most prevalent in narrative forms, and this is why he primarily considers novels. He acknowledges, not only that there are propagandist novels, but also that there are "novelistic" epics and poetry. It is important to understand this aspect of Bakhtin's definition of the novel in that heteroglossic tendencies in literature sometimes produce resistance and sometimes maintain the status quo. I will discuss this more clearly when I examine the act of reading the novel, in terms of the ways in which the reader reads him-/herself and the world while reading the novel. However, at this point it is enough to say that it is not my purpose here to argue whether or not a particular novel houses heteroglossia and which ones do it better than others. Rather, I intend to examine to what degree and in what ways heteroglossia is suppressed or brought to the forefront in the act of reading and writing. Because heteroglossia concerns the centripetal and centrifugal forces unifying and disunifying language and authorial intention, simultaneously, heteroglossia remains a potential site of resistance, disrupting the illusion of unified language and thought. Thus, it is the acts of reading and writing and how one comes to engage oneself and the world in these acts that determines to what extent the experience of the heteroglot novel can reinscribe the dominant conception of unity and stable identity or disrupts that conception. However, it is first relevant to explain how Bakhtin exposes heteroglossia within the text and authorial intentions of the novel.

In "Discourse in the Novel," Bakhtin posits three major aspects of the novel that exemplify its heteroglossic quality: the use of multiple languages and speech types, "parodic stylizations," and "hybrid constructions." Bakhtin distinguishes the common language used in a novel from that of the monologic voice of authority used in other types of literature.[6] Generally speaking, "there is no 'language of the novel' because it can assimilate all languages, including those languages characteristic of other genres."[7] Whereas the epic and poetry tend to be closed and inaccessible for dialogic interactions, the novel's use of multiple common languages enables an open system of dialogue between the different genres of discourse.[8] Common language refers to a language written down just as one might hear it in different cultural situations in society, with informal idioms, slang, and so on. In the novel, an individual's speech reflects her culture and experiences, in that there is not one speech style that is used by the author to relay what all characters say (as is the case with the epic). In this way, utilizing common language forges a move away from language as merely a carrier of a theme. Language in the novel becomes a theme in itself; it relays a message of its own—play within and between multiple voices.

Another important characteristic of heteroglossia is "parodic stylization," which concerns a novel's potential for exposing critiques of social structures and power relations by using parody, hyperbole, or other forms of ironic discourse. The novel "makes available a form of appropriating and organizing heteroglossia [in which] we find a comic-parodic reprocessing of almost all the levels of literary language."[9] Parodic stylizations, as Bakhtin explains, utilize literary discourse to direct attention to the relations of power between authorized and nonauthorized discourses.

Consider Virginia Woolf's *Orlando* and her parody of literary authority and the proper topics of literature by using more conversational (less authorized) discourse, with respect to the event of Orlando sitting in a chair, thinking:

> Life, it has been agreed by everyone whose opinion is worth consulting, is the only fit subject for novelist or biographer; life, the same authorities have decided, has nothing whatever to do with sitting still in a chair and thinking. . . . Therefore—since sitting in a chair and thinking is precisely what Orlando is doing now—There is nothing for [us to do but] recite the calendar, tell one's beads, blow one's nose, stir the fire, look out of the window, until [Orlando is] done. . . . Or suppose she had got up and killed a wasp. Then, at once, we could out with our pens and write. For there would be blood shed, if only the blood of a wasp.[10]

These parodic stylizations call into question the legitimacy of certain types of discourse over others by utilizing a form of "naïve critique." Woolf's mockery of authorized discourse and literary authority's call for "proper literary topics" illustrates parodic stylization in Bakhtin's concept of the novel, exemplifying, not only heteroglossia, but also its capacity for subversive critique.

The third major aspect of the author's style that Bakhtin analyzes in order to reveal heteroglossia is called "hybrid construction." One aspect of hybrid construction concerns what Bakhtin calls "intonational quotation marks."[11] Considered in terms of "an utterance that belongs, by its grammatical and compositional markers, to a single speaker, but that actually contains mixed within it two utterances, two speech manners, two styles, two 'languages,'" intonational quotation marks contain multiple voices within a single phrase.[12] One way I understand intonational quotation marks is by insertion of authorial opinion and critique within what appears to be descriptive. Consider, again, Woolf:

> If we compare the picture of Orlando as a man with that of Orlando as a woman we shall see that though both are undoubtedly one and the same person, there are certain changes. The man has his hand free to seize his sword; the woman must use hers to keep the satins from slipping from her shoulders. The man looks the world full in the face, *as if it were made for his uses and fashioned to his liking.*[13]

Here, the insertion of a qualitative, evaluative phrase serves to emphasize the presence of the author's subject position, world views, values, and so on within the discourse of objective description.

These many voices emerging from the author's style and the textual representation of multiple integrated discourses and meaning making also include the voices of the novel's characters. The words and actions of different characters in the novel exemplify the different ideologies in society, allowing the reader interaction with them. In *Orlando,* Woolf exhibits the differing voices of her characters, complete with their differing preconceptions of society and multiple ways of conceiving reality. One night when Orlando, now the English ambassador to Turkey, decides to throw a huge party, the event becomes somewhat chaotic. The narrator explains that though the precise event is shady, there are a few remaining, partially destroyed documents chronicling the event.

—From the diary of John Fenner Brigge: . . . Thus when the rockets began to soar into the air. . . . I came to the conclusion that this demonstration of our skill in the art of pyrotechny was valuable . . . because it impressed upon them [the] superiority of the British.

—Miss Penelope Hartopp (in a letter to a friend about the night): ". . . Ravishing! . . . Wondrous . . . gold plate . . . candelabras . . . jellies made to represent His Majesty's ships . . . swans made to represent water lilies . . . ladies' headdresses at least 6 foot high! . . ."

—From the *Gazette:* ". . . as the clock struck twelve . . . six Turks of the imperial bodyguard . . . held torches right and left . . . rockets rose up . . . a great shout went out from the people . . . next, the admiral advanced . . . placed a Collar of the Most Noble Order around [the ambassador's] neck. . . ." [14]

This example of the many characters and their varied interpretations of the evening is an invaluable illustration of multiple voices in the novel. Brigge is a classic British, Anglo-Saxon military man whose concern is the superiority of the British Empire. Miss Penelope Hartopp is engaged in different matters, seeing the evening in terms of the individuals attending the event, the luxury of the décor, and the elegant table. The *Gazette* is a voice of rationalism: this-happened, then this-happened, then this-happened, allowing for no implication or admittance that there were other ways of interpreting the evening. However, as Woolf illustrates, the *Gazette* is mistaken. So that when the reader encounters each of these characters' voices, the possibility of multiple interactions and interpretations arises and thus actively disrupts attempts to give a stable, static explanation of the event.

Not only does the text influence the experiences, dialogues and meanings of the reader, the reader herself also influences the meanings and interactions of and for the text. Therefore, each reading offers new interactions and new meanings, and in so doing, not only exposes heteroglossia in the novel, but also in each individual and society. According to Dale Bauer, "In the act of reading, we divest ourselves of the illusion of monologic self-hood. . . . We discover our own multiple identities (multivocality) against the grain of dominant ideology which fixes us as unitary subjects." [15]

Considered in this light, the acts of reading and writing can be approached as a cultural strategy and as steps towards reenvisioning and rearticulating our voice and our place in the social dialogue. The dialogics of the novel, then, by exemplifying the heteroglossia present in society, introduce the possibility of change, in that the constant interaction between the voices in the novel and those of the author and readers maintains a dynamic system, allowing no "One," single voice to silence all others.

It is important at this point to qualify the above analysis. Heteroglossia is the presence and play of multiple voices between the text, author, and reader, but the potential for creative and subversive activities requires a particular way of writing and reading oneself through writing and reading the novel. As aforementioned, the centripetal and centrifugal forces within discourse render it the case that the activities of reading and writing the novel can either reinscribe dominant monology and meaning making, so as to maintain the conception of identity and thought as unified, complete, and stable; or it can open up the potential for experimenting with self-conceptions and world conceptions that disrupt that stability and unification. One of the issues at hand here is that of moving beyond Bakhtin's description of multiple voices in the novel and in society—a description that, as critics of Bakhtin have alluded, can result in a kind of relativism regarding identities and social positions—into a recognition of, and approach to, heteroglossia that does not render invisible the concrete social barriers and privileges that reinforce some discourses, experiences, and identities as "more valid" than others.

Even if we take heteroglossia at Bakhtin's word—that is, heteroglossia celebrates and brings to the forefront multiple languages, experiences, thoughts, and identities—it still remains to be seen how heteroglossia can enable creative resistances to real world situations saturated by power relations, domination, and the oppression of every mode of thinking, speaking, writing, understanding, and acting. Addressing this issue is of paramount concern for me as I move through the remainder of this essay. As I will show, first, by examining Bakhtin's theory of the carnivalesque and the critics' responses to it, the issue revolves around not envisioning heteroglossia as an image of a better world, one full of multiplicity without hegemonic suppression of difference, but rather, that the power for resistance in heteroglossia depends on how heteroglossia is taken up in the acts of reading and writing themselves—and for my purposes, primarily in the act of reading and acting within oneself and the world through reading the novel.

It is a matter of reading as practicing processes of becoming, which can be understood utilizing aspects of Deleuze and Guattari's ontology of multiplicities. However, reading as a process of becoming is not a matter of becoming something, whether that be multiple identities or a pure multiplicitous society. It is a process of experimentation, a creative process of meaning making that expands multiple understandings of identity, exposes the illusions of unified thought and Truth discourses, and enables theorizing and acting from within those new understandings. It is a matter of how to take up reading and acting (and this can be reading and acting in the world and not simply a written text) and for what reasons. Before moving on to what Deleuze and Guattari can offer, I want to examine how far Bakhtin, himself, can take heteroglossia and its translation into experimenting and acting within society, through the theory of the "carnival."

The Carnival

Bakhtin considers heteroglossia to be the "carnivalesque" quality of the novel. The interaction of multiple voices and discourses lays the foundation for Bakhtin's carnival in that voices can be reconceived as a means of power, a power that engages dialogue, opening up discourse as fluid. "To open another's discourse is to make it vulnerable to change, to exposure, to the carnival." [16] In a society where a single ideology gains too much strength—be it religion, capitalism, education, or whatever—heteroglossia is suppressed in order to maintain the illusion of objectivity. However, in the dialogics of the novel and the opening up of discourse to engage fluidity and multivocality, heteroglossia reveals itself, thereby exposing the monological illusion.

The carnival is the site at which characters become the participants in multiple discourses rather than objects of a discourse that functions to speak for them, and Bakhtin utilizes the work of the Renaissance writer Rabelais to exemplify this feature. According to Clark and Holquist, "Rabelais's work is infamous for its breaches of good taste, and for its willful intermingling of medical, technological, and highbrow, self-consciously literary vocabularies with the crudest billingsgate." [17] The intermingling of language systems and breaches of propriety with respect to literary topics are very appealing for Bakhtin as exhibitions of the theory of dialogized heteroglossia. Thus, Rabelais is important to Bakhtin because he "turns away from stultified and artificial language of the official culture of his day and makes extensive use of the more vital, variegated, and changeable kinds of language to be found in carnival." [18]

Bakhtin develops the idea of the carnivalesque nature of heteroglossia by looking at the structure, the social situation, and the function of the carnival throughout history, but especially in Rabelais' Renaissance. Bakhtin describes this in "Discourse in the Novel":

> At a time when [epic] poetry was accomplishing the task of cultural, national, and political centralization of the verbal-ideological world in the higher official socio-ideological levels, on the lower levels, on the stages of local fairs . . . the heteroglossia of the clown sounded forth, ridiculing all "languages" and dialects, there developed the literature of the fabliaux . . . of street songs, folksayings, anecdotes, where there was no language center at all.[19]

The lack of a language center forms the basis of Bakhtin's conception of the heteroglossic nature of society, in that, with the realization of the many voices opposed to illusion of the "One" (as in the case of the clowns at the fair), the figure of authority loses its all-powerful center in these, so-called, lower levels of society, sparking new experimentations in multivocality.

In the carnival, every member is an active member. According to Bakhtin, "Carnival is not a spectacle seen by the people; they live in it, and everyone participates because its very idea embraces all the people."[20] Without the division between the passive spectators (the masses) and the privileged social actors, all can invoke their own presence—in terms of their voices and their actions—thus temporarily altering the social balance of power. And, for Bakhtin, because heteroglossia is at play in the carnival society, its discourse is transformed into a fluid discourse, able to experiment with meaning making, identity formations, and subject positions.

Like the novel's dialogism, the carnival's multivocality, in contrast to authoritarian society, opposes any claim to a closed and total language system. Bauer offers the following analysis of the fluidity of carnival language: "Bakhtin's carnival hero seeks to resist the essentializing framework 'of other people's words about [them] that might finalize and deaden them.'"[21] Such fluidity cannot house any absolutes and therefore offers alternative practices to hierarchy and monology.

Because of the novel's heteroglossic nature and its instantiation of the characteristics of the carnival as laid out above, it exemplifies the carnival "in miniature," so to speak. In this way, the carnivalesque novel is not an "event" in the sense of being something that actually organizes a structure of society, nor is it an event that is solely abstract and nonexistent in the "real" world. Rather, the novel serves as the intermediary site within which the voices of the writer and those of the reader can actively engage in interactions and subversions of domination.

Critique of Carnival as a Utopian Image

The major problem for many social philosophers with Bakhtin's theories stems from the question of how his conception is to be realized in society; some go so far as to doubt whether Bakhtin's notion of the carnival is, in fact, empowering at all. Regarding carnival as an utopian image, the argument against it is based on the following: Can a necessarily temporary situation (as Bakhtin, himself, maintains dialogism and carnival are) be a powerful resistance to dominant authority? Given the doubt surrounding this, critics have concluded that carnival, as Bakhtin describes it, merely appeases the masses and is not only tolerated by, but necessary to, the authoritative and hierarchicized paradigm's preservation of its position as dominant. Put simply, critics hold that Bakhtin's theory is weak because at the end of the carnival—in our case, the end of reading a book—the wealthy and powerful are still wealthy and powerful, and the marginalized and silenced remain marginalized and silenced. This critique gets to the heart of the issue I have raised. Does Bakhtin leave us with a lack of grounding in real social situations, and what are the consequences of this? Can heteroglossia and carnival be criticized as merely utopic relativism? It is here that we must examine to what extent these critiques hold under scrutiny.

If the carnival, conceived in terms of its utopian characteristics, cannot permanently replace a given social structure and is merely a brief interlude away from systems of domination, the question is whether, rather than being an empowering force, the carnival merely appeases the masses by allowing them to glimpse freedom for a brief time and thereby merely satisfies their need for the "feeling" of justice and equality. According to Michael Gardiner, critics of the utopian image of carnival suggest that, because these images occur within the dominant culture rather than replacing it: "Utopian images can be manipulated by mass culture in order to realize the exchange value of cultural commodities and facilitate political domination. In return for passivity and a pleasurable [if regulated] 'false consciousness,' individuals are allowed to consume degraded images of utopia, simulacra of the real thing."[22]

In the essay "Reification and Utopia in Mass Culture," Frederic Jameson argues that the mass-culture industry manipulates utopian images for the maintenance of the dominant ideology. The result of this is that even though members of society may believe that they are experiencing a true expression of freedom (whether in a festival like Mardi Gras, reading a novel, or seeing a movie), they are, in actuality, merely pacified for a while and go on with their normal (oppressed) lives until the next time they can experience their "false" freedom. Thus, according to Jameson, utopian images co-opted by the dominant ideology create the illusion of a fulfillment of social desires—freedom, equality, and so forth—whereas in reality they serve as an instrument of repression. As Jameson states, the "concept of a management of desire in social terms now allows us to think repression and wish-fulfillment together within the unity of a single mechanism, which gives and takes alike in a kind of psychic compromise . . . which strategically arouses fantasy content within careful symbolic containment structures which defuse it, gratifying intolerable, unrealizable, properly imperishable desires only to the degree to which they can again be laid to rest." [23]

Given this critique, the carnival could also be seen as nothing more than a form of escape for members of society who are temporarily released from an oppressive system, and, in this way, it can be just as dangerous to a struggle for freedom as is the dominant culture in that it serves to imprison the oppressed in an unrealizable future, impeding their ability to move on to alternate solutions.

At first glance, the critique of carnival, based on Jameson's concern that images that occur within a society undermine or resist attempts to replace them, seems to hold up to scrutiny. However, I contend that Bakhtin's conception of carnivalesque heteroglossia should not be discarded so quickly. This will require clarification of Bakhtin's emancipatory vision of the carnival through an alternate reading via Deleuze and Guattari. I will argue that the above critique misses the point of Bakhtin's conceptions of heteroglossia and the carnival, that is, their potential to produce strategies for engaging in subversive practices of creative experimentation. It is a matter of understanding Bakhtin's carnival not as a utopian image in the strictest sense, but, rather, by means of Deleuze and Guattari's theory of becoming, as an "anti-utopian utopia." The critics of carnival tend to envision it as a finalized, totalizing blueprint of an ideal or perfect society. However, my alternate reading interprets Bakhtin's carnival as fundamentally opposed to such a view of utopia.

Carnival as Anti-Utopian Processes of Becoming

The critiques of Bakhtin's carnival as a utopian image, as I described above, proceed from traditional ways of conceiving utopia as a finalized blueprint. However, there is an alternate way to conceive of Bakhtin's carnival as a utopia that rejects all traditional definitions and characterizations, a conception to which the criticisms of utopian images cannot apply. Gardiner utilizes the work of Tom Moylan[24] in order to conceive of Bakhtin's carnival as a "critical utopia," emphasizing the functions of criticizing society, traditional utopias, and itself, as well as linking ideological criticism to an experimentation with alternatives—that is, linking critique with affirmation. To a similar end, Deleuze and Guattari are useful in conceiving of the carnival as an anti-utopian utopia, in terms of its fluidity, futuricity, and becoming. I will show that Bakhtin's carnival cannot be considered a traditional utopia, a plan for a better world. Rather, carnival is the very *practice* of experimentation and becoming, and its social effectiveness lies in its capacity for that practice and not in its ability or nonability to give the "right" answer for the solution of social ills.

The key to understanding what Deleuze and Guattari can offer us for an enhanced view of carnival is their connection to Bakhtin's view of the dynamic quality and fluidity of heteroglossia. For Bakhtin, the carnival has no end or beginning; it is always in a state of becoming what is "not-yet." According to Bakhtin, in *Problems of Dostoevsky's Poetics,* "the carnival sense of the world also knows no period, and is, in fact, hostile to any sort of conclusive conclusion: all endings are merely new beginnings; carnival images are reborn again and again . . . nothing conclusive has yet taken place in the world, the ultimate word of the world and about the world has not yet been spoken, the world is open and free, everything is still in the future and will always be in the future." [25]

Bakhtin's emphasis on the perpetual futuricity of the carnival reveals that he envisions an open and ever-changing system. Ironically, Morson and Emerson accuse Bakhtin of using this conception of carnival as a formal device to realize an attitude of "unremitting skepticism and unending change without a goal." [26] Morson and Emerson are dissatisfied with Bakhtin's carnival precisely because it cannot fill the role of a traditional utopia. Gardiner explains that they critique Bakhtin's carnival on the grounds that "the overall tenor of Bakhtin's thought is anti-utopian: [Bakhtin] eschews pure harmony, identity, and stability and instead privileges complexity, difference, and the everyday, what [Morson and Emerson] call 'prosaics.'" [27] And they are quite correct in their assessment of Bakhtin's "prosaics." Prosaics is, for Bakhtin, the unfinished dialogue so necessary to the conception of the carnival. However, the strength of this unfinished dialogue must be made clear.

In the chapter of *A Thousand Plateaus* titled "Becoming-Intense, Becoming-Animal, Becoming-Imperceptible . . ." Deleuze and Guattari distinguish between three "lines" relevant to their understanding of the relation between the individual and the social: the molar line, the molecular line, and a nomadic line. The molar line refers to the line that divides, orders, and hierarchicizes. Molar identities are segmented; they are thus conceived as autonomous, without reliance on other identities to define them. A molar line, in relation to society, can be found in hierarchized systems that constitute clear distinctions between classes, ages, professions, and so on. A molar line cannot, in itself, be the focus of any analysis of becoming in that it is a finalized system of identities. Although Deleuze and Guattari return to the molar line in order to explain that all three lines do, in fact, function simultaneously and conjunctively (similarly to the way I understand centripetal and centrifugal forces within language), in this present exemplification I will begin my analysis of becoming with the second line—the molecular.

As Elizabeth Grosz explains in "A Thousand Tiny Sexes," the molecular line "forms connections and relations beyond the rigidity of the molar line. It is composed of fluid lines, which map processes of becoming, change, movement, and reorganization." [28] The molecular line, for Deleuze and Guattari, is the site of becoming. In contrast to molar entities, molecular becoming cannot be realized by assuming an autonomous identity. There is no conception of identity-as-such on the molecular line. Rather, one engages in processes of becoming by emitting the particles that make up particular functions of particular identities. Deleuze and Guattari argue that "You become-animal only if, by whatever means or element, you emit corpuscles that enter the relation of movement and rest of the animal particles, or what amounts to the same thing, that enter the zone of proximity of the animal molecule." [29]

Here, the animal particles organize in terms of animal interests and functions. As Dorothea Olkowski characterizes this, to become animal would be to take up these functions. [30] Becoming, in this sense, is a mode of organization based on functioning, on activity, on practices. This notion of molecular becoming is essential to the conception of a nonstatic system of relations of bodies and of societies. For Deleuze and Guattari, an entity is not a totalized individual. It is a manifestation of certain qualities, all of which are subject to and capable of change. The individual, then, "must be understood as a series of flows, energies, movements, and capacities, a series of fragments or segments capable of being linked together in ways other than those that congeal it into an identity." [31] Olkowski explains that "these links can be organized and reorganized as they take on new functions, new interests, and so forth." [32]

Moreover, becoming, in its constant reintegrations, is immediately relational and, for this reason, social. [33] For Deleuze and Guattari, there is no mediation between individuals and society, or between societies; each are constantly destabilized, disordered and able to form new arrangements. The conception of the multiple fragments that join together to form an individual and social entity precisely encapsulates Deleuze and Guattari's view of multiplicitous becoming. "A multiplicity [is] . . . an everchanging, nontotalizable collectivity, an assemblage defined, not by its abiding identity or

principle of sameness over time, but through its capacity to undergo per-
mutations and transformations, that is, its dimensionality." [34] Such a notion
of molecular entities and multiplicities resonates with Bakhtin's view of the
carnival in that carnival is not defined as a totalized system with a finalized
goal or telos. Rather, the carnival encompasses fluidity. In this way, the carnival must be seen as a molecular entity itself, considering that its own per-
petuality in terms of its changing voices with changing heteroglossia denies
the possibility for a distinct identity, autonomously individuated.

Deleuze and Guattari theorize a third line relevant to the relation between the individual and the social—the nomadic line. [35] Here, Deleuze
and Guattari offer a more complex look into what exactly makes up an entity. They move beyond defining an entity in terms of its elements (from the
second, molecular), to a definition of entities in terms of a more intricate
conception of multiplicities. According to Deleuze and Guattari, "A multiplicity is defined not by its elements. . . . It is defined by the number of dimensions it has; it is not divisible, it cannot lose, gain a dimension without
changing its nature. . . . It amounts to the same thing to say that each multiplicity is already composed of heterogeneous terms in symbiosis, and that
a multiplicity is continually transforming itself into a string of other multiplicities, according to its thresholds and doors." [36] These dimensions constitutive of multiplicities are explained in detail by Deleuze and Guattari in
terms of what they call "the anomalous." In this line, multiplicities are
understood not by their separation by borders, but by their openness to
other multiplicities' borders, dimensions, boundaries—that is, they are
defined by their thresholds and doors. These multiplicities create infinite
webs of connections in that all multiplicities are joined by their borders
which are amorphous—capable of changing borders with others, creating
new boundaries and therefore, new multiplicities. [37] According to Deleuze
and Guattari, "being expresses in a single meaning all that differs. What we
are talking about is not the unity of substance but the infinity of the modi-
fications that are part of one another on this unique plane of life." [38]

What this concept produces is an idea of becoming that is so interconnected, yet so capable of change that it resists any totalizing tendencies and
remains fundamentally opposed to any concept of autonomous identity.
Moreover, its capabilities and disposition to change, and its repositioning
of amorphous borders ensures that alterations in the structures of the multiplicities occur infinitely. [39]

Given this brief foray into lines of becoming, let us revisit Bakhtin's critics and consider the question of whether or not Bakhtin's carnival, in its
temporality, can only appease the masses and maintain the status quo. The
fluidity of Bakhtin's carnival is so opposed to a traditional conception of
utopia that a critique along the lines of Jameson's critiques of utopia has

solely to do with traditional conceptions of utopia and fails to consider the alternative anti-utopian possibilities in carnival. Bakhtin's theory exposes a fluid system of difference that exists in an intermediary aesthetic realm. The aesthetic realm, Bakhtin argues, is where lies the real power of carnival. It is simply a matter of understanding that Bakhtin's fluid carnival cannot be conceived as a material organization. It is rather a process, an ongoing practice of engaging multiple integrations, functions, and activities of becoming. It must remain "temporary" for there is nothing, that is, no *thing*, to institute in society and maintain. Carnival is a practice of ceaseless interaction and reconfiguration into new systems of relations. The dialogics of the novel is a site for this ongoing practice. It is a site to realize creative— that is generative, new—conceptions of difference within a fluid system, rather than a closed absolute system in which it is impossible to achieve anything new. It is a becoming in precisely the way that Deleuze and Guattari conceptualize becoming, in that the carnival practices constant reorganizations, makes new linkages, and creates new systems of relations that themselves are always fluid and becoming what is not-yet.

The carnival exists within a system of domination as a means of active resistance. Deleuze maintains that even within the most dominating and closed system, there remains a crack—a gap, a fissure—that resists totalization. Speaking of Artaud and cinema primarily, but also of literature, Deleuze credits these aesthetic realms "not with the power to make us think the whole, but on the contrary, with a 'dissociative force' which would introduce . . . a hole in appearances . . . a fissure, a crack." [40] He claims that in literature (and film), the gaps cease to be relegated to an invisible status and are brought to the forefront. These resistant gaps are the carnival. They are the sites for resistance, for a system of relations not based on hierarchy and stability, but on fluid transformative disintegrations and reconfigurations between all members of the social field, where creative reorganizations—becoming—are possible. Heteroglossia in the novel exposes a crack in society where the dominant monology has no center, no stable ground. The dissociative force is the ongoing process of disintegration/reconfiguration of multiple voices, and through this process, it ensures that the dominant monology can never be total. It is a matter of ceaselessly returning to the cracks in the dominant system, engaging in encounters with their perpetual multiplicities and becoming in order to bring the cracks to the forefront and subvert the conceptions of identities and discourse based on categorization, stabilization, and oppression.

I believe it is here that Jameson's inability to consider the insidious, subversive power of experimentation enabled by utopian images is problematized. He himself maintains that in the manipulated utopian image, there is, at once, both a fantastical—that is, imaginative—fulfillment of desire and a containment of that desire. For Bakhtin and for Deleuze and Guattari, however, the containment is never complete, never total, because the fantastical, the imaginative, exposes cracks and continually causes these cracks to widen. The focus for them is towards those cracks, and the carnival is the activity therein.

It is precisely, here, in the conception of carnival as the practice of becoming, as a process of experimentation, wherein lie the possibilities that Morson and Emerson, Jameson, and others deny. It is also here that I find the most useful possibilities in Bakhtin's theories for thinking about how to engage heteroglossia. As I stated earlier, Bakhtin's heteroglossia and carnival often seem not to take into account the concrete social barriers to "free and familiar contact." Returning to the example from Woolf's *Orlando* of the multiple interpretations of the events of a party, it would appear that to claim this as heteroglossic would deny that different interpretations have different levels of credibility and authority in the real world. However, there are several points to consider with respect to this issue.

Given the analysis of the carnivalesque quality of heteroglossia and its expanded meaning garnered from Deleuze and Guattari's concept of becoming, a critique of heteroglossia and carnival for not adequately taking into account the material, real power relations within society misses the point. They are activities of the reader and writer of experimenting with the cracks of the dominant discourses and ideologies of meaning making. If this is the case, then it becomes a matter of *how* one reads (and writes) the novel and for what purposes. What experiences, meanings, and identities does the reader bring to the reading, and what is her purpose in reading? There are, of course, ways of reading a novel (or the world) that will maintain the dominant mode of thinking and being—reading to reaffirm or reify one's stable identity and the unification of dominant ideology and Truth discourse. For example, one can read the instance of the multiple interpretations of the party in *Orlando* and understand the interpretations as reaffirming the validity of the newspaper account. But if one engages the reading on the basis of experimentation and new ways of meaning making, for the purpose of acting as a nonunified subject, and for the purposes of exposing and creating spaces within which to theorize and act, the heteroglossic tendencies and centrifugal forces of language will become paramount and will expose those creative possibilities through the act of reading the text and the act of experimenting with the heteroglossia within dominant discourse and society.

I use the phrase "reading oneself reading the text"[41] to indicate the necessity of approaching the heteroglossic text and society with the realization of, and the responsibility that comes from, the multiple voices within one's own identity—to engage with the multiple voices of the text and society and to experiment with how the voices react to, expand, engage, dismiss, or ignore the multiplicitous identities within the reader. To understand how to engage the novel is to move beyond evaluating its possibilities in terms of whether or not it can be instantiated in society, or whether or not it, itself, maintains, or is critical of, the existent relations of power, oppression, and domination within society. Reading the novel becomes a process of becoming precisely because it can enable practices of expanding meaning coming from the multiple interactions with and dialogues between the reader, the author, and the text.

It is at this point that I find it also possible to address to what extent considering together Bakhtin's heteroglossia and Deleuze and Guattari's concept of becoming can help reclaim what Deleuze and Guattari offer me as a feminist theorist—both as a reader of literature and, perhaps more importantly, within ideological domination of discursive frameworks. Most of the time, when I read Deleuze and Guattari, I find that there is little that speaks to me as a feminist philosopher, a woman who works within the concrete, real barriers to validity, credibility, and authority, and whose meaning-making activities and experiences of myself are circumscribed by ideologies, discourses, and structural constraints. Indeed, it often seems to me that to theorize about pure heterogeneous multiplicities and becoming renders invisible the social reality that ideological and discursive understandings stabilize identities and Truth making only under the condition that the Other is fragmented and marginalized. At the same time, however, I work from the assumption that these ideological, structural, and discursive frameworks are never complete, and so, given that, I work to discover strategies of acting within the world and within dominant monologies to disrupt the illusions of completeness and fixedness. To this end, I find great possibilities within Deleuze and Guattari's notion of becoming. What I have found is that, although Deleuze and Guattari work from conceptual frameworks that sometimes seem too far removed from real social situations, grounding them by Bakhtin's conceptions of heteroglossia and carnival, I am able to make use of their theories in real theoretical and social practices and experimentations.

I maintain that by understanding the carnival as a location for becoming, we may understand Deleuze and Guattari's articulations of "becoming woman" and "becoming minority" in such a way that they do not require that women and minorities "cease being, so that they can become." Because the carnival of becoming occurs within the cracks of an existent system of relations, it serves as a site for experimentation without the threat of disappearing. Becoming woman, then, is an ongoing creative practice rather than a question of being or not-being.

It is a matter for me of reading the novel recognizing my social location and those of the other voices, not to reify my subject position, but rather to encounter and to practice experimentations with the tools of other discourses and other experiences. To actively engage the world and texts— not just novels, but also the dominant discourses that define and mediate authority and Truth within the academic worlds I inhabit—in such a way that I am able move in between these subject positions in order to expand the meanings and understandings I am able to make, to expand the locations from which I am able to speak, and to recognize those discourses from which I have been excluded from speaking. It is a matter of using the tools that have been made available to me for purposes they were not intended— to write, read, and speak within the dominant discourses that have circumscribed my location, not to reify my identity or the dominant discourses themselves, but rather to theorize and act within the centrifugal forces of those discourses that constantly reconfigure meanings and practices.

I began this chapter with some of my concerns about moving within academic discourses, not only in my own work, but also in working with students to develop their own abilities to move in this world. And as I think through what it means to read oneself through reading the novel and/or world, in terms of practicing experimentations of becoming, I have found that teaching students to write critically and powerfully requires teaching them strategies for reading with an eye for the carnival in texts and in themselves. Becoming accountable and responsible for the meanings we make and to think through the reasons for making them and the social and personal factors that influence those reasons and those meanings becomes a matter of making the classroom a crack in the university, where discourse is fluid, meanings are drawn from multiple discourses and worlds of experience that are then thought through in relation with each other and with the dominant discourse of academia whose authority can then be brought into question and experimented on with movements between the discourses and worlds. Whether it be experimentations with reading and writing with different discursive styles, experimentations with interactions with students and teachers, experimentations with the cracks of the texts itself, where intentional or unintentional meanings break down, or collaborative responsibility for the frame, commitment, and purpose of the class, the issue at hand concerns the very real dilemma of moving between worlds of experience as a necessary practice for creative and critical thinking and acting not only in the classroom, but also in the world.

Notes

Introduction, by Dorothea Olkowski

1. Henri Bergson, *Matter and Memory,* trans. Nancy Margaret Paul and W. Scott Palmer (New York: Zone Books, 1988), 81.

2. Bergson, *Matter and Memory,* 83.

3. Michèle Le Doeuff, "Women and Philosophy," in *French Feminist Thought, A Reader,* ed. Toril Moi (Oxford: Basil Blackwell, 1987), 181–209. Le Doeuff sees this as an example of how men students, like women, fall into amorous relations with their teachers, but only women students remain trapped by these relations of power.

4. Le Doeuff, "Women and Philosophy," 188.

5. Simone de Beauvoir, *Memoirs of a Dutiful Daughter,* cited in Michèle Le Doeuff, *Hipparchia's Choice, An Essay Concerning Women, Philosophy, Etc,* trans. Trista Selous (Oxford: Basil Blackwell, 1991), 136.

6. Le Doeuff, *Hipparchia's Choice,* 137.

7. Debra Bergoffen, The Philosophy of *Simone de Beauvoir Gendered Phenomenologies, Erotic Generosities* (Albany, N.Y.: SUNY Press, 1997), 11.

8. Hélène Cixous, "The Laugh of the Medusa," in *Critical Theory since 1965,* ed. Hazard Adams and Leroy Searle (Tallahassee, Fla.: Florida State University Press, 1986), 308–9.

9. Cixous, "The Laugh of the Medusa," 309.

10. Cixous, "The Laugh of the Medusa," 309.

11. Cixous, "The Laugh of the Medusa," 316, 317.

12. Leroy Searle, "Afterward: Criticism and the Claims of Reason," in *Critical Theory since 1965,* 856–72.

13. Searle takes the addition of these disciplines to the roster to be a problem for literary criticism in the United States, but certainly it has equally been a problem for philosophy.

14. Jacques Derrida, "*Che cos'è la poesia,*" originally in the Italian journal *Poesia* 1, no. 11 (November 1988).

Philosophy and Gender, by Hazel E. Barnes

1. Jean Grimshaw has discussed this distinction in *Philosophy and Feminist Thinking* (Minneapolis: University of Minnesota Press, 1986), chapter 2, "The 'Maleness' of Philosophy."

2. These words appear as the first part of the title of Eva C. Keul's study of Greek sexism, *The Reign of the Phallus: Sexual Politics in Ancient Athens* (New York: Harper and Row, 1985).

3. I am thinking, for example, of ethical problems posed in connection with the education of preschool children (whether at home or in child-care centers). Within the broad field of applied philosophy we find a host of questions that are not the concerns of women exclusively

but arise in areas where women have been deeply engaged but seldom heard: the question of when, if ever, war and violence are justified; generational conflicts; and the rights and responsibilities of women and men respectively in sexual matters and in the context of new patterns of maternity and paternity. Other basic issues I will bring up in what follows.

4. It was, of course, William James who introduced "the more inclusive claim" as a formal concept into ethical discussions, but the idea behind it seems to me as old as ethics itself.

5. I have discussed these same three points, though somewhat differently, in an article titled "Sartre and Feminism: Aside from *The Second Sex* and All That," in *Rereading the Canon: Feminist Interpretations of Jean-Paul Sartre,* ed. Julien S. Murphy (University Park, Pa.: Pennsylvania State University Press, 1999).

6. I quote here from the title of an influential book: Mary Field Belensky, Blythe McVicker Clinchy, Nancy Rule Goldberger, and Jill Mattuck Tarule, *Women's Ways of Knowing: The Development of Self, Voice, and Mind* (New York: Basic Books, 1986).

7. Martin S. Weinberg, Colin J. Williams, and Douglas W. Pryor, *Dual Attraction: Understanding Bisexuality* (New York: Oxford University Press, 1994).

8. I am indebted to Robert V. Stone and Elizabeth A. Bowman, who have had access to these unpublished papers and have discussed, in two articles, Sartre's attempt there to work out an ethics consistent with the view of Marxism he held in the 1960s. See "Dialectical Ethics: A First Look at Sartre's Unpublished 1964 Rome Lecture Notes," *Social Text: Theory/Culture/Ideology* (winter/spring 1986): 195–215; and "Sartre's Morality and History: A First Look at the Notes for the Unpublished 1965 Cornell Lectures," in *Sartre Alive,* ed. Ronald Aronson and Adrian Van den Hoven (Detroit: Wayne State University Press, 1991), 53–82.

From My Menagerie to Philosophy, by Hélène Cixous

1. Translated by Keith Cohen. "*Che cos'è la poesia,*" orig. in Italian journal *Poesìa* (Ed. Crocetti) 1, no. 11 (November 1988). *Istrice* is the Italian word for hedgehog, or porcupine. See Peggy Kamuf's illuminating commentary on her translation of this passage (which I have modified slightly) in *A Derrida Reader: Between the Blinds,* (New York: Columbia University Press, 1991), 221–23, especially the sound and image of "the beast caught in the strictures" of translation.

2. Telephone conversation:

"It's me, your ass," he says.
She is surprised because she thought that she was the ass:
"So you're like my ass?"
"I love it infinitely."
"But I didn't say: do you like my ass. I said: You're like my ass??"
"Ah yes! But just a little one. And I have big ears."
"In the end you are my whole menagerie."
My greatest difficulty is in going from my menagerie to philosophy.

Retained in French at author's request, due perhaps to the unavoidable drollery of *âne* as "ass."—[Trans. note]

3. Thea is Cixous's cat. [Trans. note]

4. *(Re)connaissance:* the French word for gratitude or recognition (*reconnaissance*) is built on the word for knowledge or consciousness (*connaissance*). [Trans. note]

House and Home, by Iris M. Young

I am grateful to David Alexander, Robert Beauregard, Edward Casey, Dolores Hayden, Dorothea Olkowski, and Geraldine Pratt for helpful comments on earlier versions of this paper. I also benefited from a discussion of the paper at the University of Pittsburgh women's writing group, including Jean Carr, Nancy Glazener, Paula Kane, Margaret Marshall, and Marianne Novy. This essay is reprinted from Iris Marion Young, *Intersecting Voices*. Copyright © 1997 by Princeton University Press. Reprinted by permission of Princeton University Press.

1. Martin Heidegger, "Building, Dwelling, Thinking," in *Poetry, Language, Thought,* trans. Albert Hofstadter (New York: Harper and Row, 1971). Hereafter cited as BDT.

2. Compare Edward Casey, *Getting Back into Place. Toward a Renewed Understanding of the Place-World* (Bloomington, Ind.: Indiana University Press, 1993), 112. Casey also notes (pp. 176–77) that Heidegger slides into identifying dwelling with construction even though he begins with a wider scope for building

3. Hannah Arendt also theorized building as a fundamental aspect of human meaning. She distinguishes between labor, activity useful for production and consumption of the means of living, and work, the construction of artifacts that transcend mere life because they are made to be permanent Thus, for Arendt, the moment of founding is the primordial moment of action. Through the construction of edifices people create a built environment, a civilization, by means of which they emerge as thinking and speaking subjects. See Hannah Arendt, *The Human Condition* (Chicago: University of Chicago Press. 1958).

4. Aliye Pekin Celik, "Women's Participation in the Production of Shelter," and Victoria Basolo and Michelle Moral, "Women and the Production of Housing: An Overview," both in Hemalata C. Dandekar, *Shelter Women and Development: First and Third World Perspectives* (Ann Arbor, Mich.: George Wahr Publishing Co., 1993).

5. Caroline O. N. Moser, "Women, Human Settlements, and Housing: A Conceptual Framework for Analysis and Policy-Making," in *Women, Human Settlements, and Housing,* ed. Caroline O. N. Moser and Linda Peake (London: Tavistock Publications, 1987); Irene Tinker, "Beyond Economics: Sheltering the Whole Woman," in *Engendering Wealth and Well-Being,* ed. Blumberg, Rakowski, Tinker, and Maneton (Boulder, Colo.: Westview Press, 1995), 261–84.

6. Luce Irigaray, *An Ethics of Sexual Difference* (Ithaca, N.Y.: Cornell University Press, 1993), 101. Hereafter cited as *ESD.*

7. One of the classic statements of this idea is Herbert Marcuse's *One Dimensional Man* (Boston: Beacon Press, 1964); see also Stuart Ewen, *Captains of Consciousness* (New York: McGraw-Hill, 1976).

8. Simone de Beauvoir, *The Second Sex,* trans. H. M. Parshley (New York: Random House, 1952), 451.

9. D. J. Van Lennep, "The Hotel Room," in *Phenomenological Psychology: The Dutch School,* ed. Joseph J. Kockelmans (Dordrecht: Martinus Nijhoff, 1987), 209–15.

10. Ibid., 211.

11. Casey, *Getting Back into Place,* 120.

12. On the distinction between nostalgia and memory, see Gayle Greene. "Feminist Fiction and the Uses of Memory," *Signs* 16, no. 2 (winter 1991): 290–321.

13. See Keya Ganguly, "Migrant Identities: Personal Memory and the Construction of Self-hood," *Cultural Studies* 6, no. 1 (January 1992): 27–19; and Susan Thomason, "Suburbs of Opportunity: The Power of Home for Migrant Women" (proceedings of the Postmodern City Conference, Sydney University, 1993).

14. See Dolores Hayden, *The Power of Place* (Cambridge, Mass.: MIT Press, 1995).

15. Governments all over the world in both developed and developing countries have been cutting social services and allowing prices for basic foodstuffs to rise. The result is usually more domestic work for women. See Haleh Afshar and Carolyne Dennis, *Women and Adjustment Politics in the Third World* (New York: St. Martin's Press, 1993).

16. Biddy Martin and Chandra Talpade Mohanty, "Feminist Politics: What's Home Got to Do with It?" in *Feminist Studies/Cultural Studies,* ed. Teresa de Lauretis (Bloomington, Ind.: Indiana University Press, 1986), 191–212.

17. Teresa de Lauretis, "Eccentric Subjects: Feminist Theory and Historical Consciousness," *Feminist Studies* 16, no. 1 (spring 1990): 115–50.

18. Bonnie Honig, "Difference, Dilemmas, and the Politics of Home," *Social Research* 61, no. 3 (fall 1994): 563–97.

19. See Bernice Johnson Reagon, "Coalition Politics: Turning the Century," in *Home Girls: A Black Feminist Anthology,* ed. Barbara Smith (New York: Kitchen Table: Women of Color Press, 1983), 356–69. Reagon criticizes the attempt to seek the comforts of home in politics, but as I read her she does not reject the values of home.

20. Martin and Mohanty, "Feminist Politics," 196.

21. Ibid.

22. de Lauretis, "Eccentric Subjects," 138.

23. Honig, "Difference," 585.

24. bell hooks, "Homeplace: A Site of Resistance," in *Yearning: Race, Gender and Cultural Politics* (Boston: South End Press, 1990), 42.

25. Ibid., 43.

26. Benedict Anderson, *Imagined Communities Reflections on the Origin and Spread of Nationalism* (London: New Left Books, 1983).

27. Compare Jeremy Waldron, "Homelessness and the Issue of Freedom," in *Liberal Rights: Collected Papers 1981–1991* (Cambridge, Mass.: Cambridge University Press, 1993), 309–38.

28. Seyla Benhabib affirms this individuating function of home and privacy in her discussion of the need for feminists to retain a certain meaning to a distinction between public and private. See Benhabib, *The Reluctant Modernism of Hannah Arendt* (London: Sage, 1996), 213.

29. For a feminist defense of privacy as the fight to inviolate personality, see Jean L. Cohen. "Democracy, Difference and the Right of Privacy," in *Democracy and Difference: Contesting the Boundaries of the Political,* ed. Seyla Benhabib (Princeton, N.J.: Princeton University Press, 1996).

30. Anita Allen, *Uneasy Access* (Totowa, N.J.: Rowman and Allenheld, 1988).

Splitting the Subject, by Gail Weiss

Copyright © 1998. From *Body Images* by Gail Weiss. Reproduced by permission of Taylor & Francis/Routledge, Inc.

1. Iris Young, "Throwing Like a Girl: A Phenomenology of Feminine Body Comportment, Motility, and Spatiality," in *Throwing Like a Girl and Other Essays in Feminist Philosophy and Social Theory* (Bloomington, Ind.: Indiana University Press, 1990).

2. Ibid., 142.

3. Quoted by Young, *Throwing Like a Girl,* 141.

4. Young notes that these "exceptional" girls are quite often athletes who have learned how to make the most effective use of their bodies while engaging in sports activities. It is less clear how a boy would come to throw "like a girl," because there are few, if any, advantages that come from this latter, more constricted, throwing style. My hope is that the implementation of Title IX in the United States, the law that guarantees equal access to sports training and facilities for boys and girls, will either eliminate the denigrating ascription "throwing like a girl" altogether or lead to its radical revaluation as a way of maximizing, as opposed to minimizing, one's bodily potential.

5. In the discussion that follows I will use the terms *masculine* and *feminine* as gender markers for two distinct styles of bodily comportment. The use of these terms is not intended to be exhaustive in the sense of picking out all of the relevant features that constitute what is commonly referred to as *masculinity* and *femininity* respectively.

6. When I was in fifth grade, those of us who self-identified as tomboys refused to walk in either the girls' or the boys' line to march out to recess. Instead, wearing shorts under our skirts, we walked defiantly between the two columns in a veritable "no-man's" land that made the boys snicker in amusement and the other girls either scowl or regard us with awe and envy. Presumably recognizing this as a passing "fad," which indeed ended as soon as enough girls

moved over into "our space" to turn our middle line into a "girls' line" once again, our teacher permitted us this gesture of symbolic defiance. We were too young to recognize the significance of this early (failed) refusal of our gendered role.

In the twenty-five years that have elapsed since I marched in that transitional space, I have come to exhibit all of the contradictory modalities that Young describes in her essay. I do, indeed, throw "like a girl," and that it is extremely difficult to change my bodily style to one that is less restricted. And, when I think about my own daughter's future, I know that I do not want her to exhibit these same contradictory bodily modalities. I do not want her to throw, carry, bend, and lift "like a girl," but I also would like to see a way of rejecting these constricting bodily styles while maintaining pride in one's gender. It is this latter project of affirming the positive aspects of gender identity that we must, as feminists, pursue further without at the same time essentializing that identity or rendering any aspect of it invulnerable to critical analysis.

7. Young defines these three contradictory modalities of bodily comportment as follows. Ambiguous transcendence refers to the way in which, while seeking to perform a given task, a woman often simultaneously "lives her body as a burden which must be dragged and prodded along and at the same time protected." (*Throwing Like a Girl,* 148) Inhibited intentionality "simultaneously reaches toward a projected end with an "I can" and witholds its full bodily commitment to that end in a self-imposed "I cannot." (ibid.) Discontinuous unity is identified by Young as a "subset" of inhibited intentionality whereby "the part of the body that is transcending toward an aim is in relative disunity from those that remain immobile" (ibid.).

8. Young, *Throwing Like a Girl,* 150.

9. Examples of such activities include learning to play a new sport such as tennis, golf, or swimming where careful focus on the body's motility, comportment, and spatiality is required. Of course, the goal of such activity is to transform the acquired skills into bodily habits so that such close attention to the body is no longer needed. Nonetheless, it would seem strange to identify the bodily self-reference required for learning a new sport with the contradictory bodily modalities described by Young and/or to claim that the process of learning a new sport is more immanent because of this self-reference than the activity of playing that sport once the requisite skills have been acquired.

10. Young, *Throwing Like a Girl,* 155.

11. Luce Irigary, *Speculum of the Other Woman,* trans. Gillian C. Gill (Ithaca, N.Y.: Cornell University Press, 1974, 1985).

12. Young, *Throwing Like a Girl,* 155.

13. Ibid.

14. Bartky, 1990, 23; my emphasis.

15. Kim Chernin's popular 1981 book *The Obsession: The Tyranny of Slenderness* (New York: HarperCollins Publishers), provides wonderful examples of the seductiveness of the media images of women that bombard us on a daily basis. Chernin also discusses the self-hatred that often arises in response to one's awareness that one "falls short" of the cultural beauty standard.

16. Young, *Throwing Like a Girl,* 164.

17. Ibid. Young notes early on in her essay that she is only speaking to the situation of those women who have chosen their pregnancy "either as an explicit decision to become pregnant or at least as choosing to be identified with and positively accepting of it" (161). Hence, the description of pregnant existence offered in this essay makes no claims to universality; in fact, Young claims that this description currently can apply only to a minority rather than the majority of pregnant women in contemporary society. In an important sense, then, the positive description of the "split" subject offered in this essay presents a utopian vision of what pregnancy can and should embody.

18. Ibid., 161.

19. Ibid., 163–64.

20. *The Random House Dictionary of the English Language* (New York: Random House Publishers, 1973), 738.

21. Young, *Throwing Like a Girl,* 169.

22. Ibid., 166.

23. Ibid., 180.

24. Ibid., 182.

25. Ibid.

26. Maurice Merleau-Ponty, *The Visible and the Invisible,* ed. Claude Lefort, trans. Alphonso Lingis (Evanston, Ill.: Northwestern University Press, 1968), 255–56.

27. Young, *Throwing Like a Girl,* 184.

28. Ibid., 184.

29. Judith Butler, *Bodies That Matter: On the Discursive Limits of "Sex"* (New York: Routledge, 1993). The two senses of immateriality that I am thinking about here are: (1) non-material and (2) insignificant and both have been associated with the (all too mysterious) do-main of the imaginary.

30. Young, *Throwing Like a Girl,* 186.

31. Ibid.

32. Not the least of them is Young's unmarked move from gendered experience to a "sexed" imagination. Are only females capable of exhibiting this female imagination? Do all females exhibit it? There seems no reason why the narcissistic pleasure women take in clothes and fan-tasies about clothes are not also experienced my many men, if not through clothes, then per-haps through other cultural commodities such as cars and televisions, or even through strong identifications with athletic teams, individual athletes, and particular sports.

33. Young, *Throwing Like a Girl,* 189.

34. Ibid., 191; my emphasis.

35. Ibid., 195–196.

36. Ibid., 201.

37. Ibid., 200.

38. Mike Featherstone focuses on how strategies of body maintenance help to solidify the view of the body itself as a commodity in his 1991 essay, "The Body in Consumer Culture," in *The Body: Social Process and Cultural Theory,* ed. Mike Featherstone, M. Hepworth, and B. S. Turner (London: Sage, 1991). Today one can find almost as many advertisements for the improvement of men's bodies as women's bodies. The difference in the advertising strategies, however, is striking. For women, bodily transformation is most often presented as a successful strategy for "catching" or "retaining" a man. For men, bodily transformation is much more frequently depicted as a means of achieving health, wealth, and general well-being.

39. Young, *Throwing Like a Girl,* 201.

40. Lingerie sections in large department stores offer frequent reminders to women with un-dersized, oversized, or prosthetic breasts how "unnatural" their breasts really are, because it is hard to find bras that stray outside the range of the culturally established breast ideal.

41. It is interesting that Freud never focused very much on female breasts in his discussion of psychosexual development (except as the primary source of oral stimulation and satisfac-tion for the infant), but instead concentrated on female genitalia. The clitoris was negatively associated by him with a diminished and inferior penis, and the vagina itself was a pure lack or absence of the desired organ altogether, indeed, the very sign and threat of its castration. The abundant plenitude of the mother's breasts and their eroticism for both infant and mother itself challenges any psychoanalytic interpretation of female sexuality as founded upon lack, and thereby challenges the hegemony of a phallic construction of female sexuality in psycho-analytic theory. Rather than develop the positive significance of the intense sexual gratification provided by the mother's breasts, Freud instead chose to focus on the negative psychical con-sequences of the mother's withdrawal of the breast from the infant during weaning.

42. Wendy Chapkis, *Beauty Secrets: Women and the Politics of Appearance* (Boston: South End Press, 1986).

43. Ibid., 26.

44. Ibid.

45. Ibid.

46. Ibid., 27.

47. Paul Schilder, *The Image and Appearance of the Human Body: Studies in the Constructive Energies of the Psyche* (New York: International Universities Press, 1935, 1950).

Simone de Beauvoir, by Debra B. Bergoffen

1. Simone de Beauvoir, *The Second Sex,* trans. H. M. Parshley (New York: Vintage Books, 1974), 301.

2. Beauvoir, *Second Sex,* 317.

3. Jacques Lacan, *The Seminar of Jacques Lacan: Book VII The Ethics of Psychoanalysis, 1959–1960,* trans. Dennis Porter (New York: W. W. Norton & Company, 1992), 202.

4. Beauvoir, *Second Sex,* 313.

5. Ibid., 308.

6. Ibid., 313–14.

7. Ibid., 63.

8. Simone de Beauvoir, *The Ethics of Ambiguity,* trans. Bernard Frechtman (New York: Philosophical Library, 1948), 35–40.

9. See, for example, Jean François Lyotard, "The Sign of History," trans. Geoff Bennington in *The Lyotard Reader,* ed. Andrew Benjamin (Cambridge: Basil Blackwell, 1989), 393–411.

10. Beauvoir, *Second Sex,* 450.

11. Ibid., 810.

12. Simone de Beauvoir, *The Coming of Age,* trans. Patrick O'Brian (New York: Random House, 1983), 472–74, 521.

13. Beauvoir, *Second Sex,* XXIV–XXV.

Love and the Labor of the Negative, by Morny Joy

1. L. Irigaray, *Speculum of the Other Woman,* trans. Gillian Gill (Ithaca, N.Y.: Cornell University Press, 1985), 215–26. Women did not qualify for inclusion in this dynamic contest of master and slave, even as an allegory to the attainment of self-consciousness. See H. Raven, "Has Hegel Anything to Say to Feminists?" in *Feminist Interpretations of G. W. F. Hegel,* ed. P. Jagentowicz Mills (University Park, Pa.: Pennsylvania University Press, 1996), 242–43.

2. See the conclusion of Raven's "Has Hegel Anything to Say to Feminists?" 246, which charts this problematic aspect of Hegel's thought.

3. The final stage of Hegel's dialectic is variously described in his works. The individuality or self-consciousness ultimately attained (as *Geist*/spirit) is also understood as an enrichment or precision at a more refined level of the initially posited general universal. In this essay, I have referred to this stage by the word *universality* to distinguish it from universal statements and universalism, which is a crucial and controversial aspect of Irigaray's work, to refer to the state that Irigaray implies when she states that women should achieve the perfection of their gender or the universal. When Irigaray refers to women attaining the universal, what she has in mind is actually the mode of universality described above.

4. See M. Whitford, *Luce Irigaray: Philosophy in the Feminine* (New York: Routledge, 1991), 37–38. Irigaray's initial studies were exercises in ways to disrupt the dominant mode of masculine symbolic authority.

5. P. Jagentowicz Mills, "Hegel's Antigone," in *Feminist Interpretations of G. W. F. Hegel,* ed. P. Jagentowicz Mills (University Park, Pa.: Pennsylvania University Press, 1996), 84.

6. Irigaray's use of the term *gender* and its relation to her earlier use of the word *sexué* (translated as *sexuate*) in L. Irigaray, *Je, Tu, Nous: Toward a Culture of Difference,* trans. A. Martin (New York: Routledge, 1993), 53, is of particular importance. Initially she had seemed to confine her distinction of the sexes to the term *sexué* as indicating sexual difference in a generalized sense. As it occurred in her early works, it was understood in a disruptive and deconstructive manner, seeking to provide the space for a form of women's identity that had not been previously recognized. This was not an essential difference (Schor, "This Essentialism Which Is Not One"). It had certain affinities with the Heideggerian notion of difference (T. Chanter, *Ethics of Eros: Irigaray's Rewriting of the Philosophers* [New York: Routledge, 1995], 131–46). The term *gender* is particularly evident in the collection of essays, *Sexes and Genealogies.* In fact, in the essay, "The Universal as Mediation" (Irigaray, *Je, Tu, Nous,* 127), there is the rare occurrence of a footnote noting a change in the nature of her application of the term. It nonetheless must be noted that Irigaray is not particularly consistent in her usage, and the words *sex* and *gender* are often employed interchangeably. See L. Irigaray, *I Love to You,* trans. A. Martin (New York: Routledge, 1996), 62.

7. Ibid., 27.

8. Ibid., 13.

9. L. Irigaray, *Sexes and Genealogies,* trans. Gillian Gill (New York: Columbia University Press, 1993), 132.

10. Irigaray, *I Love to You,* 139.

11. Ibid., 22.

12. Ibid., 13.

13. Irigaray, *Sexes and Genealogies,* 179.

14. L. Irigaray, *This Sex Which Is Not One,* trans. C. Porter with C. Burke (Ithaca, N.Y.: Cornell University Press, 1985), 94–98.

15. Irigaray, *Speculum of the Other Woman,* 224.

16. Irigaray, *Je, Tu, Nous,* 82.

17. L. Irigaray, *Thinking the Difference,* trans. K. Montin (New York: Routledge, 1994), 79.

18. Irigaray, *Je, Tu, Nous,* 86.

19. With reference to law, Irigaray presumably has the French civil code in mind (Irigaray, *I Love to You,* 131, 53–54).

20. S. de Beauvoir, *The Second Sex,* trans. H. M. Parshley (New York: Vintage Books, 1974), 249.

21. Irigaray, *I Love to You,* 107.

22. Whitford, *Luce Irigaray,* 96.

23. J. Scott, *Only Paradoxes to Offer: French Feminists and the Rights of Man* (Cambridge, Mass.: Harvard University Press, 1996), 1–18.

24. L. Irigaray, *An Ethics of Sexual Difference,* trans. Carolyn Burke and Gillian Gill (Ithaca, N.Y.: Cornell University Press, 1993), 5.

25. Irigaray, *I Love to You,* 39. Irigaray has also characterized this exercise as one of becoming divine. See "Divine Women" in L. Irigaray, *Sexes and Genealogies,* 57–72.

26. See Irigaray, *Thinking the Difference,* 98–112; Irigaray, *I Love to You,* 26, 130–31, 135–36.

27. Ibid., 24.

28. Ibid., 107.

29. Ibid., 144–45.

30. See also N. Schor, "French Feminism as Universalism," *Differences* 7, no. 1 (1995): 21. I will understand *essentialism* as referring to timeless, inherent, all-pervasive qualities or tendencies pertaining to objects or organisms. *Universalism,* however, has more to do with a concrete conceptual perspective that is of a classifcatory nature that could be either generic or specific to a historical period. (It is in this latter sense that Irigaray employs the universal as a designation.)

31. Irigaray, *Sexes and Genealogies,* 147.

32. Irigaray, *I Love to You*, 112.

33. Schor, "French Feminism as Universalism," 34.

34. Irigaray, *I Love to You*, 48.

35. Schor, "French Feminism as Universalism," 33–34; S. Heath, "The Ethics of Sexual Difference," *Discourse* 12, no. 2 (1990): 147–49.

36. In *I Love to You*, Irigaray states, "Sexual difference is an immediate natural given and it is a real and irreducible component of the universal. The whole of humankind is composed of men and women and nothing else. The problem of race is, in fact, a secondary problem—except from a geographical point of view?—which means we cannot see the wood for the trees, and the same goes for other cultural diversities—religious, economic and political ones. Sexual difference probably represents the most universal question we can address" (47).

37. Irigaray, *I Love to You*, 143.

38. The question is whether Irigaray has moved beyond her earlier descriptions, which supported women's embrace of other women (L. Irigaray, *This Sex Which Is Not One*, 203–18). P. Cheah and E. Grosz, in "The Future of Sexual Difference: An Interview with Judith Butler and Drucilla Cornell," *Diacritics* 1 (1998): 28–30, argue that her notion of sexual difference remains sufficiently fluid to allow for this. Although there remain grounds for such a reading, Irigaray's repudiation of lesbian relationships as not yet having supportive social structures that thus permit the required engagement with otherness—and thus as not promoting universality—is quite adamant (Irigaray, *I Love to You*, 3, 5, 145–46).

39. Irigaray, *I Love to You*, 106.

40. Ibid., 145.

41. Ibid., 29.

42. Ibid., 138.

43. Ibid., 145.

44. Ibid., 13.

45. Ibid., 105.

46. Ibid.

47. Ibid., 102.

48. Ibid., 29–30.

49. Ibid., 147.

50. Whitford, *Luce Irigaray*, 84.

51. See E. Grosz, *Jacques Lacan: A Feminist Introduction* (New York: Routledge, 1990), 170.

52. Irigaray, *I Love to You*, 106.

53. Ibid., 26.

54. M. Joy, "What's God Got to Do with It?" in *Bodies, Lives, Voices: Essays on Gender and Theology*, ed. K. O'Grady, A. Gilroy, and J. Gray (Sheffield: Sheffield Academic Press, 1998), 231–65.

55. Irigaray, *This Sex Which Is Not One*, 158–63.

56. Scott, *Only Paradoxes to Offer*, 5.

57. V. Kirby, *Telling Flesh: The Substance of the Corporeal* (New York: Routledge, 1997), 68–81.

"The Sum of What She Is Saying," by Helen A. Fielding

1. Luce Irigaray, *An Ethics of Sexual Difference*, trans. and ed. Carolyn Burke and Gillian C. Gill (Ithaca, N.Y.: Cornell University Press, 1993), 143–44. Originally published in French as *Ethique de la différence sexuelle* (Paris: Editions de Minuit, 1984), 135–36.

2. Elizabeth Grosz, *Volatile Bodies* (Bloomington, Ind.: Indiana University Press, 1994), 9. Cited henceforth as *Volatile*.

3. Maurice Merleau-Ponty, "Eye and Mind," trans. Carleton Dallery, in *The Primacy of Perception*, ed. James Edie (Evanston, Ill.: Northwestern University Press, 1994), 187. Originally published as *L'oeil et l'esprit* (Paris: Gallimard, 1964), 85.

4. Samuel B. Mallin, *Art Line Thought* (Dordrecht: Kluwer Publishers, 1996), 313–413. Cited henceforth as *Art*.

5. Naomi Schor, "Introduction," in *The Essential Difference*, ed. Naomi Schor and Elizabeth Weed (Bloomington, Ind.: Indiana University Press, 1994), ix. Cited henceforth as "Intro."

6. Teresa de Lauretis, "The Essence of the Triangle or, Taking the Risk of Essentialism Seriously: Feminist Theory in Italy, the U.S., and Britain," in *The Essential Difference*, ed. Naomi Schor and Elizabeth Weed (Bloomington, Ind.: Indiana University Press, 1994), 2–3. Cited henceforth as "Essence."

7. de Lauretis, "Essence," 3.

8. Schor, "Intro.," xi.

9. Diana Fuss, *Essentially Speaking* (New York: Routledge, 1989), 114.

10. Diana Fuss, "Reading Like a Feminist," in *The Essential Difference*, 100.

11. Joan Scott, "Experience," in *Feminists Theorize the Political*, ed. Judith Butler and Joan W. Scott (New York: Routledge, 1992), 37.

12. Gayatri Spivak, "In a Word. *Interview*," in *The Essential Difference*, 153.

13. Maurice Merleau-Ponty, *Phenomenology of Perception*, trans. Colin Smith, ed. Forrest Williams (London: Routledge and Kegan Paul, 1963), 198–99. Originally published in French as *Phenomenologie de la perception* (Paris: Gallimard, 1976), 231. Cited henceforth as *Phenomenology*.

14. Merleau-Ponty, *Phenomenology*, 139/161. (Note: where the reference includes a "/," the English translation is given first, the French original follows the "/.")

15. Mallin, *Art*, 313–413.

16. Grosz, *Volatile*, 95.

17. Samuel B. Mallin, *Merleau-Ponty's Philosophy* (New Haven, Conn.: Yale University Press, 1979), 7–107.

18. Grosz, *Volatile*, xi.

19. Maurice Merleau-Ponty, *Visible and the Invisible*, trans. Alphonso Lingis (Evanston, Ill.: Northwestern University Press, 1969), 159. Originally published in French as *Visible et l'invisible* (Paris: Gallimard, 1979), 197. Cited henceforth as *Visible*.

20. Ibid., 109/148.

21. Dionne Brand, *Bread Out of Stone*, (Toronto: Coach House Press, 1994), 169–70. Cited henceforth as *Bread*.

22. Ibid., 13–14.

23. Gilles Deleuze and Félix Guattari, *A Thousand Plateaus, Capitalism and Schizophrenia*, trans. Brian Massumi (Minneapolis: University of Minnesota Press, 1987).

24. Merleau-Ponty, *Visible*, 115/154.

25. Maurice Merleau-Ponty, "Indirect Language and the Voices of Silence," trans. Richard C. McCleary, in *Signs*, ed. James Edie (Evanston, Ill.: Northwestern University Press, 1964), 61.

26. Merleau-Ponty, *Visible*, 113/152; Mallin, *Art*, 21.

27. Mallin, *Art*, 233–234.

28. Merleau-Ponty, *Visible*, 266/319.

29. Brand, *Bread*, 171.

30. Merleau-Ponty, *Visible*, 152/199.

31. Ibid., 149/196.

32. Marcel Proust, *Swann's Way: Part Two*, trans. C. K. Scott Moncrieff (London: Chatto & Windus, 1941), 184.

33. Ibid., 186.

34. Merleau-Ponty, *Visible*, 119/159.

35. Ibid., 152/199.
36. Merleau-Ponty, *Phenomenology,* 144/169.
37. Merleau-Ponty, *Visible,* 119/160.
38. Fuss, *Essentially Speaking.*
39. Merleau-Ponty, *Visible,* 249/303.
40. Ibid., 127/169
41. Ibid., 125–126/167.
42. Ibid., 153/200.

Making the Phenomenological Reduction Experientially Real, by Monika Langer

1. Maurice Merleau-Ponty, "Preface" to *Phenomenology of Perception,* trans. Colin Smith (Atlantic Highlands, N.J.: Humanities Press, 1961), viii.
2. Ibid., xi–xiv.
3. Ibid., xviii, xx.
4. Ibid., xx, xxi.
5. Merleau-Ponty, *Phenomenology of Perception,* 456.
6. Maurice Merleau-Ponty, "Cézanne's Doubt," in *Sense and Non-Sense,* trans. Hubert L. Dreyfus and Patrician Allen Dreyfus (Evanston, Ill.: Northwestern University Press, 1964), 19.
7. René Descartes, "First Meditation: What Can Be Called in Question," in *Philosophical Writings,* ed. and trans. Elizabeth Anscombe and Peter Thomas Geach (London: Thomas Nelson and Sons Ltd., 1970), 61–65. See also Descartes's "Reply" to Hobbes's "First Objection" to the "First Meditation" (*Philosophical Writings,* 127).
8. Merleau-Ponty, "Cézanne's Doubt," 16, 19, 17.
9. Ibid., 19.
10. Merleau-Ponty, "Preface," xix. (See also xx.)
11. Maurice Merleau-Ponty, "The Primacy of Perception and Its Philosophical Consequences," in *The Primacy of Perception and Other Essays,* ed. and trans. James M. Edie (Evanston, Ill.: Northwestern University Press, 1964), 25.
12. Ibid.
13. Merleau-Ponty, "Cézanne's Doubt," 16.
14. Samuel Mallin, *Art Line Thought* (Dordrecht: Kluwer Academic Publishers, 1996), 262.
15. Ibid., 263.
16. Merleau-Ponty, "Cézanne's Doubt," 22.
17. Neil Evernden, *The Natural Alien: Humankind and Environment* (Toronto: University of Toronto Press, 1985), 127.
18. Ibid., 126.
19. Merleau-Ponty, "Cézanne's Doubt," 13–16.
20. Ibid., 12–20.
21. Ibid., 15, 21, 17.
22. Maurice Merleau-Ponty, "Eye and Mind," in *Primacy of Perception and Other Essays,* 159–190.
23. Merleau-Ponty, "Cézanne's Doubt," 19–20; "Le Doute de Cézanne," 32–34.
24. Merleau-Ponty, "Cézanne's Doubt," 16.
25. Emily Carr, "Fresh Seeing," in *Fresh Seeing* (Toronto: Clarke, Irwin & Co. Ltd., 1972), 8, 9.
26. Ibid., 11, 14.
27. Ibid., 14, 20.
28. Emily Carr, "The Something Plus in a Work of Art," in *Fresh Seeing* (Toronto: Clarke, Irwin & Co. Ltd., 1972), 27, 28, 34.
29. Ibid., 30, 34.

30. Carr, "Fresh Seeing," 7, 8.

31. Carr, "Something Plus in a Work of Art," 33.

32. Emily Carr, *Hundreds and Thousands: The Journals of Emily Carr* (Toronto: Clarke, Irwin & Co. Ltd., 1966), 199–200.

33. Ibid., 179.

34. Carr, "Fresh Seeing," 11.

35. Carr, *Hundreds and Thousands,* 267. (See also the earlier entry of June 12th on 242.)

36. Jeffner Allen, "An Introduction to Patriarchal Existentialism Accompanied by a Proposal for a Way Out of Existential Patriarchy," *Philosophy and Social Criticism* 8, no. 4 (winter 1981): 459.

37. Mallin, *Art Line Thought,* 335. See also 314, 334 ff.

38. Ibid., 268.

39. Allen, "Introduction to Patriarchal Existentialism," 460, 461.

40. Ibid., 461.

Disappropriations, by Penelope Deutscher

All citations of untranslated French material are the author's translations.

1. Jacques Derrida, *Of Grammatology,* trans. Gayatri Spivak (Baltimore: Johns Hopkins University Press, 1976), 229. Cited henceforth as *Grammatology.*

2. Robert Bernasconi, "No More Stories, Good or Bad: de Man's Criticisms of Derrida on Rousseau," in *Derrida: A Critical Reader,* ed. David Wood (Oxford: Polity Press, 1992), 137–66, 143. Cited henceforth as "No More."

3. Paul de Man, *Blindness and Insight* (Oxford: Oxford University Press, 1971), 102–41. Cited henceforth as *Blindness.*

4. Paul de Man, *Allegories of Reading* (New Haven, Conn.: Yale University Press, 1979), 237. Cited henceforth as *Allegories.*

5. In the case discussed by de Man, the "difficulty" is that Rousseau both undermines the reliability of the "inner voice of conscience" as potentially open to error, possibly the product of the existing social milieu (de Man, 1979, 224), and also tells us to rely on and to follow our inner convictions. The apparent "control" of Rousseau over this instability is suggested because Rousseau himself poses this contradiction as the problem, on the basis of which he himself then queries the epistemological status of inner conviction (*Allegories,* 229). Thus, in the case of the contradictions inherent in the "Profession de foi" in *Emile,* de Man does explain the contradiction as part of Rousseau's deconstructive project. For de Man, Rousseau draws upon the slippage between, for example, his account of our reliance on inner judgment, and his account of the unreliable basis of inner judgment, precisely as a means of putting our reliance on inner judgment into question (237).

6. Sarah Kofman, *The Enigma of Woman,* trans. Catherine Porter (Ithaca, N.Y.: Cornell University Press, 1985), 101n. 1. Cited henceforth as *Enigma.*

7. Neither Derrida nor Irigaray would deny that Rousseau and Freud are "deconstructive," but they mean this in the sense of the gloss Derrida gives to de Man's comment that "there is no need to deconstruct Rousseau" (*Blindness,* 139). On Derrida's gloss: "there is always already deconstruction, at work *in* works. . . . Texts deconstruct *themselves* by themselves" (Jacques Derrida, *Memoirs for Paul de Man,* trans. C. Lindsay, J. Culler, and E. Cadava [New York: Columbia University Press, 1986], 123, cited in "No More," 153).

8. Notice that, in this sense, we would expect *any* deconstructive reading to be seen by Kofman as appropriative. It would be seen as a misidentification of the way in which the text in question (here, the Freudian text, but presumably any text) is already deconstructive.

9. Sarah Kofman with Roland Jaccard, "Apprendre aux hommes a tenir parole—portrait de Sarah Kofman" in *Le Monde* (27–28 April 1986): vii. Cited henceforth as "Apprendre."

10. Sarah Kofman, *Explosion II: Les enfants de Nietzsche* (Paris: Galilée, 1993), 372.

11. For a short discussion of the readings of Freud by Kofman and Irigaray, see Kelly Oliver, *Womanizing Nietzsche: Philosophy's Relation to the "Feminine"* (New York: Routledge, 1995), 12ff.

12. Gayatri Spivak, *In Other Worlds: Essays in Cultural Politics* (New York: Routledge, 1988), 149.

13. Monique Schneider, "Le regard et la femme," *Les Cahiers du grif* (new series) 3: 39–72.

14. Elizabeth Grosz, *Sexual Subversions, Three French Feminists* (Sydney: Allen and Unwin, 1989), 109.

15. Luce Irigaray, *This Sex Which Is Not One*, trans. Catherine Porter (Ithaca, N.Y.: Cornell University Press, 1985), 76. Cited henceforth as *This Sex*. Cited and discussed in Margaret Whitford, *Luce Irigaray, Philosophy in the Feminine* (New York: Routledge, 1991), 71. Cited henceforth as *Irigaray*.

16. Luce Irigaray, *Marine Lover of Friedrich Nietszche*, trans. Gillian Gill (New York: Columbia University Press, 1991), 11. Cited henceforth as *Marine*.

17. Sarah Kofman with Alice Jardine, "Sarah Kofman," in *Shifting Scenes: Interviews on Women, Writing, and Politics in Post-68 France,* ed. Alice Jardine and Anne M. Menke (New York: Columbia University Press, 1991), 104–12.

18. Ann Smock, "Translator's Introduction," in Sarah Kofman, *Rue Ordener, Rue Labat,* trans. Ann Smock (Lincoln, Neb.: University of Nebraska Press, 1996), vii–xiii.

19. Sarah Kofman, *Nerval: Le charme de la répétition, lecture de Sylvie,* (Lausanne: L'Age d'homme, 1979), 12.

20. See Natalie Alexander on Kofman's reading of Kant, "Rending Kant's Umbrella: Kofman's Diagnosis of Ethical Law," in *Engimas: Essays on Sarah Kofman,* ed. Penelope Deutscher and Kelly Oliver (Ithaca, N.Y.: Cornell University Press, 1999), 143–58.

21. Sarah Kofman with Eyelyne Ender, "Interview avec Sarah Kofman 22 mars 1991. Subvertir le philosophique *ou* Pour un supplément de jouissance," *Compar(a)ison* 1: 9–26, 12. Cited henceforth as "Interview."

22. Sarah Kofman, *The Childhood of Art,* trans. Winifred Woodhull (New York: Columbia University Press, 1988), 142–43.

23. Sarah Kofman, *Camera Obscura: De L'idéologie* (Paris: Galilée, 1973), 69. Partially translated in 1993.

24. Sarah Kofman, *Nietzsche et la scéne philosophique,* 2d ed. (Paris: Galilée, 1986). Partially translated in "Descartes Entrapped," in *Who Comes After the Subject?* ed. Eduardo Cadava, Peter Connor, and Jean-Luc Nancy (New York: Routledge, 1988), 178–97 and in "Baubô: Theological Perversion and Fetishism," in *Nietzsche's New Seas: Explorations in Philosophy, Aesthetics and Politics,* ed. Michael Allen Gillespie and Tracy B. Strong (Chicago: University of Chicago Press, 1988), 175–202. Cited henceforth as *Nietzsche*.

25. Sarah Kofman, *Nietzsche and Metaphor,* trans. Duncan Large (London: Athlone Press, 1993), 2. Cited henceforth as *Metaphor*.

26. Duncan Large, "Translator's Introduction," in Sarah Kofman, *Nietzsche and Metaphor,* xxii.

27. Richard H. Weisberg, "De Man Missing Nietzsche: *Hinzugedichtet* Revisited," in *Nietzsche as Postmodernist: Essays pro and contra,* ed. Clayton Koelb (Albany, N.Y.: SUNY Press, 1990), 111–26, 313n. 17; 312n. 21; 313n. 30.

28. The French acronym for a corporation or company (ltd, of "limited liability"). See Jacques Derrida, *Limited Inc.,* trans. S. Weber and J. Mehlman (Evanston, Ill.: Northwestern University Press, 1988), 36.

29. See Moira Gatens, *Imaginary Bodies: Ethics, Power and Corporeality* (London: Routledge, 1996); also Genevieve Lloyd, *The Man of Reason: "Male" and "Female" in Western Philosophy* (London: Methuen, 1981); and Michèle Le Doeuff, *The Philosophical Imaginary,* trans. Colin Gordon (London: Athelone Press, 1989).

30. Luce Irigaray, "Ecce Mulier? Fragments," in *Nietzsche and the Feminine,* ed. Peter J. Burgard (Charlottesville, Va.: University of Virginia Press, 1994), 316–31, 319.

Becoming-Imperceptible as a Mode of Self-Presentation, by Tamsin Lorraine

Reprinted from Tamsin Lorraine, *Irigaray and Deleuze: Experiments in Visceral Philosophy.* Copyright © 1999 Cornell University. Used by permission of the publisher, Cornell University Press.

1. See Iris M. Young, "Humanism, Gynocentrism and Feminist Politics," in *Throwing Like a Girl and Other Essays in Feminist Philosophy and Social Theory* (Bloomington, Ind.: Indiana University Press, 1990), 73–91; also Alison Jaggar, *Feminist Politics and Human Nature* (Totowa, N.J.: Rowman and Allanheld, 1983).

2. See Rosi Braidotti, *Patterns of Dissonance: A Study of Women in Contemporary Philosophy* (New York: Routledge, 1993), and Iris Young, *Throwing.*

3. Elizabeth Grosz, *Volatile Bodies: Toward a Corporeal Feminism* (Bloomington, Ind.: Indiana University Press, 1994), 9.

4. See, for example, Jessica Benjamin, *The Bonds of Love: Psychoanalysis, Feminism, and the Problem of Domination* (New York: Pantheon Books, 1988); Nancy Chodorow, *The Reproduction of Mothering: Psychoanalysis and the Sociology of Gender* (Berkeley, Calif.: The University of California Press, 1978); Juliet Mitchell, *Psychoanalysis and Feminism* (New York: Vintage Books, 1974); and Teresa Brennan, ed., *Between Feminism and Psychoanalysis* (New York: Routledge, 1989).

5. See Elizabeth Grosz, *Volatile Bodies;* Rosi Braidotti, *Patterns of Dissonance, Nomadic Subjects: Embodiment and Sexual Difference in Contemporary Feminist Theory* (New York: Routledge Press, 1994), and "Toward a New Nomadism: Feminist Deleuzian Tracks; or, Metaphysics and Metabolism," in *Gilles Deleuze and the Theater of Philosophy*, ed. Constantin V. Boundas and Dorothea Olkowski (New York: Routledge, 1994); also Moira Gatens, "Through a Spinozist Lens: Ethology, Difference, Power," in Paul Patton, ed. *Deleuze, A Critical Reader* (London: Blackwell Press, 1998).

6. Gilles Deleuze, *Negotiations 1972–1990*, trans. Martin Joughin (New York: Columbia University Press, 1995), 144.

7. Gilles Deleuze and Félix Guattari, *Anti-Oedipus: Capitalism and Schizophrenia*, trans. Robert Hurley, Mark Seem, and Helen R. Lane (Minneapolis: University of Minnesota Press, 1983).

8. Gilles Deleuze and Félix Guattari, *A Thousand Plateaus: Capitalism and Schizophrenia*, trans. Brian Massumi (Minneapolis: University of Minnesota Press, 1987), 12.

9. Gilles Deleuze and Claire Parnet, *Dialogues*, trans. Hugh Tomlinson and Barbara Habberjam (New York: Columbia University Press, 1987). Cited henceforth as *Dialogues*.

10. Gilles Deleuze and Félix Guattari, *What Is Philosophy?* trans. Hugh Tomlinson and Graham Burchell (New York: Columbia University Press, 1994), 147. Cited henceforth as *What Is?*

11. Paul Patton, "Anti-Platonism and Art," in *Gilles Deleuze and the Theater of Philosophy* (New York: Routledge, 1994), 144–45. Cited henceforth as "Anti-Platonism."

12. Daniel W. Smith, "Deleuze's Theory of Sensation: Overcoming the Kantian Duality," in *Deleuze, A Critical Reader* (London: Blackwell Press, 1998), 30. Cited henceforth as "Sensation."

13. Gilles Deleuze, *Kant's Critical Philosophy: The Doctrine of the Faculties*, trans. Hugh Tomlinson and Barbara Habberjam (Minneapolis: University of Minnesota Press, 1984), xii.

14. Gilles Deleuze, *Difference and Repetition*, trans. Paul Patton (New York: Columbia University Press, 1994), 146. Cited henceforth as *Difference.*

Between the Visible and the Articulable, by Ewa Plonowska Ziarek

1. The following Foucault's works will be cited parenthetically:
Discipline and Punish: The Birth of Prison, trans. Alan Sheridan (New York: Random House, 1977) as *DP.*

"The Discourse on Language," in *The Archeology of Knowledge and the Discourse on Language,* trans. A. M. Sheridan Smith (New York: Pantheon Books, 1972) as *DL.*

The History of Sexuality, vol. 1, trans. Robert Hurley (New York: Random House, 1978) as *HS.*

"Nietzsche, Genealogy, History," in *Language, Counter-Memory, Practice,* ed. Donald F. Bouchard, trans. Sherry Simon (Ithaca, N.Y.: Cornell University Press, 1977) as *NGH.*

The Use of Pleasure, vol. 2 of *The History of Sexuality,* trans. Robert Hurley (New York: Random House, 1990) as *UP.*

2. See, in particular, Hilary Radner's illuminating discussion of the contradictory interplay of the disciplinary technologies and the practices of self in the feminine popular culture in *Shopping Around: Feminine Culture and the Pursuit of Pleasure* (New York: Routledge, 1995); the work of Susan Bordo on eating disorders and the production of the slender body in *Unbearable Weight: Feminism, Western Culture and the Body* (Berkeley, Calif.: University of California Press, 1993) and her analysis of the normalizing function of the cultural images of beauty and physical perfection in the context of gender and race in *Twilight Zones: The Hidden Life of Cultural Images from Plato to O. J.* (Berkeley, Calif.: University of California Press, 1997);

Sandra Lee Bartky's discussion of new disciplines regulating female bodies in "Foucault, Femininity, and the Modernization of Patriarchal Power," in *Feminism and Foucault: Reflections on Resistance,* ed. Irene Diamond and Lee Quinby (Boston: Northeastern University Press, 1988), 61–86; and Jennifer Terry "Body Invaded: Medical Surveillance of Women as Reproducers," *Socialist Review* 19 (1989): 13–43. For an informative synopsis of the feminist appropriations of Foucault, see Monique Deveaux, "Feminism and Empowerment: A Critical Reading of Foucault," *Feminist Interpretations of Michel Foucault,* ed. Susan J. Hekman (University Park, Pa.: Pennsylvania State University Press, 1996), 211–38. For the discussion of Foucault's analysis of the role of race and racism in the formation of biopower, see Ann Laura Stoler, *Race and the Education of Desire: Foucault's History of Sexuality and the Colonial Order of Things* (Durham, N.C.: Duke University Press, 1995).

3. Honi Fern Haber, *Beyond Postmodern Politics: Lyotard, Rorty, Foucault* (New York: Routledge, 1994), 78.

4. As Francis Bartkowski writes, Foucault exposes the irony of "movements of liberation, which, even as they operate, are constrained by the power-knowledge-pleasure apparatus." "Epistemic Drift in Foucault," *Feminism and Foucault,* 46.

5. Lois McNay, *Foucault: A Critical Introduction* (New York: Continuum, 1994), 102.

6. Francis Bartkowski, "Epistemic Drift in Foucault," 44.

7. As Foucault explains, "Where there is power, there is resistance, and yet, or rather consequently, this resistance is never in a position of exteriority in relation to power" (*HS,* 95).

8. For the discussion of freedom in Foucault as a contextualized practice rather than an attribute of the subject, see Wendy Brown, *States of Injury: Power and Freedom in Late Modernity* (Princeton, N.J.: Princeton University Press, 1995), 3–30 and Jana Sawicki's excellent essay "Feminism, Foucault, and the 'Subjects' of Power and Freedom," in *Feminist Interpretations of Michel Foucault,* 159–78. For the notion of resistance as freeing of difference see Susan Hekman, "Editor's Introduction," in *Feminist Interpretations of Michel Foucault,* 10–11, and her earlier *Gender and Knowledge: Elements of a Postmodern Feminism* (Boston: Northeastern University Press, 1990), 182–86.

9. For a critique of this reading of Foucault, see Judith Butler, *Bodies That Matter: On the Discursive Limits of "Sex"* (New York: Routledge, 1993), 8–10.

10. For an interesting contribution to the debate about the usefulness of Foucault for feminism, see, for instance, Amy Allen, "Foucault on Power: Theory for Feminists," *Feminist Interpretations of Michel Foucault,* 265–81. However, because of the lack of an explicit discussion of how power is actualized in historical formations, Allen ends up with two contradictory

notions of power in Foucault, neither of which in itself is useful for feminism: free circulation of forces on the one hand, and the states of domination on the other hand in which individuals are unable to exercise power at all (277).

11. There are of course some notable exceptions, in particular, the work of Judith Butler, devoted from the outset to the elaboration of the theory of agency within the Foucauldian framework.

12. Nancy Hartsock, "Foucault on Power: A Theory for Women?" *Feminism/Postmodernism*, ed. Linda Nicholson (New York: Routledge, 1989), 167. For a more recent critique of the limitation of Foucault's theory for the projects of liberation see her "Postmodernism and Political Change: Issues for Feminist Theory" *Feminist Interpretations of Michel Foucault*, 39–55.

13. Friedrich Nietzsche, *On the Genealogy of Morals,* trans. Walter Kaufmann (New York: Random House, 1969), 77–78.

14. Jacques-Alain Miller, "Jeremy Bentham's Panoptic Device," *October* 41 (1987): 5–6.

15. Joan Copjec, *Read My Desire: Lacan Against Historicism* (Cambridge, Mass.: MIT Press, 1994), 41.

16. Foucault, *The Archeology Of Knowledge,* 157.

17. Gilles Deleuze, *Foucault,* trans. Seán Hand (Minneapolis: University of Minnesota Press, 1988), 62. Subsequent references will be cited parenthetically as *F.*

18. Peg Elizabeth Birmingham, "Arendt/Foucault: Power and the Law," *Transitions in Continental Philosophy,* ed. Arleen B. Dallery, Stephen Watson, and Marya Bower (Albany, N.Y.: SUNY Press, 1994), 23–24.

19. Judith Butler, *The Psychic Life of Power* (Stanford, Calif.: Stanford University Press, 1997), 29.

20. For an illuminating discussion of Nietzsche's concept of the body and its influence on Foucault, see Elizabeth Grosz, "Nietzsche and the Stomach of Knowledge," *Nietzsche, Feminism and Political Theory,* ed. Paul Patton (London: Routledge, 1993), 49–70.

21. Butler, *Bodies That Matter,* 34.

22. Ibid., 35.

23. As Nietzsche writes, "Mechanical activity and what goes with it—such as absolute regularity, punctilious and unthinking obedience, a mode of life fixed once and for all, fully occupied time . . . how subtly the ascetic priest has known how to employ them in the struggle against pain!" *On the Genealogy of Morals,* 134.

24. Bordo, *Twilight Zones,* 9. See also Radner's analysis of the codification of the body parts in exercise routine in *Shopping Around,* 154.

25. Ibid., 145.

26. Ibid., 173.

27. Ibid., 146.

28. Nietzsche, *On Genealogy of Morals,* 58–59.

29. Michel Foucault, *The Order of Things,* trans. Alan Sheridan (New York: Pantheon, 1972), 328.

30. McNay, *Foucault,* 102–3.

31. Butler, *The Psychic Life of Power,* 86.

32. Nietzsche, *On the Genealogy of Morals,* 45–46.

33. For a further discussion of the genealogy of the soul in Nietzsche, see Elizabeth Grosz, "Nietzsche and the Stomach for Knowledge," 49–70; Judith Butler, *The Psychic Life of Power,* 63–78, and Alan Schrift, *Nietzsche's French Legacy: A Genealogy of Post Structuralism* (New York: Routledge, 1995), 44–48.

34. Butler, *The Psychic Life of Power,* 65.

35. Nietzsche, *On the Genealogy of Morals,* 161.

36. Louis Althusser, "Ideology and Ideological State Apparatuses," *Lenin and Philosophy and Other Essays* (New York: Monthly Review Press, 1970), 170–77.

37. Furthermore, disciplinary apparatus fails to produce the "ideological effect" Althusser describes as the obviousness of freedom. Although it is true that the law presupposes the freedom of will, delinquency introduces an involuntary causality, which explains the crime in terms of pathology: the criminal "is linked to his offence by a whole bundle of complex threads (instincts, drives, tendencies, character)" (*DP,* 253).

38. Friedrich Nietzsche, *The Will to Power,* trans. Walter Kaufmann (New York: Vintage, 1968), 270.

39. Michel Foucault, "Two Lectures," *Power/Knowledge: Selected Interviews and Other Writings 1972–1977,* ed. Colin Gordon, trans. Colin Gordon et al. (New York: Pantheon, 1980), 108.

Carnival, by Jane Drexler

I would like to thank the following people for their comments and conversations regarding this essay: Jennifer Litzenberger, Tabor Fisher, Taze Yanick, Hasana Sharp, Nick Veroli, The Resistant Negotiations Workshop at SUNY-Binghamton with Maria Lugones, and most especially Dorothea Olkowski (whose invaluable conversations, advice, and encouragement directly affects the continuing success of this project).

1. See Josephine Donovan, "Style and Power," in *Feminism, Bakhtin, and the Dialogic,* ed. Dale M. Bauer and Susan Jaret McKinstrey (New York: State University of New York Press, 1991).

2. Gary Saul Morson and Caryl Emerson, *Mikhail Bakhtin: Creation of a Prosaics,* (Stanford, Calif.: Stanford University Press, 1990). For the basis of the critiques against Bakhtin's carnival as a utopian image, see Frederic Jameson, "Reification and Utopia in Mass Culture," in *Social Text* 1 (1979). The aspects of these critiques will be discussed at length in the third section of this paper.

3. For an extensive analysis and commentary on feminist critiques of Gilles Deleuze and Félix Guattari, see Dorothea Olkowski, *Gilles Deleuze and the Ruin of Representation* (Berkeley, Calif.: University of California Press, 1999), primarily chapter 2, "Can a Feminist Read Deleuze and Guattari?"

4. Mikhail Bakhtin, "Discourse in the Novel," in *The Dialogic Imagination,* trans. Caryl Emerson and Michael Holquist, ed. Michael Holquist (Austin, Tex.: University of Texas Press, 1981), 263.

5. Ibid., 272.

6. Ibid., 301.

7. Katerina Clark and Michael Holquist, *Mikhail Bakhtin* (Cambridge, Mass.: Harvard University Press, 1984), 294.

8. Mikhail Bakhtin, "Epic and Novel," in *The Dialogic Imagination,* trans. Caryl Emerson and Michael Holquist, ed. Michael Holquist (Austin, Tex.: University of Texas Press, 1981).

9. Bakhtin, "Discourse," 301.

10. Virginia Woolf, *Orlando: A Biography* (New York: Harcourt Brace and Company, 1928), 267.

11. Mikhail Bakhtin, "From the Prehistory of Novelistic Discourse," in *The Dialogic Imagination,* 44–51.

12. Bakhtin, "Discourse," 304.

13. Woolf, *Orlando,* 188; my emphasis.

14. Ibid., 128–129.

15. Dale Bauer, "Gender in Bakhtin's Carnival," in *Feminisms: An Anthology of Literary Theory and Criticism,* ed. Robyn R. Warhol and Diane Price Herndl (Piscataway, N.J.: Rutgers University Press, 1997), 713.

16. Ibid., 710.

17. Clark and Holquist, *Mikhail Bakhtin,* 296.

18. Ibid., 317.

19. Bakhtin, "Discourse," 273.

20. Mikhail Bakhtin, *Rabelais and His World,* trans. Helene Iswolsky (Bloomington, Ind.: Indiana University Press, 1984), 7.

21. Bauer, "Gender," 716.

22. Michael Gardiner, "Bakhtin's Carnival: Utopia as Critique," in *Critical Studies: Bakhtin, Carnival and Other Subjects: Selected Papers from the Fifth International Bakhtin Conference,* ed. Myriam Diaz-Diocaretz (Atlanta: Rodopi Press, 1993), 25.

23. Jameson, "Reification and Utopia," 141.

24. Tom Moylan, *Demand the Impossible: Science Fiction and the Utopian Imagination* (London: Methuen Press, 1986).

25. Mikhail Bakhtin, *Problems with Dostoevsky's Poetics,* trans. Caryl Emerson (Minneapolis: University of Minnesota Press, 1984), 165–66.

26. Morson and Emerson, *Mikhail Bakhtin,* 67.

27. Gardiner, "Bakhtin's Carnival," 32.

28. Elizabeth Grosz, "A Thousand Tiny Sexes: Feminism and Rhizomatics," in *Gilles Deleuze and the Theatre of Philosophy,* ed. Constantin V. Boundas and Dorothea Olkowski (New York: Routledge, 1994), 204.

29. Gilles Deleuze and Félix Guattari, *A Thousand Plateaus: Capitalism and Schizophrenia,* trans. Brian Massumi (Minneapolis: University of Minnesota Press, 1980), 274.

30. Dorothea Olkowski, personal correspondence.

31. Grosz, "A Thousand Tiny Sexes," 197.

32. Olkowski, personal correspondence.

33. Ibid.

34. Grosz, "A Thousand Tiny Sexes," 192.

35. Deleuze and Guattari, *A Thousand Plateaus,* 251.

36. Ibid., 249.

37. Ibid., 243–50.

38. Ibid., 254.

39. Thanks to Dorothea Olkowski for her comments and conversations concerning the above section.

40. Gilles Deleuze, *Cinema 2: The Time Image,* trans. Hugh Tomlinson and Robert Galeta (Minneapolis: University of Minnesota Press, 1989), 167.

41. I have borrowed this phrase from my conversations with Jennifer Lutzenberger, at SUNY-Binghamton, fall 1998.

Bibliography

COMPILED BY HELEN A. FIELDING

In gathering together this bibliography, my goal was to find feminist writings that enacted contemporary French philosophy. This bibliography captures much of what has come out in the area of feminist French philosophy, but does not promise to be exhaustive. Because Joan Nordquist and others have produced extensive bibliographies on the works of Kristeva, Irigaray, and Cixous, I have only included the secondary literature for these philosophers. Where possible, the entries have been divided according to the language used initially by the author. The Anglo-American grouping sweeps up not only those authors from England, the United States, Canada, and Australia, but also those philosophers from other countries who write or publish in English. This section is by far the largest, indicating not only how important French philosophy has been for English-speaking feminist philosophers, but also that feminist philosophy has extended institutional support in these countries. The French grouping covers for the most part not only French authors but also philosophers from French-speaking Canada, Belgium, and Switzerland. Included in the German grouping are the works of philosophers from Germany, Austria, and Switzerland.

Allen, Jeffner. "An Introduction to Patriarchal Existentialism Accompanied by a Proposal for a Way Out of Existential Patriarchy." *Philosophy and Social Criticism* 8, 4 (winter 1981): 447–65.

Carr, Emily. *Fresh Seeing*. Toronto: Clarke, Irwin & Co. Ltd., 1972.

———. *Hundreds and Thousands: The Journals of Emily Carr*. Toronto: Clarke, Irwin & Co. Ltd., 1966.

Descartes, René. *Philosophical Writings*. Translated by Elizabeth Anscombe and Peter Thomas Geach. London: Thomas Nelson and Sons Ltd., 1970.

Evernden, Neil. *The Natural Alien: Humankind and Environment*. Toronto: University of Toronto Press, 1985.

Mallin, Samuel. *Art Line Thought*. Dordrecht: Kluwer Academic Publishers, 1996.

Merleau-Ponty, Maurice. *Phenomenology of Perception*. Translated by Colin Smith. London: Routledge and Kegan Paul, 1962.

———. *The Primacy of Perception and Other Essays*. Translated and edited by James M. Edie. Evanston, Ill.: Northwestern University Press, 1964.

———. *Sense and Non-Sense.* Translated by Hubert L. Dreyfus and Patricia Allen Dreyfus. Evanston, Ill.: Northwestern University Press, 1964.

Bakhtin, Mikhail. *The Dialogic Imagination.* Translated by Caryl Emerson and Michael Holquist. Edited by Michael Holquist. Austin, Tex.: University of Texas Press, 1981.

———. *Problems with Dostoevsky's Poetics.* Translated by Caryl Emerson. Minneapolis: University of Minnesota Press, 1984.

———. *Rabelais and His World.* Translated by Helene Iswolsky. Bloomington, Ind.: Indiana University Press, 1984.

Bauer, Dale, and Susan J. McKinstrey, eds. *Feminism, Bakhtin, and the Dialogic.* New York: State University of New York Press, 1991.

Boundas, Constantin V., and Dorothea Olkowski, eds. *Gilles Deleuze and the Theatre of Philosophy.* New York: Routledge, 1994.

Clark, Katerina, and Michael Holquist. *Mikhail Bakhtin.* Cambridge, Mass.: Harvard University Press, 1984.

Danow, David. *The Thought of Mikhail Bakhtin: From Word to Culture.* New York: St. Martin's Press, 1991.

Deleuze, Gilles. *Cinema 2: The Time Image.* Translated by Hugh Tomlinson and Robert Galeta. Minneapolis: University of Minnesota Press, 1989.

Deleuze, Gilles, and Félix Guattari. *A Thousand Plateaus: Capitalism and Schizophrenia.* Translated by Brian Massumi. Minneapolis: University of Minnesota Press, 1987.

Diaz-Diocaretz, Myriam, ed. *Critical Studies: Bakhtin, Carnival and Other Subjects: Selected Papers from the Fifth International Bakhtin Conference.* Atlanta: Rodopi Press, 1993.

Jameson, Frederic. "Reification and Utopia in Mass Culture." *Social Text* 1 (1979).

Morson, Gary Saul, and Caryl Emerson. *Mikhail Bakhtin: Creation of a Prosaics.* Stanford: Stanford University Press, 1990.

Moylan, Tom. *Demand the Impossible: Science Fiction and the Utopian Imagination.* London: Methuen Press, 1986.

Olkowski, Dorothea. *The Ruin of Representation.* Berkeley: University of California Press, 1999.

Woolf, Virginia. *Orlando: A Biography.* New York: Harcourt Brace and Company, 1928.

Warhol, Robyn R., and Diane Price Herndl, eds. *Feminisms: An Anthology of Literary Theory and Criticism.* New Brunswick, N.J.: Rutgers University Press, 1997.

Simone de Beauvoir: Disrupting the Metonymy of Gender

Beauvoir, Simone de. *The Ethics of Ambiguity.* Translated by Bernard Frechtman. New York: Philosophical Library, 1948.

———. "Must We Burn Sade?" Translated by Annette Michelson. *The Marquis de Sade.* New York: Grove Press, 1966.

———. *The Second Sex.* Translated by H. M. Parshley. New York: Vintage Books, 1974.

Freud, Sigmund. *Three Essays on the Theory of Sexuality.* Translated by James Strachey. New York: Basic Books, 1962.

Lacan, Jacques. *The Seminar of Jacques Lacan, Book VII, The Ethics of Psychoanalysis 1959–1960.* Translated by Dennis Porter. New York: W. W. Norton, 1992.

Lyotard, Jean Francois. *The Lyotard Reader.* Edited by Andrew Benjamin. Cambridge: Basil Blackwell, 1989.

Anglo-American Sources

Adams, Parveen. "Representation and Sexuality." *m/f* 1 (1978): 65–82.

Adams, P., and Jeff Minson. "The 'Subject' of Feminism." *m/f* 2 (1978): 44–61.

Adlam, Diana. "Introduction to Irigaray." *Ideology and Consciousness* 1 (1977): 57–61.

Ainley, Alison. "The Ethics of Sexual Difference." In *Abjection, Melancholia and Love: The Work of Julia Kristeva,* edited by John Fletcher and Andrew Benjamin. New York: Routledge, 1990.

———. "French Feminist Philosophy: de Beauvoir, Kristeva, Irigaray, Le Doeuff, Cixous." In *Twentieth-Century Continental Philosophy,* edited by Richard Kearney. London: Routledge, 1994.

Aladjem, Terry K. "The Philosopher's Prism: Foucault, Feminism, and Critique." *Political Theory* 9, 2 (1991): 227–91.

Alcoff, Linda. "Cultural Feminism Versus Post-Structuralism: The Identity Crisis in Feminist Theory." *Signs: Journal of Women in Culture and Society* 13, 3 (1988): 405–36.

———. "Dangerous Pleasures: Foucault and the Politics of Paedophilia." In *Feminist Interpretations of Michel Foucault,* edited by Susan J. Hekman. University Park, Pa.: Pennsylvania State University Press, 1996.

———. "Feminist Politics and Foucault: The Limits to a Collaboration." In *Crises in Continental Philosophy,* edited by Arleen B. Dallery and Charles E. Scott. Albany, N.Y.: State University of New York Press, 1990.

———. "Phenomenology, Poststructuralism and Feminist Theory: On the Concept of Experience." In *Feminist Phenomenology,* edited by Lester Embree and Linda Fisher. Dordrecht: Kluwer, forthcoming.

Alexander, Anna. "The Eclipse of Gender: Simone de Beauvoir and the Différance of Translation." *Philosophy Today* 41, 1 (1997): 112–22.

Allen, Amy. "Foucault on Power: A Theory for Feminists." In *Feminist Interpretations of Michel Foucault,* edited by Susan J. Hekman. University Park, Pa.: Pennsylvania State University Press, 1996.

Allen, Jeffner. "An Introduction to Patriarchal Existentialism: A Proposal for a Way Out of Existential Patriarchy." *Philosophy and Social Criticism* 8:4 (1981): 447–65. Revised and expanded in *The Thinking Muse,* edited by Jeffner Allen and Iris Marion Young. Bloomington, Ind.: Indiana University Press, 1989.

———. "Poetic Politics: How the Amazons Took the Acropolis." *Hypatia* 3, 2 (1988): 107–22.

———. "A response to a letter from Peg Simons, December 1993." In *Feminist Interpretations of Simone de Beauvoir,* edited by Margaret A. Simons. University Park, Pa.: Pennsylvania State University Press, 1995.

———. *Sinuosities: Lesbian Poetic Politics.* Bloomington, Ind.: Indiana University Press, 1996.

Allen, Jeffner, and Iris Marion Young, eds. *The Thinking Muse: Feminism and Modern French Philosophy.* Bloomington, Ind.: Indiana University Press, 1989.

Ansell-Pearson, Keith. "Nietzsche, Women and Political Theory." In *Nietzsche, Feminism and Political Theory,* edited by Paul Patton. London: Routledge, 1993.

Antonopoulos, Anna. "Writing the Mystic Body: Sexuality and Textuality in the écriture féminine of Saint Catherine of Genoa." *Hypatia* 6, 3 (1991): 185–207.

Arens, Katherine. "Between Hypatia and Beauvoir: Philosophy as Discourse." *Hypatia* 10, 4 (1995): 46–75.

Armour, Ellen T. "Crossing the Boundaries Between Deconstruction, Feminism and Religion." In *Feminist Interpretations of Jacques Derrida,* edited by Nancy J. Holland. University Park, Pa.: Pennsylvania State University Press, 1997.

———. "Deconstruction and Feminist Theology: Toward Forging an Alliance with Derrida and Irigaray." Ph.D. diss., Vanderbilt University, 1993.

———. "Questions of Proximity: 'Woman's Place' in Derrida and Irigaray." *Hypatia* 12, 1 (1997): 63–78.

Arp, Kristana. "Beauvoir's Concept of Bodily Alienation." In *Feminist Interpretations of Simone de Beauvoir,* edited by Margaret J. Simons. University Park, Pa.: Pennsylvania State University Press, 1995.

Assister, Alison. *Enlightened Women: Modernist Feminism in a Postmodern Age.* New York: Routledge, 1996.

Atack, Margaret. "The Other Feminist." *Paragraph* 8 (1986): 25–39.

Bair, Deirdre. "Simone de Beauvoir: Politics, Language, and Feminist Identity." *Yale French Studies* 72 (1986): 149–62.

Balbus, I. "Disciplining Women: Foucault and Feminist Discourse." *Praxis International* 5, 4 (1986): 466–83.

Barnes, Hazel E. "Beauvoir and Sartre: The Forms of Farewell." *Philosophy and Literature* 19 (1985): 21–40.

———. "Sartre and Sexism." *Philosophy and Literature* 14, 2 (1990): 340–47.

Barrett, Michèle, and Mary McIntosh. "Christine Delphy: vers un féminisme matérialiste?" *Nouvelle Questions Feministes* 4 (1982): 35–49.

Bartkowski, Frances. "Epistemic Drift in Foucault." In *Feminism & Foucault,* edited by Irene Diamond and Lee Quinby. Boston: Northeastern University Press, 1988.

———. "Feminism and Deconstruction: 'A Union Forever Deferred.'" *Enclitic* 4, 2 (1980): 70–77.

———. "The Question of Ethics in French Feminism." *Berkshire Review* 21 (1986): 22–29.

———. "Speculations on the Flesh: Foucault and the French Feminists." In *Power, Gender, Values,* edited by Judith Genova. Edmonton: Academic Printing and Publishing, 1987.

Bartky, Sandra Lee. *Femininity and Domination: Studies in the Phenomenology of Oppression.* New York: Routledge, 1990.

———. "Foucault, Femininity, and the Modernization of Patriarchal Power." In *Feminism & Foucault,* edited by Irene Diamond and Lee Quinby. Boston: Northeastern University Press, 1988.

———. "Narcissism, Femininity and Alienation." *Social Theory and Practice* 8 (1982): 127–43.

Benhabib, Seyla. "Epistemologies of Postmodernism: A Rejoinder to Jean-François Lyotard." *New German Critique* 33 (1984): 103–26.

———. "Feminism and Postmodernism: an Uneasy Alliance." *Praxis International* 11, 2 (1995): 137–49.

———. "'Die Quellen des Selbst' in der zeitgenössischen feministischen Theorie." Translated by Julika Tillmanns and Amata Schneider-Ludorff. *Die Philosophin* 6, 11 (1995): 12–32.

———. *Situating the Self: Gender, Community and Postmodernism in Contemporary Ethics.* New York: Routledge, 1992.

———. "Subjectivity, Historiography, and Politic." In *Feminist Contentions,* edited by Seyla Benhabib et al. New York: Routledge, 1995.

Benhabib, Seyla et al. *Feminist Contentions: A Philosophical Exchange.* New York: Routledge, 1995. First published as *Der Streit um Differenz: Feminismus und Postmoderne in der Gegenwart.* Frankfurt a.M.: Fisher Taschenbuch Verlag, 1993.

Berg, Elizabeth. "Escaping the Cave: Irigaray and Her Feminist Critics." In *Literature and Ethics,* edited by Gary Wihl and David Williams. Toronto: University of Toronto Press, 1988.

———. "The Third Woman." *Diacritics* 12 (1982): 11–20.

Berg, Maggie. "Luce Irigaray's 'Contradictions': Poststructuralism and Feminism," *Signs: Journal of Women in Culture and Society* 17, 1 (1991): 50–70.

Bergoffen, Debra. "From Husserl to de Beauvoir: Gendering the Perceiving Subject." *Metaphilosophy* 27, 1–2 (1996): 53–62.

———. "Intentionale Ängste bekämpfen." Translated by Irmgard Scherer. In *Phänomenologie und Geschlechterdifferenz,* edited by Silvia Stoller and Helmuth Vetter. Vienna: Wiener Universitätsverlag, 1997.

———. "The Look as Bad Faith." *Philosophy Today* 36, 3 (1992): 221–27.

———. "Out from Under: Beauvoir's Philosophy of the Erotic." In *Feminist Interpretations of Simone de Beauvoir,* edited by Margaret A. Simons. University Park, Pa.: Pennsylvania State University Press, 1995.

———. *The Philosophy of Simone de Beauvoir: Gendered Phenomenologies, Erotic Generosities.* Albany, N.Y.: State University of New York Press, 1997.

———. "Queering the Phallus." In *Disseminating Lacan,* edited by David Pettigrew and François Raffoul. Albany, N.Y.: State University of New York Press, 1996.

Bernheimer, Charles. "Penile Reference in Phallic Theory." *differences: a journal of feminist cultural studies* 4, 1 (1992): 116–32.

Berry, Philippa. "The Burning Glass: Paradoxes of Feminist Revelation in *Speculum.*" In *Engaging with Irigaray,* edited by Carolyn Burke, Naomi Schor, and Margaret Whitford. New York: Columbia University Press, 1994.

———. "Woman and Space According to Kristeva and Irigaray." In *Shadow of Spirit,* edited by Philippa Berry and Andrew Wernick. New York: Routledge, 1992.

Bickford, Susan. "Why We Listen to Lunatics: Anti Foundational Theories and Feminist Politics." *Hypatia* 8, 2 (1993): 104–23.

Bigwood, Carol. *Earth Muse: Feminism, Nature, and Art.* Philadelphia: Temple University Press, 1993.

———. "Renaturalizing the Body (With the Help of Merleau-Ponty)." *Hypatia* 6, 3 (1991): 54–73.

Birmingham, Peg. "Feminist Fictions: Discourse, Desire and the Law." *Philosophy and Social Criticism* 22, 4 (1996):81–93.

———. "Toward an Ethic of Desire: Derrida, Fiction, and the Law of the Feminine." In *Feminist Interpretations of Jacques Derrida,* edited by Nancy J. Holland. University Park, Pa.: Pennsylvania State University Press, 1997.

Black, Nancy. "Psychoanalysis and Femininity." *Structuralist Review* 1, 2 (1978): 90–96.

Bordo, Susan. "Anorexia Nervosa: Psychopathology as the Crystallization of Culture." In *Feminism & Foucault,* edited by Irene Diamond and Lee Quinby. Boston: Northeastern University Press, 1988.

———. "The Body and Reproduction of Femininity: A Feminist Appropriation of Foucault." In *Gender/Body/Knowledge: Feminist Reconstructions of Being and Knowing,* edited by Alison M. Jaggar and Susan R. Bordo. New Brunswick, N.J.: Rutgers University Press, 1989.

———. "Docile Bodies, Rebellious Bodies: Foucauldian Perspectives on Female Psychopathology." *Writing and the Politics of Difference,* edited by Hugh Silverman. Albany, N.Y.: State University of New York, 1991.

———. "Feminism, Postmodernism, and Gender-Scepticism." In *Feminism/Postmodernism,* edited by Linda J. Nicholson. New York: Routledge, 1990.

———. "Postmodern Subjects, Postmodern Bodies." *Feminist Studies* 18, 1 (1992): 159–75.

———. *Unbearable Weight: Feminism, Western Culture, and the Body.* Berkeley: University of California Press, 1993.

Bove, Carol. "The Politics of Desire in Kristeva." *Boundary 2* 12, 2 (1984): 217–29.

Braidotti, Rosi. "Body-Images and the Pornography of Representation." In *Knowing the Difference,* edited by Kathleen Lennon and Margaret Whitford. London: Routledge, 1994.

———. "Embodiment, Sexual Difference and the Nomadic Subject." *Hypatia* 8, 1 (1993): 1–13.

———. "The Ethics of Sexual Difference: The Case of Foucault and Irigaray." *Australian Feminist Studies* 3 (1987): 1–14.

———. "Ethics Revisited: Women in/and Philosophy." In *Feminist Challenges: Social and Political Theory,* edited by Carole Pateman and Elizabeth Gross. Sydney: Allen and Unwin, 1986.

———. "Interview: Feminism by any Other Name." *differences: a journal of feminist cultural studies* 6, 2 & 3 (1994): 35–39.

———. *Nomadic Subjects: Embodiment and Sexual Difference in Contemporary Feminist Theory.* New York: Columbia University Press, 1994.

———. "Nomadism with a Difference: Deleuze's Legacy in a Feminist Perspective." *Man and World* 29, 3 (1996): 305–14.

———. "Of Bugs and Women: Irigaray and Deleuze on the Becoming-Woman." In *Engaging with Irigaray,* edited by Carolyn Burke, Naomi Schor, and Margaret Whitford. New York: Columbia University Press, 1994.

———. "Organs Without Bodies," *differences: a journal of feminist cultural studies* 1, 1 (1989): 147–61.

———. *Patterns of Dissonance.* New York: Routledge, 1991.

———. "Patterns of Dissonance: Women and /in Philosophy." In *Feministische Philosophie,* edited by Herta Nagl-Docekal. Vienna: R. Oldenbourg Verlag, 1990.

———. "The Politics of Ontological Difference." In *Between Feminism and Psychoanalysis,* edited by Teresa Brennan. London: Routledge, 1989.

———. "Power, Sexuality, and the Feminine in Contemporary French Philosophy: A Feminist Analysis." In *Was Philosophinnen denken III,* edited by Brigitte Weisshaupt. Zürich: Ammann Verlag.

———. "The Subject in Feminism." *Hypatia* 6, 2 (1991): 155–72.

———. "Toward a New Nomadism: Feminist Deleuzian Tracks: or, Metaphysics and Metabolism." In *Gilles Deleuze and the Theater of Philosophy,* edited by Constantin V. Boundas and Dorothea Olkowski. New York: Routledge, 1994.

Brennan, Teresa. *Beyond Feminism and Psychoanalysis.* London: Routledge, 1988.

Brodrib, Somer. "Les Immatériaux: A Feminist Critique of Postmodernism." In *Against Patriarchal Thinking,* edited by Maja Pellikaan-Engel. Amsterdam: VU University Press, 1992.

Brodzki, Bella, and Celeste Schenk. "Criticus Interruptus: Uncoupling Feminism and Deconstruction." In *Feminism and Institutions: Dialogues on Feminist Theory,* edited by Linda Kauffmann. Cambridge, Mass.: Cambridge University Press, 1989.

Brosman, Catharine Savage. *Simone de Beauvoir Revisited*. Boston: Twayne, 1991.

Brown, Beverly, and Parveen Adams. "The Feminine Body and Feminist Politics." *m/f* 3 (1979): 33–50.

Burchill, Louise. "Du Spatium chez Platon et chez Kant au dehors post-phénoménologique: lecture à partir du féminin comme scheme dans la philosophie française contemporaine." Ph.D. diss., Université de Paris VII, 1997.

———. "Either/or: Peripeteia of an Alternative in Jean Baudrillard's *De la Séduction*." In *Seduced and Abandoned*, edited by André Frankovits. Sydney: Feral Press, 1984.

———. "Ex-posing the Feminine in French Philosophy." In *Views from the Hill*, edited by M. Chalk. Melbourne: S.B.G.G.S., 1995.

———. "Post-scène Carmen." *Les cahiers du Grif* 32 (1985).

———. "Post-script Carmen: The discourse in and on the feminine." *Misch Masch* 2 (1985).

Burke, Carolyn. "Introduction to Luce Irigaray's 'When Our Lips Speak Together.'" *Signs: Journal of Women in Culture and Society* 6, 1 (1980): 66–68.

———. "Irigaray through the Looking Glass," *Feminist Studies* 7, 2 (1981): 288–306.

———. "Report from Paris: Women's Writing and the Women's Movement." *Signs: Journal of Women in Culture and Society* 3, 4 (1978): 843–54.

———. "Rethinking the Maternal." In *The Future of Difference*, edited by Hester Eisenstein and Alice Jardine. Boston: G. K. Hall, 1980.

———. "Romancing the Philosophers: Luce Irigaray." *The Minnesota Review* 29, 3 (1987): 103–14.

———. "Translation Modified: Irigaray in English." In *Engaging with Irigaray*, edited by Carolyn Burke, Naomi Schor, and Margaret Whitford. New York: Columbia University Press, 1994.

Burke, Carolyn, and Jane Gallop. "Psychoanalysis and Feminism in France." In *The Future of Difference*, edited by Hester Eisenstein and Alice Jardine. Boston: G. K. Hall, 1980.

Burke, Carolyn, Naomi Schor, and Margaret Whitford, eds. *Engaging with Irigaray: Feminist Philosophy and Modern European Thought*. New York: Columbia University Press, 1994.

Burman, Erica. *Differing with Deconstruction: A Feminist Critique*. Manchester, 1992.

Butler, Judith. "Bodies That Matter." In *Engaging with Irigaray*, edited by Carolyn Burke, Naomi Schor, and Margaret Whitford. New York: Columbia University Press, 1994.

———. *Bodies That Matter: On the Discursive Limits of "Sex."* New York: Routledge, 1993.

———. "The Body Politics of Julia Kristeva," *Hypatia* 3, 3 (1989): 104–18.

———. "Contingent Foundation: Feminism and the Question of "Postmodernism." *Praxis International* 11, 2 (1991): 150–65.

———. *Excitable Speech: Contemporary Sciences of Politics*. New York: Routledge, 1996.

———. "Foucault and the Paradox of Bodily Inscriptions." *The Journal of Philosophy* 86, 11 (1989): 601–7.

———. *Gender Trouble*. New York: Routledge, 1991.

———. "Gender Trouble, Feminist Theory, and Psychoanalytic Discourse." In *Feminism/Postmodernism*, edited by Linda J. Nicholson. New York: Routledge, 1991.

———. "Gendering the Body: Beauvoir's Philosophical Contributions." In *Women, Knowing and Reality: Explorations in Feminist Philosophy*, edited by Ann Garry and Marilyn Pearsall. Boston: Unwin Hyman, 1989.

———. "Imitation and Gender Insubordination." In *Inside/Out: Lesbian Theories, Gay Theories,* edited by Diana Fuss. New York: Routledge, 1991.

———. "Introduction: Against Proper Objects." *differences: a journal of feminist cultural studies* 6, 2 & 3 (1994): 1–26.

———. "The Lesbian Phallus and the Morphological Imaginary." *differences: a journal of feminist cultural studies* 4, 1 (1992): 133–71.

———. "Phantasmatische Identifzierung und die Annahme des Geschlechts." In *Geschlechterverhältnisse und Politik,* edited by Katharina Pühl. Frankfurt a/M: Suhrkamp, 1994.

———. "Postkriptum, April 1997." Translated by Silvia Stoller. In *Phänomenologie und Geschlechterdifferenz,* edited by Silvia Stoller and Helmuth Vetter. Vienna: Wiener Universitätsverlag, 1997.

———. *The Psychic Life of Power: Theories in Subjectivism.* Stanford: Stanford University Press, 1997.

———. "Sexual Ideology and Phenomenological Description: A Feminist Critique of Merleau-Ponty's." In *The Thinking Muse,* edited by Jeffner Allen and Iris Marion Young. Bloomington, Ind.: Indiana University Press, 1989.

———. "Sexual Inversions." In *Feminist Interpretations of Michel Foucault,* edited by Susan J. Hekman. University Park, Pa.: Pennsylvania State University Press, 1996.

———. "Sexuelle Differenz als eine Frage der Ethik." In *Macht Geschlechter Differenz,* edited by Wolfang Müller-Funk. Vienna: Picus Verlag, 1994.

———. *Subjects of Desire: Hegelian Reflections in Twentieth Century France.* New York: Columbia University Press, 1987.

———. "Variations on Sex and Gender: Beauvoir, Wittig, and Foucault." *Praxis International* 5 (1986): 505–16.

Butler, Judith, and Joan W. Scott. *Feminists Theorize the Political.* New York: Routledge, 1992.

Caldwell, Anne. "Fairy Tales for Politics: Unworking Derrida through Irigaray." *Philosophy Today* 41, 1 (1997): 40–50.

Caputo, John D. "Dreaming of the Innumerable." In *Derrida and Feminism,* edited by Ellen K. Feder, Mary C. Rawlinson, and Emily Zakin. New York: Routledge, 1997.

Chanter, Tina. "Antigone's Dilemma." In *Re-Reading Lévinas,* edited by Robert Bernasconi and Simon Critchley. London: Athlone Press, 1991.

———. *Ethics of Eros: Irigaray's Rewriting of the Philosophers.* New York: Routledge, 1995.

———. "Female Temporality and the Future of Feminism." In *Abjection, Melancholia and Love: The Work of Julia Kristeva,* edited by John Fletcher and Andrew Benjamin. New York: Routledge, 1990.

———. "Feminism and the Other." In *The Provocation of Lévinas,* edited by Robert Bernasconi. London: Routledge, 1988.

———. "Kristeva's Politics of Change: Tracking Essentialism with the Help of a Sex/Gender Map." In *Ethics, Politics and Difference in Julia Kristeva's Writing,* edited by Kelly Oliver. New York: Routledge, 1993.

———. "On Not Reading Derrida's Texts: Mistaking Hermeneutics, Misreading Sexual Difference, and Neutralizing Narration." In *Derrida and Feminism,* edited by Ellen K. Feder, Mary C. Rawlinson, and Emily Zakin. New York: Routledge, 1997.

Chase, Cynthia. "Desire and Identity in Lacan and Kristeva." In *Feminism and Psychoanalysis,* edited by Richard Feldstein and Judith Roof. Ithaca, N.Y.: Cornell University Press, 1989.

———. "The Witty Butcher's Wife: Freud, Lacan, and the Conversion of Resistance to Theory." *Modern Language Notes* 100 (1987): 989–1013.

Chisholm, Dianne. "Irigaray's Hysteria." In *Engaging with Irigaray,* edited by Carolyn Burke, Naomi Schor, and Margaret Whitford. New York: Columbia University Press, 1994.

Circelli, Carmelina. "In the Fullness of Time: An Ontological Analysis of Women, Emotion and Dance-movement in Light of the Philosophy of Maurice Merleau-Ponty and Martin Heidegger." Ph.D. diss., York University, 1989.

Cocks, Joan. *The Oppositional Imagination: Feminism, Critique and Political Theory.* London: Routledge, 1989.

Colebrook, Claire. "Feminist Philosophy and the History of Feminism: Irigaray and the History of Western Metaphysics" *Hypatia* 12, 1 (1997): 79–98.

Collins, Margery, and Christine Pierce. "Holes and Slime: Sexism in Sartre's Psychoanalysis." In *Women and Philosophy: Toward a Theory of Liberation,* edited by Carol C. Gould and Marx W. Wartofsky. New York: Putnam, 1980.

Conley, Verena Andermatt. "Féminin et écologie." In *Du Féminin,* edited by Mireille Calle. Cap-Saint-Ignace, Québec: Édition le Griffon d'argile, 1992.

———. *Hélène Cixous.* Hemel Hempstead: Harvester Wheatsheaf, 1992.

———. *Hélène Cixous: Writing the Feminine.* Lincoln, Nebr.: University of Nebraska Press, 1984.

———. "Kristeva's China." *Diacritics* 5:25–30.

———. "Missexual Mystery." *Diacritics* 7, 2 (1975): 70–82.

Coole, Diana. "Beyond Equality and Difference: Julia Kristeva and the Politics of Negativity." In *Denken der Geschlechterdifferenz,* edited by Herta Nagl-Docekal and Herlinde Pauer-Studer. Vienna: Wiener Frauenverlag, 1990.

Cope, Karin. "Plastic Actions: Linguistic Strategies and 'Le corps lesbien.'" *Hypatia* 6, 3 (1991): 74–96.

Cornell, Drucilla. *Beyond Accommodation: Ethical Feminism, Deconstruction and the Law.* New York: Routledge, 1991.

———. "Civil Disobedience and Deconstruction." In *Feminist Interpretations of Jacques Derrida,* edited by Nancy J. Holland. University Park, Pa.: Pennsylvania State University Press, 1997.

———. "Feminist Challenges: A Response." *Philosophy and Social Criticism* 22, 4 (1996): 109–18.

———. "Gender, Sex, and Equivalent Rights." In *Feminists Theorize the Political,* edited by Judith Butler and Joan W. Scott. New York: Routledge, 1992.

———. *The Imaginary Domain: Abortion, Pornography, and Sexual Harassment.* New York: Routledge, 1995.

———. *The Philosophy of the Limit.* New York: Routledge, 1992.

———. "Rethinking the Time of Feminism." In *Feminist Contentions,* edited by Seyla Benhabib et al. New York: Routledge, 1995.

———. "What Is Ethical Feminism?" In *Feminist Contentions,* edited by Seyla Benhabib et al. New York: Routledge, 1995.

———. "Where Love Begins: Sexual Difference and the Limit of the Masculine Symbolic." In *Derrida and Feminism,* edited by Ellen K. Feder, Mary C. Rawlinson, and Emily Zakin. New York: Routledge, 1997.

Cornell, Drucilla and Adam Thurschwell. "Feminism, Negativity, Intersubjectivity." *Praxis International* 5, 4 (1986): 484–504.

Cornell, Sarah. "Hélène Cixous and les Etudes Fèminine." In *The Body and the Text,* edited by Helen Wilcox, Keith McWatters, Ann Thompson, and Linda R. Williams. New York: Harvester Wheatsheaf, 1990.

Creet, M. J. "Speaking in Lesbian Tongues: Monique Wittig and the Universal Point of View." *Resources for Feminist Research* 16 (1987): 16–20.

Crowder, Diane. "Amazons and Mothers? Monique Wittig, Hélène Cixous and Theories of Women's Writing." *Contemporary Literature* 24, 2 (1983): 117–44.

Daggers, Jenny. "Luce Irigaray and 'Divine Women': A Resource for Postmodern Feminist Theology." *Feminist Theology* 14 (1997): 35–50.

Dallery, Arleen B. "The Politics of Writing (the) Body: écriture féminine." In *Gender/ Body/Knowledge: Feminist reconstructions of Being and Knowing,* edited by Alison Jaggar and Susan Bordo. New Brunswick, N.J.: Rutgers University Press, 1989.

———. "Sexual Embodiment: Beauvoir and French Feminism." *Women's Studies International Forum* 8, 3 (1985): 197–208.

David, Anthony. "Le Doeuff and Irigaray on Descartes." *Philosophy Today* 41, 3/4 (1997): 367–82.

de Lauretis, Teresa. *Alice Doesn't.* Bloomington, Ind.: Indiana University Press, 1984.

———. "Eccentric Subjects: Feminist Theory and Historical Consciousness." *Feminist Studies* 16, 1 (1990): 115–50.

———. *Sexual Difference: A Theory of Socio-symbolic Practice.* Bloomington, Ind.: Indiana University Press, 1990.

———. *Technologies of Gender.* Bloomington, Ind.: Indiana University Press, 1986.

———. "Upping the Anti (sic) in Feminist Theory." In *Conflicts in Feminism,* edited by Marianne Hirsch and Evelyn Fox Keller. New York: Routledge, 1990.

Derksen, Louise, D. "The Ambiguous Relationship between Feminism and Postmodernism." In *Against Patriarchal Thinking,* edited by Maja Pellikaan-Engel. Amsterdam: VU University Press, 1992.

Deutscher, Penelope. "At Home in Philosophy: Michèle le Doeuff's Gritty Vignettes." In *The Philosophy of Michèle le Doeuff,* edited by Max Deutscher. Atlantic Highlands, N.J.: Humanity Books, 2000.

———. "The Body: New Feminisms of Embodiment." In *Oxford Companion to Australian Feminism,* edited by B. Caine, M. Gatens, E. Grahame et al. Oxford: Oxford University Press, forthcoming.

———. "Complicated Fidelity: Kofman's Freud (Reading Childhood of Art with Enigma of Woman)." In *Enigmas,* edited by Penelope Deutscher and Kelly Oliver. Ithaca, N.Y.: Cornell University Press, 1999.

———. "Eating the Words of the Other: Philosophical Accounts of Erotics, Ethics and Cannibalism in Pedagogy." In *The Teacher's Breasts: Proceedings of the Jane Gallop Seminar,* edited by J. Matthews, 31–45. Canberra: H.R.C, A.N.U., 1993.

———. "French Feminist Philosophers on Law and Public Policy: Michèle Le Doeuff and Luce Irigaray." *Australian Journal of French Studies.* 34, 1 (1997): 24–44.

———. "Irigaray Anxiety." *Radical Philosophy* 80 (1996): 6–16.

———. " 'Is It Not Remarkable That Nietzsche. Should Have Hated Rousseau?' Woman, Femininity: Distancing Nietzsche from Rousseau." In *Nietzsche, Feminism and Political Theory,* edited by P. Patton. London: Routledge, 1993.

———. "Luce Irigaray and Her 'Politics of the Impossible.'" In *Forms of Commitment: Intellectuals in Contemporary France: Monash Romance Studies,* edited by B. Nelson. 1 (1995): 141–56.

———. " 'The Only Diabological Thing about Women': Luce Irigaray on Divinity," *Hypatia* 9, 4 (1994): 88–111.

————. *Yielding Gender: Feminism, Deconstruction and the History of Philosophy.* New York: Routledge, 1997.

Deutscher, Penelope, and Kelly Oliver, eds. *Enigmas: Essays on Sarah Kofman.* Ithaca, N.Y.: Cornell University Press, 1999.

Deveaux, Monique. "Feminism and Empowerment: A Critical Reading of Foucault." *Feminist Studies* 20, 2 (1994): 223–47.

Diamond, Irene, and Lee Quinby, eds. *Feminism and Foucault.* Boston: Northeastern University Press, 1988.

Dietz, Mary G. "Introduction: Debating Simone de Beauvoir." *Signs: Journal of Women in Culture and Society* 18, 1 (1992): 74–78.

Diprose, Rosalyn. *The Bodies of Women: Ethics, Embodiment, and Sexual Difference.* London: Routledge, 1994.

————. "Generosity: Between Love and Desire." *Hypatia* 13, 1 (1998): 1–20.

————. "In Excess: The Body and the Habit of Sexual Difference." *Hypatia* 6, 3 (1991): 156–71.

————. "Performing Body-Identity." *Writings on Dance* 11/12 (1994): 6–15.

————. "The Use of Pleasure in the Constitution of the Body." *Australian Feminist Studies* 5 (1987): 95–103.

Diprose, Rosalyn, and Robyn Ferrell, eds. *Cartographies: Poststructuralism and the Mapping of Bodies and Spaces.* Sydney: Allen and Unwin, 1991.

Duren, Brian. "Cixous' Exorbitant Texts." *SubStance* 10, 2 (1981): 39–51.

Edelstein, Marilyn. "Metaphor, Meta-Narrative and Mater-Narrative in Kristeva's 'Stabat Mater.'" In *Body/Text in Julia Kristeva: Religion, Women and Psychoanalysis,* edited by David Crownfield. Albany, N.Y.: State University of New York Press, 1992.

————. "Toward a Feminist Postmodern 'Polethique': Kristeva on Ethics and Politics." In *Ethics, Politics and difference in Julia Kristeva's Writing,* edited by Kelly Oliver. New York: Routledge, 1993.

Elliot, Patricia. *From Mastery to Analysis: Theories of Gender in Psychoanalytic Feminism.* Ithaca, N.Y.: Cornell University Press, 1991.

————. "Politics, Identity, and Social Change: Contested Grounds in Psychoanalytic Feminism." *Hypatia* 10 (1995): 41–55.

Enns, Diane. "'We Flesh': Re-Membering the Body Beloved," *Philosophy Today* 39, 3–4 (1995): 263–79.

Evans, Martha Noel. "Portrait of Dora: Freud's Case History as Reviewed by Hélène Cixous." *SubStance* 36 (1982): 64–71.

Feder, Ellen K., Mary C. Rawlinson, and Emily Zakin, eds. *Derrida and Feminism: Recasting the Question of Woman.* New York: Routledge, 1997.

Feder, Ellen K., and Emily Zakin. "Flirting with the Truth: Derrida's Discourse with 'Woman' and Wenches." In *Derrida and Feminism,* edited by Ellen K. Feder, Mary C. Rawlinson, and Emily Zakin. New York: Routledge, 1997.

Felman, Shoshana. "Rereading Femininity." *Yale French Studies* 62 (1981): 19–44.

————. "To Open the Question." *Yale French Studies* 55, 6 (1977): 5–10.

————. "Women and Madness: The Critical Phallacy." *Diacritics* 5, 4 (1975): 2–10.

Feral, Josette. "Antigone, or the Irony of the Tribe." *Diacritics* 8, 3 (1978): 2–14.

————. "The Powers of Difference." In *The Future of Difference,* edited by Hester Eisenstein and Alice Jardine. Boston: G. K. Hall, 1980.

————. "Toward a Theory of Displacement." *SubStance* 32 (1981): 52–64.

Ferguson, Ann. "Can I Choose Who I Am? And How Would That Empower Me? Gender, Race, Identities, and the Self." In *Women, Knowledge and Reality: Explorations in Feminist Philosophy,* edited by Ann Garry and Marilyn Pearsall. New York: Routledge, 1996.

——. "Lesbian Identity: Beauvoir and History." In *Hypatia Reborn: Essays in Feminist Philosophy,* edited by Aziha Y. Al-Hibri and Margaret A. Simons. Bloomington, Ind.: Indiana University Press, 1990.

Ferguson, Kathy. "Interpretation and Genealogy in Feminism." *Signs: Journal of Women in Culture and Society* 16, 2 (1991): 322–39.

Ferrell, Robyn. "The Passion of the Signifier and the Body in Theory." *Hypatia* 6, 3 (1991): 172–84.

Fielding, Helen. "Beyond the Surface: Toward a Feminist Phenomenology of the Body-as-Depth." Ph.D. diss., York University, 1996.

——. "Grounding Agency in Depth: The Implications of Merleau-Ponty's Thoughts for the Politics of Feminism." *Human Studies* 19, 2 (1996): 175–84.

Fisher, Linda. "Phänomenologie und Feminismus." Translated by Silvia Stoller. In *Phänomenologie und Geschlechterdifferenz,* edited by Silvia Stoller and Helmuth Vetter. Vienna: Wiener Universitätsverlag, 1997.

Fisher, Linda, and Lester Embree, eds. *Feminist Phenomenology.* Dordrecht: Kluwer, forthcoming.

Findlay, Heather. "Is There a Lesbian in This Text? Derrida, Wittig and the Politics of the Three Women." In *Coming to Terms: Feminism, Theory, Politics,* edited by Elizabeth Weed. New York: Routledge, 1989.

Fink, Laurie A. *Feminist Theory, Women's Writing.* Ithaca, N.Y.: Cornell University Press, 1992.

Finn, Geraldine. *Why Althusser Killed His Wife: Essays on Discourse and Violence.* Atlantic Highlands, N.J.: Humanities Press, 1996.

Finn, Geraldine, and Eleanor M. Godway, eds. *Who Is This We? Absence of Community.* Montreal: Black Rose Books, 1994.

Flax, Jane. *Disputed Subjects: Essays on Psychoanalysis, Subjects, Politics and Philosophy.* New York: Routledge, 1993.

——. "The End of Innocence." In *Feminists Theorize the Political,* edited by Judith Butler and Joan W. Scott. New York: Routledge, 1992.

——. "Postmodernism and Gender Relations in Feminist Theory." *Signs: Journal of Women in Culture and Society* 12, 4 (1987): 621–43.

——. *Thinking Fragments: Psychoanalysis, Feminism, and Postmodernism in the Contemporary West.* Berkeley: University of California Press, 1989.

Fraser, Nancy. "False Antitheses: A Response to Seyla Benhabib and Judith Butler." *Praxis International* 11, 2 (1991): 166–77.

——. 1997. "The Force of Law: Metaphysical or Political?" In *Feminist Interpretations of Jacques Derrida,* edited by Nancy J. Holland. University Park, Pa.: Pennsylvania State University Press, 1997.

——. "Foucault's Body-Language: A Post-Humanist Political Rhetoric?" *Salmagundi* 61 (1983): 55–70.

——. "Introduction." *Hypatia: Special Issue on French Feminist Philosophy* 3, 3 (1989): 1–10.

——. "Michel Foucault: A 'Young Conservative'?" *Ethics* 96, 1 (1985): 165–84.

——. "Pragmatism, Feminism, and the Linguistic Turn." In *Feminist Contentions,* edited by Seyla Benhabib et al. New York: Routledge, 1995.

——. *Unruly Practices: Power, Discourse, and Gender in Contemporary Social Theory.* Minneapolis: University of Minnesota Press, 1989.

———. "The Uses and Abuses of French Discourse Theories for Feminist Politics." *Boundary* 2 17, 2 (1990): 82–101.

Fraser, Nancy, and Sandra Lee Bartky, eds. *Revaluing French feminism: Critical Essays on Difference, Agency, and Culture.* Bloomington, Ind.: Indiana University Press, 1990.

Fraser, Nancy, and Linda J. Nicholson. "Social Criticism without Philosophy: An Encounter between Feminism and Postmodernism." In *Feminism/Postmodernism,* edited by Linda J. Nicholson. New York: Routledge, 1990.

Freeman, Barbara. "Irigaray at 'The Symposium': Speaking Otherwise." *Oxford Literary Review* 8, 1–2 (1986): 170–77.

———. "Plus-Corps-Donc-Plus-Écriture: Hélène Cixous and the Mind-Body Problem." *Paragraph* 11, 19 (1988): 58–70.

Fuchs, Jo-Ann P. "Female Eroticism in 'The Second Sex.'" *Feminist Studies* 6 (1980): 304–13.

Fullbrook, Kate, and Edward Fullbrook. "Sartre's Secret Key." In *Feminist Interpretations of Simone de Beauvoir,* edited by Margaret A. Simons. University Park, Pa.: Pennsylvania State University Press, 1995.

———. *Simone de Beauvoir: A Critical Introduction.* Oxford: Polity, 1997.

Fuss, Diana. *Essentially Speaking: Feminism, Nature and Difference.* New York: Routledge, 1989.

———. "Essentially Speaking: Luce Irigaray's Language of Essence." *Hypatia* 3, 3 (1989): 62–80.

Gallop, Jane. "French Theory and the Seduction of Feminism." *Paragraph* 8 (1986): 19–24.

———. "The Ladies Man." *Diacritics* 6 (1976): 28–34.

———. "Quand nos lèvres s'écrivent: Irigaray's Body Politic." *Romantic Review* 74 (1983): 77–83.

———. *Reading Lacan.* Ithaca, N.Y.: Cornell University Press, 1985.

———. *Thinking through the Body.* New York: Columbia University Press, 1988.

———. " 'Women' in Spurs and Nineties Feminism." *Diacritics* 25, 2 (1995): 126–34.

Gatens, Moira. "A Critique of the Sex/Gender Distinction." In *A Reader in Feminist Knowledge,* edited by Sneja Gunew. London: Routledge, 1990.

———. *Feminism and Philosophy: Perspectives on Difference and Equality.* Bloomington, Ind.: Indiana University Press, 1991

———. *Imaginary Bodies: Ethics, Power and Corporeality.* New York: Routledge, 1996.

———. "Power, Bodies and Difference." In *Destabilizing Theory: Contemporary Feminist Debates,* edited by Michèle Barret and Anne Phillips. Stanford, Calif.: Stanford University Press, 1992.

———. "Towards a Feminist Philosophy of the Body." In *Crossing Boundaries: Feminism and the Critique of Knowledges,* edited by Barbara Caine, E. A. Grosz, and Marie de Lepervanche. Sydney: Allen and Unwin, 1988.

Gauthier, Lorraine. "Truth as Eternal Metaphoric Displacement: Traces of the Mother in Derrida's Patricide." *Canadian Journal of Political and Social Theory* 13, 1–2 (1989).

Gibbs, Anna. "Cixous and Gertrude Stein." *Meanjin* 38 (1979): 281–93.

Graybeal, Jean. "Joying in the Truth of Self-Division." In *Body/Text in Julia Kristeva: Religion, Women and Psychoanalysis,* edited by David Crownfield. Albany, N.Y.: State University of New York Press, 1992.

———. "Kristeva's Delphic Proposal: Practice Encompasses the Ethical." In *Ethics, Politics and Difference in Julia Kristeva's Writing*, edited by Kelly Oliver. New York: Routledge, 1993.

———. *Language and the "The Feminine" in Nietzsche and Heidegger*. Bloomington, Ind.: Indiana University Press, 1990.

Greene, Naomi. "Sartre, Sexuality and the Second Sex." *Philosophy and Literature* (1980): 199–211.

Grooten, Angea. "A Futile Controversy Postmodernism and Feminism: United in Difference." In *Against Patriarchal Thinking*, edited by Maja Pellikaan-Engel. Amsterdam: VU University Press, 1992.

Grosz, Elizabeth. "Bodies and Knowledges: Feminism and the Crisis of Reason." In *Feminist Epistemologies*, edited by Linda Alcoff and Elizabeth Potter. New York: Routledge, 1993.

———. "The Body of Signification." In *Abjection, Melancholia and Love: The Work of Julia Kristeva*, edited by John Fletcher and Andrew Benjamin. London: Routledge, 1990.

———. "Conclusion: A Note on Essentialism and Difference." In *Feminist Knowledge: Critique and Construct*, edited by Senja Gunew. London: Routledge, 1989.

———. "Contemporary Theories of Power and Subjectivity." In *Feminist Knowledge: Critique and Construct*, edited by Sneja Gunew. London: Routledge, 1990.

———. "Derrida and the Limits of Philosophy." *Thesis Eleven* 14 (1986): 26–42.

———. "Derrida, Irigaray and Deconstruction." *Intervention* 20 (1986): 70–81.

———. "Desire and the Body in Recent French Feminism." *Intervention* 21/22 (1988): 28–34.

———. "The Hetero and the Homo: The Sexual Ethics of Luce Irigaray." In *Engaging with Irigaray*, edited by Carolyn Burke, Naomi Schor, and Margaret Whitford. New York: Routledge, 1992.

———. "The In(ter)vention of Feminist Knowledges." In *Crossing Boundaries: Feminisms and the Critique of Knowledges*, edited by Barbara Caine, E. A. Grosz, and Marie de Lepervanche. Sydney: Allen and Unwin, 1988.

———. "Irigaray and Sexual Difference." *Australian Feminist Studies* 2 (1986): 63–77.

———. *Jacques Lacan: A Feminist Introduction*. London: Routledge, 1990.

———. "Language and the Limits of the Body: Kristeva and Abjection." In *Future Fall: Excursions into Post-modernity*, edited by Elizabeth Grosz and T. Thredgold et al. Sydney: Pathfinder Press, 1987.

———. "A Note on Essentialism and Difference." In *Feminist Knowledge: Critique and Construct*, edited by Sneja Gunew. London: Routledge, 1990.

———. "Notes towards a Corporeal Feminism." *Australian Feminist Studies* 5 (1987): 1–17.

———. "Ontology and Equivocation: Derrida's Politics of Sexual Difference." *Diacritics* 25, 2 (1995): 115–25. Also in *Feminist Interpretations of Jacques Derrida*, edited by Nancy J. Holland. University Park, Pa.: Pennsylvania State University Press, 1997.

———. "Philosophy, Subjectivity and the Body: Kristeva and Irigaray." In *Feminist Challenges*, edited by Elizabeth Grosz and Carole Pateman. Sydney: Allen and Unwin, 1986.

———. *Sexual Subversions: Three French Feminists*. Boston: Allen and Unwin, 1989.

————. *Space, Time and Perversion.* New York: Routledge, 1995.

————. "A Thousand Tiny Sexes: Feminism and Rhizomatics." In *Gilles Deleuze and the Theater of Philosophy,* edited by Constantin V. Boundas and Dorothea Olkowski. New York: Routledge, 1994.

————. *Volatile Bodies: Towards a Corporeal Feminism.* Bloomington, Ind.: Indiana University Press, 1994.

Grosz, Elizabeth, and Elspeth Probyn, eds. *Sexy Bodies: The Strange Carnalities of Feminism.* New York: Routledge, 1995.

Haas, Lynda. "Of Waters and Women: The Philosophy of Luce Irigaray." *Hypatia* 8, 4 (1993): 150–59.

Haber, Honi Fern. "Foucault Pumped: Body Politics and the Muscled Woman." In *Feminist Interpretations of Michel Foucault,* edited by Susan J. Hekman. University Park, Pa.: Pennsylvania State University Press, 1996.

Haddock, Charlene Seigfried. "Second Sex: Second Thoughts." In *Hypatia Reborn: Essays in Feminist Philosophy,* edited by Aziha Y. Al-Hibri and Margaret A. Simons. Bloomington, Ind.: Indiana University Press, 1990.

Halsema, Annemie J. M. "Sexual Difference and Negativity: Irigaray, Derrida and Adorno." In *Against Patriarchal Thinking,* edited by Maja Pellikaan-Engel. Amsterdam: VU University Press, 1992.

Harding, Sandra. "Feminism, Science, and the Anti-Enlightenment Critiques." In *Feminism/Postmodernism,* edited by Linda J. Nicholson. New York: Routledge, 1990.

————. *The Science Question in Feminism.* Ithaca, N.Y.: Cornell University Press, 1986.

Hartsock, Nancy. "Foucault on Power: A Theory for Women." In *Feminism/Postmodernism,* edited by Linda J. Nicholson. New York: Routledge, 1986.

————. "Postmodernism and Political Change: Issues for Feminist Theory." *Cultural Critique* 14 (1989–90): 15–33.

Harvey, Irene. *Derrida and the Economy of Différance.* Bloomington, Ind.: Indiana University Press, 1986.

Hatcher, Donald L. "Existential Ethics and Why It's Immoral to Be a Housewife." *Journal of Value Inquiry* 23 (1989): 59–68.

Heinämaa, Sara. "What Is a Woman? Butler and Beauvoir on the Foundations of Sexual Difference." *Hypatia* 12, 1 (1997): 20–39.

Hekman, Susan J., ed. *Feminist Interpretations of Michel Foucault.* University Park Pa.: The Pennsylvania State University Press, 1996.

————. *Gender and Knowledge: Elements of a Postmodern Feminism.* Boston: Northeastern University Press, 1990.

————. "Reconstituting the Subject: Feminism, Modernism and Postmodernism." *Hypatia* 6, 2 (1991): 44–63.

Hengehold, Laura. "An Immodest Proposal: Foucault, Hysterization, and the 'Second Rape.'" *Hypatia* 9, 3 (1994): 88–107.

————. "Rape and Communicative Agency: Reflections in the Lake at L——." *Hypatia* 8, 4 (1993): 56–71.

Hirsh, Elizabeth. "Back in Analysis: How to Do Things with Irigaray." In *Engaging with Irigaray,* edited by Carolyn Burke, Naomi Schor, and Margaret Whitford. New York: Columbia University Press, 1994.

Hirsh, Elizabeth, and Gary A. Olson. "'Je—Luce Irigaray': A Meeting with Luce Irigaray." *Hypatia* 10, 2 (1995): 93–114.

Hodge, Joanna. "Feminism and Post-Modernism: Misleading Divisions Imposed by the Opposition between Modernism and Post-Modernism." In *The Problems of Modernity: Adorno and Benjamin,* edited by Andrew Benjamin. London: Routledge, 1989.

———. "Irigaray Reading Heidegger." In *Engaging with Irigaray,* edited by Carolyn Burke, Naomi Schor, and Margaret Whitford. New York: Columbia University Press, 1994.

Holland, Nancy J., ed. *Feminist Interpretations of Jacques Derrida.* University Park, Pa.: Pennsylvania State University Press, 1997.

———. "Introduction to Kofman's Rousseau's Phallocentric Ends." *Hypatia* 3, 3 (1989): 119–22.

———. *Is Women's Philosophy Possible?* Savage, Md.: Rowman and Littlefield, 1990.

———. "The Treble Clef/t: Jacques Derrida and the Female Voice." In *Philosophy and Culture: Proceedings of the XVIIth World Congress of Philosophy.* Vol. 2. Montreal: Éditions Montmorency, 1988.

Hollywood, Amy M. "Beauvoir, Irigaray, and the Mystical." *Hypatia* 9, 4 (1994): 158–85.

Holmund, Christine. "The Lesbian, the Mother, the Heterosexual Lover: Irigaray's Recodings of Difference." *Feminist Studies* 17 (1991): 283–308.

Holveck, Eleanore. "Can a Woman Be a Philosopher? Reflections of a Beauvoirian Housemaid." In *Feminist Interpretations of Simone de Beauvoir,* edited by Margaret A. Simons. University Park, Pa.: Pennsylvania State University Press, 1995.

Huntington, Patricia. "Toward a Dialectical Concept of Autonomy: Revisiting the Feminist Alliance with Poststructuralism." *Philosophy and Social Criticism* 21, 1 (1995): 37–55.

Idt, Geneviève. "Simone de Beauvoir's Adieux: A Funeral Rite and a Literary Challenge." In *Sartre Alive,* edited by Ronald Aronson. Detroit: Wayne State University Press, 1991.

Ince, Kate. "Questions to Luce Irigaray." *Hypatia* 11, 2 (1996): 122–40.

Jackson, Stevi. *Christine Delphy.* London: Sage Publications, 1996.

Jaeger, Suzanne M. "Beauty and the Breast: Dispelling Significations of Feminine Sensuality in the Aesthetics of Dance." *Philosophy Today* 41, 2 (1997): 270–76.

Jardine, Alice A. *Gynesis: Configurations of Woman and Modernity.* Ithaca, N.Y.: Cornell University Press, 1985.

———. "Interview with Simone de Beauvoir." *Signs: Journal of Women in Culture and Society* 5, 2 (1979): 224–36.

———. "Introduction to Julia Kristeva's 'Women's Time.'" *Signs: Journal of Women in Culture and Society* 7, 1 (1981): 5–12.

———. "Opaque Texts and Transparent Contexts: The Political Difference of Julia Kristeva." In *The Poetics of Gender,* edited by Nancy K. Miller. New York: Columbia University Press, 1986.

———. "Pre-texts for the Transatlantic Feminist." *Yale French Studies* 6, 2 (1981): 220–36.

———. "Theories of the Feminine: Kristeva." *Enclitic* 4, 2 (1980): 5–15.

———. "Woman in Limbo: Deleuze and His (Br)others." *SubStance* 44/45 (1984): 46–60.

Johnson, Pauline. "Feminism and Difference: The Dilemmas of Luce Irigaray." *Australian Feminist Studies* 6 (1988): 87–96.

Jones, Ann Rosalind. "Inscribing Femininity: French Theories of the Feminine." In *Making a Difference: Feminist Literary Criticism,* edited by Gayle Green and Coppelia Kahn. London: Methuen, 1985.

———. "Julia Kristeva on Femininity: The Limits of a Semiotic Politics." *Feminist Review* 18 (1984): 56–73.

———. "Writing and Body: Toward an Understanding of L'Écriture Féminine." *French Studies* 7 (1981): 73–85.

Jones, Kathleen B. "On Authority: Or, Why Women Are Not Entitled to Speak." In *Feminism & Foucault,* edited by Irene Diamond and Lee Quinby. Boston: Northeastern University Press, 1988.

Jonte-Pace, Diane. "Situating Kristeva Differently: Psychoanalytic Readings of Women and Religion." In *Body/Text in Julia Kristeva: Religion, Women and Psychoanalysis,* edited by David Crownfield. Albany, N.Y.: State University of New York Press, 1992.

Jouve, Nicole Ward. "Hélène Cixous: From Inner Theatre to World Theatre." In *The Body and the Text,* edited by Helen Wilcox, Keith McWatters, Ann Thompson, and Linda R. Williams. New York: Harvester Wheatsheaf, 1990.

Joy, Morny. "Equality or Divinity: A False Dichotomy?" *Journal of Feminist Studies on Religion* 6 (1990): 9–24.

Kamuf, Peggy. "Deconstruction and Feminism: A Repetition." In *Feminist Interpretations of Jacques Derrida,* edited by Nancy J. Holland. University Park, Pa.: Pennsylvania State University Press, 1997.

Kamuf, Peggy, and Nancy K. Miller. "Parisian Letter: Between Feminism and Deconstruction." In *Conflicts in Feminism,* edited by Marianne Hirsch and Evelyn Fox Keller. New York: Routledge, 1990.

Kaufmann McCall, Dorothy. "Simone de Beauvoir: Questions of Difference and Generation." *Yale French Studies* 72 (1986): 121–32.

———. "Simone de Beauvoir, 'The Second Sex,' and Jean-Paul Sartre." *Signs: Journal of Women in Culture and Society* 4, 2 (1979): 209–23.

Kearns, Cleo. "Kristeva and Feminist Theology." In *Transfigurations: Theology and the French Feminists,* edited by Maggie C. W. Kim, Susan M. St. Ville, and Susan M. Simonaitis. Minneapolis: Fortress, 1993.

Keef, Terry. *Simone de Beauvoir: A Study of Her Writings.* Totowa, N.J.: Barnes and Noble, 1983.

———. "Women's Mauvaise foi in Simone de Beauvoir's 'The Second Sex.'" In *The Body and the Text,* edited by Helen Wilcox, Keith McWatters, Ann Thompson, and Linda R. Williams. New York: Harvester Wheatsheaf, 1990.

Keller, Catherine. "Feminism and the Ethic of Inseparability." In *Women's Consciousness, Women's Conscience: A Reader in Feminist Ethics,* edited by Barbara Hilkert Andolsen, Christine E. Gudorf, and Mary D. Pellauer. San Francisco: Harper and Row, 1987.

Kim, Maggie C. W., Susan M. St. Ville, and Susan M. Simonaitis, eds. *Transfigurations: Theology and the French Feminists.* Minneapolis: Fortress, 1993.

Kintz, Linda. "The Dramaturgy of The Subject(s): Refinding the Deconstruction and Construction of the Subject to Include Gender Materiality." Ph.D. diss., University of Oregon, 1986.

———. "In-different Criticism." In *The Thinking Muse,* edited by Jeffner Allen and Iris Marion Young. Bloomington, Ind.: Indiana University Press, 1989.

Kirby, Vicki. "Corporeal Habits: Addressing Essentialism Differently." *Hypatia* 6, 3 (1991): 4–24.

———. "Feminisms and Postmodernisms: Anthropology and the Management of Difference." *Anthropological Quarterly* 66, 3 (1993): 127–33.

———. *Telling Flesh, the Substance of the Corporeal.* New York: Routledge, 1997.

Klaw, Barbara. "Sexuality in Beauvoir's 'Les Mandarins.'" In *Feminist Interpretations of Simone de Beauvoir,* edited by Margaret A. Simons. University Park, Pa.: Pennsylvania State University Press, 1995.

Klobucka, Anna. "Hélène Cixous and the Hour of Clarice Lispector." *SubStance* 73 (1994): 41–62.

Kozel, Susan. "The Diabolical Strategy of Mimesis: Luce Irigaray's Reading of Maurice Merleau-Ponty." *Hypatia* 11, 3 (1996): 114–29.

Kraüs, Sonia. "Simone de Beauvoir entre Sartre et Merleau-Ponty." Translated by Anne-Dominique Balmes. *Les Temps Modernes* 45, 520 (1989): 81–103.

Kruks, Sonia. "Gender and Subjectivity: Simone de Beauvoir and Contemporary Feminism." *Signs: Journal of Women in Culture and Society* 18, 1 (1992): 89–110. Also published as "Genre et subjectivité: Simone de Beauvoir et féminisme contemporaine." *Nouvelles Questions Feministes* 14, 1 (1993): 3–28.

———. "Identity Politics and Dialectical Reason: Beyond an Epistemology of Provenance." *Hypatia* 10, 2 (1995):1–22.

———. "Introduction: A Venerable ancestor? Re-Reading Simone de Beauvoir." *Women & Politics* 11, 1 (1991): 54.

———. "Simone de Beauvoir: Teaching Sartre about Freedom." In *Sartre Alive,* edited by Ronald Aronson. Detroit: Wayne State University Press, 1991.

Kuhn, Annette. "Introduction to Hélène Cixous's 'Castration or Decapitation.'" *Signs: Journal of Women in Culture and Society* 7, 1 (1981): 36–40.

Kuykendall, Eleanor H. "Introduction to 'Sorcerer Love,' by Luce Irigaray." *Hypatia* 3, 3 (1989): 28–31.

———. "Questions for Julia Kristeva's Ethics of Linguistics." In *The Thinking Muse,* edited by Jeffner Allen and Iris Marion Young. Bloomington, Ind.: Indiana University Press, 1989.

———. "Sex, Gender, and the Politics of Difference." In *Writing and the Politics of Difference,* edited by Hugh Silverman. Albany, N.Y.: State University of New York, 1991.

———. "Simone de Beauvoir and Two Kinds of Ambivalence in Action." In *The Thinking Muse,* edited by Jeffner Allen and Iris Marion Young. Bloomington, Ind.: Indiana University Press, 1989.

———. "The Subjectivity of the Speaker." In *The Question of the Other,* edited by Arleen B. Dallery and Charles E. Scott. Albany, N.Y.: State University of New York Press, 1989.

———. "Subverting Essentialism." *Hypatia* 6, 3 (1991): 208–17.

———. "Toward an Ethic of Nurturance: Luce Irigaray on Mothering and Power." In *Mothering: Essays in Feminist Theory,* edited by Joyce Trebilcot. Totowa, N.J.: Rowman and Allanheld, 1983.

Langer, Monika. "A Philosophical Retrieval of Simone de Beauvoir's 'Pour Une Morale de l'ambiguité.'" *Philosophy Today* 38, 2 (1994): 181–90.

Lazaro, Reyes. "Feminism and Motherhood: O'Brien vs. Beauvoir." *Hypatia* 1, 2 (1986): 87–102.

Leland, Dorothy. "Lacanian Psychoanalysis and French Feminism: Toward an Adequate Political Psychology." *Hypatia* 3, 3 (1989): 81–103.

Léon, Céline T. "Beauvoir's Woman: Eunuch or Male?" In *Feminist Interpretations of Simone de Beauvoir,* edited by Margaret A. Simons. University Park, Pa.: Pennsylvania State University Press, 1995.

Lindsay, Cecile. "L'Un e(s)t l'Autre: The Future of Differences in French Feminism." *L'ésprit créateur* 29, 3 (1989): 21–35.

Lloyd, Moya. "A Feminist Mapping of Foucauldian Politics." In *Feminist Interpretations of Michel Foucault,* edited by Susan J. Hekman. University Park, Pa.: Pennsylvania State University Press, 1996.

Lorraine, Tamsin. *Irigaray and Deleuze: Experiments in Visceral Philosophy.* Ithaca, N.Y.: Cornell University Press, 1999.

Lowe, Lisa. "'Des Chinoises': Orientalism, Psychoanalysis and Feminine Writing." In *Ethics, Politics and Difference in Julia Kristeva's Writing,* edited by Kelly Oliver. New York: Routledge, 1993.

Lydon, Mary. "Foucault and Feminism: A Romance of Many Dimensions." *Humanities in Society* 5, 3/4 (1982): 245–56.

Lyon, Elisabeth. "Discourse and Difference." *Camera Obscura* 3–4 (1979): 14–20.

Ludeman, Brenda. "Julia Kristeva: The Other of Language." In *The Judgement of Paris: Recent French Theory in a Local Context,* edited by Kevin Murray. North Sydney: Allen and Unwin, 1992.

Lundgren-Gothlin, Eva. "Simone de Beauvoir and Ethics." *History of European Ideas* 19, 4–6 (1994): 899–903.

Mackenzie, Catriona. "Simone de Beauvoir: Philosophy and/or the Female Body." In *Feminist Challenges: Social and Political Theory,* edited by Carole Pateman and Elizabeth Grosz. Boston: Northeastern University Press, 1986.

Mahon, Joseph. "Existentialism, Feminism and Simone de Beauvoir." *History of European Ideas* 17, 5 (1993): 651–58.

Manning, Robert J. "Thinking the Other Without Violence? An Analysis of the Relation Between the Philosophy of Lévinas and Feminism." *Journal of Speculative Philosophy* (1991): 132–43.

Marchak, C. "The Joy of Transgression: Bataille and Kristeva." *Philosophy Today* 34, 4 (1990): 354–63.

Marks, Elaine. "Transgressing the (In)cont(in)ent Boundaries: The Body in Decline." In *Yale French Studies* 72 (1986): 181–200.

Marks, Elaine, and Isabelle Courtivron, eds. *New French Feminisms.* New York: Schocken Books, 1980.

Martin, Biddy. "Feminism, Criticism, and Foucault." In *Feminism & Foucault,* edited by Irene Diamond and Lee Quinby. Boston: Northeastern University Press, 1988.

Martin, Thomas. "Sartre, Sadism and Female Beauty Ideals." *Australian Feminist Studies* 11, 24 (1996): 243–52.

Matthews, Eric. "Recent French Feminists." In *Twentieth-Century French Philosophy,* edited by Eric Matthews. New York: Oxford University Press, 1996.

McAfee, Noelle. "Abject Strangers: Toward an Ethics of Respect." In *Ethics, Politics and difference in Julia Kristeva's Writing,* edited by Kelly Oliver. New York: Routledge, 1993.

McCallum, E. L. "Technologies of Truth and the Function of Gender in Foucault." In *Feminist Interpretations of Michel Foucault,* edited by Susan J. Hekman. University Park, Pa.: Pennsylvania State University Press, 1996.

McCance, Dawne. "Julia Kristeva and the Ethics of Exile." *Tessera* 8 (1988): 23–39.

———. "Kristeva and the Subject of Ethics." *Resources for Feminist Research* 17, 1/2 (1990): 18–22.

———. "L'écriture limité: Kristeva's Postmodern Feminist Ethics." *Hypatia* 11, 2 (1996): 141–60.

McDermott, Patrice. "The Epistemological Challenge of Post-Lacanian French Feminist Theory: Luce Irigaray." *Women and Politics* 7, 3 (1987): 47–64.

McLane, Janice. "The Voice on the Skin: Self-Mutilation and Merleau-Ponty's Theory of Language." *Hypatia Special Issue: Women and Violence* 11, 4 (1996): 107–18.

McMillan, Elizabeth. "Female Difference in the Texts of Merleau-Ponty." *Philosophy Today* 31, 4 (1987): 359–66.

McNay, Lois. "The Foucauldian Body and the Exclusion of Experience." *Hypatia Special Issue: Feminism and the Body* 6, 3 (1991): 124–39.

———. *Foucault and Feminism: Power, Gender, and the Self.* Oxford: Polity, 1993.

McWhorter, Ladelle. "Is There Sexual Difference in the Work of Georges Bataille?" *International Studies in Philosophy* 27, 1 (1995): 33–41.

Mehuron, Kate. "Flesh Memory/Skin Practice." *Research in Phenomenology* 23 (1993): 73–91.

———. "An Ironic Mimesis." In *The Question of the Other,* edited by Arleen B. Dallery and Charles E. Scott. Albany, N.Y.: State University of New York Press, 1989.

———. "Sentiment Recuperated: The Performative in Women's AIDS-Related Testimonies." In *Feminist Interpretations of Jacques Derrida,* edited by Nancy J. Holland. University Park, Pa.: Pennsylvania State University Press, 1997.

Meltzer, Françoise. "Transfeminisms." In *Transfigurations: Theology and the French Feminists,* edited by Maggie C. W. Kim, Susan M. St. Ville, and Susan M. Simonaitis. Minneapolis: Fortress, 1993.

Meyers, Diana. "Moral Reflection: Beyond Impartial Reason." *Hypatia* 8, 3 (1993): 21–47.

———. *Subject and Subjectivity: Psychoanalytic Feminism and Moral Philosophy.* New York: Routledge, 1994.

———. "The Subversion of Women's Agency in Psychoanalytic Feminism: Chodorow, Flax, Kristeva." In *Revaluing French Feminism,* edited by Nancy Fraser and Sandra Lee Bartky. Bloomington, Ind.: Indiana University Press, 1990.

Miller, Nancy K. "Parables and Politics: Feminist Criticism in 1986." *Paragraph* 8 (1986): 40–54.

Mitchell, Juliet, and Jacqueline Rose, eds. Translated by Jacqueline Rose. *Feminine Sexuality: Jacques Lacan and the école freudienne.* New York: W. W. Norton and Co., 1985.

Moi, Toril. "Ambiguity and Alienation in 'The Second Sex.'" *Boundary 2* 19, 12 (1992): 96–112.

———. "Patriarchal Thought and the Drive for Knowledge." In *Between Feminism and Psychoanalysis,* edited by Teresa Brennan. London: Routledge, 1989.

———. *Sexual/Textual Politics: Feminist Literary Theory.* London: Methuen, 1985.

———. *Simone de Beauvoir: The Making of an Intellectual Woman.* Cambridge: Blackwell, 1994.

Morgan, Amy. "Journeys in the Neighbourhood of Heidegger and Cixous." *Ellipsis* 1, 1 (1989): 1–35.

Morgan, Kathryn Pauly. "Romantic Love, Altruism, and Self-Respect." *Hypatia* 1, 1 (1986): 117–48.

Morris, Meaghan. "The Pirate's Fiancée: Feminists and Philosophers, or Maybe Tonight It'll Happen." In *Feminism & Foucault,* edited by Irene Diamond and Lee Quinby. Boston: Northeastern University Press, 1988.

Morris, Phyllis. "The Lived Body: Some Patterns of Identification and Otherness." *Journal of the British Society for Phenomenology* 13 (1982): 216–25.

Mortensen, Ellen. *The Feminine and Nihilism: Luce Irigaray with Nietzsche and Heidegger.* Oslo: Scandinavian University Press, 1994.

———. "Irigaray and Nietzsche: Echo and Narcissus Revisited?" In *The Fate of the New Nietzsche*, edited by Keith Ansell-Pearson and Howard Caygill. Avebury: Aldershot, 1993.

———. "Woman's Untruth and le féminin: Reading Luce Irigaray with Nietzsche and Heidegger." In *Engaging with Irigaray*, edited by Carolyn Burke, Naomi Schor, and Margaret Whitford. New York: Columbia University Press, 1994.

Mortley, Raoul. *French Philosophers in Conversation: Lévinas, Schneider, Serres, Irigaray, Le Doeuff, Derrida*. New York: Routledge, 1991.

Muraro, Luisa. "Female Genealogies." In *Engaging with Irigaray*, edited by Carolyn Burke, Naomi Schor, and Margaret Whitford. New York: Columbia University Press, 1994.

Murphy, Julien. "Beauvoir and the Algerian War: Toward a Postcolonial Ethics." In *Feminist Interpretations of Simone de Beauvoir*, edited by Margaret A. Simons. University Park, Pa.: Pennsylvania State University Press, 1995.

———. "The Look in Sartre and Rich." *Hypatia* 2, 2 (1987): 113–24.

Nask, Kate. "The Feminist Production of Knowledge: Is Deconstruction a Practice for Women?" *Feminist Review* 17 (1994): 65–77.

Nicholson, Linda J., ed. *Feminism/Postmodernism*. New York: Routledge, 1990.

Nye, Andrea. *Feminist Theory and the Philosophies of Man*. London: Croom Helm, 1988.

———. "The Hidden Host: Irigaray and Diotima at Plato's Symposium." *Hypatia* 3, 3 (1989): 45–61.

———. "Preparing the Way for a Feminist Praxis." *Hypatia* 1, 1 (1986): 101–16.

———. "The Unity of Language." *Hypatia* 2, 2 (1987): 95–111.

———. "The Voice of Serpent: French Feminism and Philosophy of Language." In *Women, Knowledge and Reality: Explorations in Feminist Philosophy*, edited by Ann Garry and Marilyn Pearsall. New York: Routledge, 1996.

———. "Woman Clothed with the Sun: Julia Kristeva and the Escape from/to Language." *Signs: Journal of Women in Culture and Society* 12, 4 (1987): 664–86.

O'Connor, Noreen. "The An-Arche of Psychotherapy." In *Abjection, Melancholia and Love: The Work of Julia Kristeva*, edited by John Fletcher and Andrew Benjamin. New York: Routledge, 1990.

Okely, Judith. *Simone de Beauvoir*. New York: Pantheon, 1986.

Oliver, Kelly. "Alterity within Berman's 'Persona': Face to Face with the Other." *Journal of Value Inquiry* 29, 4 (1995): 521–32.

———, ed. *Ethics, Politics and Difference in Julia Kristeva's Writing*. New York: Routledge, 1993.

———. *Family Values: Subjects between Nature and Culture*. New York: Routledge, 1997.

———. "The Gestation of the Other in Phenomenology." *Epoche* 3, 1 & 2 (1995): 79–116.

———. "Julia Kristeva's Feminist Revolutions." *Hypatia* 8, 3 (1993): 94–114.

———. "Julia Kristeva's Outlaw Ethics." In *Ethics, Politics and Difference in Julia Kristeva's Writing*, edited by Kelly Oliver. New York: Routledge, 1993.

———. "Julia Kristeva's Speaking Body." In *Transitions in Continental Philosophy*, edited by Arleen Dallery and Stephen Watson. Albany, N.Y.: State University of New York Press, 1994.

———. "Kristeva's Imaginary Father and the Crisis in the Paternal Function." *Diacritics* 21, 2/3 (1991): 43–63.

———. "The Maternal Operation: Circumscribing the Alliance." In *Derrida and Feminism,* edited by Ellen K. Feder, Mary C. Rawlinson, and Emily Zakin. New York: Routledge, 1997.

———. "Nietzsche's Abjection." In *Nietzsche and the Feminine,* edited by Peter J. Burgard. Charlottesville, Va.: University Press of Virginia, 1994.

———. "The Plaint of Ariadne: Luce Irigaray's Amante Marine de Friedrich Nietzsche." In *The Fate of the New Nietzsche,* edited by Keith Ansell-Pearson and Howard Caygill. Avebury: Aldershot, 1993.

———. *Reading Kristeva: Unravelling the Double Bind.* Bloomington, Ind.: Indiana University Press, 1993.

———. *Womanizing Nietzsche: Philosophy's Relation to the 'Feminine.'* New York: Routledge, 1995.

Olkowski, Dorothea. "Bodies in the Light: Relaxing the Imaginary in Video." In *Thinking Bodies,* edited by Juliet Flower MacCannell and Laura Zakarin. Stanford: Stanford University Press, 1994.

———. "Body, Knowledge, and Becoming-Woman, Morpho-logic in Deleuze and Irigaray." In *Feminism and Gilles Deleuze,* edited by Ian Buchanan and Claire Colebrook. London: Blackwell, forthcoming.

———. "Chiasm, The Interval of Sexual Difference in Irigaray and Merleau-Ponty." In *Re-Reading Merleau-Ponty, Essays Beyond the Continental-Analytic Divide,* edited by Lawrence Hass and Dorothea Olkowski. Atlantic Highlands, N.J.: Humanity Books, 2000.

———. "Difference and the Ruin of Representation in Gilles Deleuze." In *Sites of Vision: The Discursive Construction of Vision in the History of Philosophy,* edited by David Michael Levin. Cambridge, Mass.: MIT Press, 1997.

———, ed. *Feminist Enactments of French Philosophy,* Ithaca, N.Y.: Cornell University Press, 2000.

———. "Flows of Desire and the Body-Becoming." In *Making Futures: Explorations in Time, Memory, and Becoming,* edited by Elizabeth Grosz. Ithaca, N.Y.: Cornell University Press, 1999.

———. *Gilles Deleuze and the Ruin of Representation.* Berkeley: University of California Press, 1999.

———. "Kolossos: The Measure of a Man's Cize." In *Feminist Interpretations of Jacques Derrida,* edited by Nancy J. Holland. University Park, Pa.: Pennsylvania State University Press, 1997.

———. "Materiality and Language: Butler's Interrogation of the History of Philosophy." *Philosophy and Social Criticism* 23, 3 (1997): 37–53.

———. "Phenomenology and Feminism." In *The Edinburgh Encyclopedia of Continental Philosophy,* edited by Simon Glendinning. Edinburgh: Edinburgh University Press, 1999.

———. "Words of Power and the Logic of Sense." In *Feminist Approaches to Logic,* edited by Marjorie Hass and Rachel Joffe Falmagne. New York: Roman and Littlefield, 1999.

Opel, Frances. "'Speaking of Immemorial Waters': Irigaray with Nietzsche." In *Nietzsche, Feminism and Political Theory,* edited by Paul Patton. London: Routledge, 1993.

Oppenheim, Lois. "The Ontology of Language in a Post-Structuralist Feminist Perspective: Explosive Discourse in Monique Wittig." In *Poetics of the Elements in Human Condition II: The Airy Elements in Poetic Imagination,* edited by Ann Imieniecka. Dordrecht: Kluwer, 1988.

Ormiston, Gayle L. "Traces of Derrida: Nietzsche's Image of Women." *Philosophy Today* (summer 1984): 178–87.

Pajaczkowska, Claire. "Introduction to Kristeva." *m/f* 5/6 (1981): 149–57.

Penrod, Lynn Kettler. *Hélène Cixous*. New York: Twayne Publishers, 1996.

———. "Hélène Cixous: lectures initiatiques, lectures centrifuges." In *Du Féminin*, edited by Mireille Calle. Cap-Saint-Ignace, Québec: Édition le Griffon d'argile, 1992.

Pilardi, Jo-Ann. "Female Eroticism in the Works of Simone de Beauvoir." *Feminist Studies* 6, 2 (1980): 304–13.

———. "Feminists Read 'The Second Sex.'" In *Feminist Interpretations of Simone de Beauvoir*, edited by Margaret A. Simons. University Park, Pa.: Pennsylvania State University Press, 1995.

———. "Philosophy Becomes Autobiography: The Development of the Self in the Writings of Simone de Beauvoir." In *Writing the Politics of Difference*, edited by Hugh J. Silverman. Albany, N.Y.: State University of New York Press, 1991.

Plotnitsky, Arkady. "The Medusa's Ears: The Question of Nietzsche, the Question of Gender, and Transformations of Theory." In *Nietzsche and the Feminine*, edited by Peter J. Burgard. Charlottesville, Va.: University Press of Virginia, 1994.

Pluhacek, Stephen, and Heidi Bostic. "Thinking Life as Relation." *Man and World* 29 (1996): 343–60.

Poovey, Mary. "Feminism and Deconstruction." *Feminist Studies* 14, 1 (1988): 51–65.

Porter, Laurence. "Writing Feminism: Myth, Epic and Utopia in Monique Wittig's 'Les guérillières.'" *L'ésprit créateur* 29, 3 (1989): 92–100.

Preston, Beth. "Merleau-Ponty and Feminine Embodied Experience." *Man and World* 29, 2 (1996): 167–86.

Probyn, Elspeth. "Bodies and Anti-Bodies: Feminism and the Postmodern." *Cultural Studies* 1, 3 (1987): 349–61.

———. "This Body Which Is Not One: Speaking an Embodied Self." *Hypatia* 6, 3 (1991): 111–24.

Quick, James Robert. "'Pronom' 'She'—Luce Irigaray's Fluid Dynamics." *Philosophy Today* 36, 3 (1992): 199–209.

Rabine, Leslie. "Ecriture Feminine as Metaphor." *Cultural Critique* 8 (1987/1988): 19–44.

———. "Essentialism and Its Contexts: Saint-Simonian and Post-Structural Feminists." *differences: a journal of feminist cultural studies* 1, 2 (1989): 105–23.

Radhakrishnan, R. "Feminist Historiography and Post-Structuralist Thought: Intersections and Departures." In *The Difference Within: Feminism and Critical Theory*, edited by Elizabeth Meese and Alice Parker. Amsterdam, Philadelphia: John Benjamin's Publishing Company, 1989.

Ragland-Sullivan, Ellie. "Jacques Lacan: Feminism and the Problem of Gender Identity." *SubStance* 36 (1982): 6–20.

Rawlinson, Mary C. "Levers, Signatures, and Secrets: Derrida's Use of Woman." In *Derrida and Feminism*, edited by Ellen K. Feder, Mary C. Rawlinson, and Emily Zakin. New York: Routledge, 1997.

Reineke, Martha J. "Lacan, Merleau-Ponty, and Irigaray: Reflections on a Specular Drama." *Auslegung* 14 (1987): 67–85.

———. "Life-Sentences: Kristeva and the Limits of Modernity." *Soundings* 71, 4 (1988).

———. "'This is My Body': Reflections on Abjection, Anorexia and Medieval Women Mystics." *Journal of the American Academy of Religion* 58, 2 (1990): 245–65.

Robinson, Lillian S. "Introduction to Christine Fauré's 'Absent from History' and 'The

Twilight of the Goddesses,' of the Intellectual Crisis of French Feminism." *m/f* 7, 1 (1981): 68–70.

Robinson, Sally. "Misappropriations of the 'Feminine.'" *SubStance* 59 (1989): 48–70.

Rodgers, Catherine. "Elisabeth Badinter and the Second Sex: An Interview." *Signs: Journal of Women in Culture and Society* 21, 1 (1995): 147–62.

Rofougaran, Fariba. "Les corps dans l'oeuvre de Monique Wittig." Ph.D. diss., University of California at Santa Cruz, 1983.

Rössler, Beate. "Subjects at Cross Purposes: The Debate Between Feminism and Postmodernism." *European Journal of Philosophy* 3, 3 (1995): 299–312.

Rorty, Richard. "Feminism, Ideology, and Deconstruction: A Pragmatist View." *Hypatia* 8, 2 (1993): 96–103.

Rose, Jacqueline. *Sexuality in the Field of Vision.* London: Verso, 1986.

Rowley, Hazel, and Elizabeth Grosz. "Psychoanalysis and Feminism." In *Feminist Knowledge: Critique and Construct,* edited by Sneja Gunew. London: Routledge, 1990.

Sankovitch, Tilde. "Hélène Cixous: The Pervasive Myth." In *French Women Writers and the Book: Myths of Access and Desire,* edited by Tilde Sankovitch. Syracuse, N.Y.: Syracuse University Press, 1988.

Sawicki, Jana. *Disciplining Foucault: Feminism, Power and the Body.* London: Routledge, 1991.

———. "Feminism, Foucault, and 'Subjects' of Power and Freedom." In *Feminist Interpretations of Michel Foucault,* edited by Susan J. Hekman. University Park, Pa.: Pennsylvania State University Press, 1996.

———. "Foucault and Feminism: Toward a Politics of Difference." *Hypatia* 1, 2 (1986): 23–36.

———. "Foucault, Feminism and Questions of Identity." In *The Cambridge Companion to Foucault,* edited by Garry Gutting. Cambridge: Cambridge University Press, 1994.

———. "Identity Politics and Sexual Freedom: Foucault and Feminism." In *Feminism & Foucault,* edited by Irene Diamond and Lee Quinby. Boston: Northeastern University Press, 1988.

Schiach, Morag. *Hélène Cixous: A Politics of Writing.* London: Routledge, 1991.

———. "Their 'Symbolic' Exists, It Holds Power—We, the Sowers of Disorder, Know It Only Too Well." In *Between Feminism and Psychoanalysis,* edited by Teresa Brennan. London: Routledge, 1989.

Schor, Naomi. "Dreaming Dissymmetry: Barthes, Foucault, and Sexual Difference." In *Men in Feminism,* edited by Alice Jardine and Paul Smith. New York: Routledge, 1987.

———. "This Essentialism Which Is Not One: Coming to Grips with Irigaray." *differences: a journal of feminist cultural studies* 1, 2 (1989): 38–58.

———. "Introduction." In *The Essential Difference,* edited by Naomi Schor and Elizabeth Weed. Bloomington, Ind.: Indiana University Press, 1994.

———. "Previous Engagements: The Receptions of Irigaray." In *Engaging with Irigaray,* edited by Carolyn Burke, Naomi Schor, and Margaret Whitford. New York: Columbia University Press, 1994.

Schor, Naomi, and Elizabeth Weed. *The Essential Difference.* Bloomington, Ind.: Indiana University Press, 1994.

Schrift, Alan D. "On the Gynaecology of Morals: Nietzsche and Cixous on the Logic of the Gift." In *Nietzsche and the Feminine,* edited by Peter J. Burgard. Charlottesville, Va.: University Press of Virginia, 1994.

Schwab, Gail. "Mother's Body, Father's Tongue: Mediation and the Symbolic Order." In *Engaging with Irigaray,* edited by Carolyn Burke, Naomi Schor, and Margaret Whitford. New York: Columbia University Press, 1994.

Schutte, Ofelia. "A Critique of Normative Heterosexuality: Identity, Embodiment, and Sexual Difference in Beauvoir and Irigaray." *Hypatia* 12, 1 (1997): 40–62.

———. "Irigaray on the Problem of Subjectivity." *Hypatia* 6, 2 (1991): 64–76.

Schwab, Gail. "Women and the Law in Irigarayan Theory." *Metaphilosophy* 27, 1–2 (1996): 146–77.

Scott, Joan W. "Deconstructing Equality-Versus-Difference: Or, the Uses of Poststructuralist Theory for Feminism." *Feminist Studies* 14, 1 (1988): 33–50.

Seigfried, Charlene H. "Gender-Specific Values." *Philosophical Forum* 15 (1984): 425–42.

Sellers, Susan. *Hélène Cixous: An Introduction.* Oxford: Polity, 1996.

———. *Language and Sexual Difference. Feminist Writings in France.* London: MacMillan Education Ltd., 1991.

———. "Learning to Read the Feminine." In *The Body and the Text,* edited by Helen Wilcox, Keith McWatters, Ann Thompson, and Linda R. Williams. New York: Harvester Wheatsheaf, 1990.

Shaktini, Namascar. "Displacing the Phallic Subject: Monique Wittig's Lesbian Writing." *Signs: Journal of Women in Culture and Society* 8, 1 (1982): 29–44.

Sheets-Johnstone, Maxine. "Corporeal Archetypes and Power: Preliminary Clarifications and Considerations of Sex." *Hypatia* 7, 3 (1992): 39–76.

———. *The Roots of Power: Animate Form and Gendered Bodies.* Chicago: Open Court, 1994.

———. *The Roots of Thinking.* Philadelphia: Temple University Press, 1990.

Shildrick, Margrit. *Leaky Bodies and Boundaries: Feminism, Postmodernism and (Bio)ethics.* London: Routledge, 1997.

———. "Women, Bodies and Consent." In *Against Patriarchal Thinking,* edited by Maja Pellikaan-Engel. Amsterdam: VU University Press, 1992.

Siebers, Tobin. "The Ethics of Sexual Difference." In *The Ethics of Criticism,* edited by Tobin Siebers. Ithaca, N.Y.: Cornell University Press, 1988.

Simons, Jon. "Foucault's Mother." In *Feminist Interpretations of Michel Foucault,* edited by Susan J. Hekman. University Park, Pa.: Pennsylvania State University Press, 1996.

Simons, Margaret A. "Beauvoir and Sartre: The Philosophical Relationship." *Yale French Studies* 72 (1986): 165–79.

———, ed. *Feminist Interpretations of Simone de Beauvoir.* University Park, Pa.: Pennsylvania State University, 1995.

———. "Lesbian Connections: Simone de Beauvoir and Feminism." *Signs: Journal of Women in Culture and Society* 18, 1 (1992): 136–61.

———. "The Second Sex: From Marxism to Radical Feminism." In *Feminist Interpretations of Simone de Beauvoir,* edited by Margaret A. Simons. University Park, Pa.: Pennsylvania State University Press, 1995.

———. "Sexism and the Philosophical Canon: On Reading Beauvoir's 'The Second Sex.'" *Journal of the History of Ideas* 51, 3 (1990): 487–503.

———. "The Silencing of Simone de Beauvoir: Guess What's Missing from the Second Sex." *Women's Studies International Forum* 6, 5 (1983): 559–64.

———. "Two Interviews with Simone de Beauvoir." *Hypatia* 3, 3 (1989): 11–27.

Simpson-Zinn, Joy. "The Différance of L'Écriture Féminine." *Chimeres: A Journal of French and Italian Literature* 18, 1 (1985): 77–93.

Singer, Linda. "Bodies—Pleasures—Powers." *differences: a journal of feminist cultural studies* 1, 1 (1989): 45–65.

——. *Erotic Welfare: Sexual Theory and Politics in the Age of the Epidemic,* edited by Judith Butler and Maureen MacGrogan. New York: Routledge, 1993.

——. "Feminism and Postmodernism." In *Feminists Theorize the Political,* edited by Judith Butler and Joan W. Scott. New York: Routledge, 1992.

——. "Interpretation and Retrieval Rereading Beauvoir." *Women's Studies International Forum* 8, 3 (1985): 231–38.

——. "True Confessions: Cixous and Foucault on Sexuality and Power." In *The Thinking Muse,* edited by Jeffner Allen and Iris Marion Young. Bloomington, Ind.: Indiana University Press, 1989.

Smith, Janet Farrell. "Possessive Power." *Hypatia* 1, 2 (1986): 103–20.

Smith, Paul. "Julia Kristeva et al. or, Take Three of More." In *Feminism and Psychoanalysis,* edited by Richard Feldstein and Judith Roof. Ithaca, N.Y.: Cornell University Press, 1989.

Soper, Kate. "Feminism, Humanism, and Postmodernism." *Radical Philosophy* 55 (1990): 11–17.

Spelman, Elizabeth. *Inessential Woman: Problems of Exclusion in Feminist Thought.* Boston: Beacon, 1988.

——. "Simone de Beauvoir and Women: Just Who Does She Think 'We' Is?" In *Discovering Reality: Feminist Perspectives on Epistemology, Metaphysics, Methodology, and Philosophy of Science,* edited by Sandra Harding and Merill Hintikka. Dordrecht: D. Reidel Publishing Company, 1991.

Spivak, Gayatri Chakravorty. "Cixous sans frontières." In *Du Féminin,* edited by Mireille Calle. Cap-Saint-Ignace, Québec: Édition le Griffon d'argile, 1992.

——. 1983. "Displacement and the Discourse of Woman." In *Displacement: Derrida and After,* edited by Mark Krupnick. Bloomington, Ind.: Indiana University Press, 1992.

——. "Echo." *New Literary History* 24, 1 (1993): 17–43.

——. "Feminism and Deconstruction, Again: Negotiating with Unacknowledged Masculinism." In *Between Feminism and Psychoanalysis,* edited by Teresa Brennan. London: Routledge, 1989.

——. "French Feminism in an International Frame." *Yale French Studies* 62 (1981): 154–84.

——. "French Feminism Revisited: Ethics and Politics." In *Feminists Theorize the Political,* edited by Judith Butler and Joan W. Scott. New York: Routledge, 1992.

——. "In a Word: Interview." *differences: a journal of feminist cultural studies* 1, 2 (1989): 124–56.

——. *In Other Worlds: Essays in Cultural Politics.* New York: Methuen, 1987.

——. "A Response to 'The Difference within Feminism and Critical Theory.'" In *The Difference Within: Feminism and Critical Theory,* edited by Elizabeth Meese and Alice Parker. Amsterdam: John Benjamin's Publishing Company, 1989.

Stanton, Domna C. "Difference on Trial: A Critique of the Maternal Metaphor in Cixous, Irigaray, and Kristeva." In *The Poetics of Gender,* edited by Nancy K. Miller. New York: Columbia University Press, 1986.

——. "Language and Revolution: The Franco: American Dis-connection." In *The Future of Difference,* edited by Hester Eisenstein and Alice Jardine. Boston: G. K. Hall, 1990.

Stenstad, Gail. "Anarchic Thinking." *Hypatia* 3, 2 (1988): 87–100.

Stern, Lesley. "Introduction to Plaza." *m/f* 4 (1980): 21–27.

Still, Judith. "A Feminine Economy: Some Preliminary Thoughts." In *The Body and the*

Text, edited by Helen Wilcox, Keith McWatters, Ann Thompson, and Linda R. Williams. New York: Harvester Wheatsheaf, 1990.

Stratton, Teri. "Head Aches or Headless: Who Is Poet Enough?" *Hypatia* 7, 2 (1992): 109–19.

Strong, B. "Foucault, Freud, and French Feminism: Theorizing Hysteria and Theorizing the Feminine." *Literature and Psychology* 35, 4 (1989): 10–26.

Suleiman, Susan. "Writing and Motherhood." In *The (M)other Tongue: Essays in Feminist Psychoanalytic Interpretation.* Ithaca, N.Y.: Cornell University Press, 1985.

Sullivan, Shannon. "Domination and Dialogue in Merleau-Ponty's Phenomenology of Perception." *Hypatia* 12, 1 (1997): 1–19.

Thomas, Jennifer. "The Question of Derrida's Women." *Human Studies* 16, 1/2 (1993): 163–76.

Thomas, Sue. "Difference, Intersubjectivity, and Agency in the Colonial and Decolonizing Spaces of Hélène Cixous's 'Sorties.'" *Hypatia* 9, 1 (1994): 53–69.

Tibbett, Frederick. "Irigaray and the Languages of Wittgenstein." *Critical Matrix* 4 (1988): 83–110.

Trinh T. Minh-ha. *Woman, Native, Other.* Bloomington, Ind.: Indiana University Press, 1989.

———. *When the Moon Waxes Red.* New York: Routledge, 1991.

Turcotte, Louise. Forward to *The Straight Mind and Other Essays,* by Monique Wittig. Boston: Beacon Press, 1992.

van Rossum-Guyon, F., and M. Diaz-Diocaretz, eds. *Hélène Cixous: Chemins d'une écriture.* Amsterdam: Editions Rodopoi, 1990.

Vasseleu, Cathryn. "The Face Before the Mirror Stage." *Hypatia* 6, 3 (1991): 140–55.

———. *Textures of Light: Vision and Touch in Irigaray, Lévinas and Merleau-Ponty.* London: Routledge, 1997.

Vintges, Karen. "'The Second Sex' and Philosophy." In *Feminist Interpretations of Simone de Beauvoir,* edited by Margaret A. Simons. University Park, Pa.: Pennsylvania State University Press, 1995.

———. *Philosophy as Passion: The Thinking of Simone de Beauvoir.* Translated by Anne Lavelle. Bloomington, Ind.: Indiana University Press, 1996.

Walker, Michelle. "Silence and Reason: Woman's Voice in Philosophy." *Australasian Journal of Philosophy* 71, 4 (1993): 400–24.

Ward, Graham. "Divinity and Sexuality: Luce Irigaray and Christology." *Modern Theology* 12, 2 (1992): 221–37.

Ward, Julia K. "Beauvoir's Two Senses of 'Body' in the 'The Second Sex.'" In *Feminist Interpretations of Simone de Beauvoir,* edited by Margaret A. Simons. University Park, Pa.: Pennsylvania State University Press, 1995.

Weed, Elizabeth, ed. *Coming to Terms.* New York: Routledge, 1989.

———. "The Question of Style." In *Engaging with Irigaray,* edited by Carolyn Burke, Naomi Schor, and Margaret Whitford. New York: Columbia University Press, 1994.

Weedon, Chris. *Feminist Practice and Poststructuralist Theory.* Oxford: Basil Blackwell, 1987.

Weir, Alison. "Identification with the Divided Mother: Kristeva's Ambivalence." In *Ethics, Politics and difference in Julia Kristeva's Writing,* edited by Kelly Oliver. New York: Routledge, 1993.

———. *Sacrificial Logics: Feminist Theory and the Critique of Identity.* New York: Routledge, 1996.

Weiss, Gail. *Body Images: Embodiment as Intercorporeality.* New York: Routledge, 1999.

———. "Creative Agency and Fluid Images: A Review of Iris Young's 'Throwing Like a

Girl and Other Essays in Feminist Philosophy and Social Theory.'" *Human Studies* 17, 4 (1994–95): 471–78.

Welch, Sharon "The Truth of Liberation Theology: Particulars of a Relative Sublime." In *Feminism & Foucault,* edited by Irene Diamond and Lee Quinby. Boston: Northeastern University Press, 1988.

Wenzel, Hélène Vivienne. "Introduction to Luce Irigaray's 'And the One Doesn't Stir without the Other.'" *Signs: Journal of Women in Culture and Society* 7, 1 (1981): 56–59.

———. "The Text as Body/Politics: An Appreciation of Monique Wittig's Writings in Context." *Feminist Studies* 7, 2 (1981): 264–87.

Whitford, Margaret. "Irigaray, Utopia, and the Death Drive" In *Engaging with Irigaray,* edited by Carolyn Burke, Naomi Schor, and Margaret Whitford. New York: Columbia University Press, 1994.

———. "Irigaray's Body Symbolic." *Hypatia* 6, 3 (1991): 97–110.

———. "Luce Irigaray and the Female Imaginary: Speaking as a Women." *Radical Philosophy* 43 (1986): 3–8.

———. *Luce Irigaray: Philosophy in the Feminine.* New York: Routledge, 1991.

———. "Luce Irigaray's Critique of Rationality." In *Feminist Perspectives in Philosophy,* edited by Morwenna Griffiths. Bloomington, Ind.: Indiana University Press, 1988.

———. "Re-reading Irigaray." In *Between Feminism and Psychoanalysis,* edited by Teresa Brennan. London: Routledge, 1989.

———. "Speaking as Woman: Luce Irigaray and the Female Imaginary." *Radical Philosophy* 43 (1986): 3–8.

Wilcox, Helen, Keith McWatters, Ann Thompson, and Linda R. Williams, eds. *The Body and the Text: Hélène Cixous Readings and Teachings.* New York: Harvester Wheatsheaf, 1990.

Williams, Caroline. "Feminism, Subjectivity and Psychoanalysis: Towards a (Corpo)real Knowledge." In *Knowing the Difference,* edited by Kathleen Lennon and Margaret Whitford. London: Routledge, 1994.

Williams, Linda L. "Woman as Rupture?" *International Studies in Philosophy* 25, 2 (1993): 129–34.

Wingenbach, E. C. "Sexual Difference and the Possibility of Justice: Irigaray's Transformative Politics." *International Studies in Philosophy* 28, 1 (1996): 117–34.

Winnubst, Shannon. "Exceeding Hegel and Lacan: Different Fields of Pleasure within Foucault and Irigaray." *Hypatia* 14, 1 (1999): 13–37.

Wiseman, Mary Bittner. "Renaissance Madonnas and the Fantasies of Freud." *Hypatia* 8, 3 (1993): 115–35.

Wiseman, Susan. "'Femininity' and the Intellectual in Sontag and Cixous." In *The Body and the Text,* edited by Helen Wilcox, Keith McWatters, Ann Thompson, and Linda R. Williams. New York: Harvester Wheatsheaf, 1990.

Wright, Elizabeth. "Thoroughly Postmodern Feminist Criticism." In *Between Feminism and Psychoanalysis,* edited by Teresa Brennan. London: Routledge, 1989.

Woodhull, Winnie. "By Myriad Constellations: Monique Wittig and the Writing of Women's Experience." In *Power, Gender, Values,* edited by Judith Genova. Edmonton: Academic Print. & Pub, 1987.

———. "Sexuality, Power and the Question of Rape." In *Feminism & Foucault,* edited by Irene Diamond and Lee Quinby. Boston: Northeastern University Press, 1988.

Wynn, Francine. "The Embodied Chiasmic Relationship of Mother and Infant." *Human Studies* 20, 2 (1997): 253–70.

———. "The Mother-Infant Relationship: Holding and Being Held." Ph.D. diss., York University, 1996.

Xu, Ping. "Irigaray's Mimicry and the Problem of Essentialism." *Hypatia* 10, 4 (1995): 76–89.

Young, Iris Marion. "Humanism, Gynocentrism and Feminist Politics." *Women's Studies International Forum* 8, 3 (1985): 173–83.

———. "The Ideal of Community and the Politics of Difference." *Social Theory and Practice* 12, 1 (1986).

———. "Pregnant Embodiment: Subjectivity and Alienation." *The Journal of Medicine and Philosophy* 9, 1 (1984): 45–62.

———. "Review Essay: Sexual Ethics in the Age of Epidemic." *Hypatia* 8, 3 (1993): 184–93.

———. *Throwing Like a Girl and Other Essays in Feminist Philosophy and Social Theory.* Bloomington, Ind.: Indiana University Press, 1990.

———. "Throwing Like a Girl: A Phenomenology of Feminine Body Comportment, Motility, and Spatiality." *Human Studies* 3 (1980): 137–56.

Zerilli, Linda M. G. "Between Materialism and Utopianism: Reflections on the Work of Drucilla Cornell." *Philosophy and Social Criticism* 22, 4 (1996): 95–108.

———. "'I Am a woman': Female Voice and Ambiguity in 'The Second Sex.'" *Women and Politics* 11, 1 (1991): 93–108.

———. "A Process without a Subject: Simone de Beauvoir and Julia Kristeva on Maternity." *Signs: Journal of Women in Culture and Society* 18, 1 (1992): 111–35.

———. "Rememoration or War? French feminist narrative and the Politics of Self-Representation." *differences: a journal of feminist cultural studies* 3, 1 (1991): 1–19.

Ziarek, Ewa. "At the Limits of Discourse: Heterogeneity, Alterity, and the Maternal in Kristeva's thought." *differences: a journal of feminist cultural studies.*" *Hypatia* 7, 2 (1992): 91–108.

———. "Kristeva and Lévinas: Mourning, Ethics and the Feminine." In *Ethics, Politics and difference in Julia Kristeva's Writing,* edited by Kelly Oliver. New York: Routledge, 1993.

Ziarek, Ewa Plonowska. "From Euthanasia to the Other of Reason." In *Derrida and Feminism,* edited by Ellen K. Feder, Mary C. Rawlinson, and Emily Zakin. New York: Routledge, 1997.

French Sources

Armengaud, Françoise. "Provenances de la pensée, Femmes/Philosophie. Les Cahiers du Grif." *Nouvelles Questions Feministes* 13, 2 (1992): 8–14.

Badiou, Alain. "L'amour est-il le lieu d'un savoir sexué." In *L'exercise du savoir et la différence des sexes,* edited by Geneviève Fraisse. Paris: Éditions L'Harmattan, 1991.

Badinter, Elisabeth. *L'amour en plus: Histoire de l'amour maternel, 17e-20e siècle.* Paris: Flammarion, 1980.

———. *Emilie, Emilie: L'ambitien feminine au 18e siècle.* Paris: Flammarion, 1983.

———. "Femmes, vous lui devez tout!" *Le nouvel observateur* 39 (1986): 18–24.

———. *L'un est l'autre: Des relations entre hommes et femmes.* Paris: Odile Jacob, 1986.

———. *XY, de l'identité masculine.* Paris: Odile Jacob, 1992.

Balibar, François. "La femme d'Einstein." In *Le sexe des sciences,* edited by Françoise Collin. Paris: Éditions Autrement, 1992.

———. "'Traduire,' dit-elle. La traduction, une affaire de femmes?" In *L'exercise du savoir et la différence des sexes,* edited by Geneviève Fraisse. Paris: Éditions L'Harmattan, 1991.

———. "Y a-t-il une science féminine?" In *Le sexe des sciences,* edited by Françoise Collin. Paris: Éditions Autrement, 1992.

Bastoen, France. "Cle d'un genre?" *Horizons Philosophiques* 6, 1 (1995): 75–100.

Benchelah, Anne-Catherine. "Le courage de penser." *Cahiers Internationaux de symbolisme: Penser au féminin* 65–66–67 (1990): 149–57.

Blanckaert, Claude. "La science de la femme: une affaire d'hommes." In *Le sexe des sciences,* edited by Françoise Collin. Paris: Éditions Autrement, 1992.

Boons, Marie-Claire. "L'exil amoureux." *Les cahiers du Grif: La dépendance amoureuse* 31 (1985): 41–62.

Braidotti, Rosi. "Théories des études féministes: quelques expériences contemporaines en Europe." *Les cahiers du Grif* 45 (1990): 29–50.

———. "U-topies: des non-lieux post-modernes." *Les cahiers du Grif: Nouvelle pauvreté nouvelle société* 30 (1985): 51–61.

Braidotti, Rosi, Oristelle Bonis, and Martine Menès. "Des reconversions libidinales—Femmes en fin de droits?" *Les cahiers du Grif: L'Indépendance Amoreuse* 32 (1985): 37–57.

Braidotti, Rosina. "Feminisme et Philosophie: La philosophie contemporaine comme critique du pouvoir par rapport à la Pensée Feministe." Ph.D. diss., Université de Paris, 1981.

Calle, Mireille, ed. *Du Féminin.* Cap-Saint-Ignace, Québec: Édition le Griffon d'argile, 1992.

———. "L'écrire-penser d'Hélène Cixous." In *Du Féminin,* edited by Mireille Calle. Cap-Saint-Ignace, Québec: Édition le Griffon d'argile, 1992.

Cassin, Barbara. "Le désordre philosophique." *Les Cahiers du Grif: Provenances de la pensée, Femmes/Philosophie* 46 (1992): 13–20.

Chabot, Marc, and Sylvie Chaput. "La Varieté et le Manque." *Horizons Philosophiques* 6, 1 (1995): 59–74.

Chalier, Catherine. "Ethics and the Feminine." In *Re-Reading Lévinas,* edited by Robert Bernasconi and Simon Critchley. London: Athlone Press, 1991.

———. "Éthique et féminin." *Les cahiers du Grif: L'Indépendance amoreuse* 32 (1985): 121–31.

———. *Figures du Féminin: Lecture d'Emmanuel Lévinas.* Paris: La nuit surveillée, 1982.

———. *Les Matriarches: Sarah, Rebecca, Rachel et Léa.* Paris: Éditions du Cerf, 1985.

———. "Le secret qui nous habite." *Les Cahiers du Grif: Provenances de la pensée, Femmes/Philosophie* 46 (1992): 29–40.

Charraud, Nathalie. "Sujet apparent, sujet réel." In *Le sexe des sciences,* edited by Françoise Collin. Paris: Éditions Autrement, 1992.

Cloutier, Yvan. "Par-delà de féminisme: pour une éthique sartrienne de la pluralité des points de vue." *Philosophiques* 21, 2 (1994).

Collin, Françoise. "Au Revoir." *les cahiers du Grif* 22/23 (1978).

———. "La Condition Natale." In *Égalité et différence des sexes,* edited by Louise Marcil-Lacoste. Québec: Acfas, 1986.

———. "Le corps se ribiffe." *Les cahiers du Grif* 11 (1976): 49–58.

———. "Ces Études qui son 'pas tout,' Fecondité et limites des études féministes." *Les cahiers du Grif* 45 (1990): 81–94.

———. "Inconnu à l'adresse." *Les cahiers du Grif: L'Indépendance amoreuse* 32 (1985): 107–14.

———. "Le livre et le code: de Simone de Beauvoir à Thérèse d'Avila." *Les cahiers du Grif* 2 (1997): 9–19.

————. "Parmi les femmes et les sciences." In *Le sexe des sciences,* edited by Françoise Collin. Paris: Éditions Autrement, 1992.

————. "Praxis de la différence." *Les Cahiers du Grif: Provenances de la pensée, Femmes/Philosophie* 46 (1992): 125–42.

————. "Polyglo(u)ssons." *Les cahiers du Grif* 12 (1976): 23–28.

————. "Repenser l'éthique." *Cahiers du Grif* 29 (1984): 97–99.

————, ed. *Le sexe des sciences.* Paris: Éditions Autrement, 1992.

Comesana, Gloria. "L'alterité chez Sartre et les rapports femme-homme." Ph.D. diss., Université de la Sorbonne, 1977.

David-Ménard, Monique. "La folie dans la raison pure." *Les Cahiers du Grif: Provenances de la pensée, Femmes/Philosophie* 46 (1992): 41–46.

————. "Geschlechtlicher Unterschied und Philosophische Methode." In *Was Philosophinnen Denken II,* edited by Manon Andreas-Griesebach/Brigitte Weisshaupt. Zurich: Ammann Verlag, 1986.

————. "Hommes et femmes: une question philosophique?" In *L'exercise du savoir et la différence des sexes,* edited by Geneviève Fraisse. Paris: Éditions L'Harmattan, 1991.

David-Ménard, Monique, Geneviève Fraisse, and Michel Tort. "L'exercice du savoir et la différence des sexes." In *L'exercise du savoir et la différence des sexes,* edited by Geneviève Fraisse. Paris: Éditions L'Harmattan, 1991.

Defromont, Françoise."L'Epopée du corps." In *Hélène Cixous: Chemins d'une écriture,* edited by F. van Rossum-Guyton and M. Diaz-Diocaretz. Amsterdam: Editions Rodopoi, 1990.

————. "Faire la femme, différence sexuelle et énonciation." *Fabula* 5 (1985): 95–112.

Delphy, Christine. "Libération des femmes ou droits corporatistes des mènes?" *Nouvelles Questions Feministes* 16–17–18 (1991): 93–118.

————. "Nos amis et nous: Les foundements cachés de quelques discours pseudo-féministes." *Questions Feministes* 1 (1977): 21–50.

————. "Un féminisme matérialiste est possible." *Nouvelles Questions Feministes* 4 (1982): 51–86.

Denis, Marie. "Corps et âme." *Cahiers Internationaux de symbolisme: Penser au féminin* 65–66–67 (1990): 39–45.

Dhavernas, Marie-Josèphe. "Je ne suis pas celle que vous pensez. " In *Le sexe des sciences,* edited by Françoise Collin. Paris: Éditions Autrement, 1992.

Le Doeuff, Michèle. "Ants and Women, or Philosophy without Borders." *Philosophy* 21 (1987): 41–54.

————. *L'étude et le rouet: des Femmes, de la Philosophie etc.* Paris: Éditions du seuil, 1989. Also as *Hipparchia's Choice: An Essay Concerning Women, Philosophy, etc.* Translated by Trista Selous. Oxford, England: Blackwell, 1991.

————. "Gens de Science: Essai sur le déni de mixité." *Nouvelles Questions Feministes* 13, 1 (1992): 5–37.

————. "Mastering a Woman: The Imaginary Foundation of a Certain Metaphysical Order." In *Transitions in Continental Philosophy,* edited by Arleen B. Dallery and Stephen H. Watson with Elizabeth Marya Bower. Albany, N.Y.: State University of New York Press, 1994.

————. "Operative Philosophy: Simone de Beauvoir and Existentialism." *Ideology and Consciousness* 6 (1979): 47– 57.

————. *The Philosophical Imaginary.* Translated by Colin Gordon. Stanford: Stanford University Press, 1990.

————. "The Public Employer." Translated by Colin Gordon. *m/f* 9 (1984): 3–17.

284   *Bibliography*

———. "Sartre: L'unique sujet Parlant." *Esprit: Traversée du XXe Siecle* 89 (1984): 181–91.

———. "Simone de Beauvoir and Existentialism." *Feminist Studies* 6 (1980): 277–89.

———. "Simone de Beauvoir: Falling into (Ambiguous) Line." Translated by Margaret A. Simons. In *Feminist Interpretations of Simone de Beauvoir,* edited by Margaret A. Simons. University Park, Pa.: Pennsylvania State University Press, 1995.

———. "Women and Philosophy." In *French Feminist Thought: A Reader,* edited by Toril Moi. Oxford: Blackwell, 1987.

Duchen, Claire, ed. and trans. *French Connections: Voices from the Women's Movement in France.* Amherst: The University of Massachusetts Press, 1987.

Duroux, Françoise. "Des passions et de la compétence politique." *Les Cahiers du Grif: Provenances de la pensée, Femmes/Philosophie* 46 (1992): 103–24.

El Himdy, Ilhame. "Parole de Femme." *Horizons Philosophiques* 6, 1 (1995): 123–26.

Emerton, Karin. "La Femmes et la Philosophie: La mise en discours de la différences sexuelle dans la philosophie contemporaine." Ph.D. diss., Université de Paris 1, 1987.

d'Eaubonne, Françoise. *Feminin et Philosophie: Une allergie historique.* Paris: Éditions Samizdat, 1996.

———. *Une Femme nommée Castor: Mon amie Simone de Beauvoir.* Paris: Éditions Encre, 1986.

Escoubas, Eliane. "L'amour de la philosophie." *Les Cahiers du Grif: Provenances de la pensée, Femmes/Philosophie* 46 (1992): 7–12.

Fauré, Christine. "Absent from History." Translated by Lillian S. Robinson. *Signs: Journal of Women in Culture and Society* 7, 1 (1980): 71–80.

———. "The Twilight of the Goddesses or the Intellectual Crisis of French Feminism." Translated by Lillian S. Robinson. *Signs: Journal of Women in Culture and Society* 7, 1 (1981): 81–86.

Féral, Josette. "Du texte au sujet: conditions pur une écriture et un discours au féminin." *Revue de l'Université d'Ottawa* 50, 1 (1980): 39–46.

Fraisse, Geneviève. *La différence des sexes.* Paris: Presses Universitaires de France, 1996.

———. "La différence des sexes, une différénce historique." In *L'exercise du savoir et la différence des sexes,* edited by Geneviève Fraisse. Paris: Éditions L'Harmattan, 1991.

———. "Feministische Singularität—Kritische Historiographie der Geschichte des Feminismus in Frankreich." *Feministische Studien* 4, 2 (1985): 134–40.

———. "La lucidité des philosophes." *Les Cahiers du Grif: Provenances de la pensée, Femmes/Philosophie* 46 (1992): 75–88.

———. *Muse de la Raison. La démocratie exclusive et la différence des sexes.* Aix-en-Provence: Éditions Gallimard, 1989. Also as *Reason's Muse: Sexual Difference and the Birth of Democracy.* Translated by Jane Marie Todd. Chicago: University of Chicago Press, 1994.

———. "Raison de l'espèce, raison de l'esprit." In *Le sexe des sciences,* edited by Françoise Collin. Paris: Éditions Autrement, 1992.

———. "Über die Geschichtlichkeit der Geschlecter Differenz." Translated by Ursula Konnertz. *Die Philosophin—Geschichte* 4, 7 (1993): 19–22.

———. "Zur Geschichtlichkeit des Geschlechterunterschieds—eine Philosophische Untersuchung." Translated by Wolfram Bayer and Bodo Schulze. In *Denken der Geschlechterdifferenz,* edited by Herta Nagl-Docekal and Herlinde Pauer-Studer. Vienna: Wiener Frauenverlag, 1990.

———. "Zwiefacher Verstand und die eine Natur: Grundlagen der Geschlechterdifferenz." Translated by Gabriele Krüger-Wirrer. *Die Philosophin: Das Geschlecht in der Philosophie* 1, 2 (1990): 7–16.

Fraisse, Geneviève, et al. *L'exercise du savoir et la différence des sexes.* Paris: Éditions L'Harmattan, 1991.

Gagnebin, Jeanne-Marie. "Les joueuses de flûte." *Les Cahiers du Grif: Provenances de la pensée, Femmes/Philosophie* 46 (1992): 21–28.

Gagnon, Madeleine. "Remonter l'Absence." *Horizons Philosophques* 6, 1 (1995): 43–47.

Godard, Linda. "Pour une Nouvelle Lecture de la Question de la Femme: Essai à partir de la pensée de Jacques Derrida." *Philosophiques* 12, 1 (1985): 147–64.

Goldstein, Catherine. "On ne naît pas mathématicien." In *Le sexe des sciences,* edited by Françoise Collin. Paris: Éditions Autrement, 1992.

Goux, Jean-Joseph. "Luce Irigaray Versus the Utopia of the Neutral Sex." In *Engaging with Irigaray,* edited by Carolyn Burke, Naomi Schor, and Margaret Whitford. New York: Columbia University Press, 1994.

Gruber, Eberhard. "Quant au neutre." In *Du Féminin,* edited by Mireille Calle. Cap-Saint-Ignace, Québec: Édition le Griffon d'argile, 1992.

Guillaumin, Colette. "Pratique du pouvoir et idée de nature (I) L'appropriation des femmes." *Questions Féministes* 2 (1978): 5–30.

———. "Pratique du pouvoir et idée de nature (II) Le discours de la nature." *Questions Féministes* 3 (1978): 5–30.

———. "Question de différence." *Questions Féministes* 6 (1979): 3–21.

———. *Sexe, Race et Pratique du Pouvoir: L'idée de Nature,* Paris: côté-femmes éditions, 1992. Translated as *Racism, Sexism and Power, and Ideology.* London: Routledge, 1995.

Huston, Nancy. "L'attribut invisible: (re) collage en dix morceaux." *Le Genre Humain: le masculine* 10 (1984): 139–53.

Ivekovi, Rada. *Aberrations: le devenir-femme d'Auguste Comte.* Paris: Flamarion, 1978.

———. *L'Enigme de la femme: La femme dans les textes de Freud.* Paris: Galilee, 1980. Also as *The Enigma of Woman: Woman in Freud's Writings.* Translated by Catherine Porter. Ithaca, N.Y.: Cornell University Press, 1985.

———. *Lectures de Derrida.* Paris: Galilee, 1984.

———. "Die Postmoderne und das Weibliche in der Philosophie." In *Feministische Philosophie,* edited by Herta Nagl-Docekal. Vienna: R. Oldenbourg Verlag, 1990.

———. "La question des femmes." *Les Cahiers du Grif: Provenances de la pensée, Femmes/Philosophie* 46 (1992): 65–74.

———. *Le Respect des femmes: Kant et Rousseau.* Paris: Galilee, 1982.

———. "Rousseau's Phallocratic Ends." Translated by Mara Dukats. *Hypatia* 3, 3 (1989): 119–22.

———. *Le sexe de la Philosophie: Essai dur Jean-François Lyotard et le féminin.* Paris: Éditions L'Harmattan, 1997.

———. "La sexuation de la première personne du singulier." In *Orients: critique de la raison post-moderne.* Paris: Noël Blandin, 1992.

———. "Voir/entendre." *Les Cahiers du Grif: Provenances de la pensée, Femmes/Philosophie* 46 (1992): 89–96.

Laborie, Françoise. "Femmes, embryons et hommes de sciences." In *Le sexe des sciences,* edited by Françoise Collin. Paris: Éditions Autrement, 1992.

Laroche-Parent, Madeline. "La femme (dite barée) selon l'approche Lacanienne." *Philosophiques* 12, 1 (1985): 165–76.

Leclerc, Annie. "Fragments d'Ecriture." *Horizons Philosophiques* 6, 1 (1995): 19–36.

———. *Parole de Femme.* Paris: Éditions Grasset, 1974.

———. "Penser au féminin." *Horizons Philosophiques* 6, 2 (1996): 111–18.

Lejeune, Claire. "Ecriture et l'arbre du milieu." *Les Cahiers du Grif* 7 (1975): 35–41.

――. "Réenfanter la poésie." *Cahiers Internationaux de symbolisme: Penser au féminin* 65–66–67 (1990): 57–70.

Lemoine-Luccioni, Eugénie. "La pensée dans les défilés du sex." *Cahiers Internationaux de symbolisme: Penser au féminin* 65–66–67 (1990): 117–26.

de Lesseps, Emmanuèle. "le fait féminin et moi?" *Questions Féministes* 5 (1979): 3–28.

――. "Hétérosexualité et féminisme." *Questions Féministes* 7 (1980): 55–69.

――. "Sexisme et racisme." *Questions Féministes* 7 (1980): 95–102.

Levaux, Michéle. "Simone de Beauvoir, une Feministe Exceptionnelle." *Etudes* 360 (1984): 493–98.

Lilar, Suzanne. *Le Malentendu du "Deuxième Sexe."* Paris: Presses Universitaires de France, 1969.

Marrero, Mara Negrón. "Comment faire pour écrire; Gesture póetiquement ou comment faire pour ne pas oublier." In *Hélène Cixous: Chemins d'une écriture,* edited by F. van Rossum-Guyton and M. Diaz-Diocaretz. Amsterdam: Editions Rodopoi, 1990.

Maybon, Marie-Pierre. "Le Mal de Mère." *Horizons Philosophiques* 6, 1 (1995): 127–29.

Montrelay, M. "Inquiry into Feminity." *m/f* 1 (1978).

Morosoli, Michéle. "Les avatars de la différence." *Philosophiques* 11, 2 (1984): 389–414.

Mouffe, Chantal. "Feminism, Citizenship, and Radical Democratic Politics." In *Feminists Theorize the Political,* edited by Judith Butler and Joan W. Scott. New York: Routledge, 1992.

Nahoum-Grappe, V. "Regards croisés sur la différence: l'esthétique du corps." *Sociétés: Utopie* 21 (1988): 21–25.

de Nooy, J. "Double Jeopardy: A Reading of Kristeva's 'Le Text Clos.'" *Southern Review* 21, 2 (1988): 15–168.

de Nooy, Juliana. "Entre Autres: Derrida, Kristeva et la limite entre." Ph.D. diss., Université de Paris 7, 1990.

Orphir, A. *Regards féminins. Condition féminine et création littéraire.* Paris: Denoël-Gonthier, 1976.

Pastre, Geneviève. *De l'amour lesbien. Femmes en mouvement.* Paris, 1980

Peiffer, Jeanne. "Femmes savantes, femmes de sciences." In *Le sexe des sciences,* edited by Françoise Collin. Paris: Éditions Autrement, 1992.

Plaza, Monique. "La même mère." *Questions Féministes* 7 (1980): 71–94.

――. "Our Costs and Their Benefits." Translated by W. Harrison. *m/f* 4 (1980): 28–39.

――. "Our Dangers and Their Compensation: Rape: The Will Not to Know of Michel Foucualt." *Feminist Issues* 1, 3 (1981): 25–35.

――. "Pouvoir 'Phallomorphique' et psychologie de 'femme.'" *Questions Feministes* 1 (1977): 91–119. Also as " 'Phallomorphic Power' and the Psychology of 'Woman.'" *Ideology and Consciousness* 4 (1978): 5–36.

Poissant, Louise. "Pour l'Immobilisme?" *Philosophiques* 12, 1 (1985): 133–46.

Proust, François. "Les noms secrets." *Les Cahiers du Grif: Provenances de la pensée, Femmes/Philosophie* 46 (1992):143–158.

Remy, Monique. "Cixous en langues ou les jeux de la féminité." In *Hélène Cixous: Chemins d'une écriture,* edited by F. van Rossum-Guyton and M. Diaz-Diocaretz. Amsterdam: Editions Rodopoi, 1990.

――. "L'utopie amazonienne." *Cahiers Internationaux de symbolisme: Penser au féminin* 65–66–67 (1990): 159–71.

Revault d'Allonnes, Myriam. "L'homme d'Aristote." *Les Cahiers du Grif: Provenances de la pensée, Femmes/Philosophie* 46 (1992): 97–102.

Rousseau-Dujardin, Jacqueline. "Compositeur au féminin." In *L'exercise du savoir et la différence des sexes,* edited by Geneviève Fraisse. Paris: Éditions L'Harmattan, 1991.

———. "Hors de soi." *Cahiers du Grif: La dépendance amoureuse* 31 (1985): 7–10.

Roy, Marie-Françoise. "Mathématiciennes." In *Le sexe des sciences,* edited by Françoise Collin. Paris: Éditions Autrement, 1992.

Saint-Germain, Christian. "Le texte de l'absente: féminin et différence dans la modernité." *Philosopher* 10 (1990–1991): 73–83.

Sartiliot, Claudette. "L'éclatement des genres." In *Du Féminin,* edited by Mireille Calle. Cap-Saint-Ignace, Québec: Édition le Griffon d'argile, 1992.

Schneider, Monique. "En-deçà du visage." *Les Cahiers du Grif: Provenances de la pensée, Femmes/Philosophie* 46 (1992): 47–64.

Servais, Christine. "La lettre d'amour: et la femme est jetée là où elle tomb." *Cahiers Internationaux de symbolisme: Penser au féminin* 65–66–67 (1990): 173–83.

Setti, Nadia. "Les noms de l'amour." In *Hélène Cixous: Chemins d'une écriture,* edited by F. van Rossum-Guyton and M. Diaz-Diocaretz. Amsterdam: Editions Rodopoi, 1990.

Sissa, Giulia. "On parvient péniblement à enfanter la connaissance." In *L'exercise du savoir et la différence des sexes,* edited by Geneviève Fraisse. Paris: Éditions L'Harmattan, 1991.

Slama, Béatrice. "Entre amour et écriture." In *Hélène Cixous: Chemins d'une écriture,* edited by F. van Rossum-Guyton and M. Diaz-Diocaretz. Amsterdam: Editions Rodopoi, 1990.

Stengers, Isabelle. "Un autre regard: réapprendre à rire." In *Le sexe des sciences,* edited by Françoise Collin. Paris: Éditions Autrement, 1992.

Tort, Michel. "Ce qu'un sexe sait de l'autre." In *L'exercise du savoir et la différence des sexes,* edited by Geneviève Fraisse. Paris: Éditions L'Harmattan, 1991.

Wittig, Monique. *Le Corps Lesbien.* Paris: Minuit, 1973. Also as *The Lesbian Body.* Translated by David Le Vay. London: Peter Owen, 1975.

———. *Les Guérillères.* Paris: Les Éditions de Minuit. Also as *Les Guérillères,* 1969. Translated by David LeVay. New York: Viking 1971.

———. *L'Opoponax.* Paris: Minuit, 1964. Also as *The Opoponax.* Translated by Helen Weaver. New York: Simon and Schuster, 1966.

———. "La Pensée Straight." *Questions Féministes* 7 (1980): 45–53.

———. "Un jour mon prince viendra." *Questions Féministes* 2 (1978): 31–39.

———. *The Straight Mind and Other Essays.* Boston: Beacon Press, 1992.

Wittig, Monique with Sande Zeig. *Brouillon pour un dictionnaire des amantes.* Paris: Grasset, 1976. Also as *Lesbian Peoples: Material for a Dictionary.* New York: Avon, 1979.

———. "Le Voyage sans fin." *Vlasta 4, Supplement* (1985).

Zéphir, Jacques. *Le Néo-féminisme de Simone de Beauvoir.* Paris: Denoël and Gonthier, 1982.

German Sources

Bischof, Rita. "Waren, Körper, Sprache." *Die Schwarze Botin* 2 (1977): 23–28.

Brander, Stephanie: "Philosophinnen in Gespräch: Hannah Arendt, Simone de Beauvoir—eine fiktive Begegnung." *Die Philosophin: Feministische Theorie—Philosophie—Universität* 1, 1 (1990): 57–73.

Busch, Alexandra. "Der metaphorische schleier des ewig Weiblichen—Zu Luce Irigarays Ethik der sexuellen Differenz." In *Feministischer Kompaß, patriarchales Gepäck. Kritik konservativer Anteile in neueren feministischen Theorien,* edited by Ruth Großmaß and Christiane Schmerl. Frankfurt a.M.: Campus-Verlag, 1989.

Cavarero, Adriana. "Schauplätze der Einzigartigkeit." Translated by Petra Plieger. In *Phänomenologie und Geschlechterdifferenz,* edited by Silvia Stoller and Helmuth Vetter. Vienna: Wiener Universitätsverlag, 1997.

Deuber-Mankowsky, Astrid. "In unendlicher Distanz zu sich selbst: Sarah Kofmans Denken der radikalen Alterität." *Die Philosophin* 8, 15 (1997): 24–43.

———. "Von neuen Welten und weiblichen Göttern. Zu Luce Irigarays 'Ethique de la difference sexuelle.'" In *Weiblichkeit in der Moderne. Ansätze feministischer Vernunftkritik,* edited by Ursula Konnertz and Judith Conrad. Tübingen: Editions Diskord, 1986.

Duden, Barbara. *Der Frauenleib als öffentlicher Ort: vom Mißbrauch des Begriffs Leben.* Hamburg: Luchterhand Literatur Verlag GmbH., 1991. Also as *Disembodying Women: Perspectives on Pregnancy and the Unborn.* Translated by Lee Hoinacki. Cambridge, Mass.: Harvard University Press, 1993.

———. *Geschichte unter der Haut.* Stuttgart: Ernst Klett Verlage GmbH u. Co. KG., 1987. Also as *The Woman Beneath the Skin: A Doctor's Patients in Eighteenth-Century Germany.* Translated by Thomas Dunlap. Cambridge, Mass.: Harvard University Press, 1991.

Erdle, Birgit R. "Bezeugen, verstehen, vergleichen. Spuren der Tradition der Erinnerung in Sarah Kofmans 'Parole suffoquées?'" *Die Philosophin: Umgang mit der Tradition* 6, 12 (1995): 38–52.

Funk, Julika, and Elfi Bettinger. "Weiblichkeit als Maskerade und der Fetisch Phallus." *Die Philosophin: Fetisch. Frau* 7, 13 (1996): 31–53.

Gast, Lili. "Der Körper auf den Spuren des Subjekts: Psychoanalytische Gedanken zu einer Schicksalsgemeinschaft in dekonstruktiven Turbulenzen." *Die Philosophin: Körper* 5, 10 (1994): 27–49.

Giuliani, Regula. "Körpergeschichten zwischen Modellbildung und haptischer Hexis—Thomas Laqueur und Barbara Duden." In *Phänomenologie und Geschlechterdifferenz,* edited by Silvia Stoller and Helmuth Vetter. Vienna: Wiener Universitätsverlag, 1997.

———. "Der übergangene Leib: Simone de Beauvoir, Luce Irigaray und Judith Butler." In *Phänomenologische Forschungen: Neue Folge 2,* edited by Ernst Wolfgang Orth und Karl-Heinz Lembeck. Freiburg: Verlag Karl Alber, 1997.

Gunzenhäuser, Randi. "Gibt es eine Position außerhalb des Diskurses? Zu Michel Foucault und Donna Haraway." In *'Verwirrung der Geschlechter,'* edited by Erika Haas. Munich: Profil, 1995.

Gürtler, Sabine. "Der Begriff der Mutterschaft in 'Jenseits des Seins.' Zur phänomenologischen Begründung der Sozialität des Subjekts bei Emmanuel Lévinas." *Deutsche Zeitschrift für Philosophie* 4 (1994): 653–70.

———. "Eine Metaphysik der Geschlechterdifferenz bei Emmanuel Lévinas." In *Phänomenologische Forschungen, Neue Folge 1,* edited by Ernst Wolfgang Orth and Karl-Heinz Lembeck. Freiburg: Verlag Karl Alber, 1996.

———. "Emmanuel Lévinas, Die Bedeutung der Geschlechterdifferenz für das Denken des Anderen." *XVI. Deutscher Kongreß für Philosophie: Neue Realitäten.* Berlin, 1993.

———. "Für ein männliches Wesen!!! Das Problem einer geschlectlichen Markierung des Autorsubjekts im Philosophischen Diskurs am Beispiel des Denkens von Emmanuel Lévinas." *Die Philosophin: Paradigmen des Männlichen* 4, 8 (1993): 36–56.

————. "Gipfel und Abgrund—Die Kritik von Luce Irigaray an Emmanuel Lévinas' Verständnis der Geschlechterdifferenz." In *Phänomenologie und Geschlechterdifferenz,* edited by Silvia Stoller and Helmuth Vetter. Vienna: Wiener Universitätsverlag, 1997.

————. "Gleichheit, Differenz, Alterität: Das Denken von Emmanuel Lévinas als Herausforderung für den feministischen Diskurs." *Feministische Studien* 1, 1 (1994): 70–83.

Haas, Erika, ed. *'Verwirrung der Geschlechter': Dekonstruktion und Feminismus.* Munich: Profil, 1995.

Hagemann-White, Carol. "Simone de Beauvoir und der existentialistische Feminismus." In *Traditionen—Brüche. Entwicklungen feministischer Theorie,* edited by Gudrun-Axeli Knapp and Angelika Wetterer. Freiburg: Kore, 1992.

Herbrand, Susanne and Sandrina Khaled. *Geschlectherdiffere(ä)nz. Zur Feminisierung des philosophischen Diskurses.* Pfaffenweiler: Centaurus-Verlagsgesellschaft, 1994.

Heselhaus, Herrad. "Luce Irigaray—'Weiblichkeit' widerer(er)finden, Feministische Theorie zwischen Essentialismus, Dekonstruktion und Kreativität." In *'Verwirrung der Geschlechter,'* edited by Erika Haas. Munich: Profil, 1995.

Hiltman, Gabriela. "Einen Text gebären—Körperbilder in Hélène Cixous' Déluge: Bildbeschreibung." *Die Philosophin: Körper* 5, 10 (1994): 50–68.

Kadi, Ulrike. "Berührungen einer Grenze: Eine Haut und ein Ich. In *Näherungen des Realen,* edited by Brigitta Keintzel. Vienna: Turia und Kant, forthcoming.

————. *Bilderwahn. Arbeit am Imaginären.* Vienna: Turia and Kant, 1998.

————. "Der Wahnsinn—ein Weib? Das Weib . . . ein Wahnsinn: Bemerkungen zu Paranoia, Jacques Lacan und (der) Frau." *Script* 7 (1995): 3–8.

Klefinghaus, Sybille. "Über Luce Irigaray." *Die schwarze Botin* 14/15 (1980): 12–17.

Klinger, Cornelia. "Zwei Schritte vorwärts, einer Zurück—und ein vierter darüber hinaus. Die Etappen feministischen Auseinandersetzung mit der Philosophie." *Die Philosophin: Umgang mit der Tradition* 6, 12 (1995): 81–97.

Konnertz, Ursula. "Simone de Beauvoir. Der Entwurf einer feministischen Ethik—ein gescheitertes Experiment?" In *Weiblichkeit in der Moderne. Ansätze feministischer Vernunftkritik,* edited by Ursula Konnertz and Judith Conrad. Tübingen: Edition Diskord, 1986.

Kuster, Friederike. "Luce Irigarays Ethik der sexuellen Differenz." In *Phänomenologische Forschungen, Neue Folge 1,* edited by Ernst Wolfgang Orth and Karl-Heinz Lembeck. Freiburg: Verlag Karl Alber, 1996.

Landweer, Hilge. "Herausforderung Foucault." *Die Philosophin: Geschichte* 4, 7 (1993): 8–18.

Liebsch, Katharina. *Vom Weib zur Weiblichkeit? Psychoanalytische Konstruktionen in feministischer Theorie.* Bielefeld: Kleine, 1994.

List, Elisabeth. "Feministsches Denken im Spektrum der Gegenwartsphilosophie." *Deutsche Zeitschift für Philosophie* 34 (1991): 514–27.

————. "Das lebendige Selbst—Leiblichkeit, Subjektivität und Geschlecht." In *Phänomenologie und Geschlechterdifferenz,* edited by Silvia Stoller and Helmuth Vetter. Vienna: Wiener Universitätsverlag, 1997.

————. *Die Präsenz des Anderen. Theorie und Geschlechterpolitik.* Frankfurt am Main: Suhrkamp, 1993.

————. "Wissende Körper—Wissens Körper—Maschinen Körper: zur Semiotik der Leiblichkeit." *Die Philosophin: Körper* 5, 10 (1994): 9–26.

Lorey, Isabell. "Der Körper als Text und das aktuelle Selbst: Butler und Foucault." *Feministische Studien* 11, 2 (1993): 10–23.

Maihofer, Andrea. *Geschlecht als Existenzweise.* Frankfurt am Main: Ulrike Helma Verlag, 1995

Menke, Bettina. "Dekonstruktion der Geschlechteropposition—das Denken der Geschlechterdifferenz. Derrida." In *'Verwirrung der Geschlechter,'* edited by Erika Haas. Munich: Profil, 1995.

———. "Verstellt—der Ort der 'Frau.' Ein Nachwort." In *Dekonstruktiver Feminismus. Literaturwissenschaft in Amerika,* edited by Barbara Vinken. Frankfurt a/M: Edition Suhrkamp, 1992.

Meyer, Eva. "Theorie der Weiblichkeit. Heterogenität, Negativität, sujet zéreologique." *Die schwarze Botin* 6 (1978): 31–39.

Meyer, Ursula. *Einführung in die Feministische Philosophie.* Aachen: ein-Fach-verlag, 1992.

Nagl-Docekal, Herta, and Herlinde Pauer-Studer, eds. *Denken der Geschlechterdifferenz.* Vienna: Wiener Frauenverlag, 1990.

Pechriggl, Alice. "Corps transfigurés. Stratifications de l'imaginaire des sexes/genres." Ph.D. diss., EHESS, 1997.

———. "Der Einfall der Einbildung als ontologischer Aufbruch. Vom Novum zur Veränderung so mancher Verhältnisse, nicht zuletzt desjenigen der Geschlechter." In *Die Institution des Imaginären. Zur Philosophie von Cornelius Castoriadis,* edited by A. Pechriggl and K. Reitter. Vienna: Turia & Kant, 1991.

Postl, Gertrude. "The Postmodern Discourse on Technology and the Female Body: A Feminist Approach to Lyotard and Baudrillard." In *2nd European Feminist Research Conference: Feminist Perspectives on Technology, Work and Ecology,* edited by Tina Eberhart and Christina Wächter. Graz, 1994.

———. *Weibliches Sprechen: Feministische Entwürfe zu Sprache und Geschlecht.* Vienna: Passagen Philosophie, 1991.

Rauschenbach, Brigitte. "Erkenntnispolitik als Feminismus." *Die Philosophin: Umgang mit der Tradition* 6, 11 (1995): 33–49.

———. "Gleichheit, Widerspruch, Differenz. Denkformen als Politkformen." *Die Philosophin: Paradigmen des Männlichen* 4, 8 (1993): 57–86.

Rendtorff, Barbara. *Geschlecht und symbolische Kastration. Über Körper, Matrix, Tod und Wissen.* Königstein: Ulrike Helmer Verlag, 1996.

Runte, Annette. *Kultur—Natur—Differenz in der feministischen Diskussion in Frankreich.* Frankfurt a.M., 1989.

———. "Lippenblüterinnen unter dem Gesetz. Über die feministische Diskussion in Frankreich: Luce Irigaray, Hélène Cixous, Cathérine Clément, Julia Kristeva." *Die schwarze Botin* 5 (1977): 35–42.

———. "Passion oder Segregation? Philosophisches Differenzdenken und poetische Kulturkritik am Beispiel von Monique Wittig und Luce Irigaray." *Die schwarze Botin* 29 (1985): 10–19

Schällibaum, Ursula. *Geschlechter Differenz und Ambivalenz: Ein Vergleich zwischen Luce Irigaray und Jaques Derrida.* Vienna: Passagen-Verlag, 1991.

Seifert, Edith. *Was will das Weib? Zu Begehren und Lust bei Freud und Lacan.* Weinheim: Quadriga Verlag, 1987.

Stoller, Silvia and Helmuth Vetter. "Einleitung." In *Phänomenologie und Geschlechterdifferenz,* edited by Silvia Stoller and Helmuth Vetter. Vienna: Wiener Universitätsverlag, 1997.

———, eds. *Phänomenologie und Geschlechterdifferenz.* Vienna: Wiener Universitätsverlag, 1997.

Tuohimaa, Sinikka. "Feministische Theorienbildung zwischen Strukturalismus und Dekonstruktionismus." *Zeitschrift für Semiotik* 11, 4 (1989): 377–89.

Vasterling, Veronica. "Dekonstruktion der Identität—Zur Theorie der Geschlechter-differenz bei Derrida." In *Phänomenologie und Geschlechterdifferenz,* edited by Silvia Stoller and Helmuth Vetter. Vienna: Wiener Universitätsverlag, 1997.

Vinken, Barbara. "Dekonstruktiver Feminismus—Eine Einleitung." In *Dekonstruktiver Feminismus. Literaturwissenschaft in Amerika,* edited by Barbara Vinken. Frankfurt a/M: Edition Suhrkamp, 1992.

———, ed. *Dekonstruktiver Feminismus. Literaturwissenschaft in Amerika.* Frankfurt a/M: Edition Suhrkamp, 1992.

Volkening, Heide. "Lektüredifferenzen—sometimes displacement helps. Eine Meta-phern—analyse der Debatte um den dekonstruktiven Feminismus." In *Leitbilder, Vexierbilder und Bildstörungen: Über die Orientierungsleistung von Bildern in der feministischen Geschlechterdebatte,* edited by Ruth Großmaß und Christiane Schmerl. Frankfurt a.M.: Campus Verlag, 1996.

Wagner, Ina. "Feministische Technikkritik und Postmoderne." In *Feministische Vernunft-kritik. Ansätze und Traditionen,* edited by Ilona Ostner and Klaus Lichtblau. Frank-furt a. M.: Campus Verlag, 1992.

Waldenfels, Bernard. "Fremdheit des anderen Geschlechts." In *Phänomenologie und Geschlechterdifferenz,* edited by Silvia Stoller and Helmuth Vetter. Vienna: Wiener Universitätsverlag, 1997.

Waniek, Eva. *Hélène Cixous—Entlang einer Theorie der Schrift.* Vienna: Turia und Kant, 1993.

———. "(K)ein weibliches Schreiben." *Die Philosophin: Feministische Ästhetik: Ge-schlechtsspezifische Wahrnehung* 3, 5 (1992): 45–59.

Weber, Elisabeth. *Verfolgung und Trauma zu Emmanuel Lévinas Autrement qu'être ou au-delà de l'essence.* Vienna: Passagen Philosophie, 1990.

Weisshaupt, Brigitte. "Schatten über der Vernunft." In *Feministische Philosophie,* edited by Herta Nagl-Docekal. Vienna: R. Oldenbourg Verlag, 1990.

———. "Zur ungedachten Dialektik von Eros und Logos: Die Ausschließung des Weib-lichen durch Logifizierung der Liebe." *Die Philosophin: Weibliches Begehren* 3, 6 (1992): 44–56.

Bibliographies Consulted

Heinz, Marion, and Sabine Doyé. *Feministische Philosophie: Bibliographie: 1970–1995.* Bielefeld: Kleine Verlag, 1996

Nordquist, Joan, ed. *French Feminist Theory: Luce Irigaray and Hélène Cixous: A Bib-liography.* Santa Cruz, Ca.: Reference and Research Services (Social Theory: A Bibli-ographic Series no. 20), 1990.

———, ed. *Julia Kristeva: A Biliography.* Santa Cruz, Ca.: Reference and Research Ser-vices (Social Theory: A Bibliographic Series no. 39), 1995.

Contributors

HAZEL E. BARNES is Professor Emeritus of Philosophy at the University of Colorado, Boulder. In addition to her noted translation of Jean-Paul Sartre's *Being and Time,* she is the author of five books and many articles on existentialism, literature, feminism, and education. Her publications include *An Existentialist Ethics* (Knopf, 1967), *The Literature of Possibility, A Study of Humanistic Existentialism* (University of Nebraska, 1959), *Sartre and Flaubert* (Chicago, 1981), and *The Story I Tell Myself* (Chicago 1997).

DEBRA B. BERGOFFEN is Professor of Philosophy and Director of the Women's Resource and Research Center at George Mason University, where she received the Distinguished Faculty Award in 1989 and the Teaching Excellence Award in 1993. Bergoffen was the Executive Co-Director of the Society for Phenomenology and Existential Philosophy (SPEP) from 1993–96. Her most recent works include "Marriage, Autonomy and the Feminine Protest," *Hypatia* (fall 1999); "Mourning, Woman and the Phallus: Lacan's Hamlet," *Cultural Semiosis* (1998); "Nietzsche Was No Feminist," *Feminist Interpretations of Friedrich Nietzsche* (Penn State, 1998); and *The Philosophy of Simone de Beauvoir: Gendered Phenomenologies, Erotic Generosities* (SUNY, 1997).

HÉLÈNE CIXOUS is Professor of Literature at the Université de Paris VIII and is the author of nearly thirty books of poetic fiction, many critical essays, and eight plays. Her work has been translated into ten languages. Her most recent work translated into English includes *First Days of the Year* (University of Minnesota, 1997), *The Hélène Cixous Reader* (Routledge, 1994), *Rootprints, Memory and Life Writing* (Routledge, 1997), and *The Terrible but Unfinished Story of Norodom Sihanouk, King of Cambodia* (University of Nebraska, 1994).

PENELOPE DEUTSCHER is Senior Lecturer in the Department of Philosophy at the Australian National University. She is the author of *Yielding Gender: Feminism, Deconstruction and the History of Philosophy* (Routledge, 1997) and co-editor, with Kelly Oliver, of *Enigmas: Essays on Sarah Kofman* (Cornell University Press, 1999).

JANE DREXLER is a Ph.D. candidate in Philosophy at SUNY Binghamton. She is writing her dissertation, *Public Space and the Politics of Resistance,* under Bat-Ami Bar On and Maria Lugones. She has given papers on health and justice in Plato, radical pedagogy, and Habermas and Marx. She teaches multicultural medical ethics and social and political philosophy.

HELEN A. FIELDING is Assistant Professor of Philosophy and Women's Studies at the University of Western Ontario. Her research and publications explore the intersections between feminist theory, technology, art, and embodied ethics. She is a recent SSHRC Postdoctoral Fellow at the Bergische University in Germany and has published on Merleau-Ponty and Foucault.

MORNY JOY is Professor of Religious Studies at the University of Calgary. She is the coeditor, with Penny Magee, of *Claiming Our Rights: Studies in Religion by Australian Women Scholars* (Flinders University Press, 1995) and coeditor, with Eva Neumaiaer Dargyay, of *Gender, Genre and Religion: Feminist Reflections* (Wilfrid Laurier Press, 1995) and has published many articles on feminist theory and religion. She is past president of the Canadian Society for the Study of Religion and Co-ordinator of the Institute for Gender Studies at the University of Calgary.

MONIKA LANGER is Associate Professor of Philosophy at the University of Victoria, British Columbia. Her principle areas of interest include continental philosophy, feminist philosophy, sociopolitical philosophy, and philosophy in literature. Her publications include *Merleau-Ponty's Phenomenology of Perception: A Guide and Commentary*. She is presently writing a book on *The Gay Science*.

TAMSIN LORRAINE is Associate Professor of Philosophy at Swarthmore College. She is the author of *Gender, Identity, and the Production of Meaning* and articles on Kristeva, Irigaray, Nietzsche, and Deleuze. Her most recent book is *Irigaray and Deleuze: Experiments in Visceral Philosophy* (Cornell University Press, 1999).

DOROTHEA OLKOWSKI is Professor and Co-Chair of Philosophy at the University of Colorado, Colorado Springs, where she founded and directed the program in Women's Studies. Her most recent publications are *Gilles Deleuze and the Ruin of Representation* (University of California, 1999) and a coedited volume, *Merleau-Ponty, Interiority and Exteriority, Psychic Life and the World* (SUNY Press, 1999). Her published work includes articles on French philosophy, feminist philosophy, and philosophy and art.

GAIL WEISS is Associate Professor of Philosophy and teaches in the graduate program in the Human Sciences at the George Washington University. She is the author of *Body Images: Embodiment as Intercorporeality* (Routledge, 1999) and the coeditor of *Perspectives on Embodiment: The Intersections of Nature and Culture* (Routledge, 1999). Her research and published work focuses on the intersections among phenomenology and existentialism, feminist theory, and philosophy of literature.

IRIS M. YOUNG is Professor of Public and International Affairs at the University of Pittsburgh, where she teaches ethics and political philosophy. She has held visiting appointments in Germany and Australia. She is the author of *Throwing Like a Girl and Other Essays in Feminist Philosophy and Social Theory* (Indiana University Press, 1990). Her most recent publication is *Intersecting Voices: Dilemmas of Gender, Political Philosophy and Policy* (Princeton University Press, 1997).

EWA PLONOWSKA ZIAREK is Associate Professor and Director of Graduate Studies in the English Department at the University of Notre Dame. She has published articles on Derrida, Kristeva, Irigaray, Lévinas, Foucault, Kafka, Benjamin, Joyce, and Marianna Hauser. She is the author of *The Rhetoric of Failure: Deconstruction of Skepticism, the Reinvention of Modernism* (SUNY, 1995) and the editor of *Gombrowicz's Grimaces: Modernism, Gender, Nationality* (SUNY, 1998). Her current book project is titled *Passionate Pursuits: Postmodern Ethics, Sexual Difference, and the Politics of Radical Democracy.*

Index